Auditing Information and Cyber Security Governance

Internal Audit and IT Audit

Series Editor: Dan Swanson

Dan Swanson and Associates, Ltd., Winnipeg, Manitoba, Canada.

The Internal Audit and IT Audit series publishes leading-edge books on critical subjects facing audit executives as well as internal and IT audit practitioners. Key topics include Audit Leadership, Cybersecurity, Strategic Risk Management, Auditing Various IT Activities and Processes, Audit Management, and Operational Auditing.

Auditing Information and Cyber Security Governance

A Controls-Based Approach

Robert E. Davis

CRC Press
Taylor & Francis Group
Boca Raton London New York

CRC Press is an imprint of the
Taylor & Francis Group, an **informa** business

First edition published 2021
by CRC Press
6000 Broken Sound Parkway NW, Suite 300, Boca Raton, FL 33487–2742

and by CRC Press
2 Park Square, Milton Park, Abingdon, Oxon, OX14 4RN

© 2021 Robert E. Davis

CRC Press is an imprint of Taylor & Francis Group, LLC

ISBN: 978-0-367-56850-4 (hbk)
ISBN: 978-1-003-09967-3 (ebk)
ISBN: 978-1-032-04448-4 (pbk)

Typeset in Sabon
by Apex CoVantage, LLC

Brief Content

Detail Content

Preface

A comprehensive entity security program deploys information assets protection (IAP) through stratified technological and non-technological controls. Controls are necessary for counteracting security threats, opportunities, and vulnerabilities in a manner that reduces potential adverse effects to defined, acceptable risk levels. "Auditing Information and Cyber Security Governance: A Controls-Based Approach" presents a methodological model in the context of normative decision theory constructs and concepts with appropriate reference to standards and the respective guidelines. Normative decision theory attempts to establish a rational framework for choosing between alternative courses of action when the outcomes resulting from the selection are uncertain. Decision theory techniques can provide determination of objectives, performance estimates, interaction assessments, and organizational analysis through the methodological application (Davis, 2017). A normative model prescribes what should exist according to an assumption or a rule.

Entity needs and associated security requirements should drive organizational control selection (Barnard & Von Solms, 2000). The entity's manager-leaders should clearly define security requirements in information security policies, and the security policies should dictate the control set that will provide the necessary information asset protection (Barnard & Von Solms, 2000). If the control set receives evaluation and certification as meeting organizational needs, the trust required for e-commerce is feasible (Barnard & Von Solms, 2000). The implications for positive social change encompass the potential to understand Information Security Governance (ISG) program systems, processes, activities, and tasks better, thus increasing the propensity for consumer trust and reducing consumers' costs (Davis, 2017). Information technology (IT) service consumers may benefit from entity manager-leaders understanding the significance of strategic alignment in designing and deploying effectual ISG that permits enhanced trust in deploying and sustaining information protection practices (Davis, 2017). Trust is a social commitment aspect (Davis, 2017; Edwards, 2013). Consumer perceptions of Internet information protection can influence trust beliefs and trusting intentions (Bahmanziari & Odom, 2015; Davis, 2017). For example, an e-commerce-related IAP incident can cause a measurable negative customer behavior influence (Arief et al., 2015; Choi & Nazareth, 2014; Davis, 2017; Lee & Lee, 2012).

The proper installation and operation of IAP technologies are critical to reducing entity risks (Sedlack & Tejay, 2011). Entity management's effectual IAP solutions are imperative to achieving trust relationships, especially with new customers (Choi & Nazareth, 2014; Davis, 2017). Control selection necessitates understanding why an IAP technology was purchased and implemented (Sedlack & Tejay, 2011). The potential exists to provide entity manager-leaders with a better understanding of the factors related to designing and deploying effectual ISG for e-commerce that enables consumer trust (Davis, 2017). A higher perceived Internet protection level leads to a greater intent to purchase products using e-commerce websites (Davis, 2017; Hartono et al., 2014).

Entity manager-leaders can improve the stakeholder trust factor in technology containing personally identifiable information through effectual ISG (Davis, 2008, 2017). Personal identity and privacy are among the most valuable intangible assets that individuals can ever own (Davis, 2008, 2017). Nonetheless, technology manipulation continually enables intentional or unintentional privacy invasions (Davis, 2008, 2017). Cyberattackers have ranged from hobbyists to spies, typically motivated by financial, personal, or political factors (Arief & Adzmi, 2015; Davis, 2017). IT-related identity theft had cost consumers over $5 billion yearly (Trautman et al., 2013). Cyber defenders could not adequately address cybercrime by only deploying technical information security solutions (Arief & Adzmi, 2015; Davis, 2017). Therefore, entity cyber defenders must consider the human factors involved in cybercrime (Arief & Adzmi, 2015; Davis, 2017).

Information security breaches are a controversial concern (Davis, 2017; Safa et al., 2016; Safa & Solms, 2016). Engagement in cybercrime may be due to the lack of deterrents or psychological factors (Davis, 2017; Holt & Bossler, 2014). Privacy invasion is only symptomatic of a critical question confronting individuals living in the information age (Davis, 2008, 2017): How can entity information security protect citizenry rights and freedom while simultaneously controlling criminal inclinations? Substantial investments can serve as an effectual information security breach deterrent if appropriately directed (Choi & Nazareth, 2014). However, more secure information assets can benefit communities through enhanced governance quality that can increase trust and reduce e-commerce use costs (Bahmanziari & Odom, 2015; Ludin & Cheng, 2014; Starbuck, 2014; Yaokumah, 2014).

Topical Fit

Information and associated technologies continue advancement toward diverse distributed configuration environments that encode, process, store, and retrieve data. The change in magnitude occurring is visible with the explosion of linked IT infrastructures connected to cloud computing service providers, blockchain deployments, and mobile computing devices. Consequently, the effect of such decentralization increases the need for the practical safeguarding of information assets.

Globally, laws and regulations attempt to ensure that organizational formations comply with a society's expectations for ethical behavior when conducting affairs. Critical to preserving stakeholder confidence in the entity's mission is security governance deployment protecting information affecting investment and expenditure decisions. Depending on societal perceptions, laws, and regulations, ratification occurs to ensure compliance with entity-safeguarding responsibilities. Interpretively, where government-enforced statutes overlap entity governance, audit practice coverage is typically necessary for verifying compliance mandate implementation (Davis, 2008).

Intended Audience

Potential information and cybersecurity governance engagement members should have the appropriate audit proficiency. Generally, when governance audit objectives involve a wide range of information system functions, assigned audit personnel should have extensive organizational knowledge and a proper understanding of related processes. Audit personnel can acquire proper knowledge and understanding through reading and comprehending relevant literature.

The intent of "Auditing Information and Cyber Security Governance: A Controls-Based Approach" is to create quality reference material for assurance service practitioners to enable addressing protection mandates. Therefore, this book is appropriate for entity employees interested in ensuring or verifying the design and deployment of pertinent information security and cybersecurity governance. External auditors, internal auditors, Chief Security Officers, Chief Compliance Officers, Chief Information Officers, Chief Information Security Officers, cybersecurity professionals, and control self-assessment personnel will find this book an informative and authoritative audit practice resource. Through reviewing this book's content, the reader will

1. understand the adaptive balance between sound management and applied technology,
2. identify the general activities and responsibilities associated with conducting information security and cybersecurity governance audits, and
3. acquire insightful considerations and tools for information security and cybersecurity governance audit planning, study, testing, reporting, and follow-up.

Book Organization

Collectively, in this book, the author expects readers to have basic assurance practice knowledge for enabling appropriate consideration of the role auditors play in assuring an entity's information security program. The author's content design gives readers various factors and aids in audit planning to understand how to better evaluate information security and cybersecurity governance auditable units. It also allows auditors to understand various processes, activities, and tasks required to initiate, document, and compile an audit engagement report. Moreover, this book contains an overview of program development and deployment, control environment responsibilities, and generally accepted management processes. Organizationally, "Auditing Information and Cyber Security Governance: A Controls-Based Approach" has an eight-chapter segmentation.

- Chapter 1 focuses on the effect of entity governance, ISG, and Cyber Security Governance as management tools for appropriate information and technology security.
- Chapter 2 discusses entity-centric considerations for the control environment and Government–Entity–Audit domain convergences. Additionally, Chapter 2 presents legal issues, managerial practices, control inscriptions, and technology deployments as entity risk determinants.
- Chapter 3 addresses the planning, organizing, orchestration, directing, and controlling cycle in managing ISG, enabling a well-informed and reasonable sense of certainty that information risks and controls appropriately balance.
- Chapter 4 conveys Governance Tree tier-five level activities supporting Governance Tree tier-four processes for effectual ISG.
- In Chapter 5, the author discusses responsibility delegation and counterproductive workplace behavior. Chapter 5 also provides IT incident response team insights, employee development strategies, and an overview of entity IT audit team activities.
- Chapter 6 discusses supply chain partners and managed service providers considering IAP risks. Chapter 6 also presents critical service provider audit issues.
- Chapter 7 presents how to apply important IT audit methods from a system perspective when examining ISG managerial processes.
- Chapter 8 presents how to apply important IT audit methods from a system perspective when examining CSG operational processes.

References

Arief, B., & Adzmi, M. A. B. (2015). Understanding cybercrime from its stakeholders' perspectives: Part 2: Defenders and victims. *IEEE Security & Privacy, 13*(2), 84–88. https://doi.org/10.1109/MSP.2015.44

Arief, B., Adzmi, M. A. B., & Gross, T. (2015). Understanding cybercrime from its stakeholders' perspectives: Part 1: Attackers. *IEEE Security & Privacy, 13*(1), 71–76. https://doi.org/10.1109/MSP.2015.19

Bahmanziari, T., & Odom, M. D. (2015). Prospect theory and risky choice in the ecommerce setting: Evidence of a framing effect. *Academy of Accounting & Financial Studies Journal, 19*(1), 85–106. http://www.alliedacademies.org

Barnard, L., & Von Solms, R. (2000). A formalized approach to the effective selection and evaluation of information security controls [abstract]. *Computers & Security, 19*(2), 185–194. https://doi.org/10.1016/S0167-4048(00)87829-3

Choi, J., & Nazareth, D. L. (2014). Repairing trust in an e-commerce and security context: An agent-based modeling approach. *Information Management & Computer Security, 22,* 490–512. https://doi.org/10.1108/IMCS-09-2013-0069

Davis, R. E. (2008). *IT auditing: Assuring information assets protection.* Pleier.

Davis, R. E. (2017). *Relationship between corporate governance and information security governance effectiveness in United States corporations* (Publication No. 10603383) [Doctoral study, Walden University]. ProQuest Dissertations Publishing.

Edwards, C. K. (2013). *A framework for the governance of information security* (Publication No. 3607548) [Dissertation, Nova Southeastern University]. ProQuest Dissertations Publishing.

Hartono, E., Holsapple, C. W., Kim, K. Y., Na, K. S., & Simpson, J. T. (2014). Measuring perceived security in B2C electronic commerce website usage: A respecification and validation. *Decision Support Systems, 62,* 11–21. https://doi.org/10.1016/j.dss.2014.02.006

Holt, T. J., & Bossler, A. M. (2014). An assessment of the current state of cybercrime scholarship. *Deviant Behavior, 35,* 20–40. https://doi.org/10.1080/01639625.2013.822209

Lee, M., & Lee, J. (2012). The impact of information security failure on customer behaviors: A study on a large-scale hacking incident on the Internet. *Information Systems Frontiers, 14,* 375–393. https://doi.org/10.1007/s10796-010-9253-1

Ludin, I. H. B. H., & Cheng, B. L. (2014). Factors influencing customer satisfaction and e-loyalty: Online shopping environment among the young adults. *Management Dynamics in the Knowledge Economy, 2,* 462–471. www.managementdynamics.ro

Safa, N. S., & Solms, R. V. (2016). An information security knowledge sharing model in organizations. *Computers in Human Behavior, 57,* 442–451. https://doi.org/10.1016/j.chb.2015.12.037

Safa, N. S., Solms, R. V., & Furnell, S. (2016). Information security policy compliance model in organizations. *Computers & Security, 56,* 70–82. https://doi.org/10.1016/j.cose.2015.10.006

Sedlack, D. J., & Tejay, G. P. (2011). Improving information security through technological frames of reference. *Proceedings of the Southern Association for Information Systems Conference, USA: Southern Association for Information Systems,* 153–157. https://aisel.aisnet.org/sais2011/30

Starbuck, W. H. (2014). Why corporate governance deserves serious and creative thought. *Academy of Management Perspectives, 28,* 15–21. https://doi.org/10.5465/amp.2013.0109

Trautman, L. J., Triche, J., & Wetherbe, J. C. (2013). Corporate information technology governance under fire. *Journal of Strategic and International Studies, 8*(3), 105–114. www.isisworld.org

Yaokumah, W. (2014). Information security governance implementation within Ghanaian industry sectors: An empirical study. *Information Management & Computer Security, 22,* 235–250. https://doi.org/10.1108/IMCS-06-2013-0044

Chapter 1

Security Governance

Abstract

Dependence on information by for-profit and not-for-profit organizational formations continues to expand. However, distinguishing information security from cybersecurity is a perspective issue. Contextually, information security means protecting information and information systems from unauthorized access, use, disclosure, modification, disruption, and destruction. In contrast, cybersecurity focuses on protecting IT that acquires, stores, manipulates, manages, moves, controls, displays, switches, interchanges, or transmits digitally encoded data. In contrast, Information Security Governance (ISG) necessitates taking the expanded view that the entity's data, information, and derived knowledge must receive appropriate protection without regard to the acquisition, handling, processing, transport, or storage method. Chapter 1 focuses on the effect of entity governance, ISG, and Cyber Security Governance as management tools for appropriate information and technology security.

Introduction

Information usually obtains value when considered usable in decision-making (Davis, 2008a). Security is a prominent component within organizational governance that enables fulfilling a stakeholder expectation (Brotby, 2009; Davis, 2017; Flores et al., 2014). Part of the stakeholder security expectation is satisfied through appropriate Information Security Governance (ISG; Davis, 2008a, 2013). Properly constructed and implemented, ISG supports stakeholder expectations concerning management's explicit or implicit fiduciary responsibilities (Davis, 2008a, 2011, 2017).

Loyalty to the person or group (i.e., principal) tasking the duty is a fiduciary expectation (Davis, 2008a). Consequently, personal interests do not supersede a fiduciary duty, and the fiduciary must not profit from the position unless the principal consents (Davis, 2008a). Therefore, a fiduciary should avoid engaging in activities where personal interests and fiduciary duty are conflictive and situations where the fiduciary duty conflicts with another fiduciary duty (Davis, 2008a). Moreover, a fiduciary should not seek personal benefit from the fiduciary position without expressing principal knowledge and consent (Davis, 2008a).

Control is the exercise of directing or restraining influence (Avison, 2007). An organization's information security controls comprise the procedures adopted or devised to furnish management with some degree of comfort regarding the achievement of protection objectives for information assets. An entity's management should, and in several countries do, have a legal responsibility to implement adequate control systems for preventing, detecting, and conditionally correcting errors, mistakes, omissions, irregularities, and illegal acts (Davis, 2006, 2008a).

ISG should address creating and implementing a "system of security controls" that enable ethical and legal managerial responsibilities fulfillment for information assets protection (IAP). Ethically, management must protect an entity's information assets from potential internal and external threats that can compromise confidentiality, integrity, or availability in order to preserve organization, presentation, and utilization value (Ahmad et al., 2014; Brotby, 2006; Davis, 2008a, 2017; Whitman & Mattord, 2012). Legally, within an entity's information security control system, explicitly or implicitly, management as fiduciary agents are responsible and accountable for deploying controls that prevent, deter, detect, and correct unacceptable actions (Davis, 2008a).

Management's information systems related to due care drives appropriate information security due-diligence activities that emanate from fiduciary responsibilities (Boyson, 2014; Davis, 2008a, 2017; Whitman & Mattord, 2012). Instituting and sustaining information safeguarding necessitate a comprehensive program addressing cyber threats that can thwart organizational mission achievement (Ahmad et al., 2014; Davis, 2017; Kushwaha, 2016; Mohare & Lanjewar, 2012). Information security breaches can originate from external or internal actions (Crossler et al., 2013; Davis, 2017; Silic & Back, 2014). Therefore, responsible information technology (IT) manager-leaders should ensure ethical behavior by every individual interacting with the organization's information systems through effectual ISG (Boyson, 2014; Davis, 2017). However, organizational IAP breaches have decreased value appropriation (Clark & Harrell, 2013; Silic & Back, 2014).

IAP should be an entity's uppermost concern because IT security incidents can compromise the confidentiality, integrity, or availability of financial and operational systems (Davis, 2008a). Sources of IAP threats can be a person, thing, or event (Davis, 2008a). Scholars and practitioners have synopsized that information security is no longer mainly a technology issue needing operational IT personnel handling but rather more of a governance concern (Davis, 2017; Julisch, 2013; Mohare & Lanjewar, 2012; Whitman & Mattord, 2012).

No single theoretical or practice approach can encompass organizational governance diversity. The Governance Tree framework aims to mobilize and facilitate applying a controls approach in a shared practitioner program while increasing comparability reflecting different scholarly perspectives. The framework allows scholars and practitioners to investigate and apply the drivers, forms, causal mechanisms, and organizational governance pathways, considering the effects on regulatory capacity, performance, and outcomes. This chapter presents the discernible ISG perspectives and evolution. The discussions in this chapter also define cybersecurity reflecting a contextually based understanding and Cyber Security Governance integration insights. Moreover, this chapter advances the organizational governance research agenda by illustrating the Governance Tree framework's applicability within empirical contexts.

Governance Perspectives

Organizational governance can supply a framework for ethical decision-making and managerial action predicated on transparency, accountability, and defined roles (Marnewick & Labuschagne, 2011). Implicit expectations for effective governance reside in the fiduciary relationship between stakeholders' and organizational managements' adherence to shared morality values (Davis, 2008a, 2017). Morality values link to principles and standards (Bagozzi et al., 2009; Northouse, 2013). Values of stakeholders and managements typically address morality regarding overall image perceptions and detailed edicts consisting of regulatory guides for behavior (Bagozzi et al., 2009; Ferrell, 2005). Internationally, a fiduciary duty is considered the highest care standard imposed through law or equity (Davis, 2008a).

Fiduciary relationship establishment may be an expectancy by the entrusting party or decreed by law or regulation (Davis, 2008a). Commonly, fiduciary relationships can exist for professionals, agents, executors, trustees, guardians, and entity employees (Brotby, 2006; Davis, 2008a). Salient fiduciary relationship features are loyalty, good faith, and trust at the entity employee level (Davis, 2008a). Loyalty is faithfulness to the obligating principal (Davis, 2008a). Good faith represents a veracious intention to abstain from taking unfair advantage of another (Davis, 2008a). Trust reflects confidence reposed in one person to manage or safeguard entrusted property for another's benefit (Davis, 2008a).

Ethical values affect fiduciary loyalty, good faith, and trust. As a set of moral principles, ethics can represent the science of social duty or rules of responsibility drawn from personal duty science (Davis, 2008a). Additionally, ethics can reference a system of rules and principles concerning the duty or the practice linking a social action class (Davis, 2008a). Deontological ethics only considers rational judgments in determining if an action is right or wrong (Bagozzi et al., 2009; Northouse, 2013). In contrast, teleological ethics for a decision to act considers potential outcomes, and virtue ethics focuses primarily on moral character aspects (Bagozzi et al., 2009). Commonly ethical behavior sustains principle–agent fiduciary relationships (Davis, 2008a).

Integrity values also affect fiduciary loyalty, good faith, and trust (Davis, 2008a). Integrity can be considered a set of moral values that reflect the state or quality encompassing honesty, moral principles, uprightness, and sincerity (Davis, 2008a). Typically, integrity results when individuals receive high ethical and behavioral standard communications and practice enforcement (Davis, 2008a). Organizational integrity standards should include administrative actions for removing or reducing incentives and temptations that might prompt employees to engage in dishonest, illegal, or immoral behavior (Davis, 2008a). Organizational governance is a means to attempt controlling contemptible individual and group actions to benefit entity continuity.

Governance assists in satisfying stakeholder expectations concerning managerial responsibilities (Davis, 2008a, 2017). Stakeholder identification (Gil-Lafuente & Paula, 2013) and applying value analysis (Harrison & Wicks, 2013) assist in assessing entity-level strategy and organizational culture alignment (Davis, 2017). Derivatively, the alignment of stakeholder values and organizational values depends on effectively and efficiently pursuing the defined mission while strictly adhering to espoused entity values (Davis, 2017). Alignment exists and is sustainable considering stakeholder values when an entity can furnish products or services supporting acceptable value creation (Chou, 2015; Davis, 2017; Di Gregorio, 2013) and value appropriation (Davis, 2017; Di Gregorio, 2013). Stakeholder value creation and appropriation are derivable from the relevance and quality of products and services, affiliation utility, organizational justice cognitions, and opportunity cost perceptions (Harrison & Wicks, 2013). Values alignment construct deviation by organizational management could result in stakeholder dissatisfaction generating perceptions that competitors offer a stronger value proposition (Davis, 2017).

Information assets contain or can contain data (Davis, 2012, 2017) that may be subject to dishonest, illegal, or immoral behavior. Organizational management needs to address IAP at the governance level to mitigate technology deployment informational risks (Davis, 2017; Yaokumah, 2013). However, the managerial perspective for ISG has diverging views concerning accountability (Williams et al., 2013). On the one hand, some practitioners and scholars considered ISG responsibilities to be an IT governance accountability subfunction (Gheorghe, 2010). On the other hand, some practitioners and scholars considered ISG to have discrete function accountability to those responsible for entity governance (Williams et al., 2013).

Without regard to whether management views ISG as a program directly supporting entity governance or an IT governance program subset, IAP is necessary (Davis, 2017). In meeting the needed IAP, information security perspectives must address managerial and technical aspects (Silic & Back, 2014). An adaptive balance between rational management and applied technology enables appropriate information security (Ahmad et al., 2014; Brotby, 2006; Davis, 2017; Safa & Von Solms, 2016). Organizational management's development and deployment of reasonable information security policies and procedures permit ensuring appropriate IAP, while efficaciously applied information security technology can increase IAP effectiveness in addressing potential internal and external threats (Ahmad et al., 2014; Davis, 2017).

Rational Management

Management is the act of achieving organizational objectives through the use of available resources. In other words, management is an interactive function that entails planning, organizing, orchestrating, directing, and controlling activities in an organizational setting (Davis, 2008a; Kotter, 2001; Maccoby, 2000; Northouse, 2013). Sound management practice approach to IAP is unavoidable given information systems and associated technology continue increasing in complexity (Bahl & Wali, 2014; Davis, 2008a).

Typically, primary purposes of information systems are useful data collection, reliable input processing, and timely output dissemination (Davis, 2008a). Information systems' integration design and deployment should include appropriate control measures to achieve management's objectives (Davis, 2008a). A controls-based approach for information systems operates according to a prescribed or bounded set of criteria. Therefore, an entity's management should consider IAP as a service requirement that ensures expected delivery and support by applying relevant information criteria (Davis, 2008a). An entity's information delivery and support deployment should adequately address effectiveness, efficiency, confidentiality, integrity, availability, compliance, and reliability criteria (Davis, 2008a), where the generally accepted principles for information security are confidentiality, integrity, and availability (Arief et al., 2015; Samonas & Coss, 2014).

Classically, managers receive assignments to function at various authority, responsibility, and accountability levels (Davis, 2008a). Managerial authority, responsibility, and accountability delegation usually occur after considering the following facts:

- Authority provides the power or right to give commands, enforce obedience, initiate action, or make final decisions (Davis, 2008a, 2011). How organizational assignments occur as well as how reporting relationships and authorization hierarchy establishments transpire depend on authority status (Davis, 2008b). Managerial authority invokes leadership responsibilities for activities within the assigned authority domain (Davis, 2008b). An entity's policies and procedures for assigning authority for activities affect the understanding of established reporting relationships and designated authorization authority (Davis, 2008b).
- Responsibility is an obligation to account for or answer for something or someone (Davis, 2008a). Responsibility is generally an appointed authority corollary (Davis, 2008a, 2008b). A sufficient responsibility assignment milieu includes communications and policies directed at ensuring all organizational employees understand the entity's objectives, knowledge regarding how individual actions interrelate and contribute to adopted objectives, as well as recognition of how and for what they will be held accountable (Davis, 2008b). Additionally, policies relating to appropriate organizational practices, essential personnel knowledge and experience, and resources provided for carrying out duties are vital components of assigning responsibility (Davis, 2008b).
- Accountability permits ensuring appropriately administered authority within the assigned responsibilities' context (Davis, 2008a, 2008b, 2017). Accountability institutes the obligation to answer for a responsibility conferred or implied (Davis, 2008a,

2008b). Employee accountability affects the responsibility for meeting standards (Davis, 2008a, 2008b, 2017). When accountability is remiss, standards become ineffective measurement tools (Davis, 2008a, 2008b, 2017).

Organizational power stems from meanings, resources, processes, and systems (Kolkowska & Dhillon, 2013). Leadership involves using authority to aid followers in dealing with conflicting values that emerge in organizational environments and social cultures (Northouse, 2013). Manager-leaders as fiduciaries ensure performance, commitment, or orchestration to minimize organization discontinuity risks. Employee power granting can occur through managerial authority (Davis, 2008a, 2017). IAP responsibility delegation is necessary (Davis, 2008a, 2017; Posey et al., 2014). The appropriate amount of authority must transfer with an assigned responsibility (Davis, 2008a, 2017). However, a superordinate reporting position within the entity cannot evade the ultimate accountability for delegated responsibility and authority (Davis, 2008a, 2017).

Organizational structures provide the foundation for achieving entity objectives (Davis, 2011). An entity should develop organizational structures suited to perceived needs (Davis, 2011). Entity-centric organizational structuring is partially dependent on the size and nature of forecasted outcomes. Furthermore, organizational structuring includes deploying proper authority and responsibility with adequate accountability for selected programs, systems, processes, activities, and tasks. IAP manager-leaders should address four resource classifications: people, information, processes, and infrastructure (Davis, 2008a; De Haes et al., 2013). As shown in Figure 1.1, IAP management responsibilities commonly include (a) planning, (b) organizing, (c) orchestrating, (d) directing, and (e) controlling (Davis, 2008a).

- Planning: Manager-leaders should help set objectives and establish specific achievable operational goals to accomplish objectives (i.e., Action Plan). Furthermore, superordinate manager-leaders should evaluate the operational goal expectations (i.e., Goal Achievement Indicators) and the techniques considered necessary for achievement (i.e., Performance Achievement Indicators) submitted by subordinates.
- Organizing: Manager-leaders should acquire and administrate resources reflective of the entity's control environment. Resource integration requires knowledge of the entity's organizational structures, strategies, processes, skills, personnel, superordinate goals, and styles.
- Orchestrating: Resources typically require flexible structuring to achieve goals and objectives that enable expected value creation. However, the best planning, organizing, directing, and controlling will avail nothing unless capable and sufficient personnel assignment occurs through a manager-leaders' active participation in employment practices.
- Directing: A manager-leaders' responsibility is to be proactive, not merely reactive, regarding information security. Additionally, a manager-leader should create and maintain communications and sustain assigned personnel momentum toward defined goal achievement within the entity's control environment.
- Controlling: Normally, manager-leaders are responsible for the establishment, measurement, and performance of controls. The security options for control mixture range between dynamic resource redirection and fine-tuning organizational processes.

Basic management tenets enable fiduciary responsibility standardization. Nonetheless, managerial titles vary by the entity and organizational function (Davis, 2008b). Typically, position expectations correspond to managerial status. Top-level managers are usually responsible for overall entity direction and are accountable to stakeholders. Moreover, top-level managers have the authority to establish measurable and achievable high-level

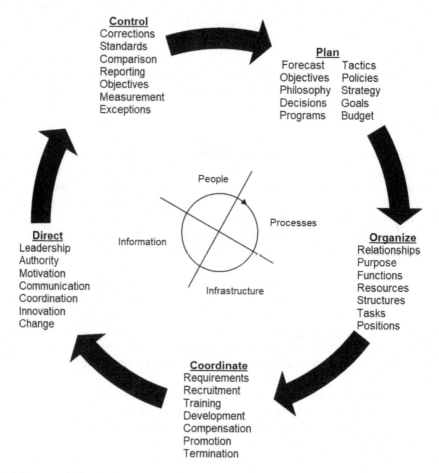

Figure 1.1 Managerial Responsibilities Model.

Note: Adapted from *IT Auditing: IT Service Delivery and Support* by R. E. Davis, 2008b, Pleier. Copyright 2008 by Robert E. Davis. Adapted with permission.

goals ensuring adopted high-level objective attainment (Davis, 2008a) for programs, systems, processes, or activities.

Middle-level managers are typically responsible and accountable for designated programs, systems, or processes (Davis, 2020). Simultaneously, these managers are accountable upward regarding entity goals and objective achievement, and responsible downward as top-level management representatives (Davis, 2008a). At the lower-level management spectrum, managers are generally considered supervisors (Davis, 2008a). Supervisors are usually responsible for daily operations and direct interaction with assigned employees to create, sustain, or terminate processes or activities (Davis, 2008a). Furthermore, supervisors are generally accountable for middle-level management-assigned responsibilities (Davis, 2008a).

As with IT governance (Davis, 2011), ISG is viewable as a framework, methodology, or technique depending on the managerial abstraction level. From the framework view, ISG enables a "system of controls", assisting in assuring organizational goals and objectives' achievement. From the methodology view, ISG furnishes a description of the role entity direction and controls have in achieving information systems objectives. Moreover, from the technique view, ISG construction and use support systems, processes, activities, and tasks generating financial or reputational returns for stakeholders.

When entity management conceptualizes ISG as a framework for assisting in governance, then, structurally, the implementation should occur as an organizational program with objectives, goals, policies, procedures, standards, and rules designed to accomplish management's intentions. To drive controls, ISG should subsequently receive significant program status because of the direct effect on other program results – such as cybersecurity. Furthermore, the obtainment of control efficiency should transpire through models available to assist in deploying ISG.

Alternatively, if entity management perceives ISG as a methodology for achieving organizational information system objectives, adopted processes should provide a series of assessments enabling defining control usefulness and deployment. The adopted processes for ISG should conjunctively relate to the managerial authority, responsibility, and accountability structure sustaining established transparency. Management is usually concerned with the control costs and the benefits derived from control deployments and usage within the methodology abstraction level while achieving the strategic direction. Hence, understanding ISG roles is considered the key to managing IAP.

If, however, entity management assumes ISG provides financial and reputational benefits through appropriate techniques, potential stakeholders are presumed to rely upon governance elements. General investors have estimated the price and volume reactions to information security breach announcements based on the textual contents of the reports (Wang et al., 2013). Therefore, ascertaining information security objective effectiveness and efficiency through monitoring is rudimentary to sound practices for satisfying stakeholder expectations. In this regard, effectiveness and efficiency evaluation require measurement against established standards. The performance measures establishment should occur when standards are created or adopted. Techniques used for ISG implementation may include capability maturity modeling, budgeting, benchmarking, and gap analysis. With an organization's reputation enhanced through demonstrated profitability when employing ISG, new stakeholder attraction may accrue as a benefit.

Whatever the organizational management perspective is, overlooking the criticality of effective and efficient ISG in the current global high technology environment is not a managerial option. Considering what is at stake economically, politically, and technically for most organizations, usually justifying ISG deployment based on one of the three outlined perspectives narrows suitability and expected benefits. In the final analysis, combining the discussed individual abstraction levels may be the most appropriate support for implementing ISG. Nonetheless, a primary ISG focus is establishing a controls-based approach using normative decisions.

Applied Technology

IT security development occurs to protect the acquisition, creation, storage, use, and exchange of digitally encoded information assets against unauthorized access, misuse, malfunction, modification, destruction, or improper disclosure. IT security deployment is implementing measures designed for safeguarding digitally encoded information assets utilizing various technology configurations. Thereby, IT security attempts to preserve the value, confidentiality, integrity, availability, intended use, and the permitted processing of digitally encoded information assets.

IT security threats can be classified into two groups: internal and external. External IT threats manifest through extrinsic activities to the entity (Humaidi & Balakrishnan, 2015).

Internal IT threats manifest through intrinsic activities to the entity (Humaidi & Balakrishnan, 2015). External and internal IT hackers and crackers are a "clear and present danger" to inadequately protected information assets (Davis, 2008a). IT hackers are individuals performing activities that are generally inspired by the desire to experiment with computers for inoffensive purposes (Davis, 2008a). In contrast, IT crackers are individuals performing activities that generally have malicious intent (Davis, 2008a). Nevertheless, IT hackers and crackers activate or exploit perceived IT security vulnerabilities that may produce undesirable events or incidents (Davis, 2008a).

An IT security event may or may not be an IT security incident. However, an IT security incident is an IT security event. An IT security event is any occurrence where electronically encoded information assets may have received exposure to inappropriate activity. IT security threats are events that can inflect unauthorized harm to information assets (Davis, 2008a). If an IT security event was proven to have resulted in an IT security breach, the event is an IT security incident. Potential IT security threats that can convert to IT security incidents include, but are not limited to:

- phishing,
- spyware,
- pharming,
- piracy,
- viruses, and
- denial of service.

IT threats require evaluation, organization, and management to reduce potential entity risks utilizing available resources (Davis, 2008a). IT security resources encompass hardware, software, and firmware mechanisms that are definable as technological controls. As shown in Table 1.1, technological controls are classifiable as addressing Trust Management, Identity Management, Vulnerability Management, and Threat Management

Table 1.1 Potential IAP Technological Resources Categorized by Managerial Use

Trust Management	Identity Management	Vulnerability Management	Threat Management
Digital Rights Management	Provisioning	Trusted Operating System	Network Intrusion Detection
Digital Signature	Password Management	Network Scanner	Antivirus
Application Integrity	Authentication	Vulnerability Assessment	Host Intrusion Detection
Public Key Infrastructure	Web Access Control	Network Intrusion Prevention	Content Scanner
Virtual Private Network	Single Sign-On	Security Resource Planning	Security Event Manager
Encryption	Biometrics	Network Firewall	
		Host Application Control	
		Application Firewall	
		Software Security	

Note: Adapted from *IT Auditing: Assuring Information Assets Protection* by R. E. Davis, 2008a, Pleier. Copyright 2008 by Robert E. Davis. Adapted with permission.

(Davis, 2008a). Trust Management is an approach to ensuring the reliability of resources used for performing authorized functions (Davis, 2008a). Identity Management is the use of managerial techniques and tools for identifying objects (Davis, 2008a). Vulnerability Management is an approach to limiting weaknesses in resource-users, IT-based systems, and physical locations (Davis, 2008a). Moreover, Threat Management is an approach to identifying and responding to malicious or inappropriate activity within a computing environment (Davis, 2008a).

IAP technological criticality is proportional to an entity's IT dependency (Blakley et al., 2001). When an entity's digitally encoded information assets have risks, IAP technology deployments commonly emerge as appropriate exposure reduction measures. However, IAP technology fractionally dispositions information asset risks (Arief & Adzmi, 2015; Blakley et al., 2001). Indeed, inscribed evidence suggests that IAP technology has a partial effectiveness probability (Arief & Adzmi, 2015; Blakley et al., 2001).

Security Program Evolution

An organizational program is a complex structure because it generally consists of multiple interdependent systems that often require diverse interfaces to provide the desired product or service (Davis, 2008a). Characteristically, a program has at least one high-level objective with an organized set of goals, policies, procedures, and rules designed to accomplish a course of action (Davis, 2008a). Critical success factors identify issues needing resolutions to accomplish the program's objectives (Davis, 2008a). Critical success factors also define priority management-oriented deployment guidelines for achieving control over and within systems (Davis, 2008a). When implementing an entity-centric program for information security management, several critical success factors must be satisfied (Davis, 2008a). Critical success factors for information security management include cultural alignment, comprehensive policies, management commitment, employee support, technical expertise, effective marketing, contracting processes, appropriate training, and measurable performance (Davis, 2008a).

An Information Security Office should be responsible for developing and administering an entity's information security program (Davis, 2008b). Information security programs for computerized information systems have evolved from the technology to governance orientation (Davis, 2017). Correspondingly, the information security organizational unit has evolved from being a technology protection provider into a needed strategic safeguarding partner (Davis, 2012). During structural evolution, the information security function can and may have followed a three-stage systematic approach (Sallé, 2004): information security infrastructure management (ISIM), information security service management (ISSM), then ISG.

As shown in Figure 1.2, starting with ISIM, each subsequent evolutionary stage builds upon previously established constructs (Davis, 2008b). During the first stage, an entity's information security function primarily focuses on improving ISIM with the management employing effectiveness measurements – usually based on maximizing return on computing assets and infrastructure control (Davis, 2008b). Upon moving to the second stage, ISSM, the information security function actively identifies services clients need, focusing on planning, organizing, and orchestrating services to meet organizational requirements (Davis, 2008b). Internally and externally, during the ISSM stage, the information security function manages service delivery and support to meet quality and cost targets (Davis, 2008b). When the information security function evolves to the third stage, ISG, transformation into a real entity management partner occurs, enabling new opportunities with

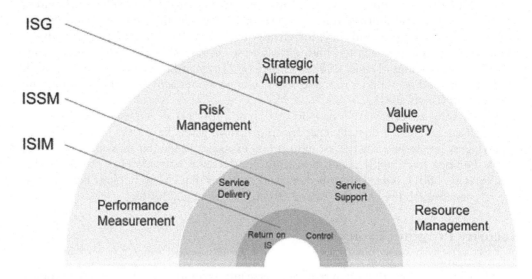

Figure 1.2 Information Security Managerial Evolution.

Note: ISIM, Information Security Infrastructure Management; ISSM, Information Security Service Management; ISG, Information Security Governance; and IS, information security.

appropriate protection mechanisms (Davis, 2008b). Once information security function reaches the ISG stage, information security processes should sustain full integration with organizational processes, thus potentially improving service quality and agility for achieving entity objectives (Davis, 2008b).

Information Security Infrastructure Management

Organizational information infrastructures typically include hardware, operating systems, configuration systems, facilities, and support structures (see Figure 1.3) that enable objective achievement (Davis, 2009b). Due to external and internal computer deviance, security infrastructure integration is a necessity for ensuring adequate IAP. Organizations commonly manage information security infrastructure through a security operations center (Davis, 2008a). An IT security infrastructure supports and enables workforce productivity through appropriate installation and monitoring (Pfaff & Ries, 2014).

Adequate information security infrastructure permits the continuance and growth of technology-based systems. An entity's information security infrastructure frequently integrates diverse software and hardware solutions, each designed to achieve a specific function. For most organizations, ISIM administrates essential protection components that enable obtaining architectural effectiveness and efficiency. As a critical ingredient to designing, deploying, and sustaining efficacy, the entity's information security infrastructure requires controls.

Controls

Systems and infrastructure design affect the controls relied on by an entity's management (Davis, 2010). Building organizational systems and infrastructure using Safeguarding-by-Design model necessitates incorporating security features that help protect data, whether at

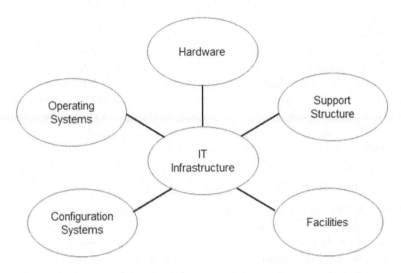

Figure 1.3 IT Infrastructure Resources.

Note: IT, information technology. Adapted from *IT auditing: Systems and infrastructure life cycle management* by R. E. Davis, 2009b, Pleier. Copyright 2009 by Robert E. Davis. Adapted with permission.

rest or in transit (Stürmer et al., 2005). Safeguarding-by-Default is a part of the Safeguarding-by-Design model where no required individual action is necessary to protect the data (Stürmer et al., 2005). Consequently, considering typical information security development costs with expressed information security project expectations is imperative (Davis, 2009b).

From a management perspective, the design and development phases of entity-centric information systems or infrastructure assets are critical points to emphasize security controls. The installing of controls before a new informational asset becomes active helps ensure deployable item reliability (Davis, 2009b). Indeed, doing an information security deployment correctly the first time is less challenging than adding controls after systems or infrastructure implementation (Davis, 2009b). Moreover, adding systems or infrastructure controls after implementation may not be feasible due to significant architectural revision costs (Davis, 2009b).

Return on Security Investment

For information security projects, financially related data is necessary to establish cost-oriented steering (Beebe et al., 2014; Davis, 2009b; Sonnenreich et al., 2006). In particular, the benefit from an investment necessitates evaluation in terms of potential realizable value and time-adjusted expected performance (Beebe et al., 2014; Davis, 2009b; Sonnenreich et al., 2006). Addressing realizable value includes calculating return on security investment as a primary gauge for determining whether to proceed with an information security project (Sonnenreich et al., 2006).

Information Security Service Management

Considering adamant stakeholder demands for continuous process improvements, overall information protection and security delivery value in terms of enabled services have become the managerial norm (Davis, 2008a). ISSM is a set of processes enabling and potentially optimizing operational requirement fulfillment while simultaneously providing strategic and tactical infrastructure management (Davis, 2008a). ISSM should be considered a quality of service administration permitting demonstrable process improvement contributions (Davis, 2008a).

Most entities contain a group of core processes (Davis, 2008b). Consistent with this view, ISSM encompasses processes for maintaining and improving service quality alignment (Davis, 2008b), which link to a protective service value system. A protective service value system allows all the component processes, activities, and tasks to work together for value creation. Information security service alignment occurs through a constant cycle of agreeing, monitoring, reporting, reviewing achievements, and initiating actions to eradicate unacceptable information security service levels.

Information Security Service Delivery

Information security service delivery necessitates effective ISSM practices. Management should design objectives and goals for information security service delivery (see Table 1.2). Regarding accomplishing objectives and goals, particular links passing through strategic, tactical, and operational management levels of functional reporting ensure alignment with the entity's mission (Davis, 2008b). High-level control objectives need identification and linkage with rationale for the development of lower-level information security objectives and goals.

Information Security Service Support

In delivering adequate services, the necessary support processes must be established and functioning consistent with entity-centric service requirements (Davis, 2008b). Information security service support comprises those disciplines that enable information security

Table 1.2 Information Security Service Delivery Domains, Objectives, and Goals

Domain	Objectives	Goals
Service Level Management	Define and manage information security service levels	Deliver information security services that comply with agreed-upon service-level requirements.
Capacity Management	Manage information security service resources	Provision of appropriate resource allocations for information security service activities.
Availability Management	Ensure continuous information security service	Sustain information security services as required by operational level agreements.
Continuity Management	Ensure information security service resilience	Provide a predetermined and agreed-upon level of information security services in the case of a disastrous event.
	Assess information security risks	
		Prioritize information security service resumption in the case of a disastrous event.
Financial Management	Manage the information security investment	Account for information security spending and attribute costs to information security services delivered for the entity.
	Identify automated information security solutions	Assist management in decisions regarding information security investments.
	Identify and allocate information security costs	
	Obtain independent information security assurance	

Table 1.3 Information Security Service Support Domains, Objectives, and Goals

Domain	Objectives	Goals
Configuration Management	Manage the information security architecture	Account for information security assets and configurations within the entity as well as associated services.
		Provide accurate information on security configurations and referential inscription.
		Provide a sound basis for other information security support processes, activities, and tasks.
		Verify the information security configuration records and correct exceptions.
Incident Management	Manage information security service incidents	Swiftly restore normal service operations.
		Minimize adverse effects on entity operations.
Problem Management	Manage information security problems	Critical information security problems are solved expeditiously.
		Reduce repetitive information security issues.
Change Management	Prepare and accredit information security modifications	Information security change accreditation occurs within the agreed time with minimal deployment risk.
Release Management	Install and accredit authorized information security changes	Only accredited information security component deployments occur.

services delivery to users. Information security service support focuses on providing daily operational level buttress. As with information security service delivery, information security service support needs objectives and goals (see Table 1.3).

Information Security Governance

ISG is a program by which entities are directed and controlled (Davis, 2008a, 2017). A formal ISG program is usually necessary for safeguarding information assets (Davis, 2012; Srivastava & Kumar, 2015) because of increased entity information incursions. The evolution of ISG processes often involves factors related to improving security functionality, efficiency, or effectiveness. An ISG program can assist in ensuring information confidentiality, integrity, availability, and compliance and in ensuring that the reliability compromises do not occur through gaps in controls (Davis, 2012). However, the information security program and associated systems, processes, and activities need regular efficacy assessments for quality and compliance with defined requirements (Davis, 2012). Monitoring and evaluating information security drive assurances through due care and due diligence (Davis, 2012). Monitoring and evaluating information security also enables managerial fiduciary oversight expectations fulfillment (Davis, 2012).

Reflective of shared information and communication requirements that sustain employee accountability consistency, governance occurs at different organizational strata, with procedures tailored for processes, with processes linking up to systems, and programs receiving objectives from the entity's oversight committee through established reporting lines (Davis, 2008a, 2017). Alternatively, designated technological resources may provide information directly to the entity's oversight committee for critical programs, systems, or processes (Davis, 2008a). Nonetheless, the governance connectivity approach options are not practical unless approved plans, as well as strategic objectives and goals, have first been conveyed within the entity's organizational structure (Davis, 2008a). Therefore, management should govern safeguarding information assets through an objectives-oriented security program or risk excessive incidents that may affect customer loyalty, financial stability, and employee morale (Davis, 2008a).

The overall objective of an ISG program should be provisioning assurance that information assets receive appropriate protection levels commensurate with their value or the risk an information asset compromise poses to the entity. Management commonly needs governance that enables organizational alignment, intrinsic value delivery, adaptive risk management, judicious resource allotments, and accurate performance measurement to accomplish protection expectations (Davis, 2008a, 2017; Mohare & Lanjewar, 2012). Management in addressing information security issues should apply:

- strategic alignment centering on ensuring entity, IT, and information security plan linkage; defining, maintaining, and validating the information security value proposition; and information security operational congruence with the entity and IT operations (Davis, 2008a, 2017). Entity manager-leaders should enhance strategic alignment attributes to achieve effectual ISG (Davis, 2017; Yaokumah & Brown, 2014). Effective strategic alignment must be dynamic, sharable, and malleable (Yaokumah & Brown, 2014) to meet entity, IT, and information security environment changes (Davis, 2008a);
- value delivery that executes the information security value proposition throughout the delivery cycle, ensuring that information security delivers benefits against the adopted entity strategy, concentrates on optimizing costs, and proves intrinsic information security value (Davis, 2008a). Effectual ISG value delivery practices recognize different investment categories that must be asymmetrically evaluated and managed (Yaokumah & Brown, 2014);
- risk management reflecting principles, processes, and approaches using a systematic application (Rasheed et al., 2015). Consequently, organizational risk management necessitates information security risk awareness by senior officials, a clear understanding of the entity's appetite for information security risks, understanding requirements to accomplish information security compliance, transparency regarding significant information security risks, and embedding internal risk management responsibilities (Davis, 2008a);
- resource management reflecting the intention for optimal investment in and the proper administration of information security resources (Davis, 2008a; Mohare & Lanjewar, 2012; Yaokumah, 2013). Resource management focus areas are information security knowledge and infrastructure processing efficiency (Davis, 2008a); and
- performance measurement practices that involve quantifying, monitoring, and reporting information security systems, processes, and related activities to ensure achievement of organizational objectives (IT Governance Institute, 2008). Minimally, performance measurement administrators track and monitor information security strategy implementations, information security project completions, information security resource utilization, information security process performance, and information security service delivery (Davis, 2008a).

Managerial aids available for deploying or enhancing an entity-centric ISG program include the United States Department of Commerce, National Institute of Standards and Technology's, Minimum Security Requirements for Federal Information and Information

Systems (Federal Information Processing Standard 200); the Organization for Economic Cooperation and Development's Guidelines for the Security of Information Systems and Networks – Towards a Culture of Security; the International Organization for Standardization/International Electrotechnical Commission's, Information Security Management System Family of Standards (ISO/IEC 27000); and ISACA's Information Security Governance: Guidance for Boards of Directors and Executive Management.

Framing Governance

Frameworks can capture oblique models (Pagani, 2013). Moreover, frameworks can serve as a tool for organizational leaders to build effective organizational programs (e.g., Atoum et al., 2014; Committee of Sponsoring Organizations of the Treadway Commission, 2013; Davis, 2008a; Sindhuja, 2014; Williams et al., 2013). Controls immersion should be transparent throughout an entity's adopted framework (Davis, 2008a) to ensure appropriate IAP. When framing governance, domains can be formed and connected through parent–child informational relationships, for example (Davis, 2008a).

Hierarchical node connectivity establishment enables foundational linkage when standard attribute sharing occurs in parent–child data relationships (Kearney & Kruger, 2013; Davis, 2011, 2017). Idiomatically, a technological hierarchical structure depicting central data collection and the dissemination points is often called a tree (Davis, 2008a). The model composition is a set of elements – known as nodes – that link as disjoint subsets (Davis, 2008a). However, unlike biological trees, technological trees have an inverted germination base, where lower-level accessibility is only achievable through top-down paths to associated elements (Davis, 2008a). Interpretively, Governance Tree dimensions enable describing managerial information and communication aspects permitting nodal family alignment (Davis, 2008a).

Entity interactions exist in various forms, including strategic, tactical, and operational mandates (Davis, 2008a). Applying the Governance Tree framework allows methodological value-driven consideration in developing and deploying aligned programs that positively affect control environment awareness and subsequent resource allocation decisions (Davis, 2008a). Governance Tree structural behavior integrates an open system approach that continually interacts with the external and internal environment through functionally adaptive mechanisms permitting organizational redirection (Davis, 2008a). Consequently, an active Governance Tree node must enable management to accurately forecast events affecting organizational plans or confront the possibility of consolidation or elimination (Davis, 2008a). Moreover, a factor stagnation within a dynamic Governance Tree node will typically cease significantly swaying managerial decisions over time (Davis, 2008a).

Tier One Governance

Governance Tree contextual comprehension permits conceptualization for a superior information security program deployment (Davis, 2008a). Figure 1.4 depicts three tiers of the Governance Tree model. Tier one of the Governance Tree represents stakeholders capable of directing or controlling entity nodal information and communication activity (Davis, 2008a). Stakeholders are groups or individuals who directly or indirectly have an interest in the entity or can influence objective achievements (Ogunsakin, 2015). If not directly, entity activities indirectly are affected by extrapolated external conditions presented in stakeholder information (Davis, 2008a). Specifically, first-tier stakeholders provide expectation information affecting linked nodes within the Governance Tree model (Davis, 2008a).

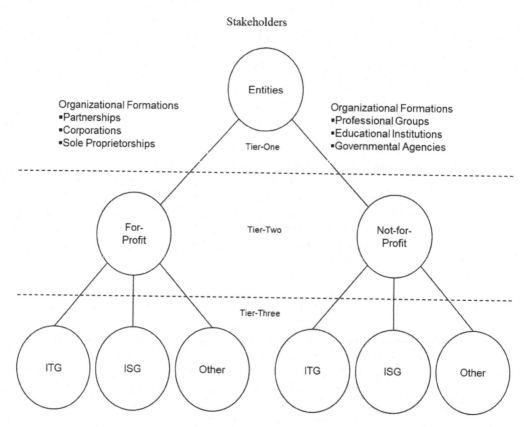

Figure 1.4 Governance Tree: First, Second, and Third Tier Structural View.

Note: ITG, Information Technology Governance; ISG, Information Security Governance. Adapted from *IT Auditing: Assuring Information Assets Protection* by R. E. Davis, 2008a, Pleier. Copyright 2008 by Robert E. Davis. Adapted with permission.

At the tier one level of the Governance Tree model, organizational formations exist as entities with a collective purpose (Davis, 2008a). The collective purpose can be for-profit or not-for-profit. Organizational formations typically occur to satisfy a perceived need for a product or service based on the available information (Davis, 2008a). Entity manager-leaders are subject to constituent stakeholders' expectations and pressures such as suppliers, customers, employees, government regulators, and shareholders (Bagozzi et al., 2009; Heracleous & Lan, 2012). Consequently, manager-leaders must often negotiate issues related to organizational potency and viability while simultaneously balancing various stakeholder needs (Bagozzi et al., 2009; Ferrell, 2005).

Governing an entity mandates management to accurately conceptualize organizational development, information criticality, and communication paths. For-profit manager-leaders tend to view value in financial terms (Davis, 2011). Contrastingly, not-for-profit manager-leaders tend to perceive value in nonfinancial terms (Davis, 2011). Governance is necessary for both organizational classifications to ensure that management pursues achieving the entity's mission ethically and legally (Davis, 2008a). Regarding information criticality and communication paths, governance conveyance frequently occurs using the entity stakeholder architectural links (Davis, 2008a).

Governance descriptions embrace language explaining incentives and relationships among oversight committee members, senior executives, and other stakeholders resulting in financial accountability, transparent responsibility, and assertion reliability (Davis, 2008a). Exercising effective governance throughout an entity requires the highest oversight committee and senior executives have a clear understanding of what to expect from entity programs, systems, and processes (Davis, 2008a). An entity's oversight committee and senior executives need to direct resource deployments, evaluate the entity's status regarding existing plans, and determine strategies as well as objectives for programs (Davis, 2008a). Organizational information and communication rely on a hierarchical data structure, with the parent Governance Tree node connecting to offspring to drive administrative cohesiveness (Davis, 2008a).

Entity tonal and nodal associations create useful decision-making structures that enable achieving objectives and goals. Information is generally the primal basis for decision-making (Davis, 2008a). However, to affect decision-making, information must be communicated through an acceptable medium (Davis, 2008a). Communication is critical for formulating, implementing, organizing, and controlling the entity-centric purpose (Davis, 2008a). Effective communication unifies and simultaneously permits environment, risk, data, and activity stratification (Davis, 2008a). Characteristically, organizational information flows through multiplexed communication networks to ensure appropriate employee direction and participation (Davis, 2008a). Conceptually, considering the Governance Tree structure, precise information using suitable communication flows to and from various horizontally linked and vertically aligned nodes (Davis, 2008a) enables organizational cohesiveness.

Tier Two Governance

For-profit organizational formations exist to generate tangible and intangible wealth for stakeholders in the tier two Governance Tree nodes (Davis, 2008a). Contrastingly, not-for-profit organizational formations exist to satisfy perceived societal needs (Davis, 2008a). Abstraction development occurs based on perceived usefulness (Davis, 2008a). The Governance Tree tier two nodes are entity-level hubs that collect, analyze, evaluate, and disseminate information (Davis, 2008a). Tier two Governance Tree information nodes are also viewable in the context of programs, systems, and processes (Davis, 2008a). Thus, pragmatically, the establishment of entity-level governance is a second-tier concentrator within the Governance Tree model that focuses on:

- designing and implementing necessary activities,
- institutionalizing risk assessments,
- providing fluid information and communication,
- ensuring performance monitoring and evaluation, as well as
- creating an appropriate control environment (Davis, 2008a).

For-Profit Governance

Strategic organizational management is often transformational and dynamic because for-profit enterprises confront various risks (Nishimura, 2006). For-profit entities can apply enterprise governance, where:

Enterprise governance is a set of responsibilities and practices exercised by the board and executive management with the goal of providing strategic direction, ensuring that objectives are achieved, ascertaining that risks are managed appropriately and verify-ing that the enterprise's resources are used [sic] responsibly.

(IT Governance Institute, 2003, p. 6)

Nonetheless, the Enterprise Governance nexus is aiding the board in identifying crucial decision-making points, understanding the organization's appetite for risk and vital per-formance drivers, and making strategic decisions (Connell et al., 2004).

Enterprise Governance must encompass the entire for-profit organizational account-ability framework (Connell et al., 2004). Controllability and disclosure are pointless without accountability (Nishimura, 2006). Therefore, for-profit enterprises should merge accountability with controllability and disclosure (Nishimura, 2006). Feed-forward and feedback control systems are necessary deployments where accountability, controllability, and disclosure are fundamental governance elements (Nishimura, 2006).

Enterprise governance represents a conceptual framework (Van der Stede, 2010; Nugroho, 2014) that integrates Corporate Governance and Business Governance aspects (Nishimura, 2006). Corporate Governance addresses organizational conformance (Connell et al., 2004; Nishimura, 2006) that covers issues such as roles, board structures, and execu-tive compensation (Connell et al., 2004). Business Governance addresses organizational performance, focusing on strategy and value creation (Connell et al., 2004; Nishimura, 2006).

Not-for-Profit Governance

Not-for-profit governance deployment gives the entity oversight committee authority to exercise administrative power on behalf of the served community (Chelliah et al., 2015). The not-for-profit oversight committee member roles are (a) setting organizational direc-tion and strategy, (b) providing organizational oversight, and (c) furnishing access to resources needed by the organization (Chelliah et al., 2015). Not-for-profit governance commonly focuses on achieving the entity's social mission and ensuring the sustainment of the entity's credibility, image, and viability (Viader & Espina, 2014). Organizational cred-ibility is fundamental for overcoming hesitant support that a not-for-profit governance may face when seeking funding (Viader & Espina, 2014). Image is an essential aspect of viability for achieving the not-for-profit entity's social mission (Viader & Espina, 2014). Nonetheless, governance frameworks used in for-profit entities may be usable in not-for-profit entities (Viader & Espina, 2014).

Not-for-profit governance covers oversight committee composition and structures, the roles and responsibilities of oversight committee members, and the relation between over-sight committee effectiveness and organizational effectiveness (Chelliah et al., 2015). Not-for-profit governance can adopt corporate governance, philanthropic governance (Viader & Espina, 2014), or cooperative governance (Cheney, 2014). Active participation of management in the oversight committee, formal management accountability to the over-sight committee, and emphasis on strategic and entrepreneurial activity characterize not-for-profit corporate governance (Viader & Espina, 2014). Not-for-profit philanthropic governance emphasizes asset and mission preservation and informal management account-ability to the oversight committee (Viader & Espina, 2014). Cooperative governance reflects financial structure, tax laws, membership type, decision-making structure, and sometimes size (Cheney et al., 2014).

As alternatives, not-for-profit governance can also rely on Traditional Governance, Policy Governance, or Results-based Governance. Traditional governance exists where the board functions parallel the responsibilities of management, and the exercised responsibilities are through a structure organized around primary management functions (Viader & Espina, 2014). In using Policy Governance, the oversight committee governs by setting policies related to organizational processes, limitations on executive power, oversight committee relationships with the Chief Executive Officer, governance style, and monitoring policy compliance (Viader & Espina, 2014). Through selection, the focus of Results-based Governance is on the oversight committee instead of management, where the oversight committee monitors progress and results achieved on approved objectives (Viader & Espina, 2014).

Tier Three Governance

Threading from the first-tier Governance Tree level, depicted linked nodes are inextricably affected by governance frameworks (Davis, 2008a). Applied governance frameworks have become an enabler for advocating stakeholder interests (Davis, 2008a). Organizational management defines expected governance effectiveness for connected subordinate nodes (Davis, 2008a). Entity continuity depends on accurate and timely external and internal environment information assessments to drive appropriate governance (Davis, 2008a). Management, especially information security management, cannot establish an adequate safeguarding posture unless root expectations are understood, and potential weaknesses, threats, and opportunities receive appropriate redress (Brotby, 2006; Davis, 2008a).

IT Governance

Entity IT governance is a top management and oversight committee responsibility (Davis, 2011). Key IT governance elements are leadership, organizational structures, and processes attempting to ensure that the entity's IT sustains and extends the entity's objectives and strategies roles (Marnewick & Labuschagne, 2011). Consequently, since organizational processes commonly integrate IT, an essential IT governance base ingredient is IT executive management (Davis, 2011; Wu et al., 2015). Generally, professionals agree that defining IT roles and responsibilities should be the first step when developing IT governance (Davis, 2011). Toward this end, roles entail assignment accountability based on the organizational structure, while responsibilities indicate activities with associated methodologies or processes for achieving organizational objectives and goals (Davis, 2011).

IT executives need to provide quality leadership when defining and then activating IT governance (Davis, 2011). IT governance leadership requires vision as well as responsibility and accountability to ensure entity continuance (Davis, 2011). Depending on the entity, accountability for defining IT governance can reside within a single person or group (Davis, 2011). Organization models available for IT governance deployment and maintenance include the following:

- Governance Initiation is applied where the IT function introduces IT governance projects through a designated panel's collective knowledge regarding achievements or projected achievements elsewhere in the entity (Davis, 2011).
- Governance Steering Committee usually is applied where representatives from various entity areas are appointed to collectively review and act upon IT governance-related issues (Davis, 2011; Wu et al., 2015).
- Governance Clearing House is applied where the IT function's chief officer has considerable, but not total, decision-making responsibility for IT governance (Davis, 2011).

- Corporate Governance Planning is applied where an IT group serves as a primary management tool in evaluating operational governance efficiency and as a task force for addressing specific governance problems (Davis, 2011).
- Governance Service Center is applied where autonomous IT governance group deployments exist within an entity's cost or responsibility centers, and executive management evaluates each group's performance (Davis, 2011).
- Governance Team is applied typically where five to seven individuals are selected as full-time group members for IT governance development and remediation (Davis, 2011).

Personnel, structures, processes, and risk management integration is foundational during the construction of an IT governance framework (Davis, 2011). Various frameworks can assist management in deploying IT governance within an entity (Davis, 2011). Frameworks available for IT governance construction include the Office of Government Commerce's IT Infrastructure Library (Gërvalla et al., 2018) and ISACA's Control Objectives for Information and Related Technology (Davis, 2011). The IT Infrastructure Library framework presents practice approaches for IT Service Management (Gërvalla et al., 2018). Distinctively, the Control Objectives for Information and Related Technology framework provisions a maturity model, as well as an IT governance framework, with a purpose to ensure the alignment of IT resources with the organizational vision and strategies (Marnewick & Labuschagne, 2011).

ISG

Although entities exist for various reasons, broadcasting information security breaches increases private and public demands to institutionalize ISG with program oversight (Davis, 2008a, 2017; Srivastava & Kumar, 2015). Effectual ISG counteracts security threats through control deployments enabling legal and ethical managerial responsibilities' fulfillment for IAP (Davis, 2017). Based on Governance Tree nodal connectivity, when properly aligned, controls represent processes, activities, or tasks within a system affected by stakeholder safeguarding expectations. Cascading down, ISG needs to address an entity's tactical and operational objectives, including performance expectations, profitability goals, and resource safeguarding (Davis, 2008a). However, ISG is a narrower concept than entity governance, although a broader concept than Cyber Security Governance.

Whether an entity exists for-profit or not-for-profit, to exercise effective governance throughout an organization, the top-level oversight committee and senior executives must clearly understand what to expect from deploying ISG (Davis, 2008a). Conceptually, considering the for-profit entity domain, ISG is a subset of enterprise governance that (a) provisions strategic direction, (b) ensures objectives' achievement, (c) manages risks appropriately, (d) uses organizational resources responsibly, and (e) monitors the successes and failures of the enterprise security program (IT Governance Institute, 2008). Similarly, not-for-profit entities can define ISG as a subset of not-for-profit governance that (a) provisions strategic direction, (b) ensures objectives' achievement, (c) manages risks appropriately, (d) uses organizational resources responsibly, and (e) monitors the successes or failures of the not-for-profit security program. Therefore, by replacing enterprise and not-for-profit with "entity" in the statements given before, the resulting general definition applies to both Governance Tree entity types when explicating ISG expected value.

ISG is a critical entity-linked node requiring a framework to ensure information assets safeguarding responsibilities receive appropriate managerial attention (Davis, 2008a). At the tier three Governance Tree level, ISG can generate significant benefits, including the following:

- stakeholder value increases for entities that practice good governance,
- effective information security policies and policies' compliance assurance,
- accountability for safeguarding information during critical organizational activities,
- a minimum assurance-level that critical decisions do not reflect flawed information,
- establishment of a structure and framework permitting allocated security resources optimization,
- protection from the increasing potential for criminal or civil liability due to information inaccuracy or the absence of due care,
- enhanced predictability and reduced uncertainty of operational execution through lowering of information security-related risks to definable and acceptable levels, and
- a firm foundation for effective and efficient risk management, process improvements, and rapid incident responses related to protecting information assets (Davis, 2008a).

With Governance Tree traversal, organizational management can easily understand and accept the necessity for ISG alignment with entity-level governance to ensure appropriate information asset safeguarding (Davis, 2008a). Managerially, ISG must sustain policies, processes, personnel, and structures adopted by the entity's oversight committee to inform, manage, monitor, and direct information security activities toward objectives achievement (Davis, 2008a, 2017). Through Governance Tree framing, information security nodal connectivity enables developing and sustaining strategically aligned information systems with the entity's objectives and goals (Davis, 2008a). However, ISG alignment with IT governance is also crucial to maintaining effective control congruency.

Considering the state of IT usage by most entity information systems, safeguarding IT resources usually requires deploying an ISG framework rendering essential IAP coverage (Davis, 2008a). An entity's management can adopt the framework suggested by Brotby (2006), which employs processes for ensuring an effective ISG system of controls. Alternatively, Williams et al. (2013) presented a more multifaceted information protection view incorporating a tiered technical and social feature set that forms and activates through governance adaptation.

Other Governance

Governance structures vary in nature and ambit (Luesebrink, 2011). An entity's governance structure provides the conduit within which activities for achieving objectives encompass planning, execution, control, and review (Davis, 2011). Organizational management develops and deploys a governance structure suited to meet perceived needs (Davis, 2011). Numerous relationships commonly exist throughout the governance structure, which may allow resource integration based on roles (e.g., Deschamps, 2013a). An entity-centric governance structure is dependent, in part, on size and the nature of activities (e.g., Deschamps, 2013b). Consequently, organizational management can institutionalize frameworks deemed necessary for achieving the entity's objectives (e.g., Stilgoe et al., 2013).

Security Governance Fusion

Given the global product and service environment, secure IT deployments are indispensable for enabling information reliability, processing efficiency, and communication expediency (Davis, 2017). Because assembled information has measurable value, data collection, processing, storage, and transmission by organizational employees need appropriate safeguarding (Davis, 2017). In safeguarding information, information security is the means for protecting information and information systems from unauthorized access, use, disclosure, modification, disruption, and destruction. Safeguarding information mandates addressing IT protection to ensure managerial due care and due diligence (Davis, 2017). IT protection is sustained through IT security. IT security is known as cybersecurity.

There are divergent opinions regarding information security and cybersecurity conceptual construct correspondence (Schatz et al., 2017). Nonetheless, as a representative definition, cybersecurity is the approach and actions associated with security risk management processes followed by organizations and governments to protect confidentiality, integrity, and availability of assets used in cyberspace (Schatz et al., 2017). The cybersecurity concept includes policies, guidelines, and collections of safeguards, technologies, tools as well as training to provide the best protection for the cyber environmental state and users (Schatz et al., 2017).

Managerially, cybersecurity is a group of practices, processes, and technologies designed and deployed to protect data, programs, devices, and networks from attack, damage, or unauthorized access (Vähäkainu & Lehto, 2019). Cybersecurity strategy development determines technologically based risks and threats, courses of action in case of a cyberattack, procedures to follow for minimizing the effects of a cyberattack, and means for catching attackers (Nastasiu, 2016). ISG is a critical aid to cybersecurity's success by ensuring that stakeholders have decision-making rights for guiding the organizational security efforts across the entity.

Understanding the ISG depth and breadth can help organizational managers supply a stable context and models adaptable or usable for Cyber Security Governance efforts. The Cyber Security Governance strategy must consider safeguarding information and computer technology. "Information is data interpretation presented in a form that furnishes value to a recipient" (Davis, 2017, p. 72). Computer technology is a capability of task accomplishment using mechanized processes, methods, or knowledge. An effective Cyber Security Governance strategy forms the foundation of an organization's approach to protecting information and computer technology. A holistic cybersecurity framework for cybersecurity strategies is available to help construct appropriate Cyber Security Governance (i.e., Atoum et al., 2014).

Cyber Security Governance also addresses specific IT requirements for entities that control and process data, which fall under the ISG domain. IT is hardware, software, services, and supporting infrastructure that manages or delivers data using electronic encoding. Information and associated technologies are assets requiring appropriate investments in protective measures to retain intrinsic value. IT permits amassing and processing large data volumes as well as inspires innovation. IT that links information systems has made intra-organizational communication almost seamless, depending on product-specificity (Davis, 2017). Within an entity's organizational structure, providing satisfactory service delivery necessitates installing a responsive cybersecurity support system. In addressing cybersecurity, service delivery and support may range from operational protection deployment to crisis response training (Davis, 2017).

Cyber Security Service Delivery for IT

Considering information systems generally are critical to enhancing productivity, there is a deployment imperative that IT provides availability with service responsiveness that meets usability demands (Davis, 2008b). Entity intricacies and IT operational complexities can result in cybersecurity issues that may necessitate speedy and systematic redress to fulfill availability requirements (Davis, 2008b). Furthermore, neither operations nor IT resides within static environments (Davis, 2008b). Thus, environmental dynamics can generate system interface alterations that require timely response and resolution to ensure continuous service delivery (Davis, 2008b). When concluded, cybersecurity service delivery is typically assessed based on satisfying user functionality expectations.

IT has enhanced control processes (Davis, 2011). IT has enabled opportunities for utilizing closed-loop control systems and provided the means for more timely corrective actions (Davis, 2011). Unfortunately, IT has also enabled the potential for a detrimental proliferation of controls (Davis, 2011). Therefore, developing an organizationally adjusted governance structure is a task requiring an in-depth understanding of the entity's internal and external environments (Davis, 2011). Specifically, conceptualizing the entity's mission and operating environment is essential when implementing good Cyber Security Governance (Davis, 2011).

Secure IT service delivery requires cybersecurity services management. Cybersecurity service delivery should provide the best possible service levels to meet entity-centric IT needs with pervasive controls. Cybersecurity pervasive controls for service delivery should minimally encompass service level management, availability management, capacity management, continuity management, and financial management.

Service Level Management of IT Security

Effectual IT cybersecurity solutions are imperative to achieve trust relationships with stakeholders (Davis, 2017). Cyber-attack proliferation threatens the confidentiality, integrity, and availability expected from IT (Chatterjee et al., 2015). Consequently, management has heightened expectations regarding cybersecurity service delivery. To remediate stakeholders' IT security apprehensions, increased quality, functionality, ease of use, continuously improving service levels, multilateral cost containment or abatement, and decreased delivery time are required typically. For cybersecurity service delivery personnel, expectations generally translate into providing appropriate service level management. Service level management is typically considered the primary managerial area that ensures promised service deliveries when and where expected at agreed-upon cost (Davis, 2008b). Assisting in the service delivery process is the service quality plan (Davis, 2008b).

Internal and external suppliers and customers need identification to enable service level management (Davis, 2008b). Descriptively, sound service level management necessitates clear interfaces and customer-centered service specifications for constructing service level requirements (Davis, 2008b). Furthermore, internal operational level agreements and contracts with external suppliers facilitate adherence to negotiated service level agreements (Davis, 2008b).

Service level management can be considered service quality monitoring and management based on key performance indicators (Davis, 2008b). Key performance indicators for service quality can range from generic availability and usage statistics to entity-centric per-interaction indicators (Davis, 2008b). Adequate service level management requires potential problem identification and alerts creation-enabling breach risk minimization (Davis,

2008b). Consequently, service level management practices should include comparing actual performance to pre-defined expectations, determining appropriate actions, and generating meaningful reports to permit service improvement (Davis, 2008b).

Capacity Management

Capacity management is the practice that ensures IT infrastructure provisioning at the right time, in the right volume, and at the right price for using IT in the most efficient manner (Davis, 2008b). Capacity management processes identify performance requirements that ensure continuous service levels and proper resource management (Davis, 2008b). Availability requirements drive capacity monitoring (Davis, 2008b). Derivatively, work-load forecasting necessitates resource scheduling to meet expected availability levels (Davis, 2008b). Sound management of capacity considers three levels: operational, service, and resource (Davis, 2008b). For achieving satisfactory capacity management, assigned cybersecurity service personnel need to

- define, plan, and manage the requirements;
- provide resources for the services;
- monitor the performance of applied resources and adjust if necessary;
- plan and implement improvements; and
- establish and maintain a capacity plan (Davis, 2008b).

Availability Management

Information availability usually mandates appropriate safeguarding (Davis, 2008a). Cybersecurity availability management reflects ensuring timely and reliable information access and use (Davis, 2008a). Accessibility and security are critical processing issues (Boritz & Datardina, 2019). However, security and availability are polar states because security aims to restrict access, whereas availability aims to facilitate access (Davis, 2008a).

For information to be complete, current, and timely, there is a necessity for user availability and accessibility following specifications as well as reclamation in a desirable form when required (Davis, 2008a). Pertinent information that is inaccessible when sought has no practical consequences for user activities or decisions, except for negatively limiting information and decision quality (Davis, 2008a). User practicality requires robust cybersecurity to render trustworthy information (Davis, 2008a). Such information must be available when needed, enable authorized user modifications, operate efficiently and effectively, and accommodate information allocation adjustments (Davis, 2008a).

Continuity Management

Continuity management of cybersecurity systems, processes, or activities should minimize adverse effects caused by disastrous and unpredictable events while focusing on sustaining core operational processes. Major management tasks need to include defining requirements and strategies for cybersecurity continuity as well as setting measures and continuity plans for cybersecurity services. Moreover, cybersecurity tasks need to encompass managing continuity procedures as well as managing emergency continuity and recovery. Cybersecurity service continuity controls ensure that when unexpected events occur, required operations continue without interruption or operational resumption is prompt, and critical as well as sensitive data remain protected (Davis, 2009a).

After a catastrophic incident or event, losing the capability to process, retrieve, and protect the information maintained electronically can significantly affect entity management's ability to accomplish the organization's mission (Davis, 2009a). For this reason, an entity should have: (a) controls in place to protect information assets as well as minimize the risk of unplanned interruptions and (b) a plan to recover critical operations should interruptions occur (Davis, 2009a). Continuity management plans should consider the activities performed at general support facilities, such as data processing centers, managed service providers, and telecommunications facilities, as well as the activities performed by users of specific IT resources (Davis, 2009a).

Following a process interruption or disaster, critical cybersecurity services need to be restored first, perhaps in a matter of hours. In contrast, the time span available for restoring non-essential services may extend to weeks. The maximum recovery time documented for each cybersecurity service will determine the type and cost of continuity arrangements necessary to meet operational expectations. Cybersecurity service recovery targets should reflect operational requirements for resource continuity and technical requirements for resource availability. When developing disaster or interruption responses, prioritized classifications should be relevant indicators of the magnitude, severity, or potential effect a situation has on an entity (Davis, 2009a).

Financial Management

Financial management processes for ISSM usually redress entity cost accounting requirements (Davis, 2008b; Sonnenreich et al., 2006) for cybersecurity. Information security cost management ensures that information security resources are obtained and sustained at the most effective price by calculating costs for providing information security; thus, enabling organizational management to understand the protection cost structure. Instituting cost management generally requires accurate program budgeting. To this end, implementing a Program Planning and Budgeting System is an appropriate method for monitoring cybersecurity investments.

Cyber Security Service Support for IT

Control systems permit the organization and management of information security (Davis, 2008a, 2010, 2020). Control systems define the processes, responsibility allocation for policy statements, and the management framework (Davis, 2008a, 2020). Selecting a security management framework defines the processes for configuration development, deployment, and evaluation of directing action plans. Furthermore, the management framework defines the reporting of security results. Because information assets are usually critical to an entity's success, control system development and deployment should occur to achieve specific entity-centric control objectives (Davis, 2008a, 2010, 2020). The control system for information security service support should address cybersecurity configuration management, incident management, problem management, change management, and release management processes.

Configuration management and change management are the primary cybersecurity service support processes enabling control objectives' achievement for cybersecurity service delivery. With the proper deployment of configuration management and change management, additional secondary cybersecurity service support provisioning can occur through incident management, problem management, and release management (Davis, 2008b). Typically, within the cybersecurity service support domain, the cybersecurity service desk function is a necessary sub-process for ensuring a responsive organizational structure (Davis, 2008b).

Configuration Management

IT security requires an essential process for enabling cybersecurity services supporting information systems (Davis, 2008b). The cybersecurity configuration management process should register, track, and report each IT security infrastructure component. IT security configuration items are discrete assets that may be functionally independent or dependent (Behr et al., 2005). Under typical circumstances, cybersecurity significant control status is attributable to an accepted belief that the initiation point for adequately managing information security services depends on clearly knowing what items constitute the entity's cybersecurity architecture (Davis, 2008b). Entities should maintain an inventory of cybersecurity configuration items usable in providing cybersecurity services (Davis, 2008b). However, maintaining a cybersecurity inventory listing can be a managerial challenge if not addressed through a process with information asset owner participation (Davis, 2008b). Considering entity information assets are continuously updated, the information security function must regulate and inscribe changes to support future maintenance situations (Davis, 2008b).

Enabling the accommodation of essential configuration management requirements is implementing and controlling the Information Security Management System containing details regarding cybersecurity infrastructure elements employable in information security services provisioning and administration (Kushwaha, 2016). Cybersecurity configuration management best-practice adoptions of inventory management and software engineering are essential. However, the Information Security Management System is more than a cybersecurity asset register when properly deployed (Kushwaha, 2016). The repository should also contain information that accurately portrays the maintenance, movement, and issues experienced with cybersecurity configuration items that enable effectual cybersecurity service practices.

Incident Management

An incident is definable as an interruption or quality reduction of IT service (Palilingan & Batmetan, 2018). Various potential IT service threats can convert to intentional or unintentional incidents requiring adequate cybersecurity service support. If restoring cybersecurity service normalcy as swiftly as possible and minimizing adverse effects on entity operations are the primary incident management process goals, support personnel performance ensures that the highest possible service quality and availability levels are maintained.

Incidents are typically unavoidable when IT is relied on to provide processual services (Davis, 2008b). Therefore, procedures for responding and recovering to normal operations are necessary (Davis, 2008a, 2008b). Incident response management includes processes to stop or contain information asset damage and gather incident data (Davis, 2008a, 2008b). Acquired data may be used during recovery to ascertain compromise extent or for criminal prosecution (Davis, 2008a, 2008b). A compromised information asset can require restoration and return to regular operation (Davis, 2008a) or replacement. Recovery may also involve exploited weakness determination and, if feasible, subsequent vulnerability eradication (Davis, 2008a, 2008b).

Managing the complex process of incident resolution to restore service as quickly as possible can be quite challenging (Davis, 2008b). The primary discernable benefits of an adequate incident handling capability are containing or repairing damage from incidents affecting usability and preventing future damage to configuration items (Davis, 2008b). Less obvious are the secondary incident handling capability benefits that include enhancing the training program, awareness program, internal communication, entity preparedness, and threat data augmentation (Davis, 2008b). For example, training and awareness enhancements are achievable through information conveying customer knowledge and real-world scenarios presented as illustrations for instructional purposes (Davis, 2008b).

Regarding security, one incident response aspect that can be especially problematic is gathering evidence to pursue legal action against suspected criminals (Davis, 2008b). Specifically, to collect evidence, an entity may need to allow an intruder or violator to continue inappropriate activities – a situation that puts information assets at continued risk (Davis, 2008b). However, once publicized, detection and prosecution fears can serve as an illegal activity deterrent for potential transgressors (Davis, 2008b).

Problem Management

Effective problem management commonly reduces the number of issues in the entity's operational environment by addressing the root causes of closed problems (Davis, 2008b). Problem management can thus be considered the resolution or prevention of issues that affect an entity's cybersecurity services. Problem management can also refer to managing issues typically logged by the entity's IT service desk function. Once an issue is considered a cybersecurity problem, an appropriate level of resources should be employed to enable timely resolution. Organizational management should contribute to decisions on prioritizing problems to ensure minimal disruption to regular operations (Davis, 2008b). Furthermore, cybersecurity service support management should provide regular reports on problem resolution progress.

A cybersecurity service problem is viewable as a demarcated and identified condition extracted from a single circumstance or many circumstances exhibiting common symptoms. Initially, the cybersecurity service problem is an unknown circumstance awaiting identification and attribution. Through successful problem root cause analysis by an analyst, unknown circumstances convert to known circumstances that generated the identified condition when a configuration item defect occurred (Davis, 2008b). Therefore, a primary problem management process objective should be ensuring cybersecurity service stability by identifying and removing known circumstances negatively affecting deployed IT. When cascaded, the primary problem management process goals are to minimize the adverse impact of known circumstances affecting cybersecurity service delivery and preventing recurring situations related to known circumstances that can affect IT. Consequently, the reactive aspect of the problem management goals is to quickly solve issues in response to one or more circumstances. In contrast, the proactive aspect of the problem management goals is to reduce the overall number of situational issues (Davis, 2008b).

An entity's cybersecurity service customers need to agree on guidelines for remedying reported problems requiring extended timeframes for resolution as well as information detailing the effect on organizational processes, other systems, and users (Davis, 2008b). Information security service support has a proactive role in identifying process or infrastructural weaknesses and areas of concern within the deployed entity's IT architecture. Once adverse trends are recognized, service problems need highlighting and corrective action needs initiation (Davis, 2008b). For instance, a known cybersecurity weakness may necessitate notifying a change in management personnel or further employee education and training initiated (Davis, 2008b).

A cybersecurity maintenance request requires the analysis of all incidents and problems generated in the entity's production environment. However, assigned cybersecurity service support personnel should make a problem evaluation the final step before correction. Sequentially, within the evaluation process, an entity's major problem management tasks should include resolving problem causes, investigating and diagnosing the root cause of the problem, identifying and inscribing known circumstances, assessing known circumstances, inscribing the known circumstances' resolution, and requesting appropriate changes (Davis, 2008b).

Change Management

Cybersecurity deployments can require change management to ensure alignment with the entity's strategy, structure, and culture (Davis, 2009b). Cyber security change management is the practice of ensuring all configuration item alterations happen in a planned and authorized manner. Change can occur for various reasons, including response to operational process needs, the availability of updated technology, technological innovations, and entity growth (Davis, 2008b). Cybersecurity changes can be permanent or temporary. However, cybersecurity change management procedures should reduce and provide adequate responses to anticipated or unanticipated incidents as well as problems.

Receiving the change request, logging the change request, assessing the incident or problem, obtaining authorization to perform the change, and planning the change are procedures that should precede change construction (Davis, 2008b). Minimally, the change request should provide the operational or technological reason behind each change; identify the specific configuration items and cybersecurity services affected by the change; identify cost estimates, risk assessment, and resource requirements; and support process approvals (Davis, 2008b). Logging the change permits tracking and inscribing the change request, which has passed initial documentation requirements (Davis, 2008b). Assessing the incident or problem provides analysis, and evaluation enables categorized change prioritization (Davis, 2008b). Cybersecurity service support should obtain proper authorizations for the change from the appropriate non-technical and technical experts responsible for change deployment to construct the change. Furthermore, change planning provides the means to ensure successful change development (Davis, 2008b).

Thorough change planning is necessary for adequate change construction, including back-out planning, change testing, and inscription updating (Davis, 2008b). Back-out planning is necessary should the change result in an unacceptable cybersecurity configuration state. Since most information systems and infrastructure are usually too large, integrated, and complicated for cybersecurity service design failure or success predicting without testing, experimentation should occur during the change process. Even a small change in a configuration item could cause a mission-critical information asset to fail or disrupt an IT service (Davis, 2008b). Furthermore, cybersecurity configuration item inscriptions affected by the change should receive updating to ensure appropriate resource use and maintenance (Davis, 2008b).

Release Management

Once change tests prove satisfactory functionality, the cybersecurity configuration items require movement to a secure staging area. Subsequently, a release request submission to the appropriate individual for production implementation should occur (Davis, 2008b). Upon notification of a successfully released change, the individual responsible for the

Information Security Management System should receive an inscribed cybersecurity update. In the end, a change review assesses change process performance and development adequacy (Davis, 2008b).

Cybersecurity release management is the practice of configuring item development, installation, and distribution controls within the control processes. Rigorous cybersecurity release builds, testing, and rollback practices significantly affect individual performance measures and the overall performance of the information assets. A primary cybersecurity release management objective is to ensure that only authorized and correct versions of cybersecurity assets are made available for operational production usage. Cascading from the primary cybersecurity release management objective, a primary cybersecurity release management goal is to ensure approved and accredited components are installed malfunction-resistant and on schedule. Consequently, the high-level activities associated with the cyber-security release process encompass release and deployment planning, release building and testing, release distribution and implementation, as well as reviewing and closing deployments.

Security Governance Insights

In using a controls-approach, security management focuses on making decisions to miti-gate risks (Davis, 2012). According to decision theories under uncertainty, individuals select an alternative that brings the highest prospect or utility (Lee & Lee, 2012). On the one hand, choice prospect or utility consists of possible selection consequences (Lee & Lee, 2012). Each consequence has a weighted subjective probability and preference (or value) for the decision-maker (Lee & Lee, 2012). As subcategorical decision theories, prospect theory and subjective expected utility theory build on the same basic structure of possible outcomes and probabilities as well as providing similar platforms (Lee & Lee, 2012).

On the other hand, prospect theory and subjective expected utility theory differ in model formulation and assumptions at the detailed level (Beebe et al., 2014; Lee & Lee, 2012). The prospect theory is a descriptive attempt to explain seemingly nonrational decisions that diverge from canonical model predictions (Beebe et al., 2014; Lee & Lee, 2012). Subjective expected utility theory is an abetted decision theory that suggests a normative decision model based on perfect rationality (Beebe et al., 2014; Lee & Lee, 2012).

Governance determines decision authorization (Weill & Ross, 2004). Governance is a pivotal link in control processes that drives institutionalization (Luesebrink, 2011). Institutionalization of organizational security confers:

- legitimacy through the development of normative knowledge structures,
- trust through establishing trusted relationships in the institutional environment, and
- authority through the legitimacy of power (Luesebrink, 2011).

For organizational security conferral acceptance, instituting and sustaining ISG require (a) comprehensive planning and organizing, (b) robust acquisitions and implementations, (c) effective delivery and support, as well as (d) continuous monitoring and evaluation to address managerial, operational, and technical issues that can thwart the success of the entity's mission (Davis, 2008a).

Planning and organizing are imperative to administrative cohesiveness (Davis, 2008a). ISG typically transpires at distinct organizational levels, with team leaders reporting to and receiving directions from assignment manager-leaders, and manager-leaders reporting to and receiving direction from executive manager-leaders (Davis, 2008a). The highest-level executive manager-leader confers with and receives direction from the entity's oversight committee (Davis, 2008a) that provides the lower-level executive manager-leaders with objective achievement expectations. Information that indicates deviation from targets will usually include recommendations for action requiring endorsement by the entity's oversight layer (Davis, 2008a).

Acquisitions and implementations are commonly necessary for appropriate information security (Davis, 2008a). Information security solutions require identification, acquisition (or development), as well as seamless operational and IT process implementation and integration to realize the information security strategy (Davis, 2008a). During an information security product or service acquisition and implementation cycle, changes and maintenance may be necessary to sustain continued service quality for affected systems or processes (Davis, 2008a).

Critical support service components contributing to security delivery value are assessing changes in and maintaining existing systems (Davis, 2008a). Required information protection changes and maintenance can emerge through various problems encountered by users (Davis, 2008a; Safa et al., 2016) or deliberate external or internal information security architecture attacks (Davis, 2008a; Safa et al., 2015). Concurrently, innovations can manifest in different forms that require managerial attention (Cegielski et al., 2013) to security service support.

Entity management needs to understand the status of organizational information systems in deciding appropriate resource deployments to meet operational requirements. When security monitoring is an extension of the entity's operating activities, and processing performance reviews occur on a real-time basis, protection degradation can receive prompt remediation for the unacceptable condition (Davis, 2008a). Characteristically, productive monitoring activities dynamically adapt to environmental factors, with each security assessment performed according to an authorized plan reflecting the evaluation type, assurance level, and information classification (Davis, 2008a).

As suggested by Figure 1.5, the formal authority of the managements affects interpersonal, informational, and decisional roles (Davis, 2008a). As a linear progression, a

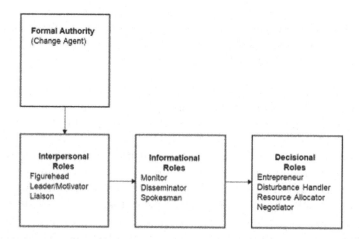

Figure 1.5 Managerial Roles' Progression.

Note: Adapted from *IT Auditing: Assuring Information Assets Protection* by R. E. Davis, 2008a, Pleier. Copyright 2008 by Robert E. Davis. Adapted with permission.

manager's interpersonal steward, leader, and liaison roles enable the informational monitor, disseminator, and spokesman roles (Davis, 2008a). In turn, the informational roles enable decisional entrepreneur, disturbance handler, resource allocator, and negotiator roles (Davis, 2008a). Listed managerial roles' adoption by the Chief Information Security Officer is typically necessary to drive an effective and efficient ISG deployment within the entity.

Formal Authority

Authority without accountability can result in corrupt practices (Davis, 2008a; Pitesa & Thau, 2013). Accountability for procedural decisions offers a way to contain the self-serving outcomes of power (Pitesa & Thau, 2013). Administrative power typically operates based on position, coercion, expertise, friendship, and rewards' control (Davis, 2008a). The higher the number of known power sources a manager has, the more likely an entity employee will be inclined to accept administrative authority (Davis, 2008a).

Making managers accountable for procedural decisions is a potent self-serving decision restrictor under moral hazard (Pitesa & Thau, 2013). Conclusively, the deployed ISG program must ensure ethical employee behavior (Davis, 2008a, 2017). Punishment severity, reward significance, and control certainty effects are serious managerial actions with an information security framework deployment (Chen et al., 2012; Kolkowska & Dhillon, 2013).

Interpersonal Roles

Managers assume organizational fiduciary responsibilities with a fiduciary duty (Bagozzi et al., 2009) for sustaining entity values. Entity values should address morality regarding an overall image perception and edicts consisting of regulatory guides for behavior (Bagozzi et al., 2009; Ferrell, 2005). Values link to the alignment of principles and standards with deontological ethics (Bagozzi et al., 2009; Northouse, 2013). Entity manager-leaders can influence moral decisions using persuasion and create a culture that bolsters, motives, and links affecting decisions (Bagozzi et al., 2009; Ferrell, 2005).

Employees are an essential group of entity stakeholders in an organization (Ogunsakin, 2015). One of the goals of information security managers is to lead subordinate employees in attaining organizational objectives (Ogunsakin, 2015). However, ISG benefits extend beyond IT risk mitigation and impact control. Good ISG can enhance an entity's service reputation, inspire employee confidence, and improve trust relationships with value chain participants. Additionally, when recovering from safeguarding incidents, appropriate information security practices can enhance efficiency through wasteful time and effort avoidance. ISG development and deployment echo how an entity's designated information security management team intends to accomplish the organizational safeguarding mission (Davis, 2008a, 2011; Whitman & Mattord, 2012).

Employee decisions are essential to achieving ISG goals (Davis, 2008a). Goal congruence is a decision quality influencer (Davis, 2008a). If decision quality is essential and subordinates do not share the same ISG goals, manager-leaders face losing control over assigned activities (Davis, 2008a), which may have detrimental organizational effects. Hence, employee goal incongruence potentially suboptimizes ISG decision quality (Davis, 2008a). Therefore, manager-leaders must ensure that employees accept and comply with ISG goals (Davis, 2008a). For which, organizational manager-leaders should acquire an in-depth understanding of the entity environment, processes, and organizational objectives to enable provisioning information security services congruent with organizational needs (Flores et al., 2014).

Informational Roles

An effective governance structure establishment includes deploying proper authority and responsibility with adequate accountability for activities. Beneficially, regarding an entity's direction and purpose, when responsibility, accountability, and authority receive proper tailoring, communication efficiency is improved through reductions in entropy and misunderstanding. Furthermore, management's IAP control monitoring deployments assist in ensuring fulfillment of the fiduciary relationships with stakeholders. As an entity-integrated resource, IT deployments should occur as managerially required and with a sufficient level of formality, coverage, and control completeness to allow IAP monitoring.

Foundationally, information construction is dependent on available data (Davis, 2008a). After that, through data processing, resulting information creates knowledge for decision-making. With IT considered indispensable for providing processing efficiencies, communication expediency, and information reliability, management should govern safeguarding information assets through the entity's ISG program. An essential element of appropriate security is protection mechanisms (Davis, 2017; Sen & Borle, 2015). There is a perception that a lack of focus and support causes information security breaches (Davis, 2017). Organizations need a balanced approach to various technical, human, and organizational information security management challenges (Singh et al., 2013).

Effective ISG covers all tangible and intangible information system elements, regardless of whether they involve employees, technology, or relationships with trading partners, customers, or third parties or not (Davis, 2017). Consequently, effectual ISG addresses safeguarding activities throughout the information life cycle within the defined data protection perimeter. System boundaries generally reflect external input and resulting output. As a prosecution avoidance mechanism, deploying an exceptional ISG framework addressing IAP can significantly reduce legal risks (Davis, 2008a).

Responsibility for a standard should directly correspond to the assigned activity (Davis, 2008a, 2017). Therefore, accountability necessitates ensuring appropriately administered authority within the assigned responsibilities' context (Davis, 2008a, 2017). The ultimate responsibility for conveying expectations rests with the entity's manager-leaders. Organizational information and communication have employee responsibility and reporting structures. Formal organizational structures can be responsible for institutionalizing social behaviors and reflecting the organizational rules, social norms, and cultural beliefs in the entity's environment, collectively known as organizational culture (Luesebrink, 2011). Formal organizational structures often reflect constructs associated with laws, regulations, policies, directives, procedures, standards, and rules (Davis, 2008a, 2017; Flores et al., 2014; Kearney & Kruger, 2013). Informal organizational structures mirror the interlocking social makeup governing how people work together in practice (Davis, 2017; Flores et al., 2014).

Decisional Roles

Implementing and maintaining an ISG structure require commitment from the entity employees at all levels and require time and resources for management and implementation. Process discipline should be a managerial concern (Davis, 2008b). However, no change, configuration, or release process is available that can guarantee security service objective achievement

(Davis, 2008b). Additionally, instituting a process-focused culture as well as monitoring and responding to process exceptions can initially affect performance levels more than adopting the latest recognized best practices (Davis, 2008b). Consequently, adequately providing a holistic information security approach should address people, information, processes, and infrastructure.

Combined, the lack of managerial intent and a sound ISG framework that includes cybersecurity means vital directions and controls are remiss within the organization. The IT function is willfully unattended if the entity's management abdicates from securing information assets, rejects creating policies and procedures, permits control deficiencies, avoids assessments, and corrective actions are nonexistent (Fay & Patterson, 2017). Under the described circumstances, management effectively embraces IT risks and associated consequences as well as disavows a strategic interest in directing and controlling information security.

Cybersecurity issues require more than managerial pretense (Fay & Patterson, 2017). If entity management accepts the need to administrate cybersecurity issues, the design and deployment decisions need to ensure best practices to govern resource allocations (Fay & Patterson, 2017). Without the discipline of assessment and corrective action, entity management leads by assuming that procedures, threat assessments, information assets, motivations, and the technology state remain constant and require no further analysis or adjustments (Fay & Patterson, 2017). Static information security management is almost as detrimental to an entity as no information security management (Fay & Patterson, 2017).

Information security manager-leaders do not have the similar degree of exposure to organizational information security breaches (Davis, 2017). Some information security manager-leaders might have not experienced an information security breach, while other information security manager-leaders may have experienced several breaches of information security (Davis, 2017). Nevertheless, the information security manager-leaders' deep knowledge acquisition permits practical IAP activities' coordination (Flores et al., 2014).

References

Ahmad, A., Maynard, S. B., & Park, S. (2014). Information security strategies: Towards an organizational multi-strategy perspective. *Journal of Intelligent Manufacturing, 25*, 357–370. https://doi.org/10.1007/s10845-012-0683-0

Arief, B., & Adzmi, M. A. B. (2015). Understanding cybercrime from its stakeholders' perspectives: Part 2: Defenders and victims. *IEEE Security & Privacy, 13*(2), 84–88. https://doi.org/10.1109/MSP.2015.44

Arief, B., Adzmi, M. A. B., & Gross, T. (2015). Understanding cybercrime from its stakeholders' perspectives: Part 1: Attackers. *IEEE Security & Privacy, 13*(1), 71–76. https://doi.org/10.1109/MSP.2015.19

Atoum, I., Otoom, A., & Ali, A. A. (2014). A holistic cyber security implementation framework. *Information Management & Computer Security, 22*, 251–264. https://doi.org/10.1108/IMCS-02-2013-0014

Avison, D., Baskerville, R., & Myers, M. D. (2007). The structure of power in action research projects. In *Information systems action research* (pp. 19–41). Springer.

Bagozzi, R. P., Sekerka, L. E., & Hill, V. (2009). Hierarchical motive structures and their role in moral choices. *Journal of Business Ethics, 90*(S4), 461–486. https://doi.org/10.1007/s10551-010-0601-3

Bahl, S., & Wali, O. P. (2014). Perceived significance of information security governance to predict the information security service quality in software service industry. *Information Management & Computer Security, 22*, 2–23. https://doi.org/10.1108/IMCS-01-2013-0002

Beebe, N. L., Young, D. K., & Chang, F. R. (2014). Framing information security budget requests to influence investment decisions. *Communications of the Association for Information Systems*, *35*(7), 134–144. https://doi.org/10.17705/1CAIS.03507

Behr, K., Kim, G., & Spafford, G. (2005). *The visible ops handbook: Starting ITIL in 4 practical steps* (Rev. 1st). Information Technology Process Institute.

Blakley, B., McDermott, E., & Geer, D. (2001, September). Information security is information risk management. *Proceedings of the 2001 workshop on New security paradigms*, 97–104. https://doi.org/10.1145/508171.508187

Boritz, J. E., & Datardina, M. (2019). *A framework for information integrity controls*. Chartered Professional Accountants of Canada.

Boyson, S. (2014). Cyber supply chain risk management: Revolutionizing the strategic control of critical IT systems. *Technovation*, *34*, 342–353. https://doi.org/10.1016/j.technovation.2014.02.001

Brotby, K. W. (2006). *Information security governance: Guidance for boards of directors and executive management* (2nd ed.). IT Governance Institute.

Brotby, K. W. (2009). *Information security governance: A practical development and implementation approach*. John Wiley & Sons.

Cegielski, C. G., Bourrie, D. M., & Hazen, B. T. (2013). Evaluating adoption of emerging IT for corporate IT strategy: Developing a model using a qualitative method. *Information Systems Management*, *30*, 235–249. https://doi.org/10.1080/10580530.2013.794632

Chatterjee, S., Sarker, S., & Valacich, J. S. (2015). The behavioral roots of information systems security: Exploring key factors related to unethical IT use. *Journal of Management Information Systems*, *31*(4), 49–87. https://doi.org/10.1080/07421222.2014.1001257

Chelliah, J., Boersma, M., & Klettner, A. (2015, January). Governance challenges for not-for-profit organisations: Empirical evidence in support of a contingency approach. *Australasian Conference on Business and Social Sciences 2015, Sydney*, 47–59.

Chen, Y., Ramamurthy, K., & Wen, K. (2012). Organizations' information security policy compliance: Stick or carrot approach? *Journal of Management Information Systems*, *29*(3), 157–188. https://doi.org/10.2753/MIS0742-1222290305

Cheney, G., Santa Cruz, I., Peredo, A. M., & Nazareno, E. (2014). Worker cooperatives as an organizational alternative: Challenges, achievements and promise in business governance and ownership. *Organization*, *21*(5), 591–603. https://doi.org/10.1177/1350508414539784

Chou, D. C. (2015). Cloud computing: A value creation model. *Computer Standards & Interfaces*, *38*, 72–77. https://doi.org/10.1016/j.csi.2014.10.001

Clark, M., & Harrell, E. C. (2013). Unlike chess, everyone must continue playing after a cyber-attack. *Journal of Investment Compliance*, *14*(4), 5–12. https://doi.org/10.1108/JOIC-10-2013-0034

Committee of Sponsoring Organizations of the Treadway Commission. (2013). *Internal control-integrated framework* (Executive Summary). www.coso.org/Pages/default.aspx

Connell, B., Mallett, R., Rochet, P., Chow, E., Savino, L., & Payne, P. (2004). *Enterprise governance: Getting the balance right*. International Federation of Accountants.

Crossler, R. E., Johnston, A. C., Lowry, P. B., Hu, Q., Warkentin, M., & Baskerville, R. (2013). Future directions for behavioral information security research. *Computers & Security*, *32*, 90–101. https://doi.org/10.1016/j.cose.2012.09.010

Davis, R. E. (2006). *IT auditing: Irregular and illegal acts*. Pleier.

Davis, R. E. (2008a). *IT auditing: Assuring information assets protection*. Pleier.

Davis, R. E. (2008b). *IT auditing: IT service delivery and support*. Pleier.

Davis, R. E. (2009a). *IT auditing: Business continuity and disaster recovery*. Pleier.

Davis, R. E. (2009b). *IT auditing: Systems and infrastructure life cycle management*. Pleier.

Davis, R. E. (2010). *IT auditing: An adaptive system*. www.amazon.com

Davis, R. E. (2011). *Assuring IT governance*. www.amazon.com

Davis, R. E. (2012). *Assuring information security*. www.amazon.com

Davis, R. E. (2013). *Assuring IT legal compliance*. Lulu.

Davis, R. E. (2017). *Relationship between corporate governance and information security governance effectiveness in United States corporations* (Publication No. 10603383) [Doctoral Study, Walden University]. ProQuest Dissertations Publishing.

Davis, R. E. (2020). *IT auditing using a system perspective.* IGI Global.

De Haes, S., Grembergen, W. V., & Debreceny, R. S. (2013). COBIT 5 and enterprise governance of information technology: Building blocks and research opportunities. *Journal of Information Systems, 27*(1), 307–324. https://doi.org/10.2308/isys-50422

Deschamps, J. (2013a, May). 9 different models in use for innovation governance. *Innovation Management.* https://innovationmanagement.se/2013/05/08/9-different-models-in-use-for-innovation-governance

Deschamps, J. (2013b, May). What is innovation governance?: Definition and scope. *Innovation Management.* https://innovationmanagement.se/2013/05/03/what-is-innovation-governance-definition-and-scope

Di Gregorio, D. (2013). Value creation and value appropriation: An integrative, multi-level framework. *The Journal of Applied Business and Economics, 15,* 39–53. www.na-businesspress.com

Fay, J. J., & Patterson, D. (2017). Managing information security. In *Contemporary security management* (4th ed., pp. 353–390). Butterworth Heinemann. https://doi.org/10.1016/B978-0-12-809278-1.00017-7

Ferrell, O. C. (2005). A framework for understanding organizational ethics. In R. A. Peterson & O. C. Ferrell (Eds.), *Business ethics: New challenges for business schools and corporate leaders* (pp. 3–17). M. E. Sharpe.

Flores, W. R., Antonsen, E., & Ekstedt, M. (2014). Information security knowledge sharing in organizations: Investigating the effect of behavioral information security governance and national culture. *Computers & Security, 43,* 90–110. https://doi.org/10.1016/j.cose.2014.03.004

Gërvalla, M., Preniqi, N., & Kopacek, P. (2018). IT Infrastructure Library (ITIL) framework approach to IT governance. *IFAC-PapersOnLine, 51*(30), 181–185. https://doi.org/10.1016/j.ifacol.2018.11.283

Gheorghe, M. (2010). Audit methodology for IT governance. *Informatica Economica, 14*(1). http://revistaie.ase.ro/

Gil-Lafuente, A., & Paula, L. B. (2013). Algorithm applied in the identification of stakeholders. *Kybernetes, 42,* 674–685. https://doi.org/10.1108/K-04-2013-0073

Harrison, J. S., & Wicks, A. C. (2013). Stakeholder theory, value, and firm performance. *Business Ethics Quarterly, 23,* 97–124. https://doi.org/10.5840/beq20132314

Heracleous, L., & Lan, L. L. (2012). Agency theory, institutional sensitivity, and inductive reasoning: Towards a legal perspective. *Journal of Management Studies, 49,* 223–239. https://doi.org/10.1111/j.1467-6486.2011.01009.x

Humaidi, N., & Balakrishnan, V. (2015). Leadership styles and information security compliance behavior: The mediator effect of information security awareness. *International Journal of Information and Education Technology, 5*(4), 311–318. https://doi.org/10.7763/IJIET.2015.V5.522

IT Governance Institute. (2003). *Board briefing on IT governance* (2nd ed.). Author.

IT Governance Institute. (2008). *Information security governance: Guidance for information security managers.* Author.

Julisch, K. (2013). Understanding and overcoming cyber security anti-patterns. *Computer Networks, 57,* 2206–2211. https://doi.org/10.1016/j.comnet.2012.11.023

Kearney, W. D., & Kruger, H. A. (2013). A framework for good corporate governance and organisational learning: An empirical study. *International Journal of Cyber-Security and Digital Forensics, 2,* 36–47. http://sdiwc.net

Kolkowska, E., & Dhillon, G. (2013). Organizational power and information security rule compliance. *Computers & Security, 33,* 3–11. https://doi.org/10.1016/j.cose.2012.07.001

Kotter, J. P. (2001). What leaders really do. *Harvard Business Review, 79*(11), 85–96. http://hbr.org/magazine

Kushwaha, P. (2016). Amalgamation of the information security management system with business-paradigm shift. *International Journal of Computer Science and Information Security, 14*(1), 105–111. https://sites.google.com/site/ijcsis

Lee, M., & Lee, J. (2012). The impact of information security failure on customer behaviors: A study on a large-scale hacking incident on the Internet. *Information Systems Frontiers, 14,* 375–393. https://doi.org/10.1007/s10796-010-9253-1

Luesebrink, M. (2011). *Institutionalization of information security governance structures in academic institutions: A case study* [Dissertation, Florida State University]. http://purl.flvc.org/fsu/fd/FSU_migr_etd-1009

Maccoby, M. (2000). Understanding the difference between management and leadership. *Research Technology Management, 43*(1), 57–59. www.iriweb.org

Marnewick, C., & Labuschagne, L. (2011). An investigation into the governance of information technology projects in South Africa. *International Journal of Project Management, 29*(6), 661–670. http://dx.doi.org/10.1016/j.ijproman.2010.07.004

Mohare, R., & Lanjewar, U. (2012). Determinants of business information security. *International Journal of Marketing and Technology, 2*(7), 203–209. www.ijmra.us

Nastasiu, C. I. (2016, July). Cybersecurity strategies in the Internet era. *Proceedings of the Scientific Conference AFASES 2*, 619–624. https://doi.org/10.19062/2247-3173.2016.18.2.19

Nishimura, A. (2006). Enterprise governance and management accounting from the viewpoint of feed forward control. *Asia-Pacific Management Accounting Journal, 1*(1), 1–17. http://arionline.uitm.edu.my

Northouse, P. G. (2013). *Leadership: Theory and practice* (6th ed.). Sage.

Nugroho, H. (2014). Conceptual model of IT governance for higher education based on Cobit 5 framework. *Journal of Theoretical & Applied Information Technology, 60*(2). www.jatit.org

Ogunsakin, O. (2015). *Employees' perceptions of managerial transformational leadership behaviors and effectiveness among information technology managers* (Publication No. 3711019) [Doctoral Study, Walden University]. ProQuest Dissertations Publishing.

Pagani, M. (2013). Digital business strategy and value creation: Framing the dynamic cycle of control points. *MIS Quarterly, 37*, 617–632. www.misq.org

Palilingan, V. R., & Batmetan, J. R. (2018). Incident management in academic information system using ITIL framework. *2nd International Conference on Innovation in Engineering and Vocational Education 2017, Manado*, 1–9. https://doi.org/10.1088/1757-899X/306/1/012110

Pfaff, O., & Ries, S. (2014). Integrating enterprise security infrastructure with cloud computing. *Journal of Internet Technology and Secured Transactions, 3*, 338–343. www.infonomics-society.org

Pitesa, M., & Thau, S. (2013). Masters of the universe: How power and accountability influence self-serving decisions under moral hazard. *Journal of Applied Psychology, 98*, 550–558. https://doi.org/10.1037/a0031697

Posey, C., Roberts, T. L., Lowry, P. B., & Hightower, R. T. (2014). Bridging the divide: A qualitative comparison of information security thought patterns between information security professionals and ordinary organizational insiders. *Information & Management, 51*, 551–567. https://doi.org/10.1016/j.im.2014.03.009

Rasheed, S., ChangFeng, W., & Yaqub, F. (2015). Towards program risk management and perceived risk management barriers. *International Journal of Hybrid Information Technology, 8*, 323–338. https://doi.org/10.14257/ijhit.2015.8.5.35

Safa, N. S., Sookhak, M., Solms, R. V., Furnell, S., Ghani, N. A., & Herawan, T. (2015). Information security conscious care behaviour formation in organizations. *Computers & Security, 53*, 65–78. https://doi.org/10.1016/j.cose.2015.05.012

Safa, N. S., & Von Solms, R. (2016). An information security knowledge sharing model in organizations. *Computers in Human Behavior, 57*, 442–451. https://doi.org/10.1016/j.chb.2015.12.037

Safa, N. S., Von Solms, R., & Furnell, S. (2016). Information security policy compliance model in organizations. *Computers & Security, 56*, 70–82. https://doi.org/10.1016/j.cose.2015.10.006

Sallé, M. (2004). *IT service management and IT governance: Review, comparative analysis and their impact on utility computing.* Hewlett-Packard.

Samonas, S., & Coss, D. (2014). The CIA strikes back: Redefining confidentiality, integrity and availability in security. *Journal of Information System Security, 10*(3), 21–45. www.jissec.org/

Schatz, D., Bashroush, R., & Wall, J. (2017). Towards a more representative definition of cyber security. *Journal of Digital Forensics, Security and Law, 12*(2), 53–74. https://doi.org/10.15394/jdfsl.2017.1476

Sen, R., & Borle, S. (2015). Estimating the contextual risk of data breach: An empirical approach. *Journal of Management Information Systems, 32,* 314–341. https://doi.org/10.1080/07421222.2015.1063315

Silic, M., & Back, A. (2014). Information security: Critical review and future directions for research. *Information Management & Computer Security, 22,* 279–308. https://doi.org/10.1108/IMCS-05-2013-0041

Sindhuja, P. N. (2014). Impact of information security initiatives on supply chain performance: An empirical investigation. *Information Management & Computer Security, 22,* 450–473. https://doi.org/10.1108/IMCS-05-2013-0035

Singh, A. N., Picot, A., Kranz, J., Gupta, M. P., & Ojha, A. (2013). Information security management (ISM) practices: Lessons from select cases from India and Germany. *Global Journal of Flexible Systems Management, 14,* 225–239. https://doi.org/10.1007/s40171-013-0047-4

Sonnenreich, W., Albanese, J., & Stout, B. (2006). Return on security investment (ROSI)-a practical quantitative model. *Journal of Research and Practice in Information Technology, 38*(1), 45–56. https://50years.acs.org.au/digital-archive/jrpit.html

Srivastava, H., & Kumar, S. A. (2015). Control framework for secure cloud computing. *Journal of Information Security, 6,* 12–23. https://doi.org/10.4236/jis.2015.61002

Stilgoe, J., Owen, R., & Macnaghten, P. (2013). Developing a framework for responsible innovation. *Research Policy, 42*(9), 1568–1580. https://doi.org/10.1016/j.respol.2013.05.008

Stürmer, I., Weinberg, D., & Conrad, M. (2005). Overview of existing safeguarding techniques for automatically generated code. *ACM SIGSOFT Software Engineering Notes, 30*(4), 1–6. https://doi.org/10.1145/1082983.1083192

Vähäkainu, P., & Lehto, M. (2019, February). Artificial intelligence in the cyber security environment. In N. van der Waag-Cowling & L. Leenan (Eds.), *ICCWS 2019 14th International Conference on Cyber Warfare and Security: ICCWS 2019* (pp. 431–440). Academic Conferences International.

Van der Stede, W. (2010, January–March). Enterprise governance. *Pakistan Institute of Public Finance Accountants Journal,* 12–13. http://pipfa.org.pk/

Viader, A. M., & Espina, M. I. (2014). Are not-for-profits learning from for-profit-organizations? A look into governance. *Corporate Governance, 14*(1), 1–14. https://doi.org/10.1108/CG-11-2012-0083

Wang, T., Ulmer, J. R., & Kannan, K. (2013). The textual contents of media reports of information security breaches and profitable short-term investment opportunities. *Journal of Organizational Computing and Electronic Commerce, 23,* 200–223. http://dx.doi.org/10.1080/10919392.2013.807712

Weill, P., & Ross, J. W. (2004). *IT governance: How top performers manage IT decision rights for superior results.* Harvard Business School Press.

Whitman, M. E., & Mattord, H. J. (2012). Information security governance for the non-security business executive. *Journal of Executive Education, 11,* 97–111. http://digitalcommons.kennesaw.edu

Williams, S. P., Hardy, C. A., & Holgate, J. A. (2013). Information security governance practices in critical infrastructure organizations: A socio-technical and institutional logic perspective. *Electronic Markets, 23,* 341–354. https://doi.org/10.1007/s12525-013-0137-3

Wu, S. P. J., Straub, D. W., & Liang, T. P. (2015). How information technology governance mechanisms and strategic alignment influence organizational performance: Insights from a matched survey of business and IT managers. *MIS Quarterly, 39*(2), 497–518. https://doi.org/10.25300/MISQ/2015/39.2.10

Yaokumah, W. (2013). *Evaluating the effectiveness of information security governance practices in developing nations: A case of Ghana* (Publication No. 3557634) [Dissertation, Capella University]. ProQuest Dissertations Publishing.

Yaokumah, W., & Brown, S. (2014). An empirical examination of the relationship between information security/business strategic alignment and information security governance domain areas. *Journal of Business Systems, Governance & Ethics, 9*(2), 50–65. https://doi.org/10.15209/jbsge.v9i2.718

Recommended Reading

Chelliah, J., Boersma, M., & Klettner, A. (2016). Governance challenges for not-for-profit organisations: Empirical evidence in support of a contingency approach. *Contemporary Management Research*, *12*(1), 3–24. https://doi.org/10.7903/cmr.14538

Dawson, J., & Thomson, R. (2018). The future cybersecurity workforce: Going beyond technical skills for successful cyber performance. *Frontiers in Psychology*, *9*(744), 1–12. https://doi.org/10.3389/fpsyg.2018.00744

De Haes, S., Van Grembergen, W., Joshi, A., & Huygh, T. (2020). *Enterprise governance of information technology: Achieving alignment and value in digital organizations* (3rd ed.). Springer.

Diesch, R., Pfaff, M., & Krcmar, H. (2020). A comprehensive model of information security factors for decision-makers. *Computers & Security*, *92*, 101747. https://doi.org/10.1016/j.cose.2020.101747

Olifer, D., Goranin, N., Kaceniauskas, A., & Cenys, A. (2017). Controls-based approach for evaluation of information security standards implementation costs. *Technological and Economic Development of Economy*, *23*(1), 196–219. https://doi.org/10.3846/20294913.2017.1280558

Chapter 2

Security Governance Environment

Abstract

Organizational formations reflect personal aims, values, expectations, and sentiments that transform into a culture. There is a link between organizational leadership, culture, climate, and the environment from a functionalist perspective. As equivalent control environment factors, management's awareness and actions express leadership and communication intensity. Moreover, governmental enactment of laws continues, and the regulatory environment has become more sophisticated due to unacceptable conduct remediation. Controlling and monitoring activities attempting to ensure acceptable risk responses include policies, directives, standards, procedures, and rules. Management's philosophy for controlling and monitoring reflects a broad range of beliefs, concepts, and attitudes that significantly affect the entity's necessary policies and determine the organizational culture. Chapter 2 discusses entity-centric considerations for the control environment and Government–Entity–Audit domain convergences. Additionally, Chapter 2 presents legal issues, managerial practices, control inscriptions, and technology deployments as entity risk determinants.

Introduction

An entity's environment represents all conditions surrounding and affecting organizational endeavors (Davis, 2008a). Most entities operate in an environment determined by perceived stakeholder values as well as the entity's values, mission, and vision (Hu et al., 2012). Additionally, community and organizational ethics and culture, applicable laws, regulations, policies, and industry practices affect entity personnel (Davis, 2008a; Hu et al., 2012; IT Governance Institute, 2003). When interacting with the environment, manager-leaders endeavor to maintain the entity culture while attempting to control external and internal factors affecting programs, systems, and processes dedicated to pursuing the entity's mission (Davis, 2008a; Steiger et al., 2014). In systems theory, the sought sustainability represents manager-leaders seeking to minimize dynamic homeostasis cultural effects (Davis, 2008a).

Contextually, dynamic homeostasis means a system is in a constant state of variable activity where an equilibrium state is achievable at some change point (Davis, 2008a). Consequently, in response, organizational unit manager-leaders generally rely on adaptive processes for appropriate coping with changing environmental circumstances (Davis, 2008a). Dynamic homeostasis is steady-state achievement through a relatively open system (Davis, 2008a). The open system condition results from receiving input outside the system that is minimally equal to the sum of system output and resource expenditure (Davis, 2008a). All organizational units are open systems to a degree because none can operate without interaction with the surrounding environment elements (Davis, 2008a).

Derivatively, an entity's established information control environment must achieve dynamic homeostasis or risk managerial chaos (Davis, 2008a).

Control planning allows forecasting the future organizational direction and critical influences as well as deriving the best strategy for accomplishing control objectives – considering the entity's strengths, weaknesses, and foreseeable trends (Davis, 2008a, 2010). Furthermore, the control planning process translates strategy into measurable and operational plans then retranslates operational plans into policies, procedures, directives, standards, and rules (Davis, 2008a, 2010; Edwards, 2013). Nonetheless, information provides entity manager-leaders with a resource for appropriately reacting to demarcated environment conditions (Davis, 2008a). Information used in the entity's environment risk assessments can determine control implementation criticality (Davis, 2008a).

Compliance demonstrates the acceptance of expected behavior. Legal compliance is an essential management fiduciary responsibility (Davis, 2008a). However, legal compliance is not enough to ensure an appropriate control environment (Davis, 2008a). Controls can facilitate information security deployment efficacy through influencing employee behaviors (Atoum et al., 2014; Davis, 2017) and IT configurations. Management needs to understand the state of the entity's control systems in deciding what control deployments are necessary to meet organizational requirements.

When contributing to entity governance, the control environment deploys organizations, personnel, policies, procedures, accounting, budgeting, reporting, and internal control reviews (Davis, 2008a, 2010, 2020). An entity's ISG program needs to impart management's control environment attitude, awareness, and actions (Davis, 2008a). External factors often affect an entity's environment (Davis, 2008b). Specific external influencers affecting an entity's ability to achieve objectives include economics, communities, governments, technologies, competitors, suppliers, and customers (Davis, 2008b). Therefore, the external environment must receive an accurate assessment before proceeding with a course of action affecting the entity's control systems (Davis, 2008b). In other words, information security management should ensure an adequate ISG program deployment (Davis, 2008a). This chapter provides primary entity environment considerations when constructing an ISG and Cyber Security Governance program.

Entity-Centric Considerations

Leadership is a crucial concept for any entity (Anderson, 2015). The meaning of the leadership concept varies based on the circumstances (Anderson, 2015). There is a link between organizational leadership, culture, climate, and the environment from a functionalist perspective (Sarros et al., 2008). Functionalist supporters aver organizational leaders are social engineers through meaningful and apparent actions or assigned emblematic positions (Sarros et al., 2008). Thus, leadership is the process or act of influencing people to strive willingly or unwillingly toward achieving group objectives and adapting to change (Northouse, 2013).

Organizational leaders have a clear incentive to identify and redress any differences or gaps between their entity's actual culture and the envisioned culture. Where there are differences or gaps between cultural values, employee attitudes can form, which hinder performance; suppress motivation; and result in greater dissatisfaction, turnover, and stress levels (Posner, 2010). Manager-leaders must comprehend their effect in advancing an organizational culture; determining the necessary programs, systems, and processes to deploy a culture; and taking the necessary action to generate a healthy organizational culture. An entity's climate and linked environment should reflect a culture promoting cross-process cooperation and teamwork, support compliance and continuous process improvement, and manage process variations well (Davis, 2008a; Haag & Cummings,

2008). The achievement of effective leadership occurs when followers perform organizational assignments reflective of cultural expectations.

Organizational culture indicates a way of thinking, behaving, or working in an entity (Davis, 2020). Though situations may change, the organizational formation culture is unlikely to be recast based on current group circumstances (Steiger et al., 2014). Nonetheless, changing the organization's culture is typically necessary to successfully engage in new product development and innovation (Büschgens et al., 2013; Dasgupta et al., 2011). Isomorphic mechanisms may be responsible for constructing social behaviors and structures through institutional change (Luesebrink, 2011). Isomorphism constrains the organizational population unit by inducing conformance to changes in the entity environment (Luesebrink, 2011). Identified methods for conformance are:

- coercive mechanisms derived from political interests concerned with the problem of legitimacy and power in response to changes in the entity's environment,
- mimetic processes derived from imitative behaviors as a response to uncertainties and changes in the entity's environment, and
- normative pressures concerned with how social behaviors and professional standards address organizational changes in the entity's environment (Luesebrink, 2011).

An organizational climate is a usual or most widespread mood or conditions in an entity relevant to policies, procedures, and practices (Chernyak-Hai & Tziner, 2014). Organizational climate perceptions are part of an active psychological process that helps employees recognize behavioral expectations and rewards (Chernyak-Hai & Tziner, 2014). An entity's climate enables or disables adequate organizational task accomplishment and group maintenance through the organizational culture (Davis, 2008a; Northouse, 2013; Sarros et al., 2008). The organizational environment affects the employee effectiveness attributions through accepted social norms in the entity's climate (Sarros et al., 2008). The organizational climate perceptions reflect employee impressions of the work environment and influence job satisfaction, levels of stress, commitment, and performance, which, in turn, have implications for overall entity productivity (Chernyak-Hai & Tziner, 2014).

An organizational environment reflects aggregate social and cultural conditions that influence employee lives (Rasheed et al., 2015). Responding to an institutional change requires strategic choices after making sense of opportunities and threats from the change, as well as power differences in relationships (Akpinar, 2017). Transference, avoidance, reduction, and acceptance are the potential types of IAP strategic responses (Davis, 2008a) to environmental changes. The type of strategic response choice predicts what will influence relationship strategy selection and the power type exercised (Akpinar, 2017). An entity's manager-leaders should respond to changes in the environment for organizational survival and success (Akpinar, 2017).

Entity Control Environment

Entity control environments reflect the highest management level's attitude, relative to conformance imperatives and performance demands (Davis, 2008a). As equivalent control environment factors, managements' awareness and actions express leadership and communication intensity (Davis, 2008a). An entity's control environment should enable appropriate control deployments (Davis, 2008a). For an entity, control encompasses all the means used to direct, restrain, govern, and monitor organizational activities (Davis, 2006, 2008a).

Entity control systems are significantly affected by the control environment (Davis, 2008b). The entity's control environment sets the governing tone and influences control technique efficacy (Davis, 2008b). An entity's manager-leaders can contribute foundational control environment factors such as values and attitudes (Davis, 2008b). Values and attitudes represent a view of what is desirable or undesirable behavior (Davis, 2008b). Behavior refers to the way one acts (Davis, 2008b). Individual and group behavior is affected by an association with purported general value systems and specific attitude endorsements (Davis, 2008b). Values and attitudes are obscure evidential concepts due to inferring intangible qualities from actual behavior, verbal descriptions, or written statements (Davis, 2008b).

At the entity level, control consciousness is influenced significantly by oversight committee members (Davis, 2008b). Being aware of the entity's environment and managerial issues, tasks, responsibilities, and organizational differences connect to control consciousness. Therefore, the ideal collective characteristics of individuals participating in entity oversight should include independence from management, experience, stature, demonstrated involvement in activities and scrutiny, appropriate situational actions, good knowledge management, effective administrative assessment techniques, as well as interaction with internal and external auditors (Davis, 2008b).

Production of practice codes and other regulations or guidance benefical in ensuring appropriate entity oversight accentuates the responsibility importance of those charged with governance (Davis, 2008b). The inscribed primary responsibilities of those charged with governance include oversight of the design and effective operation of procedures and the process for reviewing control system efficacy (Davis, 2008b). Consequently, the entity's oversight committee should direct information security manager-leaders to achieve measurable service and support value by:

- delivering appropriate service quality,
- enhancing service cost–efficiency relationships,
- enabling customer trust in services performed, and
- achieving competitive times for information security redeployments.

An entity's general IT objectives typically increase significantly when collectively considered with fiduciary responsibilities (Davis, 2008b). As shown in Table 2.1, distinct general IT objectives for an entity are achievable through various information criteria establishment that frame aligned focus on meeting entity-centric needs (Davis, 2008b). Foundationally, the IT control environment should assist in enabling the entity's governing body,

Table 2.1 Information Criteria Correspondence to IT Objectives

Criteria	Operational			IT	Compliance		
	Effectiveness	Efficiency	Economy	Reliability	Laws	Regulations	Policies
Effectiveness	X						
Efficiency		X	X				
Confidentiality				X			
Integrity				X			
Availability				X			
Compliance					X	X	X
Reliability				X			

Note: X, Applicability.

management, and all other employees in providing reasonable assurance regarding the achievement of:

- Operational efficiency that epitomizes task performance ease considering the organizational objectives (Davis, 2008b).
- Operational effectiveness in available resource use to accomplish the organizational objectives (Davis, 2008b).
- Operational economy maximizing the benefit in the cost–benefit relationship for accomplishing the organizational objectives (Davis, 2008b).
- Reliability sustainment of IT for a specific duration, within the specified environment, when pursuing organizational objectives (Davis, 2008b).
- Compliance of laws and regulations that reduce the risk of criminal or civil charges by plaintiffs, as well as fines and penalties (Davis, 2008b).
- Compliance of internal policies fulfilling management's intentions for organized units (Davis, 2008b).

Technology has and will continue to assume the change agent role and influence entity control environments (Davis, 2008a; Hirschheim & Klein, 2012; Wiener et al., 2019). Technological development and deployment have an inextricable connection to the social, political, economic, and informational factors that prevail in an entity's control environment (Davis, 2008a). Entity control environments usually govern control emphasis through assessed sensitivity, criticality, or impact (Davis, 2008a). Therefore, manager-leaders cannot afford to disregard technological advances (Davis, 2008a).

Electronically conveyed information is a primary catalyst for managerial decisions (Davis, 2008a; Wiener et al., 2019). Astute entity executives ensure IT deployments provide continuous information and processes safeguarding (Davis, 2008a). Typically, executive management does not have a responsibility to understand technical details such as the fundamentals of digital rights or electronic signature intricacies (Davis, 2008a). Moreover, information asymmetry positively relates to information security service effectiveness (Wu & Saunders, 2016). Nevertheless, top management needs to insist upon administrative information concerning security deployments, supporting evidence of existing protection processes, and furnishing proper functionality (Davis, 2008a).

There are external and internal environment stakeholders (Kinicki & Williams, 2013). Sub-categorically, the classification of external stakeholders consists of general and task environments (Kinicki & Williams, 2013). The general environment includes commercial, technological, sociocultural, demographic, political–legal, and global forces (Kinicki & Williams, 2013). Whereas the task environment encompasses employee associations, customers, suppliers, distributors, strategic allies, local communities, competitors, financial institutions, government regulators, special interest groups, and the mass media. (Kinicki & Williams, 2013). Comparatively, internal corporate stakeholders consist of employees, owners, and the entity's board of directors (Kinicki & Williams, 2013). Nonetheless, stakeholders derive value from entity affiliation utility, justice cognitions, and opportunity cost perceptions (Harrison & Wicks, 2013).

Extending agency theory to diverse settings using a deductive approach is achievable through formal institutional context recognition and incorporation encompassing the principal–agent relations into agency-based models (Wiseman et al., 2012). Combined, Stakeholder-Agency Theory explicates why manager-leaders might ignore or overlook stakeholder interests (Tashman & Raelin, 2013). Notably, researchers addressing Stakeholder-Agency Theory have argued that market frictions can cause fragmentary contracting that can misalign managerial abstractions of what and who is significant to the entity (Tashman & Raelin, 2013). For instance, the top management team may commit financial resources to deploy an entity-wide ISG program that will ensure appropriate IAP, yet the manager-leaders abstain from using safeguards or other ISG program aspects (Garba et al., 2015; Kushwaha, 2016).

Budgeting is the process for inscribing resource allocations considering planned activities (Davis, 2008a). An entity's oversight committee should ensure the earmarking of sufficient resources to sustain ISG (Davis, 2008a). Earmarking sufficient ISG resources does not demand those responsible for governance examine the integrity of the budget allocation models (Davis, 2008a). ISG performance, conformance, and objectives are institutionally contingent (Williams et al., 2013). Consequently, deployed information security programs can be entity-centric and comprehensive (Davis, 2008a; Edwards, 2013; Mohare & Lanjewar, 2012). However, manager-leaders should pursue independent opines from audit professionals regarding adequate information security resources' provisioning and use (Davis, 2008a).

Security responsibilities conveyance can occur through an entrusting party or by statutory edict (Davis, 2008a). External stakeholders or internal management are entrusting parties that delegate security responsibilities for entity assets (Davis, 2008a). In contrast, statutory edicts are enforceable laws or regulations that can impose individual or agent security responsibilities, usually with specific objective identification (Davis, 2008a). Whether consigned by an entrusting party or statutory edict, security responsibilities commonly transform into operational and technological requirements for satisfying managerial expectations, generally institutionalized through objectives and goals (Davis, 2008a).

Conceptually, organizational control goals enable achieving entity control environment objectives (Davis, 2008a). As an entity objective, the control environment should assist in enabling the governing body, management, and all other employees in providing reasonable assurance regarding information security responsibilities' achievement of:

- confidentiality that epitomizes preserving authorized restrictions addressing access and disclosure,
- integrity protection against improper modification or destruction, and
- availability sustainment permitting timely and reliable access and use (Davis, 2008a).

Protecting information assets should be the primary ISG focal point when a symbiotic entity control environment exists (Davis, 2008a). As delineated in Table 2.2, confidentiality, integrity, and availability are criteria (Davis, 2008a) represented in the information security triad model (Samonas & Coss, 2014). Manager-leaders responsible for an entity's control environment should consider security information criteria while pursuing organizational goals and objectives (Davis, 2008a). Adopting security information criteria is an enabler assisting in framing the control environment for conducting entity affairs (Davis, 2008a). Correspondingly, manager-leaders often depend on information reliability,

Table 2.2 Security Information Criteria Correspondence to Information Reliability Objective

Information Criteria	Information Reliability Objective
Confidentiality	X
Integrity	X
Availability	X

Note: X = Applicability

especially when conveying instructions, providing analysis, and responding to inquiries concerning achieving entity objectives (Davis, 2008b). Mapping generally accepted security information criteria to the information reliability objective elucidates relevance for a controlled environment that supports security information criteria when pursuing satisfying information objectives (Davis, 2008a).

Information Confidentiality Criteria

Information confidentiality value is an entity-centric issue that needs to reflect managerial expectations (Davis, 2008a). Institutionalizing confidentiality values requires employee conformance to a moral system or code that standardizes acceptable behaviors (Davis, 2008a). There is a common expectation that once assigned work responsibilities requiring organizational information use, entity-centric confidentiality values are thoroughly understood and accepted by the employee (Davis, 2008a). Just because information generation occurs within an entity does not automatically confer confidential classification (Davis, 2008a).

Sustaining IT confidentiality translates into maintaining assigned information asset privacy levels (Davis, 2008a). Appropriate confidentiality management necessitates deploying an entity-centric information asset classification system (Davis, 2008a). In considering the security informational asset classification, unauthorized data disclosure potentially resulting in an adverse effect or penalty on the entity, customers, or employees should receive confidential treatment (Davis, 2008a). Privacy in an interconnected world begins with understanding and securing information systems and IT networks. Therefore, privacy is an Information and Cyber Security Governance concern that should receive appropriate information security and cybersecurity program consideration.

Information Integrity Criteria

As with confidentiality value, information integrity value is an entity-centric issue that needs to reflect managerial expectations (Davis, 2008a). Information retains integrity if the accuracy, completeness, timeliness, validity, and processing methods receive continuous safeguarding (Flowerday & Von Solms, 2007). Generally, information integrity value correlates representational faithfulness to the condition or subject matter depicted by the content (Boritz, 2005; Davis, 2008a; Flowerday & Von Solms, 2007). Information resiliency under adverse conditions is a litmus test of adherence to accepted integrity value (Davis, 2008a).

Managerial information integrity needs to maintain durational validity, completeness, and accuracy attributes within the entity's control environment (Boritz, 2005; Davis, 2008a). Specifically, managerial information integrity must demonstrate an unimpaired, or unmarred, representation for the entire content correspondence life cycle regarding an original condition or subject matter when conducting affairs, such as conveying expectations or employee interfacing (Boritz, 2005; Davis, 2008a). Achieving information trust typically requires invoking integrity management (Davis, 2008b; Samonas & Coss, 2014). When information reflects integrity, manager-leaders establish trust and provide the basis for reliance on decisions affecting the entity (Davis, 2008a).

Information Availability Criteria

Availability and IAP are polar states because availability aims to facilitate access to information, whereas security aims to restrict access to information (Davis, 2008a). However, information availability usually mandates appropriate safeguards (Davis, 2008a). Accessibility and appropriate information security are critical processing issues (Boritz, 2005;

Davis, 2008a). For information to be current, complete, and timely, the information security personnel maintaining user availability and accessibility per specifications (Boritz, 2005; Davis, 2008a; Samonas & Coss, 2014) as well as reclamation in a desirable form when required is necessary (Boritz, 2005; Davis, 2008a).

When sought, inaccessible pertinent information has no practical consequences for user decisions or activities, except to limit quality (Boritz, 2005; Davis, 2008a). User practicality requires robust systems to render trustworthy information (Boritz, 2005; Davis, 2008a). Such systems must be available when needed, enable user configuration modifications, operate efficiently and effectively, as well as accommodate information allocation adjustments (Boritz, 2005; Davis, 2008a).

Information Reliability Objective

Generally, IT reliability represents the capability to maintain a specified acceptable level of performance under defined conditions (Davis, 2008a). Information reliability requires representational faithfulness to ensure assertions and supporting purported events agree (Davis, 2008a). Reliability measurements determine if information deployments occurred with appropriate security (Davis, 2008a). Minimally, the information contained within technology can be reliable when completeness, accuracy, and validity attributes are independently verifiable and user neutral (Boritz, 2005; Davis, 2008a). Information completeness indicates that an item contains all data elements and records needed for trusted usability (Davis, 2008a). Information accuracy reflects the exact reality data generation entered at the source or replication from a previous inscription (Davis, 2008a). Information validity implies that elemental data represent real conditions, rules, or relationships rather than physical object characteristics (Boritz, 2005; Davis, 2008a).

Achievement of data reliability occurs through confirmability. Confirmability infers how other individuals can verify data to ensure constructed information reflects understandings and experiences from actual events rather than individual preferences. An audit of information can reduce the chance of bias, thus increasing objectivity assurance for reliability.

Domain Convergence Effects

Governmental enactment of laws continues, and the regulatory environment has become more sophisticated due to unacceptable conduct remediation (Davis, 2013). Consequently, entities must have the capability to demonstrate compliance with legal mandates (Davis, 2013). The migration from manual to automated information generation has resulted in verdicts and judgments where liability, guilt, or innocence determination relied solely upon, or primarily on, electronically encoded evidence (Davis, 2013). Reliance on IT generated information as evidence raises issues and challenges from a management perspective that can require resolution through effective governance and audit (Davis, 2013).

Globally, laws and regulations ensure that entity employees comply with a society's expectations for ethical behavior when conducting organizational affairs (Brotby, 2006; Davis, 2008a). Critical to preserving stakeholder confidence in the entity's mission is governance deployments that protect information and related technologies against undesirable events (Davis, 2008a). Depending on societal perceptions, statutory ratifications occur to ensure compliance with perceived managerial, operational, and technical responsibilities for IAP (Davis, 2008a).

Interpretively, the underlined titles in Figure 2.1 name relational domains, and the content within the three circles are topical or sub-topical attributes of each domain. The government domain, which is the top-center circle, represents imposed laws and regulations. The entity domain, which is the bottom-left circle, represents governance and associated

Figure 2.1 Government– Entity – Audit Convergences.

Note: Adapted from *IT Auditing: Assuring Information Assets Protection* by R. E. Davis, 2008a, Pleier. Copyright 2008 by Robert E. Davis. Adapted with permission.

control environment, managerial, and employee considerations. In the end, the audit domain, which is the bottom-right circle, represents the practice of audits, reviews, and agreed-upon procedures. The strategic placement of the circles illustrates the significance of the interrelationship between domains. Where the government, entity, and audit circles overlap, the merged attributes are crucial in discerning organizational effects.

Government-Entity Convergence

Groups conceive rules, customs, and prevailing opinions that can convert into laws through government actions (Davis, 2008a, 2013, 2020). Compliance infers behavioral expectation acceptance (Davis, 2008a, 2013, 2020). Expected behavior acceptance requires value conformance (Davis, 2008a, 2013, 2020). Conformance is usually the goal for most societies, whether laws or regulations apply to group or individual behavior (Davis, 2008a, 2013, 2020). Internationally, nationally, or locally enforceable laws reflect official behavioral norms for a society (Davis, 2008a, 2013, 2020). The legal interpretation of laws and regulations indicates the corresponding community's sociological trends (Davis, 2008a, 2013, 2020). Like entity governance-related laws and regulations, political divisions enacting and enforcing ISG mandates provide behavioral expectation consistency for activities (Davis, 2008a, 2013, 2020). As a prosecution avoidance mechanism, deploying an exceptional ISG framework encompassing all information assets can reduce legal risks (Davis, 2008a, 2013).

Generally, primary law functions embrace influencing and enforcing conduct standards, maintaining the status quo, facilitating orderly change, providing maximum individual self-assertion, facilitating planning and reasonable expectation realization, providing social justice promotion, compromise solution provisioning, and peacekeeping (Davis, 2008a). However, the application of laws may have perceived limitations (Davis, 2008a) or extensions requiring adjudication. Moreover, a decreed behavioral conduct expectation is likely to face enforcement difficulties if the affected citizenry considers a rule unreasonable or unfair (Davis, 2008a). In contrast, governmental regulations are legally binding requirements administered through regulatory agency personnel (Davis, 2008a). Regulatory agencies are independent government commissions generally charged by government legislatures to establish and enforce specific entity standards (Davis, 2008a). Resultingly, regulatory agency compliance and enforcement address the direct monitoring and oversight of a specific individual, group, community, or industry participating in a defined activity (Davis, 2008a).

Governmentally enforceable legal mandates continuously intersect with entities organized to satisfy the perceived needs for goods or services (Davis, 2013). In most instances, courts interpret laws and regulations that apply to particular facts arising from situational disputes (Davis, 2008a). Managements laws and regulations exposition generally follow guidelines established by assessed intent of respective judicial, legislative, or executive governmental entities (Davis, 2008a). Enacted laws and regulations associated with IAP include the United States Digital Millennium Copyright Act, the Canadian Personal Information Protection and Electronic Documents Act (Davis, 2008a), and the European Union General Data Protection Regulation.

Compliance with applicable laws and regulations necessitates obeying statutory requirements to which the entity or the organizational employees are subject (Davis, 2008a). Directly or indirectly, applicable laws and regulations influence an entity's ISG control environment, administrative decisions, and employee actions (Davis, 2008a). Statutory mandates traditionally define permissible activities, recognized organizational formulations, and social responsibility that guides control environment construction (Davis, 2008a). Governments define permissible activities that determine acceptable entity and employee behaviors (Davis, 2011). Management's selection of a government-recognized organizational structure affects conduct of the affairs throughout the entity (Davis, 2011). The government-imposed social responsibility affects the amount of diligence and care expected from the entity and entity employees (Davis, 2011). Consequently, manager-leader administrative decisions require legal mandate consideration. Legal requirements drive fiduciary responsibilities and enable redress for statute violations for all entity employee noncompliance actions (Davis, 2008a).

Intersecting and interacting with governmental legal mandates are deployed entity governance structures (Davis, 2008a). Corresponding to entity stakeholder calls for fulfilling fiduciary responsibilities through appropriate governance is the increasing pressure for effective control system deployment (Davis, 2008a). To satisfy control system expectations, ISG must represent the combined people, processes, and structures implemented by the entity's highest-level oversight committee and executive management to inform, direct, manage, and monitor information security activities toward the achievement of objectives (Davis, 2008a).

Government-Audit Convergence

Governments enact laws and regulations that influence auditor conduct and impose IT audit practice requirements (Davis, 2008a). Therefore, auditors need to maintain the highest degree of integrity and conduct as well as reject any methods perceivable as unlawful, unethical, or unprofessional to obtain or execute an audit assignment (Davis, 2008a). Considering de jure assurance service standards for avoiding government-imposed mandates transgressions, practicing auditors should pursue sustaining currency with applicable IAP-related laws and regulations (Davis, 2008a). Moreover, auditors need to forego using unlicensed hardware, firmware, and software when conducting audit assignments (Davis, 2008a).

Professional prudence dictates legal mandates affecting audit practice areas require a thorough understanding by audit team members before proceeding with audit fieldwork (Davis, 2008a). Individually, auditors must review compliance with applicable statutory laws, regulations as well as contracts and, where applicable, seek legal guidance when participating in an audit (Davis, 2008a). Therefore, through preliminary discussions with a practicing attorney, an auditor can acquire sufficient knowledge to identify illegal act indicators (Davis, 2008a). However, there should be no expectation that a financial or operational auditor has the expertise of individuals whose primary responsibility is detecting and investigating illegal acts (Davis, 2008a).

Regarding compliance engagements of laws and regulations, the lead auditor has the right to believe that management established appropriate controls to prevent, deter, and detect illegal acts until evaluations and tests carried out by audit team members prove otherwise (Davis, 2008a). Professionally, audit team members must exercise due caution for disclosing information acquired during an engagement to any person other than the entity's dually appointed representatives (Davis, 2008a). Engagement information disclosure by audit team members to an individual, with or without consent, may violate a nondisclosure or confidentiality agreement for the time being in force (Davis, 2008a). Audit team members must remain vigilant throughout an engagement of the various regulatory and statutory issues applicable to the entity under audit to ensure providing reasonable assurance of compliance with information disclosure mandates (Davis, 2008a).

The most common audit practice laws and regulations influence evidence collection and retention (Davis, 2008a). For decreed legal compliance audits, if an illegal act is suspected, auditor team members must ensure the satisfaction of evidential legal mandates to successfully provide authorities with untainted items for prosecuting alleged perpetrators (Davis, 2008a). Additionally, when auditors perform engagements on an international scale, understanding various evidentiary requirements can become critical to sustaining professional audit practices (Davis, 2008a). Under most circumstances, audit evidence available to the auditor during a legal compliance audit should be persuasive rather than conclusive for demonstrating due diligence. At the same time, retention period requirements vary by jurisdiction (Davis, 2008a).

Entity–Audit Convergence

Entity governance transparency has become a contentious subject matter (Davis, 2008a, 2011; Hess, 2007). Entity governance transparency virtues link to trust and credibility (Rawlins, 2008). If manager-leaders do not impart trustworthy information, the organization risks operational discontinuity (Rawlins, 2008). Information reliability enables manager-leaders to operate the entity and exercise reporting responsibilities (Davis, 2008a). Typically, consistency is an accuracy subcategory supporting integrity for information reliability (Davis, 2008a). Consistency refers to lucid and discrete data that yields similar results in similar circumstances (Boritz, 2005; Davis, 2008a). If informational data consistency exists and supports data accuracy, and data accuracy supports information integrity, then sustained informational data consistency determines the appropriateness of a security integrity deployment that assists in meeting the information reliability objective.

Effective IAP employs vulnerability management and threat intelligence in strategic decision-making (Davis, 2008a) in achieving information reliability. Entity ISG program manager-leaders should integrate IAP that aligns strategically with operational objectives and safeguarding requirements (Davis, 2008a). Manager-leaders need to ensure IAP best-practice deployments within the ISG program (Davis, 2008a). By convention, an adequate IAP system initiates or sustains data links with the entity's IT configuration items, operational risk assessments, human resources practices, monitoring procedures, and assurance activities (Davis, 2008a). Proactive IT incident or event-defensive posturing promotes appropriate IAP standardization, performance, and compliance, not as discrete processes, but as interweaving fabrics for complete entity-centric information integrity and confidentiality attire (Davis, 2008a).

Entity security programs can implement protective measures using technological and non-technological control stratification (Davis, 2008a). IAP controls are necessary for counteracting vulnerabilities and threats in a manner that reduces potential adverse impacts to defined, acceptable risk levels (Davis, 2008a). IAP processes frequently overlap and reinforce organizational efforts to improve entity-governance, IT governance, and ISG through risk management, compliance management, operational management, as well as other critical management systems (Davis, 2008a). Directly, entity management's IAP posture has a significant effect on ISG program viability. Indirectly, ISG can influence stakeholder's assessed entity value (Davis, 2008a).

For most entities, compliance management of information and related technologies is critical to organizational continuity (Davis, 2008a). As with other organizational programs, information security compliance does not occur without managerial oversight (Davis, 2008a). Generally, an entity's oversight committee and executives periodically evaluate control system effectiveness, recommended deployments, monitoring activities, and the ability to prevent or detect irregularities and illegal acts (Davis, 2008a). Arguably, data security is the most significant element supporting information reliability. If IT is inadequately protected, data may not be appropriately processed (Davis, 2008a). Consequently, manager-leaders should continually seek to improve information security within the entity's control system (Davis, 2008a).

Information security control and assurance processes require managerial dedication to continuous improvement to ensure effectiveness and efficiency (Davis, 2008a). Many entities perform recurring network and application security assessments to demonstrate due diligence (Davis, 2008a). Information security drills can assist in evaluating designed processes and deployed controls (Davis, 2008a). Information security drills can also help ensure the meeting of service and support expectations (Davis, 2008a) when an incident or event occurs. However, assurance activities need to address different aspects of an entity's ISG program or systems at different locations or in various divisions, on separate schedules, and with varied team types (Davis, 2008a).

Assessing the current state of implemented controls may take a variety of forms (Davis, 2008a). Control self-assessments are conduits for entity monitoring (Davis, 2008a) and evaluation. Strategically planning annual control self-assessments is a sound managerial practice (Davis, 2008a). Nonetheless, following a cyclic approach to control self-assessments cannot guarantee unqualified audit reports (Davis, 2008a). Information security manager-leaders should prepare for audits through engaging control self-assessments to verify compliance with legislation, regulations, policies, directives, procedures, standards, and rules (Davis, 2008a).

When considering IAP, control self-assessments are namable as security self-assessments. Each security self-assessment exercise necessitates producing a report (Davis, 2008a). In utilizing a workshop format, the security self-assessment group consensus for discussed issues needs inscription (Davis, 2008a). Prerequisites for workshop participation should include a fundamental understanding of operational and security requirements associated with respective duties to ensure sustained confidentiality, integrity, and availability achievement through appropriate consideration of security self-assessment results (Davis, 2008a). Security self-assessment report substance creation should occur during deliberations by describing relevant risks, identifying control weaknesses, and suggesting remedial actions (Davis, 2008a). Additionally, the security self-assessment group should review the proposed final report before ending the workshop session (Davis, 2008a).

Generally, the audit function manager-leader has a responsibility for ensuring that (a) independence and objectivity are maintained in all engagement processes; (b) supportable professional judgment occurs in planning approaches, performing procedures, and reporting engagement results; (c) work conducted by personnel is professionally competent, and team members collectively have the necessary knowledge and skills; and (d) an independent peer-review is periodically performed resulting in an opinion issued as to whether the quality control system design and operation provide reasonable assurance of conforming with professional standards as well as legal mandates (Davis, 2008a). Furthermore, auditors may not be the individuals who execute an entity's information security control review (Davis, 2008a). However, auditors may subsequently assess control review quality (Davis, 2008a). In the regulatory arena, prompt corrective actions to an adverse finding can mitigate civil or criminal penalties. Thereby, prompt corrective actions to an adverse finding can potentially reduce or avoid legal risks (Davis, 2008a).

Audit personnel can foster a special relationship with security personnel since both employee types operate in the role of seeking asset-safeguarding improvements (Davis, 2008a). Similarly, auditors and security professionals can face resistance from manager-leaders due to fear, cost, or priority of tampering with fragile networks, systems, or processes (Davis, 2008a). When entity manager-leaders perceive the information security or audit personnel promote control enhancements without concern for costs or benefits, communications must ensure sufficient evidence of control effectiveness with demonstratable benefits exceeding cost (Davis, 2011). Part of the Chief Audit Executive or Audit Partner's duty is to provide the oversight committee with information that will help determine appropriate resource allocations for security (Davis, 2008a). Therefore, auditors can contribute positively to the audit-security relationship reflective of experience with explaining technical problems in operational and management terms to the oversight committee (Davis, 2008a).

Government–Entity–Audit Convergence

Where government-enforced laws and regulations overlap entity governance, audit practice coverage is usually required to verify mandated compliance (Davis, 2008a). Therefore, the Government–Entity–Audit convergence describes the central environment from which to operate ISG (Davis, 2008a). Implicit in the deployment of ISG is information security management's fiduciary relationship with stakeholders (Davis, 2008a). Commonly, stakeholder fiduciary expectations receive support from a jurisdictional legal system (Davis, 2008a). Additionally, considering most audit standards require a legal compliance risk evaluation, management can reasonably expect an audit to verify adherence to applicable legal mandates (Davis, 2008a). Full compliance with statutes, policies, directives, procedures, standards, and rules enables superior ISG (Davis, 2008a).

Managerial transparency permits monitoring and accountability for commitments and the discharge of duties (Broz, 2002) instead of opacity, cloudiness, shadiness, and an unconstrained decision-making process. The level of entity transparency is the extent of clarity, visibility, clearness, openness, and constraint manager-leaders exhibit in executing the decision-making process (Pasquier & Villeneuve, 2007). By extension, governance transparency enables further inquiry into the factors that may cloud or obscure managerial transparency (Pasquier & Villeneuve, 2007). In keeping with the promotion of good governance within for-profit or not-for-profit entities, governance transparency enables adequate measures adoption to minimize employee opacity, turbidity, irregularities, and illegal acts (Pasquier & Villeneuve, 2007).

Managerially, an appropriate entity control environment can enhance ISG efficacy (Davis, 2008a). Information security manager-leaders need to actively ensure that the control environment addresses the protection of information assets since the protection of information assets is a primary ISG component for ensuring reliable financial reporting and data privacy (Davis, 2008a). Consequently, information security manager-leaders should deploy a comprehensive risk assessment framework that assists in designing appropriate policies, procedures, standards, and rules for entity employees (Davis, 2008a).

Designing and sustaining appropriate ISG are proportionally linked to information security control deployments (Davis, 2008a). General and application control categorization aids in devising appropriate control deployments. As general and application security categories, ISG should minimally earmark network infrastructure security, logical access controls, environmental controls, risk analysis, physical access controls, and the confidential information life cycle (Davis, 2008a). General and application controls that incorporate information asset protection principles are foundationally enabled to successfully assist employees in fulfilling fiduciary security responsibilities, whether automated or manual (Davis, 2008a).

IAP is a safeguarding activity that should integrate with responsibility, authority, and accountability separation to prevent unauthorized access, modification, disclosure, as well as the destruction of information and associated technologies (Davis, 2008a). With safeguarding considered a legally enforceable fiduciary responsibility, IAP legal compliance management rates as a high-priority ISG risk subcategory (Davis, 2008a). Inept IAP legal compliance management can jeopardize an entity's ability to attract stakeholders when correlated to the regulatory noncompliance reputational repercussion (Davis, 2008a).

Statutes can impose audit practice requirements affecting ISG attestation service efforts (Davis, 2008a). Attestation engagements focus on examining, reviewing, or performing agreed-upon procedures of a subject matter or an assertion regarding a subject matter, then reporting evidentially supported results (Davis, 2008a). The attestation engagement subject matter can take many forms, including programs, systems, processes, functions, past performance, prospective conditions, or behavior (Davis, 2008a).

ISG and Cyber Security Governance necessitate subject matter consideration for external and internal audits due to the high impact on manager-leaders fulfilling safeguarding responsibilities (Davis, 2008a). Security typically is a complex and dynamic safeguarding subject (Davis, 2008a). Given the descriptive attributes associated with information security, auditors usually have a vast array of sub-topics to contemplate when performing ISG-related audits, reviews, or agreed-upon procedures (Davis, 2008a). However, the engagement's ambit and terms of reference bound the detail control objectives, methodology selections, and examination activities for assurance service (Davis, 2008a). As discrete work domains, when performing ISG or Cyber Security Governance assurance, auditors should select the most relevant material applicable to the defined audit ambit (Davis, 2008a). Simultaneously, the auditors should assess alignment with operational and IT processes, considering entity-centric control objectives and correlating acceptable management practices (Davis, 2008a).

Entity Risk Determinants

Manager-leaders are usually assessed on the basis of the ability to achieve designated operational, financial, and compliance responsibilities (Davis, 2008a). The control environment can provide discipline and structure to entity processes for appropriately addressing operational, financial, and compliance requirements (Davis, 2008a). However, the control environment reflects many factors that are entity risk determinants. Besides authority, responsibility, and accountability delegation, primary risk determinants for an entity's control environment include

- Ethics: Employee ethical values reflect organizationally enforced behavioral expectations (Davis, 2008b). There is an expectation that once assigned managerial responsibilities, the entity's ethical values are thoroughly understood and adopted by the employee (Davis, 2008b). Adopting entity-centric ethical values requires conformance to a system or code of morals that standardizes acceptable behaviors (Davis, 2008b). Nonetheless, just because a choice is acceptable, statutory or regulatory conformance does not automatically qualify the behavior as ethical (Davis, 2008b).
- Integrity: Employee integrity values, as with ethical values, are an issue reflecting organizationally enforced behavioral expectations (Davis, 2008b). Within an entity's control environment, managerial integrity should represent the state or quality of sound moral principles (Davis, 2008b). Specifically, entity manager-leaders should demonstrate uprightness, honesty, and sincerity when conducting organizational affairs, conveying information, and interfacing with employees (Davis, 2008b). By acting with integrity, manager-leaders establish trust and provide the basis for reliance on decisions affecting the entity (Davis, 2008b). Stakeholders expect manager-leaders to maintain integrity values consistent with accepted societal norms and obligations (Davis, 2008b). Entity managements' capacity to sustain compliance with laws, regulations, policies, directives, procedures, standards, and rules under adverse conditions are litmus tests of adherence to personal as well as employee integrity values (Davis, 2008b).
- Philosophy: Management's philosophy encompasses a broad range of beliefs, concepts, and attitudes that have a significant effect not only on the entity's necessary policies but also on determining the organizational culture (Davis, 2008b). Management's beliefs are the focal point for directing activities (Davis, 2008b). The manner of communicating management's philosophy affects employee behavior when accomplishing the entity's mission (Davis, 2008b). Commonly, communications rendering entity purpose and general methodological conduct inscription usually occur within a mission statement (Davis, 2008b, 2011). Architecturally, mission statements are how management translates organizational concepts into instructive information enabling consumer and employee awareness of primary organizational motivation drivers (Davis, 2008b, 2011).
- Operating style: Management's operating style is usually an extraction from devotion to tasks, symbolic behavior, and engrained cultural norms (Davis, 2008b). Within this arena, the entity-designed and deployed control systems should attempt to achieve the goals set in or comply with adopted governance rules (Davis, 2008b). Management's operating style will typically reflect, directly or indirectly, the entity-centric direction presented in items such as the mission statement, management principles, management plans, ethic codes, and conduct codes (Davis, 2008b). Consequently, the manner of communicating management's operating style also affects employee behavior (Davis, 2008b).

- Organizational structures: Organizational structures are operational segmentations, managerial layers, and constructed processes that determine how employees accomplish work (Julisch, 2013). An entity's organizational structure defines the planned, executed, controlled, and reviewed employee activities for achieving objectives (Davis, 2008b). Traditional organizational structures represent inherited, established, or conventional business architectures (Steiger et al., 2014). Less traditional entities rely on informal organizational structures using alliance building and boundary spanning managerial techniques (Foss & Dobrajska, 2015; Steiger et al., 2014). Interior and exterior environment factors influence organizational structures (Davis, 2008a; Hodgkinson et al., 2014; Sila, 2013).

- Commitment to competence: Commitment to competence is necessary for ensuring adequate leadership and quality when engaged in entity endeavors (Davis, 2008b). Knowledge management initiatives and activities enable competence (Davis, 2008b). Therefore, the employment of well qualified, capable, and fit individuals can ensure sufficient knowledge, skills, and abilities to meet an entity's needs (Davis, 2008b). Conversely, compromising commitment to employee competence for financial burden relief can lead to an entity's demise (Davis, 2008b). Minimally, within the entity, commitment to employee competence requires fostering strategic, tactical, and operational – recruiting, hiring, knowledge reviews, skills reviews, training, team development, records' management, collaborative communication systems, as well as knowledge management systems (Davis, 2008b).

- Human resources policies and practices: Human resources policies are specific courses or methods of action selected by management from alternatives, considering the environment, that guide as well as determine present and future employment decisions (Davis, 2008b). Designed human resource policies should identify specific entity human resource control processes (Davis, 2006). Moreover, human resource practices can assist in resource quality assurance (Davis, 2008a). Human resources practices relate to recruiting, orientating, training, evaluating, counseling, promoting, compensating, and remediating entity personnel (Davis, 2008b).

- Control methods over compliance with laws and regulations: If the entity's executive manager-leaders have an enforceable fiduciary duty, then subordinate organizational personnel are expected to adhere to and sustain the defined obligation (Davis, 2008a). Policies and procedures that support compliance with laws and regulations are the primary employee controls (Davis, 2008a). Employees that value compliance usually hold honesty and integrity as desirable personal traits or fear noncompliance repercussions (Davis, 2008a). However, if an entity's culture continually encourages or accepts objectives achievement over ethical behavior, legal dilemmas eventually ensue that can damage reputations and create financial losses (Davis, 2008a). Therefore, entity manager-leaders should implement control self-assessment procedures that ensure adherence to legal obligations (Davis, 2008a).

The entity's control environment replication occurs typically within an ISG program through organizational cascading (Davis, 2008a). Therefore, if an entity-level control environment maintains an acceptable risk level, so should the ISG program (Davis, 2008a). Risk assessment frequency determination for an entity control environment should occur after assessing the impact of risks, history of compliance or ethics debacles, and the likelihood of incidents (Davis, 2008a).

Concerning information asset safeguarding, integrity values, and ethical values should be considered critical control environment characteristics that dramatically impact information security (Davis, 2008a). Integrity and ethical values influence the design, administration, and monitoring efficacy of controls. An individual's total past experiences provide a perspective of values through which a person evaluates the relative merit, usefulness, or importance of things, ideas, or alternative courses of action (Davis, 2008b). Contrastingly, attitudes are more precise since they refer to a person's disposition, opinion, or mental resolution concerning objects such as things, ideas, people, or policies (Davis, 2008b). Thus, management's attitude toward information processing determines the approach to taking and monitoring risks.

Deeply ingrained in entity employment's physical and social context are security issues (Carlson, 2014; Davis, 2008a, 2017). Employee organizational justice perceptions can motivate counterproductive work behavior regarding information systems security (Davis, 2017; Willison & Warkentin, 2013). For which, entity manager-leaders should focus on information systems' security awareness and moral beliefs (Davis, 2017; Vance & Siponen, 2012). Security awareness is a process that interacts with the organizational context as well as other security management processes and elements (Davis, 2017; Tsohou et al., 2012). The monitoring of policies, user activities, network accesses, and information security protocols can furnish training enrichment opportunities (Davis, 2017; Price, 2014). Moreover, training improvements may occur through making the content especially pertinent or securing an emotional connection (Davis, 2017; Price, 2014). An entity's conduct code combined with training can influence employee conceptualizations of appropriate behaviors (Davis, 2017; Vance & Siponen, 2012).

Legal Issues

Managerial due care redresses activity responsibility, whereby due diligence includes continuously promoting compliance (Davis, 2008a). Information asset due care dictates the appropriateness of data security due diligence activities (Davis, 2008a). Functionally, an entity's information assets represent resources committed to data collection, transaction processing, data storage, or operational results communication that should perform services within legal limits (Davis, 2008a). An entity's manager-leaders, through deployed governance, must ensure due diligence by all individuals involved in the design, development, installation, operation, use, administration, or maintenance of information assets (Davis, 2008a). Therefore, managerial due care and due diligence enable compliance with IAP legal requirements (Davis, 2008a).

Information assets are categorizable as public or private, potentially containing elements protected by security, privacy, or intellectual property laws and regulations (Davis, 2008a; Tran & Atkinson, 2002). Ownership defines public and private property classification (Davis, 2008a). On the one hand, if the management of a government or a political division thereof declares organizational ownership, the information asset typically lists as public property (Davis, 2008a). On the other hand, if a non-governmental individual, group of individuals, or corporation declares ownership, the information asset is typically a private property (Davis, 2008a). Property type affects care expectations and legal requirements (Davis, 2008a).

Security is the condition of not being under threat, whereas protection is the process of keeping safe. Categorically, security infers protection (Davis, 2008a) while privacy infers confidentiality (Davis, 2008a; Findlaw, 2018). As a legal definition, privacy refers to the freedom from intrusion into personal matters or information. In contrast, confidentiality refers to personal information that is generally undisclosable unless the first party expresses consent (Findlaw, 2018). Ensuring confidential and private information protection necessitates managerial due diligence (Alcaraz & Zeadallly, 2015).

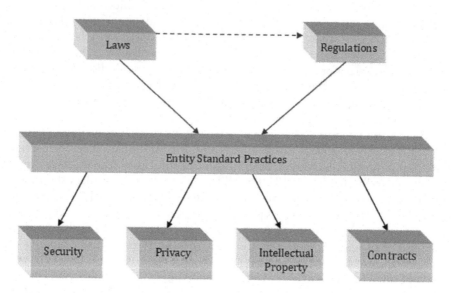

Figure 2.2 Transformation of Laws and Regulations.

Note: Adapted from *IT Auditing: Assuring Information Assets Protection* by R. E. Davis, 2008a, Pleier. Copyright 2008 by Robert E. Davis. Adapted with permission.

Throughout the world, enacted laws and regulations generally address security, privacy, intellectual property, or contracts (Davis, 2008a). Compliance with laws and regulations is vital to avoiding legal prosecution risks, resulting in various penalties and fines if an organizational employee or entity conviction occurs for breaching behavioral expectations (Davis, 2008a, 2010). For most entities, as depicted in Figure 2.2, prosecution avoidance means systematizing standard practices that cover the regulatory spectrum and decreasing legal compliance complexity (Davis, 2008a).

Security laws and regulations can decree the requisite degree of property protection, usually based on governmental interest (Davis, 2008a; Tran & Atkinson, 2002). Information security laws and regulations can describe control measures to prevent unapproved access to devices that process sensitive data (Davis, 2008a; Tran & Atkinson, 2002). Inclusively, statutory data control measures can encompass peripheral equipment considered necessary for compliant protection (Davis, 2008a; Tran & Atkinson, 2002). Consequently, IT resources' integration should occur with an approach that rebuffs potential compromises in applicable data treatment edicts for the defined subject matter (Davis, 2008a; Tran & Atkinson, 2002).

Privacy laws can dictate adherence to assurances and responsibilities associated with any information connected to an identified or identifiable data subject (Davis, 2008a; Tran & Atkinson, 2002). Personal data privacy refers to informational associations of specific individuals or identifying attributes that might be combinable with other information or data to identify an individual (Davis, 2008a; Tran & Atkinson, 2002). Sensitive personal data can include items labeled as individual preferences, habits, racial or ethnic origin, as well as financial or medical conditions (Davis, 2008a; Tran & Atkinson, 2002).

Intellectual property laws address something cognitively designed, of which the ownership or right to usage is legally protected (Davis, 2008a; Tran & Atkinson, 2002).

Intellectual property can signify knowledge-based resources that encompass information or data, resulting in intellectual capital from innovations, ideas, and designs, howsoever expressed or recorded (Davis, 2008a; Tran & Atkinson, 2002). Intellectual capital is intangible for such items as customer loyalty, product innovation, employee morale, patents, and trademarks (Commission on Guidelines, 2007; Davis, 2008a; Tran & Atkinson, 2002). Therefore, management should minimally provide and implement a policy on intellectual property rights covering custom-entity-developed-software as well as commercial-off-the-shelf-software (Davis, 2008a).

Prescriptively utilizing security, privacy, and intellectual property clauses in contractual agreements may aid in clarifying expectations as well as reducing adverse outcomes in post-facto legal disputes (Davis, 2008a). The standard entity IT service level agreement is a contractual arrangement, preferably inscribed between the IT function and users, or managed service provider, stating what each party's responsibilities are regarding a computerized system (Davis, 2008b). Service level agreements assist in defining, negotiating, and agreeing-on acceptable confidentiality, integrity, and availability requirements (Davis, 2008b). A service level agreement can also create a mutual understanding of the safeguarding measurement criteria (Davis, 2008b). When suitably structured, the service contract enables confidence in a defined amount of stability, reliability, and performance for the provided IT (Davis, 2008b).

International jurisdictions predominantly reflect geographical world division into national territories (Davis, 2008a). Within each geographical division, the established government has a sovereign right to exercise magistracy (Davis, 2008a). However, where a country's citizen commits a crime in another country, upon potential illegal act detection, problems can arise when a suspect is residing in the homeland jurisdiction during violation discovery (Davis, 2008a). Extradition laws, mutual assistance agreements, recognition and reciprocity provisions, legal proceedings' transfers, and other international cooperation may facilitate resolving jurisdiction issues during violation investigations, apprehension of perpetrators as well as court appearances (Davis, 2008a).

There generally are three main dimensions to jurisdictional decisions: procedural, substantive, and enforcement (Davis, 2008a; Kurbalija, 2016). The procedural jurisdiction dimension defines which court or state has the proper authority (Davis, 2008a; Kurbalija, 2016). The substantive jurisdiction dimension determines which rules apply to the circumstance (Davis, 2008a; Kurbalija, 2016). The dimensions of enforcement jurisdiction commonly address court decision implementation (Davis, 2008a; Kurbalija, 2016). The principal criteria employed when establishing jurisdiction in cases are the

- Personal Link: customarily considered as the state's right to govern its citizens no matter the location,
- Territorial Link: generally presented as the state's right to govern persons and property within its geographical domain, and
- Effects Link: usually defined as the state's right to rule on the economic and legal outcomes regarding a territory stemming from activities conducted elsewhere (Davis, 2008a; Kurbalija, 2016).

Since transactions, contracts, and disputes can involve parties, actions, and evidence in multiple distinct jurisdictions, entity manager-leaders need to clarify existing edicts and presumptions regarding the laws pertinent to IAP (Davis, 2008a). IAP disputes can involve complex factual situations and parties – with actions and evidence spanning multiple jurisdictions – that necessitate non-judicial means for resolution such as arbitration

(Davis, 2008a; Kurbalija, 2016). Additionally, a centralized oversight function may be beneficial to an entity with multiple-compliance scenarios. If established, the centralized oversight function should evaluate controls across all compliance arenas, interface with auditors for each compliance area, and provide direction on the most cost-effective controls maximizing total compliance (Davis, 2008a).

Even when governmental compliance requirements extend internationally, managerial responsibility to prevent and detect illegal acts continues regardless of organizational formation origin (Davis, 2008a). Given the fiduciary obligation, an entity's management can use policies, directives, procedures, standards, rules, validation, and monitoring as control conduits to obtain reasonable certainty that information-related illegal acts' prevention or detection happens on a timely basis (Davis, 2008a).

Managerial Practices

Organizational human resources' management is the process of working with and through individuals to achieve entity objectives in a dynamic environment (Davis, 2008a; Kreitner & Cassidy, 2012). Central to people management is an effective and efficient deployment of complementary resources such as information, infrastructure, and processes (Davis, 2008a; Kreitner & Cassidy, 2012). Social, political, moral, physical, and informational environment factors are a few change sources manager-leaders must anticipate before launching appropriate ISG program responses (Davis, 2008a; Kreitner & Cassidy, 2012). Therefore, manager-leaders should deploy monitoring as a continuous process for assessing control environment quality (Davis, 2008a, 2011).

Risk management should receive considerable attention from manager-leaders (Davis, 2017; Magdaraog, Jr., 2014). Hierarchically, an entity's control environment is a significant factor affecting IAP risk management (Davis, 2008a, 2017; Mohare & Lanjewar, 2012). Risk management practitioners are typically aware of control system limitations in an unethical control environment (Davis, 2008a). Therefore, after completing the control evaluation process, IAP-inherent risk and control risk need specific delineation from residual risk to assist ethical manager-leaders in understanding quantitative and qualitative control limitations (Davis, 2008a, 2017; Nazareth & Choi, 2015). Additionally, entities need to assign proper political influences concerning information security risks (Davis, 2017; Kwon et al., 2013).

Managerial monitoring of control deployments focuses on redressing environment quality, ensuring established fiduciary relationship fulfillment with stakeholders (Davis, 2008a, 2011). Control environment quality is a significant factor affecting irregular and illegal act risks (Davis, 2008a). However, there also is a relationship between control environment maturity and irregularities and illegal acts risk assessment frequency (Davis, 2008a). Thus, management should perform irregularities and illegal acts risk assessments frequently to enhance control environment maturity (Davis, 2008a). The irregular and illegal acts' risk assessment is the foundation for a proactive approach to discouraging unacceptable behaviors within an entity's activity sphere (Davis, 2008a). Moreover, the irregular and illegal acts' risk assessment (a) aids in defining the IT risk appetite, (b) enhances IT risk responses, (c) reduces IT operational aberrations, (d) identifies IT irregular or illegal act schemes, and (e) improves IT capital deployments (Davis, 2008a).

Security threats can hinder or reduce the possibility for operational and IT objective achievement, value creation, and value preservation (Davis, 2008a; Tran & Atkinson, 2002). Designing and maintaining appropriate ISG are proportionally linked to deployed IT general and application controls (Davis, 2008a). As general and application security categories, considerable risks to an entity implementing and using IT are deficient logical access controls (Kim et al., 2012; Tran & Atkinson, 2002) and weak network infrastructure security (Cowley et al., 2015; Halliday et al., 1996; Tran & Atkinson, 2002). Also, inappropriate environmental controls (Farahmand et al., 2005), misaligned risk responses, and inadequate physical access controls (Kim et al., 2012; Tran & Atkinson, 2002) are significant risks to an entity implementing and using IT. Moreover, inadequate confidential information life cycle protection (Da Veiga & Martins, 2015; Fenz et al., 2014; Halliday et al., 1996; Tran & Atkinson, 2002) is a substantial risk to an entity implementing and using IT.

Employee decisions are crucial to achieving ISG goals (Davis, 2008a, 2017). Goal congruence affects decision quality (Davis, 2008a, 2017). If decision quality is essential and if subordinates or followers do not share the same ISG goals, manager-leaders face losing control over expected activity performance (Davis, 2008a, 2017), which may have effects detrimental to the entity (Davis, 2017). Consequently, employee goal incongruence potentially suboptimizes ISG-based decision quality (Davis, 2008a, 2017). Manager-leaders must ensure that employees accept and comply with ISG goals to avoid decision suboptimization (Davis, 2008a, 2017). For which, manager-leaders should acquire an in-depth understanding of the entity's environment, processes, and objectives to enable provisioning information security services congruent with organizational needs (Davis, 2017; Flores et al., 2014). Deep knowledge obtainment by manager-leaders also permits effective orchestration of information security activities (Davis, 2017; Flores et al., 2014).

Nevertheless, entity manager-leaders may have the ability to circumvent or override a risk-based control environment that deployed control policies supported by appropriate control procedures, thus negating irregularities and illegal acts' risk assessment benefits (Davis, 2008a). A manager-leader's control procedure circumvention or override is tantamount to forsaking stakeholder fiduciary responsibility (Davis, 2008a). Justification for circumventing or overriding controls conceptualization usually applies environmental perceptions, violation cost–benefit analysis, or violation risk appetite (Davis, 2008a). Environmental perceptions represent perceived circumstances permitting an irregular or illegal activity to occur. Violation cost–benefit analysis weighs the perceived cost against the irregular or illegal act benefit. Violation risk appetite is the risk level that a violator is prepared to accept in pursuit of an objective.

Control Inscriptions

Controls encompass an entity's policies, procedures, directives, standards, rules, organizational structures, and practices providing reasonable assurance that activity performance will occur as specified by control objectives (Davis, 2008a). Management's intentions for information security are implementable manually or technologically (Davis, 2011). Policies, procedures, directives, standards, and rules direct employee activity to ensure the implementation of management's intentions throughout an entity (Davis, 2011). Entity personnel relies on established and maintained activity authority relationships to enforce management's intentions (Davis, 2011). As a sidebar, various criminal and civil charges, as well as fines and penalties, could confront an entity and employees if there are deviations from inscribed policies, procedures, directives, standards, and rules (Davis, 2011).

Deployments of policies, directives, standards, procedures, and rules should occur considering assessed efficacy in addressing managements' risk appetite (Davis, 2011). Deployed controlling and monitoring activities should reflect management's strategy for ensuring an appropriate control system (Davis, 2011). Control policies and directives are high-level

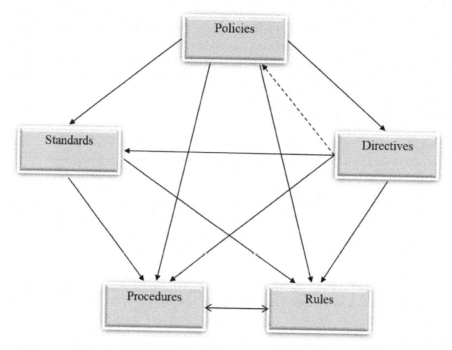

Figure 2.3 Control Selection Interaction Model.

Note: Adapted from *Assuring IT Governance* by R. E. Davis, 2011, Amazon.com. Copyright 2011 by Robert E. Davis. Adapted with permission.

governance inscription, while standards, procedures, and rules are detail-level governance inscription (Davis, 2011). Regularly, oversight committees and executive management use high-level governance inscriptions to provide general control directions (Davis, 2011). Lower-level management converts high-level governance inscriptions into detail-level governance inscriptions, ensuring control objective achievement (Davis, 2011). Developing and deploying ISG design effectiveness and efficiency can be a multidirectional, interactive, iterative, and adaptive process (see Figure 2.3; Davis, 2011).

Policies

Policies are general inscribed statements or understandings that prescribe managerial choices (Davis, 2008a; Posthuma et al., 2013). Entity-centric policies typically impose guidelines enabling routine judgment execution, consistent with current objectives (Davis, 2008a; Posthuma et al., 2013). Policy activation enables authority, leadership, motivation, communication, coordination, innovation, and change (Davis, 2008a). Strategically, policies provide specific courses or methods of action selected by manager-leaders from alternatives to guide and determine present and future decisions considering the environment (Davis, 2008a). Top-level manager-leaders should establish policies as advisories for middle-level and lower-level management decision-making (Davis, 2008a).

Information security policies prioritize data confidentiality, integrity, availability, and resulting information to achieve operational objectives. For policies and processes to work,

Table 2.3 Security Policy Affecting Control Environment Attributes

Security Policy	Control Environment Attributes			
	Ethical Values	Operating Style	Competence Commitment	Human Resources Practices
Conduct or Ethics Code	X	X		
Security Awareness Program		X		X
Security Operations Center		X		
Incident Management Program		X		X
Security Training Program		X	X	X
Broad of Directors Oversight		X	X	
Security Committee Oversight		X	X	

Note: X = Applicability

human engagement must occur. Social–organizational and psychological factors might accentuate or encourage employee compliance with information system security policies (Ifinedo, 2014). Moreover, perceived benefits can substantially influence employee non-compliance with information system policies (Vance & Siponen, 2012). IT users tend to disregard or actively circumvent policies that are difficult to understand or seem unreasonable and resist using time-consuming methods, steep learning curves, or drastically change work performance. Thus, smooth adoption by employees who work with data and information requires sensible policies that provide clear benefits and user-friendly processes.

Table 2.3 shows a conduct or ethics code, security awareness program, security operations center, incident management program, security training program, and security committee oversight represent critical policies providing managerial guidance for sustaining entity security. Ethical values, operating style, competence commitment, human resources practices are the central control environment attributes affected by the security policies. Designed policies should promote acceptable authorized conduct effectively, efficiently, and economically while providing a satisfactory degree of assurance that entity resources are suitably safeguarded (Davis, 2008a).

Policies should not provide detailed operational guidance (Davis, 2008a). Furthermore, policies need periodic reviews and appropriate revisions when circumstances change (Davis, 2008a). Policies need clear inscriptions and organization in entity handbooks, manuals, or other publications (Davis, 2008a). Control policies necessitate identifying the addressed control processes (Davis, 2008a). Systemically, policies should be accessible by all entity personnel. Supporting risk reduction activities are ISG policies providing for a:

- Conduct or Ethics Code. Since laws, regulations, and rules cannot cover all situations, entities can benefit from code statements (Davis, 2008a). The code statements should effectively communicate acceptable behaviors or values to all organizational members, including contractors and sub-contractors (Davis, 2008a). The entity code statements need to establish high standards against which individuals can measure performance (Davis, 2008a). The code statements should also communicate to individuals outside the entity that requesting behavior or value compromises by organizational members is an unacceptable practice (Davis, 2008a). Furthermore, the code statements necessitate providing enforcement methods for inscribed expectations (Davis, 2008a).

- Security Awareness Program. Entity manager-leaders must keep individuals expected to sustain compliance informed to ensure security plan effectiveness (Davis, 2008a). First-time training for new employees, contractors, and users, as well as periodic refresher training after that, is essential to maintaining security awareness (Davis, 2008a). The awareness program policy should impart the message that security is beneficial in sustaining the entity and all linked individuals (Davis, 2008a). The awareness program policy should also impart that every person connected to the entity must comply with defined security requirements (Davis, 2008a). All affected parties should have access to security policies, directives, procedures, standards, rules, and individual responsibilities (Davis, 2008a; Wiley et al., 2020). The security awareness program policy should require users to periodically sign a statement acknowledging awareness and acceptance of security responsibilities (Davis, 2008a).
- Security Operations Center. Information security is a set of processes enabling and optimizing cybersecurity services for the entity to satisfy operational requirements (Davis, 2008a; Demertzis et al., 2019). Simultaneously, the security operations center provides strategic and tactical cybersecurity infrastructure management (Davis, 2008a; Demertzis et al., 2019). Through responsibility for entity-wide information security, proactive and reactive, resource deployments for IAP can occur effectively and efficiently (Davis, 2008a; Demertzis et al., 2019).
- Incident Management Program. Security incidents can occur; therefore, a policy for responding and recovering to normal operations is necessary (Davis, 2008a). The most significant harm or disruption to information assets can emanate from intentional or unintentional actions of internally employed individuals (Davis, 2008a). Frequently, information systems experience disruption, damage, loss, or other adverse effects due to employee efforts to use or maintain IT objects (Davis, 2008a). Thus, securing reductions in harm or disruption to information asset services requires emphasizing and periodically reemphasizing defined rules-of-behavior to individuals employed by the entity (Davis, 2008a).
- Security Training Program. Manager-leaders must ensure that employees have the skills, knowledge, and abilities to carry out assigned information security responsibilities (Davis, 2008a). The security program policy should address job descriptions, periodically reassessing the adequacy of skills, annual training requirements, enrollment in professional development programs, as well as monitoring of employee training and professional development accomplishments to accomplish the job assignment expectations (Davis, 2008a).
- Entity Oversight Committee. The entity's highest oversight committee should develop entity values for dissemination (Davis, 2008a). Entity values should represent non-negotiable essential and enduring tenets that withstand compromise for financial gain or short-term expediency (Davis, 2008a). The entity's highest oversight committee must ensure that manager-leaders adopt functional values consistent with entity values (Davis, 2008a). An entity's oversight committee should also be responsible for setting high-level objectives, overseeing the planning model, measuring performance against established objectives, and revising ineffective or inefficient objectives (Davis, 2008a).
- Security Oversight Committee. The entity oversight committee should provide internal and external security controls' due diligence (Davis, 2008a). In this regard, entity oversight committees typically delegate responsibility, accountability, and authority to a security oversight committee that monitors and evaluates security controls, interfaces with auditors, and provides direction on security priorities (Davis, 2008a). In exercising due care, appointed security oversight committee members should not have managerial responsibilities within the entity during the term of service (Davis, 2008a).

Management should assume full responsibility for developing and maintaining a structural policy that establishes the entity's overall approach to ISG (Davis, 2008a). Typically, the information security manager-leader's role in policy formulation includes establishing an appropriate IAP control environment (Davis, 2008a). Within the defined framework, ISG policies need to maintain congruency with entity and technology objectives, minimizing risks by addressing asset loss limitation, timely irregularity identification, illicit act recognition, and service restoration (Davis, 2008a). A cost–benefit analysis should be the basis for adopted measures' prioritization (Davis, 2008a). Manager-leaders should also ensure that ISG policies specify the

- ambit,
- purpose,
- objectives,
- management structure,
- implementation responsibility definitions,
- implementation responsibility assignments,
- penalty definitions for failing to comply with lower-level ISG policies, and
- disciplinary actions for failing to comply with lower-level ISG policies (Davis, 2008a).

Top-down ISG policy construction typically requires procedures, standards, and rules to organize, direct, and control activities consistent with sustaining designed structural intentions (Davis, 2008a). As a logical managerial assumption, information assets are the primary protection points for ISG programs (Davis, 2008a). Entity information security policies positively affect subjective norms toward the performance of information security conscious-care behaviors (Davis, 2017; Safa et al., 2015). Nonetheless, entity manager-leaders should examine employee time spent on organizational tasks (Davis, 2017; Posey et al., 2014). High IT user workloads can create a conflict between assigned organizational tasks and information security responsibilities (Davis, 2017; Posey et al., 2014). Entity employees who feel overburdened are more likely to have lapses in information security vigilance (Davis, 2017; Posey et al., 2014). Entity management's control environment due diligence can significantly reduce IAP risks (Davis, 2008a).

Management's negligence to support and implement information security policy initiatives is usually a matter of conflicting priorities for sustaining an appropriate control environment (Davis, 2008a). Conflicting priorities resolution can occur through an entity's performance-reward systems (Davis, 2008a). Consequently, performance goals associated with information security must be reasonable and support, not impede, operational processes and deployed IT (Davis, 2008a). Priorities must be clearly defined and established in the information security strategy (Davis, 2008a). Process owners need key performance indicators approved at the highest entity oversight level to ensure goals will be effectively, consistently, and efficiently managed, monitored, and executed (Davis, 2008a).

Directives

Directives present orders or instructions (Davis, 2011). Directives serve or intend to influence, guide, or administrate actions or goals (Davis, 2011). Proxy Directives are legal inscriptions assigning decisions to another if the decision-maker cannot make decisions (Davis, 2011). When activated, entity proxy directives are interpretable as conveying fiduciary requirements to the assignee (Davis, 2011). Individuals and internal or external central authorities may issue directives (Davis, 2011). Internal directives are usually inscribed in memorandums and reflect matters requiring immediate attention (Davis, 2011). Directives should receive the same due diligence as policies.

When links between national and international arenas are under consideration, international developments have decisively affected national laws (Davis, 2008a; Kurbalija, 2016). Regional coalitions have enacted IAP-related edicts that subsequently received codification in national laws and regulations (Davis, 2008a; Kurbalija, 2016). Procedurally, most regional coalition IAP decrees are directives for presentation to member nations for federal ratification (Davis, 2008a). For this reason, with the assistance of legal counsel, information security manager-leaders must evaluate all relevant statutory and regulatory mandates in whatever jurisdictional divisions the entity operates (Davis, 2008a). Beneficially, multiple legal compliance requirement assessments enable entity-centric standard practices for satisfying expected behavior (Davis, 2008a). Practicing due care for legal matters can also equip an entity to build a compliance culture where standardization is the norm and conditionally produce an environment conducive to training entity employees in IAP (Davis, 2008a).

Standards

Designed and implemented ratiocinative information security standards are necessary (Davis, 2008a, 2017; Järveläinen, 2012). Assessing the current information security state requires comparison to accepted de facto or de jure standards for performance measurement (Davis, 2008a, 2017). Manager-leaders should establish standards as baselines for measuring a quantity, weight, extent, value, or quality (Davis, 2008a, 2011, 2017). Standards can reflect specific objectives or goals for comparison against performance (Davis, 2011, 2017). Performance measurement point selection is critical to effective standard implementation (Davis, 2008a, 2011, 2017). Information security manager-leaders need to consider the importance of complying with standards when seeking effectual ISG (Davis, 2017; Lopez, 2012; Price, 2014).

Procedures

Procedures establish methods for accomplishing an activity through specific performance. Simultaneously, procedures must comply with prescribed policies (Davis, 2011). Before designing information security, procedures, identification, and classification of processes are necessary to determine the effect on control objectives (Davis, 2011). Manager-leaders must understand and inscribe operational procedures to install an appropriate ISG framework (Davis, 2011). Control procedures need inscription and should attempt to enforce management's intentions concerning the organization. Thus, control procedures provide for the safeguarding of an entity's assets.

An entity's information security controls comprise the procedures adopted or devised to furnish management with some degree of comfort regarding the achievement of information asset protection objectives. Manager-leaders should address the effectiveness of information security controls for two main reasons. One, weaknesses in information security control procedures can lead to material misstatements in risk information. Two, adequate information security control procedures ensure prevention, detection, or correction by organizational employees of perceived potential threats to data. Where information security control procedures are considered effective, the procedures facilitate more efficient information security management.

Rules

Rules are specific and detailed guides that restrict and confine behavior (Davis, 2011). Comparatively, rules are the most straightforward operational control formulation (Davis, 2011). A rule requires a specific action expectation regarding a given situation (Davis, 2011). Manager-leaders should inscribe Rules-of-Behavior to aid in preventing employees from breaching IAP mechanisms (Davis, 2012). For deterring information security breaches, rules should delineate all individual responsibilities and expected behavior with access to the entity's information assets (Davis, 2012). Adopted Rules-of-Behavior should align with established and implemented practices regarding the usage, security, and acceptable risk levels of information assets (Davis, 2012). Thus, the Rules-of-Behavior should cover such matters as work at home situations, connection to the Internet, assignment of privileges, limitation of privileges, use of copyrighted works, unauthorized use of equipment, and individual accountability (Davis, 2012). Nonetheless, the design and deployment of information security rules should only be as stringent as needed to sustain the desired asset safeguarding level (Davis, 2012).

Technology Deployments

IT manager-leaders usually plan, orchestrate, and recommend entity information asset deployments (Davis, 2008a). Correspondingly, responsibility for planning IT protection against unauthorized use and abuse should reside with the entity's Chief Information Security Officer (Davis, 2008a; Mohare & Lanjewar, 2012). The IT protection planning responsibility may include designing methods for preventing system attacks by internal as well as external hackers and crackers who activate undesirable security events by exploiting cybersecurity weaknesses or deficiencies (Davis, 2008a). Information security manager-leader duties also typically include establishing applicable policies, procedures, and standards for information assets, based on the organizational structure (Davis, 2008a).

IT opportunities and threats need organization, evaluation, and administration to reduce potential entity risks using available resources (Barrett, 2016; Davis, 2008a; Fenz et al., 2014). Effective IAP technologies are valuable defense mechanisms for counteracting inappropriate and malicious behavior (Claycomb et al., 2012). Therefore, Chief Information Security Officers should assign responsibility for identifying and evaluating deployed configuration management tools to ensure the network infrastructure maintains data integrity, availability (Boyes, 2015), and confidentiality expectations.

Stakeholders advocate that entity manager-leaders engage in risk management of supply chain activities (Cantor et al., 2014). As a response, entity supply chain administrators should consider examining the network configuration technologies to assess vulnerabilities (Boyes, 2015). Moreover, organizational administrators should refrain from authorizing or performing knowledge sharing across the supply chain unless risk indicators are at an acceptable level for deployed protection mechanisms (Manzouri et al., 2013). In sustaining an acceptable risk level, if not deployed, an Active Directory Federation Service may be the best method to secure information across the supply chain (Manzouri et al., 2013).

Internet-based technologies enable organizational and customer advantages (Safa et al., 2016). With an ever-increasing number of entities and individuals Internet-reliant for exchanging sensitive or confidential information, appropriate message security is a technological management concern (Chatterjee et al., 2015; Davis, 2008a; Wlosinski, 2016). Security is significant for e-commerce system quality (Homsud & Chaveesuk, 2014). Serviceable e-commerce models include Business-to-Business and Business-to-Consumer architectures (Davis, 2008a; Z. Wang et al., 2013). Delineated, Business-to-Business is an e-commerce between discernibly distinct entities (Davis, 2008a) and reflect open standards (Sila, 2013). Business-to-Business links enable the exchange of services, products, or messages between entities (Davis, 2008a; Sila, 2013). However, Business-to-Business e-commerce is more vulnerable to security breaches than the legacy of external interface systems (Sila, 2013).

Electronic Data Interchange methodologies are the forerunners and pillars of Internet-integrated Business-to-Business relationships (Davis, 2008a). Business-to-Business e-commerce still relies on proprietary Electronic Data Interchange systems (Sila, 2013). Depending on activity frequency and application, Electronic Data Interchange control risks can become material (Davis, 2008a). Lack of direction, reliance on third parties, and system dependencies potentially expose an entity to additional legal, security, and operational risks with an Electronic Data Interchange deployment (Davis, 2008a).

When entity employees develop a reputation for ensuring information confidentiality, integrity, and availability, customers tend to exhibit electronic loyalty (Choi & Nazareth, 2014). Customer loyalty determines Business-to-Consumer long-term success (Homsud & Chaveesuk, 2014). A publicized information security incident can trigger retreative behaviors (Lee & Lee, 2012). An information security incident can cause a measurable negative customer behavior influence, although the effect seems mainly limited to the violating website (Lee & Lee, 2012). Perceived damage and availability of alternative purchasing sources can significantly increase victimized customer retreative behaviors (Lee & Lee, 2012). Additionally, website-relative usefulness and ease-of-use perceptions by consumers have shown limited effects in reducing retreative behaviors (Lee & Lee, 2012).

Information security addresses safeguarding activities throughout information life cycles and asset usage within the established entity protection perimeter (Davis, 2008a). Setting a security perimeter's primary objective is provisioning the ambit for entity-centric policies and protection mechanisms (Konieczny et al., 2015). The Chief Information Security Officer typically designates an IAP perimeter to manage network cybersecurity risks programmatically (Konieczny et al., 2015). For IT-based networking, the main improvements in protection mechanisms were e-mail confidentiality and e-mail user identity authentication and privacy transformation (Babrahem et al., 2015). However, with the emergence of linked information enclaves, erecting layered protective barriers preserving deployed IT configurations can introduce a tactical security quagmire (Konieczny et al., 2015; Zhao et al., 2013). Manager-leaders should consider changing the architectural model for entity IT (Konieczny et al., 2015) and employing usability heuristics (Jaferian et al., 2014) during network design to reduce potential network confounding.

Entity manager-leaders have a compelling incentive to identify and remediate any divergences between current access controls and legal obligations (Davis, 2017). Accessing information assets without permission is a criminal offense (Davis, 2008a; Sen & Borle, 2015) and civilly litigable (Romanosky et al., 2014) in most nations. Nonetheless, an elevated access control level can decrease network performance (Hayajneh et al., 2013) and security flexibility (Thomson, 2012). To prevent, detect, or correct potential security vulnerabilities, information security manager-leaders should voluntarily introduce formal cybersecurity self-assessment procedures that assure adherence to legal obligations and edicts (Davis, 2008a) as well as managerial expectations.

Executive manager-leaders lead the drive to bring-your-own-device (Thomson, 2012) and bring-your-own-technology adoption in entities to achieve a competitive advantage (Davis, 2017). Manager-leaders are typically pursuing bring-your-own-device and bring-your-own-technology-related policies for three reasons: intuitive tool knowledge, costs savings, and productivity gains (Priyadarshi, 2013). Bring-your-own-device and bring-your-own-technology in the workplace are security challenges (Olalere et al., 2015). Governance is critical to the successes of bring-your-own-device- and bring-your-own-technology-related policies (Thomson, 2012). Security governance includes furnishing control policies for bring-your-own-device and bring-your-own-technology management (Priyadarshi, 2013; Tokuyoshi, 2013). However, security issues should make manager-leaders pause in adopting bring-your-own-device and bring-your-own-technology work policies (Li & Clark, 2013; Priyadarshi, 2013; Tokuyoshi, 2013). Individually, resizing and integrating all entity security requirements into a personal device to protect work-related information can present configuration challenges (Li & Clark, 2013; Meng et al., 2015; Tokuyoshi, 2013).

Security performance measurement also becomes challenging where entity employees use authorized cloud computing environments (Avram, 2014; Herath & Herath, 2014; Kalloniatis et al., 2013). If adopted, a performance evaluation decision model allows the entity to choose whether conducting a cybersecurity audit is advantageous (Herath & Herath, 2014). Whereby, if deemed beneficial, questions can arise concerning what additional factors need consideration when engaging a third-party assurance reporting (Herath & Herath, 2014), such as data leakage during and after an audit as well as audit efficacy (Davis, 2017). Manager-leaders should adopt confidentiality schemes that furnish verifiable protection and are highly efficient in a cloud computing environment (C. Wang et al., 2013). As a remedy, authenticator and random masking technologies may ensure that a third-party auditor would not obtain any stored data content knowledge on a cloud server (C. Wang et al., 2013). Additionally, regarding efficacy, the engaged third-party auditors can perform various auditing tasks in a batch manner for better efficiency (C. Wang et al., 2013).

IT networks, virtualization, and storage are the most significant security concerns in Cloud Computing (Hashizume et al., 2013). Nevertheless, technical challenges when adopting Cloud Computing include the installed security access architecture (Rai et al., 2015). On the one hand, as a potential access remedy, using standards-based Web Single Sign-on protocols that provisions authentication requests with expressiveness and token security versatility may resolve usage issues (Pfaff & Ries, 2014). On the other hand, homomorphic encryption and proxy re-encryption schemes can prevent unauthorized data leakage when a revoked user rejoins a Cloud-based system (Samanthula et al., 2015). Consequently, entity manager-leaders should deploy a comprehensive risk assessment framework for information security to assist in the appropriate design of IAP policies, procedures, standards, and rules (Davis, 2017).

References

Akpinar, M. (2017). The exercise of power in inter-organisational relationships in response to changes in the institutional environment: Cases from the European automotive industry. *International Journal of Automotive Technology and Management*, 17(1), 51–71. https://doi.org/10.1504/IJATM.2017.082276

Alcaraz, C., & Zeadallly, S. (2015). Critical infrastructure protection: Requirements and challenges for the 21st century. *International Journal of Critical Infrastructure Protection*, 8, 53–66. https://doi.org/10.1016/j.ijcip.2014.12.002

Anderson, L. E. (2015). *Relationship between leadership, organizational commitment, and intent to stay among junior executives* (Publication No. 3708010) [Doctoral Study, Walden University]. ProQuest Dissertations Publishing.

Atoum, I., Otoom, A., & Ali, A. A. (2014). A holistic cyber security implementation framework. *Information Management & Computer Security, 22*, 251–264. https://doi.org/10.1108/IMCS-02-2013-0014

Avram, M. G. (2014). Advantages and challenges of adopting cloud computing from an enterprise perspective. *Procedia Technology, 12*, 529–534. https://doi.org/10.1016/j.protcy.2013.12.525

Babrahem, A. S., Alharbi, E. T., Alshiky, A. M., Alqurashi, S. S., & Kar, J. (2015). Study of the security enhancements in various e-mail systems. *Journal of Information Security, 6*, 1–11. https://doi.org/10.4236/jis.2015.61001

Barrett, S. (2016). *Effects of information technology risk management and institution size on financial performance* (Publication No. 10148398) [Doctoral Study, Walden University]. ProQuest Dissertations Publishing.

Boritz, J. E. (2005). IS practitioners' views on core concepts of information integrity. *International Journal of Accounting Information Systems, 6*(4), 260–279. https://doi.org/10.1016/j.accinf.2005.07.001

Boyes, H. (2015). Cybersecurity and cyber-resilient supply chains. *Technology Innovation Management Review, 5*(4), 28–34. http://doi.org/10.22215/timreview/888

Brotby, K. W. (2006). *Information security governance: Guidance for boards of directors and executive management* (2nd ed.). IT Governance Institute.

Broz, J. L. (2002). Political system transparency and monetary commitments regimes. *International Organization, 56*(4), 861–887. https://doi.org/10.1162/002081802760403801

Büschgens, T., Bausch, A., & Balkin, D. B. (2013). Organizational culture and innovation: A meta-analytic review. *Journal of Product Innovation Management, 30*(4), 763–781. https://doi.org/10.1111/jpim.12021

Cantor, D. E., Blackhurst, J., Pan, M., & Crum, M. (2014). Examining the role of stakeholder pressure and knowledge management on supply chain risk and demand responsiveness. *International Journal of Logistics Management, 25*, 202–223. https://doi.org/10.1108/IJLM-10-2012-0111

Carlson, L. V. (2014). *Worker perceptions of the relationship between information security and productivity* (Publication No. 3645776) [Dissertation, Capella University]. ProQuest Dissertations Publishing.

Chatterjee, S., Sarker, S., & Valacich, J. S. (2015). The behavioral roots of information systems security: Exploring key factors related to unethical IT use. *Journal of Management Information Systems, 31*(4), 49–87. https://doi.org/10.1080/07421222.2014.1001257

Chernyak-Hai, L., & Tziner, A. (2014). Relationships between counterproductive work behavior, perceived justice and climate, occupational status, and leader-member exchange. *Journal of Work and Organizational Psychology, 30*(1), 1–12. https://doi.org/10.5093/tr2014a1

Choi, J., & Nazareth, D. L. (2014). Repairing trust in an e-commerce and security context: An agent-based modeling approach. *Information Management & Computer Security, 22*, 490–512. https://doi.org/10.1108/IMCS-09-2013-0069

Claycomb, W. R., Huth, C. L., Flynn, L., Mcintire, D. M., & Lewellen, T. B. (2012). Chronological examination of insider threat sabotage: Preliminary observations. *Journal of Wireless Mobile Networks, Ubiquitous Computing, and Dependable Applications, 3*(4), 4–20. https://doi.org/10.22667/JOWUA.2012.12.31.004

Commission on Guidelines. (2007). *Information asset protection guideline.* ASIS International.

Cowley, J. A., Greitzer, F. L., & Woods, B. (2015). Effect of network infrastructure factors on information system risk judgments. *Computers & Security, 52*, 142–158. https://doi.org/10.1016/j.cose.2015.04.011

Dasgupta, M., Gupta, R. K., & Sahay, A. (2011). Linking technological innovation, technology strategy and organizational factors: A review. *Global Business Review, 12*(2), 257–277. https://doi.org/10.1177/097215091101200206

Da Veiga, A., & Martins, N. (2015). Information security culture and information protection culture: A validated assessment instrument. *Computer Law & Security Review, 31*, 243–256. https://doi.org/10.1016/j.clsr.2015.01.005

Davis, R. E. (2006). *IT auditing: Irregular and illegal acts.* Pleier.

Davis, R. E. (2008a). *IT auditing: Assuring information assets protection.* Pleier.

Davis, R. E. (2008b). *IT auditing: IT service delivery and support.* Pleier.

Davis, R. E. (2010). *IT auditing: An adaptive system.* www.amazon.com

Davis, R. E. (2011). *Assuring IT governance.* www.amazon.com

Davis, R. E. (2012). *Assuring information security.* www.amazon.com

Davis, R. E. (2013). *Assuring IT legal compliance.* www.amazon.com

Davis, R. E. (2017). *Relationship between corporate governance and information security governance effectiveness in United States corporations* (Publication No. 10603383) [Doctoral Study, Walden University]. ProQuest Dissertations Publishing.

Davis, R. E. (2020). *IT auditing using a system perspective.* IGI Global.

Demertzis, K., Tziritas, N., Kikiras, P., Sanchez, S. L., & Iliadis, L. (2019). The next generation cognitive security operations center: Adaptive analytic lambda architecture for efficient defense against adversarial attacks. *Big Data and Cognitive Computing, 3*(1), 6. https://doi.org/10.3390/bdcc3010006

Edwards, C. K. (2013). *A framework for the governance of information security* (Publication No. 3607548) [Dissertation, Nova Southeastern University]. ProQuest Dissertations Publishing.

Farahmand, F., Navathe, S. B., Sharp, G. P., & Enslow, P. H. (2005). A management perspective on risk of security threats to information systems. *Information Technology and Management, 6*(2–3), 203–225. https://doi.org/10.1007/s10799-005-5880-5

Fenz, S., Heurix, J., Neubauer, T., & Pechstein, F. (2014). Current challenges in information security risk management. *Information Management & Computer Security, 22*, 410–430. https://doi.org/10.1108/IMCS-07-2013-0053

Findlaw. (2018, March 18). *Is there a difference between confidentiality and privacy?* https://criminal.findlaw.com/criminal-rights/is-there-a-difference-between-confidentiality-and-privacy.html

Flores, W. R., Antonsen, E., & Ekstedt, M. (2014). Information security knowledge sharing in organizations: Investigating the effect of behavioral information security governance and national culture. *Computers & Security, 43*, 90–110. https://doi.org/10.1016/j.cose.2014.03.004

Flowerday, S., & Von Solms, R. (2007). What constitutes information integrity? *South African Journal of Information Management, 9*(4), 1–19. https://doi.org/10.4102/sajim.v9i4.201

Foss, N. J., & Dobrajska, M. (2015). Valve's way: Vayward, visionary, or voguish? *Journal of Organization Design, 4*(2), 12–15. https://doi.org/10.7146/jod.20162

Garba, A. B., Armarego, J., Murray, D., & Kenworthy, W. (2015). Review of the information security and privacy challenges in bring your own device (BYOD) environments. *Journal of Information Privacy and Security, 11*, 38–54. https://doi.org/10.1080/15536548.2015.1010985

Haag, S., & Cummings, M. (2008). *Management information systems for the information age* (Laureate Education, Inc., custom ed.). McGraw-Hill/Irwin.

Halliday, S., Badenhorst, K., & Von Solms, R. (1996). A business approach to effective information technology risk analysis and management. *Information Management & Computer Security, 4*(1), 19–31. https://doi.org/10.1108/09685229610114178

Harrison, J. S., & Wicks, A. C. (2013). Stakeholder theory, value, and firm performance. *Business Ethics Quarterly, 23*, 97–124. https://doi.org/10.5840/beq20132314

Hashizume, K., Rosado, D. G., Fernández-Medina, E., & Fernandez, E. B. (2013). An analysis of security issues for cloud computing. *Journal of Internet Services and Applications, 4*(1), 1–13. https://doi.org/10.1186/1869-0238-4-5

Hayajneh, T., Mohd, B. J., Itradat, A., & Quttoum, A. (2013). Performance and information security evaluation with firewalls. *International Journal of Security and Its Applications, 7*(6), 355–372. https://doi.org/10.14257/ijsia.2013.7.6.36

Herath, H. S., & Herath, T. C. (2014). IT security auditing: A performance evaluation decision model. *Decision Support Systems, 57*, 54–63. https://doi.org/10.1016/j.dss.2013.07.010

Hess, D. (2007). Social reporting and new governance regulation: The prospects of achieving corporate accountability through transparency. *Business Ethics Quarterly, 17*(3), 453–476. www.jstor.org

Hirschheim, R., & Klein, H. K. (2012). A glorious and not-so-short history of the information systems field. *Journal of the Association for Information Systems, 13*(4), 188–235. https://doi.org/10.17705/1jais.00294

Hodgkinson, I. R., Ravishankar, M. N., & Aitken-Fischer, M. (2014). A resource-advantage perspective on the orchestration of ambidexterity. *The Service Industries Journal*, *34*, 1234–1252. https://doi.org/10.1080/02642069.2014.942655

Homsud, S., & Chaveesuk, S. (2014). Understanding a proposed model of customer loyalty formation in B2C e-commerce. *International Journal of Future Computer and Communication*, *3*, 191–196. https://doi.org/10.7763/IJFCC.2014.V3.294

Hu, Q., Dinev, T., Hart, P., & Cooke, D. (2012). Managing employee compliance with information security policies: The critical role of top management and organizational culture. *Decision Sciences*, *43*, 615–660. https://doi.org/10.1111/j.1540-5915.2012.00361.x

Ifinedo, P. (2014). Information systems security policy compliance: An empirical study of the effects of socialisation, influence, and cognition. *Information & Management*, *51*, 69–79. https://doi.org/10.1016/j.im.2013.10.001

IT Governance Institute. (2003). *Board briefing on IT governance* (2nd ed.). Author.

Jaferian, P., Hawkey, K., Sotirakopoulos, A., Velez-Rojas, M., & Beznosov, K. (2014). Heuristics for evaluating IT security management tools. *Human-Computer Interaction*, *29*, 311–350. https://doi.org/10.1080/07370024.2013.819198

Järveläinen, J. (2012). Information security and business continuity management in interorganizational IT relationships. *Information Management & Computer Security*, *20*, 332–349. https://doi.org/10.1108/09685221211286511

Julisch, K. (2013). Leading information security. *ISACA Journal*, *6*, 27–30. www.isaca.org

Kalloniatis, C., Mouratidis, H., & Islam, S. (2013). Evaluating cloud deployments scenarios based on security and privacy requirements. *Requirements Engineering*, *18*, 299–319. https://doi.org/10.1007/s00766-013-0166-7

Kim, A. C., Lee, S. M., & Lee, D. H. (2012). Compliance risk assessment measures of financial information security using system dynamics. *International Journal of Security and Its Applications*, *6*(4), 191–200. www.sersc.org

Kinicki, A., & Williams, B. K. (2013). The manager's changing work environment & ethical responsibilities: Doing the right thing. In *Management: A practical introduction* (6th ed., pp. 74–105). McGraw-Hill Education.

Konieczny, F., Trias, E., & Taylor, N. J. (2015). SEADE: Countering the futility of network security. *Air & Space Power Journal*, *29*(5), 4–14. www.airuniversity.af.edu/ASPJ/

Kreitner, R., & Cassidy, C. (2012). *Management* (12th ed.). Houghton Mifflin.

Kurbalija, J. (2016). *An introduction to internet governance* (7th ed.). Diplo Foundation.

Kushwaha, P. (2016). Amalgamation of the information security management system with business-paradigm shift. *International Journal of Computer Science and Information Security*, *14*(1), 105–111. https://sites.google.com/site/ijcsis

Kwon, J., Ulmer, J. R., & Wang, T. (2013). The association between top management involvement and compensation and information security breaches. *Journal of Information Systems*, *27*(1), 219–236. https://doi.org/10.2308/isys-50339

Lee, M., & Lee, J. (2012). The impact of information security failure on customer behaviors: A study on a large-scale hacking incident on the Internet. *Information Systems Frontiers*, *14*, 375–393. https://doi.org/10.1007/s10796-010-9253-1

Li, Q., & Clark, G. (2013). Mobile security: A look ahead. *IEEE Security & Privacy*, *11*(1), 78–81. https://doi.org/10.1109/MSP.2013.15

Lopez, R. H. (2012). *Information data security specialists' and business leaders' experiences regarding communication challenges* (Publication No. 3503982) [Doctoral Study, Walden University]. ProQuest Dissertations Publishing.

Luesebrink, M. (2011). *Institutionalization of information security governance structures in academic institutions: A case study* [Dissertation, Florida State University]. http://purl.flvc.org/fsu/fd/FSU_migr_etd-1009

Magdaraog, Jr., G. A. (2014). Warning signs in the workplace: An analysis of risk factors in employee fraud. *The Carrington Rand Journal of Social Sciences*, *1*(1), 73–82. www.carringtonrand.com

Manzouri, M., Rahman, M. N. A., Nasimi, F., & Arshad, H. (2013). A model for securing sharing information across the supply chain. *American Journal of Applied Sciences*, *10*(3), 253–258. http://dx.doi.org/10.3844/ajassp.2013.253.258

Meng, G., Liu, Y., Zhang, J., Pokluda, A., & Boutaba, R. (2015). Collaborative security: A survey and taxonomy. *ACM Computing Surveys*, *48*, 1–42. https://doi.org/10.1145/2785733

Mohare, R., & Lanjewar, U. (2012). Determinants of business information security. *International Journal of Marketing and Technology*, *2*(7), 203–209. www.ijmra.us

Nazareth, D. L., & Choi, J. (2015). A system dynamics model for information security management. *Information & Management*, *52*, 123–134. https://doi.org/10.1016/j.im.2014.10.009

Northouse, P. G. (2013). *Leadership: Theory and practice* (6th ed.). Sage.

Olalere, M., Abdullah, M. T., Mahmod, R., & Abdullah, A. (2015). A review of bring your own device on security issues. *SAGE Open*, *5*, 1–11. https://doi.org/10.1177/2158244015580372

Pasquier, M., & Villeneuve, J. P. (2007), Organizational barriers to transparency: A typology and analysis of organizational behavior tending to prevent or restrict access to information. *International Review of Administrative Sciences*, *73*(1), 147–162. https://doi.org/10.1177/0020852307075701

Pfaff, O., & Ries, S. (2014). Integrating enterprise security infrastructure with cloud computing. *Journal of Internet Technology and Secured Transactions*, *3*, 338–343. www.infonomics-society.org

Posey, C., Roberts, T. L., Lowry, P. B., & Hightower, R. T. (2014). Bridging the divide: A qualitative comparison of information security thought patterns between information security professionals and ordinary organizational insiders. *Information & Management*, *51*, 551–567. https://doi.org/10.1016/j.im.2014.03.009

Posner, B. Z. (2010). Another look at the impact of personal and organizational values congruency. *Journal of Business Ethics*, *97*(4), 535–541. https://doi.org/10.1007/s10551-010-0530-1

Posthuma, R. A., Campion, M. C., Masimova, M., & Campion, M. A. (2013). A high performance work practices taxonomy: Integrating the literature and directing future research. *Journal of Management*, *39*(5), 1184–1220. https://doi.org/10.1177/0149206313478184

Price, J. D. (2014). *Reducing the risk of a data breach using effective compliance programs* (Publication No. 3619214) [Doctoral Study, Walden University]. ProQuest Dissertations Publishing.

Priyadarshi, G. (2013). Leveraging and securing the bring your own device and technology approach. *ISACA Journal*, *4*, 47–51. www.isaca.org

Rai, R., Sahoo, G., & Mehfuz, S. (2015). Exploring the factors influencing the cloud computing adoption: A systematic study on cloud migration. *SpringerPlus*, *4*, 197–208. https://doi.org/10.1186/s40064-015-0962-2

Rasheed, S., ChangFeng, W., & Yaqub, F. (2015). Towards program risk management and perceived risk management barriers. *International Journal of Hybrid Information Technology*, *8*, 323–338. https://doi.org/10.14257/ijhit.2015.8.5.35

Rawlins, B. (2008). Give the emperor a mirror: Toward developing a stakeholder measurement of organizational transparency. *Journal of Public Relations Research*, *21*(1), 71–99. https://doi.org/10.1080/10627260802153421

Romanosky, S., Hoffman, D., & Acquisti, A. (2014). Empirical analysis of data breach litigation. *Journal of Empirical Legal Studies*, *11*, 74–104. https://doi.org/10.1111/jels.12035

Safa, N. S., Sookhak, M., Von Solms, R., Furnell, S., Ghani, N. A., & Herawan, T. (2015). Information security conscious care behaviour formation in organizations. *Computers & Security*, *53*, 65–78. https://doi.org/10.1016/j.cose.2015.05.012

Safa, N. S., Von Solms, R., & Furnell, S. (2016). Information security policy compliance model in organizations. *Computers & Security*, *56*, 70–82. https://doi.org/10.1016/j.cose.2015.10.006

Samanthula, B. K., Elmehdwi, Y., Howser, G., & Madria, S. (2015). A secure data sharing and query processing framework via federation of cloud computing. *Information Systems*, *48*, 196–212. https://doi.org/10.1016/j.is.2013.08.004

Samonas, S., & Coss, D. (2014). The CIA strikes back: Redefining confidentiality, integrity and availability in security. *Journal of Information System Security, 10*(3), 21–45. www.jissec.org/

Sarros, J. C., Cooper, B. K., & Santora, J. C. (2008). Building a climate for innovation through transformational leadership and organizational culture. *Journal of Leadership & Organizational Studies, 15*(2), 145–158. https://doi.org/10.1177/1548051808324100

Sen, R., & Borle, S. (2015). Estimating the contextual risk of data breach: An empirical approach. *Journal of Management Information Systems, 32*, 314–341. https://doi.org/10.1080/07421222.2015.1063315

Sila, I. (2013). Factors affecting the adoption of B2B e-commerce technologies. *Electronic Commerce Research, 13*, 199–236. https://doi.org/10.1007/s10660-013-9110-7

Steiger, J. S., Hammou, K. A., & Galib, M. H. (2014). An examination of the influence of organizational structure types and management levels on knowledge management practices in organizations. *International Journal of Business and Management, 9*(6), 43–57. https://doi.org/10.5539/ijbm.v9n6p43

Tashman, P., & Raelin, J. (2013). Who and what really matters to the firm: Moving stakeholder salience beyond managerial perceptions. *Business Ethics Quarterly, 23*, 591–616. https://doi.org/10.5840/beq201323441

Thomson, G. (2012). BYOD: Enabling the chaos. *Network Security, 2012*(2), 5–8. https://doi.org/10.1016/S1353-4858(12)70013-2

Tokuyoshi, B. (2013). The security implications of BYOD. *Network Security, 2013*(4), 12–13. https://doi.org/10.1016/S1353-4858(13)70050-3

Tran, E., & Atkinson, M. (2002). Security of personal data across national borders. *Information Management & Computer Security, 10*(5), 237–241. https://doi.org/10.1108/09685220210446588

Tsohou, A., Karyda, M., Kokolakis, S., & Kiountouzis, E. (2012). Analyzing trajectories of information security awareness. *Information Technology & People, 25*, 327–352. https://doi.org/10.1108/09593841211254358

Vance, A., & Siponen, M. T. (2012). IS security policy violations: A rational choice perspective. *Journal of Organizational and End User Computing, 24*(1), 21–41. https://doi.org/10.4018/joeuc.2012010102

Wang, C., Chow, S., Wang, Q., Ren, K., & Lou, W. (2013). Privacy-preserving public auditing for secure cloud storage. *IEEE Transactions on Computers (TC), 62*, 362–375. https://doi.org/10.1109/TC.2011.245

Wang, Z., Huang, J., & Tan, B. (2013). Managing organizational identity in the e-commerce industry: An ambidexterity perspective. *Information & Management, 50*, 673–683. https://doi.org/10.1016/j.im.2013.05.002

Wiener, M., Mähring, M., Remus, U., Saunders, C., & Cram, W. A. (2019). Moving IS project control research into the digital era: The "why" of control and the concept of control purpose. *Information Systems Research, 30*(4), 1387–1401. https://doi.org/10.1287/isre.2019.0867

Wiley, A., McCormac, A., & Calic, D. (2020). More than the individual: Examining the relationship between culture and information security awareness. *Computers & Security, 88*, 1–8. https://doi.org/10.1016/j.cose.2019.101640

Williams, S. P., Hardy, C. A., & Holgate, J. A. (2013). Information security governance practices in critical infrastructure organizations: A socio-technical and institutional logic perspective. *Electronic Markets, 23*, 341–354. https://doi.org/10.1007/s12525-013-0137-3

Willison, R., & Warkentin, M. (2013). Beyond deterrence: An expanded view of employee computer abuse. *MIS Quarterly, 37*, 1–20. www.misq.org

Wiseman, R. M., Cuevas-Rodríguez, G., & Gomez-Mejia, L. R. (2012). Towards a social theory of agency. *Journal of Management Studies, 49*, 202–222. https://doi.org/10.1111/j.1467-6486.2011.01016.x

Wlosinski, L. G. (2016). Mobile computing device threats, vulnerabilities and risk factors are ubiquitous. *ISACA Journal, 4*, 45–49. www.isaca.org

Wu, Y., & Saunders, C. S. (2016). Governing the fiduciary relationship in information security services. *Decision Support Systems, 92*, 57–67. https://doi.org/10.1016/j.dss.2016.09.008

Zhao, H., Peng, Z., & Sheard, G. (2013). Workplace ostracism and hospitality employees' counterproductive work behaviors: The joint moderating effects of proactive personality and political skill. *International Journal of Hospitality Management, 33,* 219–227. https://doi.org/10.1016/j.ijhm.2012.08.006

Recommended Reading

Boritz, J. E., Datardina, M., Anderson, C., Curim, U., Henrickson, R., James, D., Livesley, R., Nayar, M., & Teed, S. A. (2019). *A framework for information integrity controls.* Chartered Professional Accountants of Canada. www.incp.org.co/wp-content/uploads/2019/09/Framework-Information-Integrity-26092019.pdf

Conteh, N. Y., & Schmick, P. J. (2016). Cybersecurity: Risks, vulnerabilities and countermeasures to prevent social engineering attacks. *International Journal of Advanced Computer Research, 6*(23), 31–38. http://dx.doi.org/10.19101/IJACR.2016.623006

Da Veiga, A., Astakhova, L. V., Botha, A., & Herselman, M. (2020). Defining organisational information security culture: Perspectives from academia and industry. *Computers & Security, 92,* 101713. https://doi.org/10.1016/j.cose.2020.101713

Stott, J. H. (2001). *Electronic systems assurance and control: eSAC model.* The Institute of Internal Auditors. www.tarrani.net/kate/docs/eSACModel.pdf

Von Solms, R., & Van Niekerk, J. (2013). From information security to cyber security. *Computers & Security, 38,* 97–102. https://doi.org/10.1016/j.cose.2013.04.004

Chapter 3

Security Governance Management

Abstract

Information and Cyber Security Governance should specify the accountability, responsibility, and authority framework for an entity. Planning is a necessary managerial process in determining IAP objectives and goals for an entity. Entity governance needs to provide the means for administrative oversight to ensure IAP risks receive appropriate treatment, while ISG manager-leaders ensure that authorized risk treatment strategy enactment occurs as intended. The organizing process transforms the IAP action plan into controllable areas and includes the grouping of activities based on efficient usage of available resources. Whereby organizational direction permits the managerial function to regulate the activities or action courses of entity personnel. Where enacted, control activities help ensure the following of management directives. Chapter 3 addresses the planning, organizing, orchestration, directing, and controlling cycle in managing ISG, enabling a well-informed and reasonable sense of certainty that information risks and controls appropriately balance.

Introduction

In fulfilling addressable security information criteria, an ISG program should include processes, activities, and tasks for assessing property (R. Davis, 2008a). The physical nature distinguishes tangible and intangible property (R. Davis, 2008a). Properties having physical existence, such as fire extinguishers and air conditioning units, are tangible (R. Davis, 2008a). Properties having no physical existence, such as patent rights and computer programs, are intangible (R. Davis, 2008a). With ownership rights, information acquired or created is classifiable as an intangible asset (R. Davis, 2008a). Intangible assets may have explicit or implicit legal retention and protection mandates imposed by governmental entities (R. Davis, 2008a). Consequently, entity manager-leaders must provide appropriate safeguards to preserve information value (R. Davis, 2008a). Moreover, entity manager-leaders must comply with applicable information-related laws, regulations, and expectations to fulfill fiduciary responsibilities (R. Davis, 2008a).

Roles and responsibilities' assignments for providing appropriate information security are typically critical to cybersecurity efficacy (R. Davis, 2008a). However, depending on the entity, IAP management roles and responsibilities may focus solely on cybersecurity (R. Davis, 2008a) or both on information security and cybersecurity. Roles and responsibilities define relationships among individuals within the entity and significantly affect control objective achievements (R. Davis, 2008a). Additionally, roles with responsibilities for security delivery and support need inscribing for accountability determination (R. Davis, 2008a).

Because documentation is a critical element in compliance, evidence regarding how data is handled and protected is necessary. Techniques for applying additional security measures, such as enabling encryption in cases where it does not exist by default, should be generated and retained. In attempting to ensure compliance, not only must entity management meet the regulatory requirements regarding data administration and protection, but also it should be able to offer evidentiary documentation supporting decisions. Evidentiary documentation includes records showing a legitimate basis for data collection and processing (and when consent is the basis, indicating obtainment according to the requirements). Keeping records of processing operations performed on data and inscribed information regarding applicable security policies, procedures, and configurations is critical to substantiating compliance.

Entity noncompliance risks are an undeniable reality (Wiley et al., 2020), where the repercussions range from significant financial penalties to reputational damage (R. Davis, 2012b). Engineering appropriate countermeasures to a security breach is typically an operational necessity (R. Davis, 2012b). Deploying an information security management system can enable correlating available information asset data to intended usage for determining security breach criticality, severity, or impact (R. Davis, 2012b). Resultingly, the information security management system permits effective response administration (R. Davis, 2012b). Considering the primary contingency management objective is to provide solutions by understanding risk factors, an appropriate response to a cybersecurity incident depends on timely, reliable information to assess the risks and apply needed resources (Davis, 2012b).

Entity manager-leaders can use alternative approaches to accomplish organizational objectives (R. Davis, 2008a). Potential leadership styles for achieving organizational objectives are participative, free rein, and autocratic (Derakhshandeh & Gholami, 2012; Nwekeaku, 2013). Participative manager-leaders emphasize considering and incorporating employee views in decisions while maintaining managerial decision authority (Derakhshandeh & Gholami, 2012; Nwekeaku, 2013; R. Davis, 2008a). Free rein manager-leaders allow employees to make their own decisions concerning subject matters (Derakhshandeh & Gholami, 2012; Nwekeaku, 2013; R. Davis, 2008a). Autocratic manager-leaders underscore decision dictating to employees (Derakhshandeh & Gholami, 2012; Nwekeaku, 2013; R. Davis, 2008a). Based on empirical evidence, most entities currently prefer applying a participative leadership style (R. Davis, 2008a). Consequently, this chapter focuses on applying a participative approach to performing an entity-wide information security risk assessment.

Planning

Planning is a formal procedure to produce a stated result through an integrated decision system (R. Davis, 2011). Management planning is typically necessary to deploy an effective and efficient ISG program (R. Davis, 2008a). However, an employee assigned overall responsibility for ISG can be an executive, senior, or junior level manager-leader (R. Davis, 2008a). At whatever the designated managerial level, the ISG manager-leader is usually accountable for developing teams, taking organizational decisions, and monitoring activities (R. Davis, 2008a). Through authority delegation, manager-leaders assume responsibility for performing information gathering, risk assessing, and determining methods to accomplish objectives and goals (R. Davis, 2008a). Management's vision, mission, and values usually convert into the planning premise (R. Davis, 2011).

Vision takes the ability to perceive something not visible and converting the conception to a projected future state (R. Davis, 2011). In some instances, vision requires mental acuteness or keen foresight (Davis, 2011). However, vision manifestation typically occurs incrementally (R. Davis, 2011). Once conceptualized, an entity manager-leader's vision needs acceptance and organization into a framework for achieving developed objectives (Davis, 2011). Envisioning the ISG program supporting the fulfillment of entity objectives is fundamental to appropriate operational creation and sustainability (R. Davis, 2011). When initiating ISG development, some key planning considerations include:

- length of time between periodic risk assessments,
- skills and qualifications of individuals designing and executing the risk evaluation,
- the extent of external and internal audit involvement in the ISG program design or operation, and
- due diligence and monitoring expectations at the executive management and oversight committee levels (R. Davis, 2008a).

For information security employees to accomplish management's organizational vision of activity requirements, they should emulate the entity's and ISG's mission (R. Davis, 2011). An entity's mission statement traditionally represents the adopted employee creed (R. Davis, 2011). Implicitly, within the accepted creed for employees are management's values (R. Davis, 2011). The entity's executive personnel and highest oversight committee should develop values for dissemination (R. Davis, 2011). Organizational values should represent nonnegotiable essential and enduring tenets barred from compromise for short-term expediency or financial gain (R. Davis, 2011). The ISG manager-leader should adopt functional values consistent with organizational values (R. Davis, 2011).

Information obtainment enables analysis (R. Davis, 2008a). However, information usefulness needs weighing against information acquisition costs (R. Davis, 2008a). When planning an ISG deployment, entity manager-leaders prioritize acquiring internal and external operating environment data (R. Davis, 2008a). As a sub-process corollary, analysis of the entity's operating environment provides planning assumptions for ISG program development (R. Davis, 2008a). Alternatively, higher-level manager-leaders may provide a strategy premise for IAP planning (R. Davis, 2008a). Management's IAP planning premise can be the entity's adopted cybersecurity policy (R. Davis, 2008a). Assumptions and premises' consideration need inclusion in the planning process and typically affect objectives, goals, and risk mitigation selection, as well as development and deployment strategies (R. Davis, 2008a).

ISG planning establishes the means to reach organizational objectives and goals (R. Davis, 2008a). An integral part of methodical planning is objectives (R. Davis, 2011). During planning, organizational objectives establishment are the end of the means-ends relationship (R. Davis, 2011). The objectives need identification and specification in the long range or strategic plans (R. Davis, 2011). Furthermore, objectives are interpretable as general statements of the entity's direction (R. Davis, 2011). During creation, as shown in Figure 3.1, inscribing objectives requires participation at various management levels (R. Davis, 2011). ISG objectives should attempt to define expected accomplishments (R. Davis, 2011). ISG goal elections should contain performance indicators for design, deployment, maintenance, and bound entity objectives (R. Davis, 2011).

As expectations, ISG objectives and goals have different contextual definitions (R. Davis, 2011). Minimally, objectives are broad, intended achievement statements supporting the organization's vision, mission, and values (R. Davis, 2011), whereby goals are specific objectives of specific processes or organizational units. Objectives and goal determination are the second activity in the ISG planning process when using a risk-based approach for determining appropriate security controls. Regarding the accomplishment of goals and objectives, clear and distinct links passing through strategic, tactical, and operational management levels (Nicho, 2018) and functional reporting levels ensure alignment with the entity's mission (R. Davis, 2008a).

High-level control objectives necessitate rationale identification and linkage to develop lower-level goals and objectives (R. Davis, 2008a). Management should inscribe

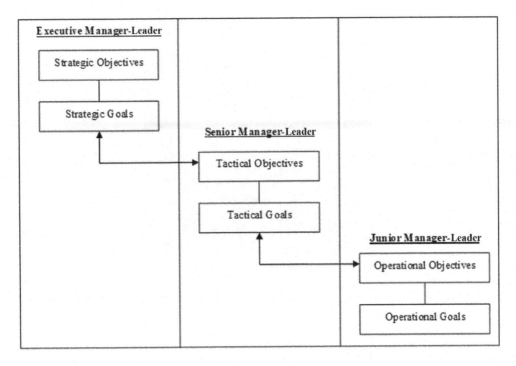

Figure 3.1 Objectives–Goals Flow by Managerial Responsibility.

Note: Adapted from *IT Auditing: IT Governance* by R. E. Davis, 2006, Pleier. Copyright 2006 by Robert E. Davis. Adapted with permission.

improvements in the entity's operations and image when setting objectives (R. Davis, 2011). Entity personnel development and cost reduction commitments should also receive inscription through a bottom-up communication network to assist in setting objectives (R. Davis, 2011). After appropriate review and approval, top-down objectives' communication is essential for creating entity direction awareness (R. Davis, 2011).

ISG objectives development should reflect the adopted vision, mission, and values accepted by the entity's manager-leaders (R. Davis, 2011). Additionally, an efficient and effective budget system should support and control the establishment of ISG objectives (Nicho, 2018). Typically, as presented in Figure 3.2, entity manager-leaders establish, or support, planning horizons designed to achieve specific time-dependent objectives (R. Davis, 2011). Depending on environmental dynamics, the long-range plan duration can be 1 to 20 years (R. Davis, 2011). The strategic plan is typically more than 1 year, the tactical plan is 1 year or less, and the operational plan addresses daily operations (R. Davis, 2011).

The ISG long-range plans should reflect management's projected or desired state of the entity (R. Davis, 2011). ISG long-range planning allows functional direction with relevant influences forecasting to derive the best strategy for achieving objectives considering organizational strengths, weaknesses, and relevant future trends (R. Davis, 2011). Determining cybersecurity control objectives emulates establishing information security objectives (R. Davis, 2011). Consequently, ISG control planning is a conduit for assessing and evaluating organizational and cybersecurity strengths and weaknesses based on entity governance philosophy of the formation's management (R. Davis, 2008a). From a holistic perspective, people, information, processes, and infrastructure are critical elements that need strategic definitions, tactical adoption, and operational execution.

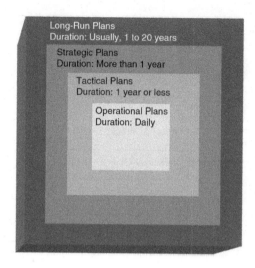

Figure 3.2 Entity Planning Modes.

Note: Adapted from *IT Auditing: IT Governance* by R. E. Davis, 2006, Pleier. Copyright 2006 by Robert E. Davis. Adapted with permission.

Strategic plans are management's assessment of what long-range plan achievements will materialize from using available resources. Strategic planning represents the highest decision-making level for determining an entity's necessary direction and purpose (R. Davis, 2011). Strategic planning enables the development of organizational objectives (R. Davis, 2011). Strategic planning has a project-orientation with a time-orientation that should help determine and address priorities for achieving organizational expectations (R. Davis, 2011). Strategies focus on controlling the entity's destiny and achieving articulated objectives (R. Davis, 2011). An entity's oversight committee should be responsible for setting high-level objectives, overseeing the ISG planning model, measuring performance against established objectives, and revising ineffective or inefficient objectives (R. Davis, 2011).

The planning process should translate strategies into measurable tactical plans (R. Davis, 2011). Lower-level organizational management should be responsible for executing the ISG strategy and operating within the ISG program model (R. Davis, 2011). Preparation, verification, and adaptation are activities directly related to tactical planning, reviewing, and changing objectives (R. Davis, 2011). The strategic planning process should convert an ISG program's vision, mission, and values into directions, objectives, strategies, activity selection, and resource allocation with appropriate tactical planning (R. Davis, 2011). ISG needs consideration as a strategic component for entity opportunities and control system enhancements (R. Davis, 2011). If properly integrated, ISG can provide a competitive advantage, customer satisfaction, increased productivity, and improved controls (R. Davis, 2011).

An operational level manager-leader oversees the day-to-day information security-related tasks in most entities (R. Davis, 2008b, 2017; Yaokumah, 2013). At the operational level, junior-level manager-leader accountability is generally to a senior-level manager-leader for fulfilling delegated operational objectives and congruent goals (R. Davis, 2008a, 2017). Operational manager-leaders emphasize economy, efficiency, and effectiveness based on administrative techniques and related subject knowledge (R. Davis, 2008b). Operational planning centers on formulating activities are required to deliver appropriate information security and maintain user functionality as defined in service level agreements (R. Davis, 2008b).

Selected strategic, tactical, and operational protective measures should ensure a properly controlled entity environment for information assets (Coertze & Von Solms, 2013; R. Davis, 2008a). Foundationally, information construction is dependent on available data (R. Davis, 2008a). Information usually obtains value through usability in decision-making (R. Davis, 2008a). Usable information also creates knowledge (R. Davis, 2008a). Conceptually, information that provides derivable knowledge requires safeguarding no matter the conveyance method (R. Davis, 2008a). Therefore, management needs to safeguard information against unauthorized use, disclosure, or modification, as well as damage or loss (R. Davis, 2008a).

Chief Information Security Officers should ensure strategy inscription for accomplishing IAP control objectives and develop an ISG program plan that will provide acceptable risk tolerance levels at a reasonable cost (R. Davis, 2008a). An ISG program plan should describe all considered IAP controls and indicate the purpose and justification for inclusion (R. Davis, 2008a). Next, before implementation, top-level management should review and approve the ISG plan to ensure sufficient organizational accountability, responsibility, and authority to deploy and sustain IAP controls (R. Davis, 2008a).

Once entity manager-leaders ratify resource requirements, IAP baseline development and deployment can occur (Brotby, 2006; R. Davis, 2008a). Protection baselines vary by information asset sensitivity, criticality, and impact valuation (Brotby, 2006; R. Davis, 2008a). However, minimally, information assets should receive protection against misuse, abuse, and destruction (R. Davis, 2008a). When implemented, IAP baselines can become managerial, technical, or operational standards applicable throughout the entity (Brotby, 2006; R. Davis, 2008a).

Security Risk Assessment

Comprehensive IAP risk assessments should occur to ensure relevant items come under consideration and receive appropriate treatment when developing or modifying an entity's ISG plans (R. Davis, 2008a). A risk assessment is the process of risk identification, risk analysis, and risk evaluation (ISO Technical Management Board Working Group, 2009). In other words, IAP risk assessments are evaluations performed to classify and appraise risks as well as determine the potential significance of a selected domain (R. Davis, 2008a). IAP risk assessment objectives should address risk management elements (R. Davis, 2008a). The primary IAP risk assessment objective is to enable recommendations for maximizing confidentiality, integrity, and availability while maintaining information functionality and usability (R. Davis, 2008a).

Regarding techniques, the ISG program's ambit determines the assessment focus, how the assessment will transpire, and assessment limits (R. Davis, 2008a). Reflective of the ISG planning premise, evaluating cost versus data collection level will help define the risk assessment effort (R. Davis, 2008a). The ISG program ambit generally dictates the risk assessment approach (R. Davis, 2008a). Simultaneously, inscribing overall and detailed control perimeters helps evaluate risk analysis process decisions and data (R. Davis, 2008a). Detailed ISG control perimeter delineation can reflect functional areas, IT environments, or physical locations (R. Davis, 2008a).

As shown in Figure 3.3, an IAP risk assessment plan should describe the predetermined objective, goals, and ambit, with sufficient supporting detail, to guide risk assessment development (R. Davis, 2008a) for generating IAP general and application controls. IAP risk assessment plans should demonstrate the consideration of applicable standards and practice statements issued by governing bodies (R. Davis, 2008a). Providing an ISG program's risk assessment nature, timing, and extent is a primary administrative

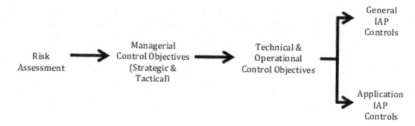

Figure 3.3 Risks–Controls Process.

Note: IAP, information assets protection. Adapted from *Ensuring Information Assets Protection* by R. E. Davis, 2009, Lulu. Copyright 2009 by Robert E. Davis. Adapted with permission.

consideration when determining the IAP ambit (R. Davis, 2008a). Potential IAP risk assessment ambits include:

- risk analysis,
- logical access,
- physical access,
- confidential information,
- IT network infrastructure, and
- environmental conditions (Davis, 2008a).

The IAP risk assessment ambit determines methods and tool selection (R. Davis, 2008a). Without exceeding the IAP ambit and the ISG program's authority or control perimeter, an IAP risk assessment can:

- identify potential new exposures,
- identify potential existing exposures,
- appraise relevant new exposures,
- appraise relevant existing exposures,
- provide potential exposures analysis,
- determine risk countermeasure costs,
- determine risk countermeasure benefits,
- establish appropriate controls, and
- establish compliance with standards (Davis, 2008a).

Furthermore, an IAP risk assessment enables classifying information by criticality, sensitivity, and impact on entity operations (R. Davis, 2008a). Comprehensive IAP risk assessments should permit adaptive and iterative processes (Nicho, 2018; R. Davis, 2008a). Therefore, ISG processes should allow movement from yearly to quarterly risk assessments to maintain established risk tolerance levels (R. Davis, 2008a) in a dynamic environment. Additionally, risk assessment performance should be capable of coming under consideration whenever there is a change in the entity's operations or use of technology or whenever outside influences affect operations (R. Davis, 2008a). However, unless mandated by law or regulation, risk assessment costs should not outweigh derivable benefits from managerial due diligence (R. Davis, 2008a).

An adopted ISG risk assessment framework is an indispensable component in focusing on information asset sensitivity, criticality, and impact (R. Davis, 2008a). Risk assessment frameworks can employ qualitative or quantitative measurements (R. Davis, 2008a). No matter what risk assessment measurement technique an analyst applies, quantitative and qualitative analysis procedures need inscription (R. Davis, 2008a).

Selectively, the Information Security Assessment Methodology; the Operational Critical Threat, Asset, and Vulnerability Evaluation; and the Federal Information Technology Security Assessment Framework are capability maturity-based models (R. Davis, 2008a). The United States National Security Agency developed the Information Security Assessment Methodology (R. Davis, 2008a). The Information Security Assessment Methodology allows examining the entity's mission, organization, security policies, security programs, information systems, and information system threats (R. Davis, 2008a). The recommendation is to organize and maintain a highly proficient information security team to accomplish the Information Security Assessment Methodology objectives (R. Davis, 2008a). The information security team's responsibilities encompass providing crisis and contingency management and training (R. Davis, 2008a). Thus, comparatively, the Information Security Assessment Methodology generates implementation costs two or three times higher than the Operational Critical Threat, Asset and Vulnerability Evaluation; and the Federal Information Technology Security Assessment Framework (R. Davis, 2008a).

A comprehensive high-level risk assessment is a starting point for designing or modifying an IAP action plan or policy (R. Davis, 2008a). Such assessments are essential to ensuring (a) all IAP threats, opportunities, and vulnerabilities receive an examination; (b) identification of the most significant risks; (c) the making of appropriate decisions regarding which risks are acceptable, avoidable, reducible, or transferable; and (d) needed information assets' enhancing, compensating, or mitigating through appropriate control deployments (R. Davis, 2008a).

General risk analysis is a formal risk assessment technique and a risk management driver and enabler (R. Davis, 2008a). Thus, dialectically, information asset risk analysis is the method selected for considering entity threats, vulnerabilities, and opportunities. IAP risk assessment is typically a complex undertaking requiring risk analysis to prioritize judicious resource allocations (R. Davis, 2008a). Risk analysis aids in integration of IAP objectives with other entity-centric objectives and requirements (R. Davis, 2008a). Furthermore, risk analysis helps design an appropriate budget for the ISG program (R. Davis, 2008a). Specifically, once the information security manager-leader appraises asset value and potential threat, vulnerability, and opportunity exposures, rational spending allocation decisions can be made for IAP (R. Davis, 2008a).

As shown in Figure 3.4, a risk analysis permits the means for assessing conceivable adversities for determining practical IAP deployments (R. Davis, 2008a). Security manager-leaders usually

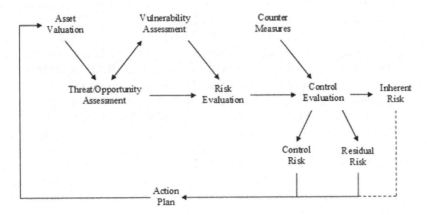

Figure 3.4 Expanded Risk Analysis Model.

Note: Adapted from *Ensuring Information Assets Protection* by R. E. Davis, 2009, Lulu. Copyright 2009 by Robert E. Davis. Adapted with permission.

complete an information asset risk analysis to ensure IAP effectiveness, relevancy, efficiency, and responsiveness to threats and opportunities (R. Davis, 2008a). The standard information asset risk analysis identifies vulnerabilities that may be exploitable by a threat (R. Davis, 2008a). Conditionally, information asset risk analysis can enable IAP baseline creation and subsequent comparisons to other identified risks (R. Davis, 2008a). Information asset risk analysis also enables identifying and mitigating unacceptable risk appetite variances (R. Davis, 2008a).

The distinction between quantitative and qualitative risk analysis is numerical value assignments to risk elements (Dellis et al., 2014; McCusker & Gunaydin, 2015; R. Davis, 2008a; Yilmaz, 2013). On the one hand, monetary or non-monetary valuations of identified information assets are the options available for quantitative risk analysis (R. Davis, 2008a). On the other hand, qualitative risk analysis only addresses nonmonetary valuations (R. Davis, 2008a) because words convey actions. However, combining quantitative and qualitative measures may be unavoidable if the preferred quantitative or qualitative measurement approach hinders fulfilling evaluation objectives (R. Davis, 2008a).

An analyst's mixed methods can help develop insights into various phenomena of interest, which are not entirely understandable with a singular quantitative or qualitative approach (Mayoh & Onwuegbuzie, 2015; Siddiqui & Fitzgerald, 2014; Venkatesh et al., 2013). Quantitative, qualitative, and mixed methods can explore, describe, or explain security-related risk elements (R. Davis, 2017). Elements associated with a risk analysis of information assets include asset value, threat frequency, vulnerability severity, organizational impact, IAP costs, IAP benefits, uncertainty, and probability (R. Davis, 2008a).

Quantitative risk analysis is a more objective valuation approach (R. Davis, 2008a). Objectively obtaining and disseminating data and information aligns with a postpositivist worldview that objectivity is essential to competent examination achievement (Christ, 2013; K. Davis, 2016; Mayoh & Onwuegbuzie, 2015; R. Davis, 2017). Generally, quantitative information asset risk analysis uses percentages, mathematical formulas, and financial values (Davis, 2008a). Impediments to applying a quantitative risk analysis approach include difficulties in identifying and assigning values to information assets and a lack of statistical data to determine threat frequencies (R. Davis, 2008a). Advantageously, when quantitative method application occurs for information assets' measurement, management's preference for equivalent valuation techniques deployment throughout the entity is customarily satisfied (R. Davis, 2008a).

Typically, an initial information asset risk estimate reflects parameter assumptions (Davis, 2008a). If warranted, the assessor can apply sensitivity analysis (Farahmand et al., 2005; R. Davis, 2008a; Syamsuddin, 2013). Sensitivity analysis is a class of methods designed to identify parameter or parameter set acuteness (Li et al., 2013). Quantitatively, sensitivity analysis addresses the uncertainty inherent in mathematical models where the model input values can vary. Through a simulation approach, quantitative sensitivity analysis of information asset risks requires formulating a situation into a mathematical model (R. Davis, 2008a). Quantitative sensitivity analysis requires that the calculated solution variance to changes in any given parameter or parameter set has determinability (R. Davis, 2008a). Consequently, the best parameter assumptions may be least sensitive to probabilistic inputs (R. Davis, 2008a).

Unilaterally, qualitative risk analysis is a more subjective valuation technique (R. Davis, 2008a). Subjectivity increases the potential for a decision reflecting a bias toward achieving the desired outcome (R. Davis, 2008a). Qualitative techniques rely on the assessor's experience or supposition ability to determine an item's significance (R. Davis, 2008a). Qualitative risk analysis identifies and ranks an information asset individually or relatively (R. Davis, 2008a). Individually, the significance determination of information assets occurs based on the owner's assessed worth (R. Davis, 2008a). Relatively, the significance determination of information assets occurs through comparison to other items (R. Davis, 2008a).

The individual risk rating parameter or parameter set importance is obtainable through performing qualitative sensitivity analysis (R. Davis, 2008a). Qualitative sensitivity analysis methods provide heuristic ratings to intuitively represent the relative sensitivity of parameters or parameter sets (Li et al., 2013). When employing a qualitative sensitivity analysis, specific information asset vulnerabilities require potential threats indexing to derive the protection risk level posed to the entity (R. Davis, 2008a). Moreover, ratings of information asset vulnerabilities, asset values, and threats or opportunities are combinable for deriving a relative qualitative risk rating (R. Davis, 2008a). IAP risk assessors can deduce relative valuations qualitatively using occurrence frequency or high watermark approach to asset values, threats or opportunities, and vulnerabilities (R. Davis, 2008a).

Asset Valuation

Information asset identification must occur to determine risk (R. Davis, 2008a). Typically, information asset identification is the precursor to sensitivity, threat, opportunity, privacy, and vulnerability risk classification and valuation (R. Davis, 2008a). A managerial risk analysis restriction for data collection, information asset classification, and information asset valuation may impose an ambit limitation on items directly aiding in achieving the entity's operational objectives (R. Davis, 2008a). However, information assets unrelated to entity operational objective achievement can compromise achieving entity operational objective realization (R. Davis, 2008a; Zhao et al., 2013).

Information asset identification permits addressing what is at risk for a protection breach (R. Davis, 2008a). Compiling or obtaining an information asset inventory with descriptive functionality should be the highest priority action item of an entity risk management committee, project team, or person solely performing information asset valuations (R. Davis, 2008a). If an information asset inventory listing is unavailable for analysis and subsequent assessment processes, management risks safeguarding malfeasance accusations that may result in criminal and civil prosecution (R. Davis, 2008a).

Classification is crucial to providing repeatable IAP since all information assessments are not equal (R. Davis, 2008a). There are numerous qualitative schemes available to classify information and related assets (R. Davis, 2008a). An accepted qualitative information security principle's classification scheme demarks confidentiality, integrity, and availability as primary data sensitivity indicators (see Table 3.1; R. Davis, 2008a). Nonetheless, information classification relies typically on:

- Sensitivity: Sensitivity is an important term to a person or entity for restricting item sharing with anyone. Singularly, information sensitivity directly relates to information confidentiality assessments (see Appendix; R. Davis, 2008a). Sensitivity measurement determination occurs based on how the information could affect compliance with laws and regulations or entity-centric processes (R. Davis, 2008a).
- Criticality: Criticality reflects how vital the item is to a person or entity. Singularly, information criticality directly relates to information integrity assessments (see Appendix; R. Davis, 2008a). Criticality measurement occurs through identical information replacement valuation (R. Davis, 2008a).
- Impact: Impact is the exposure magnitude of an item affected by an unacceptable incident or event. Singularly, information impact correlates directly to information availability requirements (see Appendix; R. Davis, 2008a). Impact measurement occurs through detrimental effect valuation (R. Davis, 2008a).

Table 3.1 Data Classification Sensitivity Indicator

Classification	Indicator
Confidentiality	There is a need to preserve data access and disclosure restrictions.
Integrity	There is a need to protect against improper data modification, corruption, or destruction.
Availability	There is a need to ensure timely and reliable data access and use.

Note: Adapted from *Ensuring Information Assets Protection* by R. E. Davis, 2009, Lulu. Copyright 2009 by Robert E. Davis. Adapted with permission.

IAP can also come under classification consideration individually or jointly for threat analysis. For instance, specific criminal activities associated with telecommunications are classifiable as disclosure, deception, disruption, or usurpation (R. Davis, 2008a), where credit card fraud, phreaking, and unauthorized data pass-through are threats. Thus, the theft of service classified as an unauthorized data pass-through is a usurpation risk for allowing the transporting of information using the technology (R. Davis, 2008a).

An information system should permit secure resource access and use to occur as intended under all circumstances. Since comprehensive information security is impossible, management should consider delineating misuse based on organizational impact to enable judicious and productive resource deployments for fulfilling managerial safeguarding responsibilities (R. Davis, 2008a). Sub-categorically, IT misuse can be classified as malicious or accidental (R. Davis, 2008a). Further, malicious or accidental IT misuse definitions should encompass reading, modification, and destruction of information (R. Davis, 2008a).

Information classification can assist in satisfying statutory and regulatory privacy mandates (R. Davis, 2008a). In completing mandatory privacy assessments, preparatory individuals can use IAP classifications to communicate protection expectations based on implied valuations and goals (R. Davis, 2008a). Moreover, information classifications can help develop appropriate information asset treatments (R. Davis, 2008a).

Once information asset identification and IAP classifications occur, valuation assessment or assignment is feasible (R. Davis, 2008a). Inscribing individual values for information assets should be a valuation process priority after identification and IAP classification (R. Davis, 2008a). Quantitative information asset valuations usually take precedence over qualitative information asset valuations (R. Davis, 2008a). An information asset valuation report should inscribe potential productivity, monetary, and stakeholder losses that may result from IAP breaches (R. Davis, 2008a). The primary purpose of preparing an information asset valuation report is to provide a range of values for use in IAP threat, vulnerability, and opportunity analysis as well as risk evaluation (R. Davis, 2008a).

Quantitative risk analysis methods usually apply absolute or relative information asset valuation models (R. Davis, 2008a). Given that information assets are tangible or intangible items, applying a monetary accounting approach is a valuation option (R. Davis, 2008a). For instance, information asset valuation determination may occur using an accounting cost or income approach (R. Davis, 2008a). When an entity's management is aware of an information asset's numerical value, resource allocation requirements for suitable protection can receive assessments based on more objective measurements (R. Davis, 2008a). However, the inability to generate or acquire quantitative data should not deter risk analysis development (R. Davis, 2008a).

A standard categorization for qualitative risk analysis is high, medium, and low when assigning information asset values (R. Davis, 2008a). Alternatively, when an additional qualitative distinction is necessary, information asset valuations of very high, high, medium, low, and very low are viable (R. Davis, 2008a). Generally, more than five valuation levels are excessive for qualitative analysis (R. Davis, 2008a). A risk assessor can design a grid to assign appropriate categorization for entity information assets when using qualitative valuations and conventional information security criteria (R. Davis, 2008a).

Entity manager-leaders who create or acquire information assets or primary users should accept responsibility for providing information asset classifications and identification (R. Davis, 2008a). However, the individual or team directly responsible for risk analysis asset valuation should perform independent information asset identification and classification verification (R. Davis, 2008a).

Threats or Opportunities Assessment

As part of the IAP threat or opportunity assessment, a threat or opportunity analysis is essential. The threat or opportunity analysis inscribes all actions and events that might adversely affect an information asset (R. Davis, 2008a). Categorical grouping of threats (Huang et al., 2007) or opportunities during an assessment can address human or nonhuman, intentional or unintentional, technological or non-technological, skillful or unskillful, as well as internal or external events or incidents (R. Davis, 2008a). When analyzing information asset threats or opportunities, assessors should consider the entity's vulnerabilities to ensure assessment completeness and accuracy (R. Davis, 2008a). As conceptualized in Figure 3.5, an IAP threat or opportunity may exist with a single vulnerability or multiple vulnerabilities (R. Davis, 2008a). Thus, to enable a robust risk response, mapping threats or opportunities to vulnerabilities is crucial for preventing or deterring undesirable events or incidents.

Broadly, security threats are events that can result in unauthorized harm to information assets (R. Davis, 2008a). Narrowly, threats to an entity's cybersecurity encompass physical environment hazards, criminal activities, privacy invasion, IT abuse, and IT misuse (R. Davis, 2008a). Potential information asset threats include eavesdropping, identity recognition manipulation, and telecommunication interference (R. Davis, 2008a). Cybersecurity threats

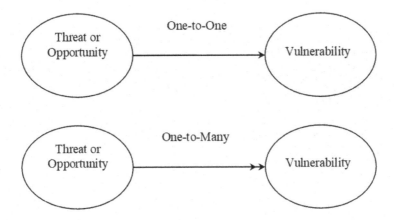

Figure 3.5 Threat or Opportunity Canonical Attribute Mappings.

Source: Adapted from *Ensuring Information Assets Protection* by R. E. Davis, 2009, Lulu. Copyright 2009 by Robert E. Davis. Adapted with permission.

can hinder or reduce entity and IT objective achievement, value creation, and value preservation (R. Davis, 2008a, 2017; Srivastava & Kumar, 2015; Tarafdar et al., 2015).

Identified threats correspond to the entity's internal and external environmental conditions (R. Davis, 2008a). Quantitatively, indicative data regarding potential IAP threats are obtainable from various reliable sources to create a threat list containing the frequency of threat occurrences, information asset descriptions, and information asset values (R. Davis, 2008a). Regardless, an opposed state can exist between the threat occurrence probability and occurrence cost for identified information assets (R. Davis, 2008a).

In contrast, manual or automation opportunities are generally considered events that can positively affect objective achievement, value creation, and value preservation (R. Davis, 2008a). Planned or unplanned circumstances can present opportunities to enhance an entity's reputation or financial position through manual or IT process deployments (R. Davis, 2008a). When favorable conditions exist, risk assessment procedure activation should occur using an appropriate opportunity analysis to maintain an acceptable security risk level and sustain appropriately deployed security controls (R. Davis, 2008a).

Depending on the quantitative technique applied, assessing IAP threats or opportunities requires using mathematical and sub-mathematical calculations (R. Davis, 2008a). To determine a single IAP threat or opportunity valuation, a threat or opportunity assessor can use the following formula:

$$ALE = SLE \times ARO \text{ (R. Davis, 2008a)} \tag{3.1}$$

ALE is the annualized loss expectancy for an information asset (R. Davis, 2008a). SLE is the single loss expectancy for an information asset (R. Davis, 2008a). ARO is the annualized rate of occurrence for an information asset-related event or incident (R. Davis, 2008a). Moreover, when determining SLE, the following formula is brought into service:

$$SLE = IAV \times RO \text{ (R. Davis, 2008a)} \tag{3.2}$$

IAV is the total information asset value (R. Davis, 2008a). RO is the occurrence rate for an information asset-related event or incident (R. Davis, 2008a). Wherefore, the RO is a necessary calculation that employs the formula:

$$RO = (IAV-UIAV)/IAV \text{ (R. Davis, 2008a)} \tag{3.3}$$

UIAV represents the unaffected information asset value segment (R. Davis, 2008a). Additionally, for the ALE calculation, ARO valuation can use the following formula:

$$ARO = 1/TF \text{ (R. Davis, 2008a)} \tag{3.4}$$

TF is the threat frequency counted in years (R. Davis, 2008a).

Vulnerability Assessment

Vulnerabilities are any weaknesses or deficiencies existing in a facility, system, or operation that can potentially allow threats to occur (Lamba, 2014; R. Davis, 2008a). Individuals, things, or characteristics can be vulnerabilities (R. Davis, 2008a). Cybersecurity vulnerabilities increase the potential for an attack occurrence, increase the potential for a successful attack, or influence the likelihood of targeted object obtainment (R. Davis, 2008a).

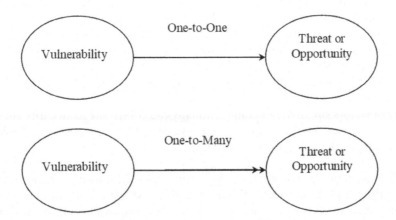

Figure 3.6 Vulnerability Canonical Attribute Mappings.

Note: Adapted from *Ensuring Information Assets Protection* by R. E. Davis, 2009, Lulu. Copyright 2009 by Robert E. Davis. Adapted with permission.

An information asset vulnerability reduction for any threat is more likely through objective- or goal-driven control deployment than by haphazard or heuristic control deployment (R. Davis, 2008a). Vulnerability assessments permit methodological examinations to determine IAP-measured adequacy and appropriateness, identify IAP deficiencies, and predict IAP proposal effectiveness (R. Davis, 2008a).

When assessors undertake an IAP vulnerability assessment, a vulnerability analysis is necessary. The vulnerability analysis inscribes all known deficiencies or weaknesses that adversely affected or might adversely affect an information asset. Categorical grouping of vulnerabilities during an assessment can address IAP adequacy, appropriateness, and existence (R. Davis, 2010, 2020). When analyzing information asset vulnerabilities, assessors should consider the entity's IAP threats or opportunities to ensure assessment completeness and accuracy (R. Davis, 2008a). As conceptualized in Figure 3.6, single or multiple threats or opportunities may exist for a known IAP vulnerability (R. Davis, 2008a). Consequently, to enable an appropriate IAP risk response, vulnerability mapping to threats or opportunities is necessary to prevent or deter undesirable events or incidents. (R. Davis, 2008a).

When an assessor undertakes a threat to vulnerability or vulnerability to threat mapping for determining the RO for events or incidents, then vulnerability values should become part of the threat assessment ALE computation (R. Davis, 2008a). During IAP vulnerability assessments, vulnerability analysis converges on consequences to target objects considering primary and secondary repercussions affecting the entity's environment (R. Davis, 2008a). Vulnerability analysis should encompass:

• defining information assets,
• classifying information assets,
• assigning significance levels to information assets,
• identifying potential threats to information assets,
• developing strategies to address problematic circumstances,
• defining responses to minimize attack consequences,
• reporting vulnerabilities to appropriate parties, and
• inscribing responses to minimize attack consequences (R. Davis, 2008a).

Like the information asset threat or opportunity assessments, external and internal indicative data regarding potential IAP vulnerabilities are obtainable from various sources to create an entity vulnerability list (R. Davis, 2008a). As a selection option, recent audit reports and vulnerability scanning results are acceptable sources when compiling an IAP vulnerability list (R. Davis, 2008a). The developed vulnerability list should minimally indicate notification dates, information asset descriptions, and information asset values (R. Davis, 2008a).

A variety of factors singularly or conjunctionally can contribute to an entity environment cultivating IAP vulnerabilities, including defective components, geographical distribution, size, complexity, or change frequency (R. Davis, 2008a).

- Defective components: Often, the design and deployment of information assets transpire without IAP as a priority (R. Davis, 2008a). Moreover, developing and deploying completely secure information assets is typically impossible, impractical (R. Davis, 2008a), or cost-prohibitive. Therefore, the lack of IAP focus and IAP deficiencies can lead to organizational vulnerabilities (R. Davis, 2008a).
- Geographical distribution: Information assets are internationally dispersible and can connect to global networks (R. Davis, 2008a). Whereby information systems accessibility can take place from anywhere in the world. For most entities, restricting geographic distribution becomes an obstacle to expected information system availability (R. Davis, 2008a) when conducting organizational affairs. Consequently, the geographical distribution of information assets to achieve expected availability may impede physical and logical access control deployments (R. Davis, 2008a).
- Size: Entity information assets can be stand-alone computers to wide area networks (R. Davis, 2008a). Programming within any technology accepting, generating, and storing information may be extensive (R. Davis, 2008a). Thus, program size can increase vulnerabilities that go undetected (R. Davis, 2008a).
- Complexity: An entity's IT may support many users and consist of an abundance of individual elements connected to networks (Garba et al., 2015; R. Davis, 2008a). Additionally, programs or systems may perform a single task or multiple tasks for a unique process or the entire entity in a hybrid, centralized, or decentralized IT environment (R. Davis, 2008a, 2017; Yaokumah, 2013). IT may also be commercial off-the-shelf software or custom-entity-developed software (R. Davis, 2008a). Relevant activities and knowledge are the most salient factors for appropriate IAP in entities (Kim et al., 2014). Lack of complete configuration knowledge underlying systems, network topologies, and multiple access points enables vulnerabilities to develop and exist unnoticed until an IAP event or incident occurs (R. Davis, 2008a).
- Change frequency: Hardware and software changes usually increase with IT configuration complexity (R. Davis, 2008a). The changing of entity applications, systems, and network connections can be a daily routine (R. Davis, 2008a). Therefore, a high change frequency can hinder the timely tracking and controlling of information assets (R. Davis, 2008a) for preventing vulnerabilities.

Information asset resource-users are people, processes, and infrastructure (R. Davis, 2008a). Computing systems and applications represent the services and processes running in the IT environment (R. Davis, 2008a). Thus, computing system vulnerabilities denote known general control prevention, detection, or correction deficiencies or weaknesses that affect IT infrastructure protection (R. Davis, 2008a). Whereas computing application vulnerabilities usually signify known protection limits provided to address unauthorized use and abuse of processes (R. Davis, 2008a). Moreover, physical locations are the areas where information assets reside (R. Davis, 2008a). Physical location vulnerabilities indicate known access restriction limitations affecting protection from people (R. Davis, 2008a).

IAP vulnerability controls limit resource-users, computing systems, computing applications, and physical location exposures (R. Davis, 2008a). Quantitatively or qualitatively, vulnerabilities are characteristically an inverse expression of implemented controls (Lamba, 2014; R. Davis, 2008a). In other words, if manager-leaders maximize controls for entity information assets, information asset vulnerabilities should be minimized (Lamba, 2014; R. Davis, 2008a). However, the vulnerability reduction rate may not be proportional to the deployed control (R. Davis, 2008a). Additionally, controls can reduce an information asset's vulnerabilities yet create other information asset vulnerabilities (R. Davis, 2008a).

Before completing an IAP vulnerability assessment, deployed IAP controls need testing to determine whether undesirable events and incidents prevent, detect, deter, or correct as intended (R. Davis, 2008a). IAP vulnerability testing permits ensuring full responsibility assignments, procedural understanding and following, and rightly functioning control mechanisms (R. Davis, 2008a). Vulnerability scanning preceding penetration testing is standard practice for illuminating potential information asset exposures (R. Davis, 2008a). Technological vulnerability scanning solutions report potential configuration weaknesses (R. Davis, 2008a). Chat software, packet injections, password crackers, and file disassemblers are standard IT penetration testing tools used to assess vulnerability.

Risk Evaluation

An IAP risk evaluation permits making decisions concerning risk materiality or significance to the entity and whether management will accept or treat each risk examined. Threats, opportunities, and vulnerability analysis are the primary risk assessment enablers permitting an effective and efficient security control system deployment (R. Davis, 2008a). However, continuous monitoring is necessary to ensure threats, opportunities, and vulnerabilities do not erode the security control system (R. Davis, 2008a). After reviewing threats, opportunities, and vulnerability assessment reports, organizational units may require IAP remediation to ensure cybersecurity expectational resilience (R. Davis, 2008a, 2017; Yaokumah & Brown, 2014). Unfortunately, simultaneously reducing IAP risks to a tolerable level for all potential IAP deficiencies or weaknesses is usually prohibitively expensive (Nazareth & Choi, 2015; R. Davis, 2008a). Given the expense limitation, a risk grading system assists in information asset deployment evaluation and prioritization (Nazareth & Choi, 2015; R. Davis, 2008a; Rubino & Vitolla, 2014).

Before applying any controls, the risk level confronting an entity is gross or raw (R. Davis, 2008a). A gross or raw risk evaluation permits awareness of potential detrimental effects regarding information assets. As conceptualized in Figure 3.7, single or multiple threats may exist for an information asset deployment opportunity (R. Davis, 2008a). During the ordinary course of performing information asset risk analysis, the assessor should consider security threats associated with an information asset deployment opportunity (R. Davis, 2008a). Thus, if undertaking a deployment opportunity makes an information asset vulnerable, and a threat can exploit the vulnerability, there is a protection risk (R. Davis, 2008a).

A risk assessor can evaluate individual IAP risks for likelihood and cost of occurrence when threats, opportunities, and vulnerability determination use quantitative methods (R. Davis, 2008a). An individual risk rating is derivable by using each Threat Assessment ALE when assigning individual information asset risk.

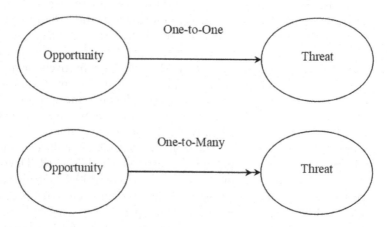

Figure 3.7 Opportunity Canonical Attribute Mappings.

Note: Adapted from *Ensuring Information Assets Protection* by R. E. Davis, 2009, Lulu. Copyright 2009 by Robert E. Davis. Adapted with permission.

Alternatively, the risk assessor can use the formula:

$$\text{IIAR} = \text{T} \times \text{V} \times \text{A (R. Davis, 2008a)} \qquad (3.5)$$

IIAR is the resulting individual information asset risk valuation. As multiplicands, T is the total individual threat valuation of the information asset, and V symbolizes the information asset's total individual vulnerability valuation. A is the total individual asset valuation of the information asset.

As previously discussed, qualitative risk analysis identifies and ranks protection mechanisms individually and relatively to impute the value for all identified information assets (R. Davis, 2008a). Critical qualitative risk evaluation elements include asset value, threat or opportunity assessment, and vulnerability assessment for each information asset (R. Davis, 2008a). In combination, the evaluation elements represent components for determining an information asset's qualitative valuation (R. Davis, 2008a). A risk assessor can evaluate individual IAP risks qualitatively using control valuations (R. Davis, 2008a). Employing the control valuation method requires an information asset's relative risk assignment based on control strength (R. Davis, 2008a). As shown in Table 3.2, control risk evaluations include inscribing the relationship between control adequacy and information asset risks for appropriate ratings (R. Davis, 2008a).

Control adequacy determination considers directness, selectivity, method-of-application, and follow-up (R. Davis, 2008a, 2020). Directness is the extent a designed or deployed control relates to a control objective (R. Davis, 2008a, 2010, 2020). Selectivity references the control repetition magnitude, distinguishing characteristics or other criteria for identifying an exception condition (R. Davis, 2008a, 2010, 2020). How the control placement occurred represents the method-of-application (R. Davis, 2008a, 2010, 2020). Control follow-up is the activities pursued upon exception condition discovery (R. Davis, 2008a, 2010, 2020).

Procedurally, if a risk assessor uses the control risk evaluation method, the most significant controls upon which IAP control adequacy resides require identification (R. Davis, 2008a). A risk assessor can then cross-reference controls to information assets (R. Davis, 2008a).

Table 3.2 Qualitative Control Strength Classifications with Descriptions

Classification	Description
Adequate	IAP control is appropriate and functioning effectively. Generally, the control element is unimpaired or, if partially impaired, is not significant enough to affect IAP control performance or functionality. Control weakness may exist, but the resulting exposure is not significant.
Needs Strengthening	IAP control is weak, resulting in an unacceptable risk level. Consequently, control element impairment is significant enough to affect activity performance or functionality. Immediate management attention is required. If left uncorrected, the situation may deteriorate to an inadequate control condition.
Inadequate	IAP control has a notable deficiency resulting in a significant risk level. Therefore, the control element impairment renders the control unreliable. Immediate corrective action is imperative.

Note: Adapted from *Ensuring Information Assets Protection* by R. E. Davis, 2009, Lulu. Copyright 2009 by Robert E. Davis. Adapted with permission.

After that, a risk assessor should indicate risk valuations for each information asset control strength on a worksheet (R. Davis, 2008a). A controls' risk evaluation can consider employing the valuation frequency, weakest link, or high watermark technique for assessing individual information asset risks (R. Davis, 2008a).

There are distinct methods available for information asset risk prioritization (R. Davis, 2008a). Nonetheless, IAP risk prioritization occurs by using comparative risk ranking. Quantitative and qualitative risk ranking necessitates assessing each information asset valuation (R. Davis, 2008a). Methods available to rank IAP risks include estimation, categorization, and serialization (R. Davis, 2008a). Estimation ranking uses potential risk dollar amount approximations to determine the degree of a single information asset risk (R. Davis, 2008a). Categorization ranking uses individual information asset risk rates to classify risk ratings in descending order by defined suite rankings (R. Davis, 2008a). Serialization ranking uses numerical values in descending order from 1 to "n" items, with 1 assigned to the highest risk and sequentially ranking lower risks reflecting individual information asset risk magnitudes (R. Davis, 2008a).

Countermeasures

IAP risk responses are the means through which entity management elects to administrate individual risks (R. Davis, 2008a). Appropriate IAP risk responses provide countermeasures for threat, opportunity, or vulnerability exposures (R. Davis, 2008a). IAP countermeasures are any action, process, device, or system that prevents, deters, detects, or corrects the adverse effects of threat, opportunity, and vulnerability exposures (R. Davis, 2008a). Nonetheless, IAP threats and vulnerabilities may present opportunities depending on risk assessor, committee, or project team creativity (R. Davis, 2008a).

High-level IAP risk strategies are classifiable as transference, avoidance, reduction, or acceptance. Transference strategies are the partial or full risk assumption by another entity (R. Davis, 2008a). Avoidance strategies devise the means for risky activity evasion. Reduction strategies are risk responses designed and deployed to decrease the impact or likelihood of incidents or events (R. Davis, 2008a). Acceptance strategies embrace IAP risk and associated consequences (R. Davis, 2008a).

Mathematically, risk probability values can range from 0 to 100% (R. Davis, 2008a). If elected, IAP transference, avoidance, and reduction strategies are risk treatments that decrease risks to less than 100% (R. Davis, 2008a) but elevate to a level greater than 0. Contrastingly, risk acceptance strategies will not affect IAP risk probability values (R. Davis, 2008a), because risk treatment is an unacceptable risk response option.

Though transference and avoidance are viable risk countermeasure candidates, risk reduction methods are the primary IAP risk strategy for most entities due to potential revenue losses when inadequate controls exist (R. Davis, 2008a). A controls-based approach to IAP risks enables ensuring acceptable entity risk level sustainment (R. Davis, 2008a). Preventive, detective, and corrective controls usually protect entity information assets (R. Davis, 2008a). Cybersecurity controls selection as technological countermeasures should reflect error frequencies, error magnitudes, and error detection costs (R. Davis, 2008a). Nonetheless, the adopted definition of entity controls affects the countermeasure selection options (R. Davis, 2008a).

Mitigating or compensating controls are classifiable as IAP risk countermeasures (R. Davis, 2008a). Mitigating controls address control weakness risks through transference, avoidance, or reduction treatment (R. Davis, 2008a, 2020). Moreover, mitigating controls lower risks corresponding directly to achieving IAP control objectives (R. Davis, 2008a). In contrast, compensating controls reflect additional control tasks, activities, or processes indirectly corresponding to accomplishing IAP control objectives (R. Davis, 2008a). However, compensating controls serve to strengthen controls directly related to IAP control objectives (R. Davis, 2008a).

Control measures available to reduce or mitigate IAP risks include bonding employees, pre-employment screening, promotion screening, segregation-of-functions, segregation-of-duties, reconciliations, activities monitoring, approval requirements, authorization requirements, document design, document use, authentication, ownership rights, and legal obligations (R. Davis, 2008a). Wherever practical, deployable control measures should contain irregularity and illegal acts prevention, deterrence, or detection methods that do not transcend the entity control perimeter (R. Davis, 2008a). When there is a need for supplement countermeasures, more than one mitigating or compensating control may be necessary for providing equivalent or comparable direct IAP (R. Davis, 2008a).

Control Evaluation

Appropriate entity IAP deployment necessitates effectual information security controls (R. Davis, 2008a). Informational threat or opportunity and vulnerability risk assessments need to provide mechanisms for alternative responses that minimize or avoid risks (R. Davis, 2008a). Management usually is concerned with the cost of controls and derivable benefits from using IAP control deployments while pursuing the entity and IT strategic direction (R. Davis, 2008a). Risk assessors should consider IAP control synergy during the risk assessment control evaluation to ensure effectiveness (R. Davis, 2008a). ISG program operating effectiveness exists if an entity's manager-leaders deploy IAP processes providing reasonable assurance of transparent control objectives and goals achievement (R. Davis, 2008a).

Entity manager-leaders may find defining and engaging compensating or mitigating controls to appropriately address risks necessary or prudent (R. Davis, 2008a). When a compensating or mitigating control is necessary for an information asset, minimally, the ISG program owner needs to inscribe a complete and convincing explanation regarding how the compensating or mitigating control supplies an appropriate capability or protection level. Moreover, the ISG program owner must inscribe a complete and convincing explanation regarding why a directly related IAP control is not sufficient (R. Davis, 2008a). The ISG program owner must also inscribe that entity management assessed and formally accepted the risk associated with employing the selected compensating or mitigating control (R. Davis, 2008a). After that, using a compensating and mitigating IAP control needs inscription in a risk register and approval by the authorizing manager-leader responsible for the information asset (R. Davis, 2008a).

Information asset control materiality or significance needs analysis to assess control effects (R. Davis, 2008a). IAP risks after applying controls require evaluation to determine the development of acceptable risk levels. Formulations can express the risk exposure factors counterbalancing the security strategy relationship when considering risk tolerance levels associated with information assets. Value Analysis examines the ongoing program, project, or process costs to determine if more beneficial resources are substitutable (R. Davis, 2008a). The value of control techniques is in conceptual representations, usefulness as interpretation instruments when determining objective accomplishment, and highlighting operational problems and weaknesses that signal the need for a risk treatment strategy (R. Davis, 2008a).

The control cost also needs weighing against the benefits derived from deploying the control (R. Davis, 2008a). A comparative analysis considers the difference between assessed risks and information protection controls (R. Davis, 2008a). Analytically, the total annual loss expectation needs comparison to the annualized IAP control cost for reducing risk (R. Davis, 2008a) by individual information assets. Cost–benefit analysis employing an expected value approach provides an objective basis for setting control value cost limits (R. Davis, 2008a). Establishing IAP control value limits establish the decision criteria for determining control investigation (R. Davis, 2008a). The limits of proceeding with designing and deploying a control need inscription to ensure that the investigation costs are less than or equal to the benefits derived (R. Davis, 2008a).

When evaluating controls, the security risk assessment team must be willing to accept spending sufficient time understanding facts and analyzing the entity in terms of skills, resources, and positions (relative to the control environment) to ferret out germane issues (R. Davis, 2008a). Risk assessment team members should begin the control evaluation by reviewing the risk evaluation and countermeasures (R. Davis, 2008a). To ensure the capturing of all pertinent information, risk evaluation and countermeasure review should occur three times. The first review is to obtain familiarization with the risk evaluation and countermeasures. During the second review, risk assessors should note essential data and information in the risk evaluation and the documentation of countermeasures. During the third review, the security risk assessment team should perform a thorough situational analysis and develop discussion questions (R. Davis, 2008a).

Pertinent IAP fact analysis may require review participator diligence in discussions to enable isolating significant threats, opportunities, or vulnerabilities from the amassed risk assessment data (R. Davis, 2008a). Review participators must continuously be vigilant regarding the entity perimeter and cognizant that the IAP control system design needs to address the entire entity configuration (R. Davis, 2008a). In the absence of using the Delphi Technique for gaining consensus, discussing IAP threats, opportunities, and vulnerabilities becomes vital and necessary for determining appropriate risk responses (R. Davis, 2008a). During the control evaluation process, review participators test ideas and concepts and evaluate analyses and potential action plans (R. Davis, 2008a). Each participant's extensive review preparation is necessary to ensure fruitful discussions (R. Davis, 2008a). Deliberations of IAP issues and questions can raise new issues and questions generated through expertise pooling and conclusions from personnel with different risk abstraction levels (R. Davis, 2008a; Tsohou et al., 2015). After completing the control evaluation process, IAP inherent risk and control risk should receive clear delineation from residual risk to help management understand control limitations (R. Davis, 2008a).

Control Risk

Identifying, rating, and ranking IAP control risks may be a paradigm change for the security risk assessment team. Control deployments do not eliminate IAP risks (Barton et al., 2016; R. Davis, 2008a). However, controls can aid in managing IAP risks (R. Davis, 2008a). Regarding ISG risk management, IAP control risk is the possibility that the control will not prevent, detect, or correct an undesirable incident or event (R. Davis, 2008a). Axiomatically, control risk inversely corresponds to the relevant information asset control (R. Davis, 2008a). Hence, on a quantitative scale ranging from 0 to 1, if the control risk is approaching 1, then the control is approaching 0 (R. Davis, 2008a, 2010). Alternatively, when using a qualitative control risk scale, the inverse correspondence to control addresses a nonnumerical range (R. Davis, 2008a, 2010).

Entity control systems are governance requirement projections that can have misconceived control elements because control structuring is dependent on the architectural frame-of-reference (Magdaraog, Jr., 2014; R. Davis, 2008a, 2017). Stemming from managerialism, constructed control mechanisms may only minutely affect market inefficiencies and resulting governance issues (Raelin & Bondy, 2013). Furthermore, entity-centric control systems may embrace mistaken assumptions regarding required control assurance levels to satisfy stakeholders (R. Davis, 2008a, 2017). Insularly, employing risk-based IAP controls may also do little to enhance stakeholder fiduciary confidence in the entity personnel because manager-leaders typically can override deployed controls (R. Davis, 2008a). The security risk assessment team should consider control system limitations in an unethical control environment and enable a reasonable person to deduce that controls are a risk source (R. Davis, 2008a).

Residual Risk

Residual risk is the remaining information asset exposure after control deployments as risk reductions (R. Davis, 2008a; Rubino & Vitolla, 2014) for a threat, opportunity, or vulnerability. Reporting residual risks separate from control risks can crystallize the entity's risk appetite (R. Davis, 2008a). Reporting residual risk separate from control risks can also ensure the formal acceptance of IAP residual risks by manager-leaders (Fenz et al., 2014). Thus, through residual risk reporting, manager-leaders can determine if IAP residual risks are within an acceptable level (Barton, 2014) or need additional risk treatment.

Inherent Risk

IAP inherent risk is the exposure in the absence of risk treatment (Rubino & Vitolla, 2014). IAP inherent risk considers the nature of the information asset, prior history, and the nature of materiality or significance (R. Davis, 2008a). IAP inherent risks can receive separate inscriptions from other residual risks (R. Davis, 2008a; Rubino & Vitolla, 2014). After that, inherent risk ratings and ranking can enable IAP action plan development (R. Davis, 2008a).

Action Plan

Once risk assessment team members reach a prioritization agreement, the next logical risk assessment activity is IAP action plan development (R. Davis, 2008a). Planning is necessary before any managerial ISG program function can comply with the established risk appetite (R. Davis, 2008a). Action plans supply instructions for achieving specific objectives or goals through procedures, available resources, and monitoring activities (Luecke, 2005). An action plan demonstrates entity managements' desire to transfer, avoid, reduce, or accept

IAP risks (R. Davis, 2008a). IAP action planning translates strategy into measurable tactical and operational expectations (R. Davis, 2008a). Moreover, IAP action planning retranslates expectations into policies, procedures, directives, standards, and rules (R. Davis, 2008a). Functionally, the selection of ISG program goals precedes the design of policies and procedures (R. Davis, 2008a).

Action procedures provide direction while addressing assignment ownership, identifying every expected action, ambit limitations, and task timetable. A practical action plan includes determining the necessary resources, identifying organizational interlocks, setting performance measures, and predicting economic effects (Luecke, 2005). When ISG program team members become familiar with all risk assessment elements and acknowledge satisfaction with the control evaluation, action plan development can commence (R. Davis, 2008a). The newly formulated action plan may call for changes in strategic countermeasure decisions (R. Davis, 2008a). A complete root strategy reformulation may be necessary (R. Davis, 2008a). Alternatively, circumstances may call for a plan that includes a well-developed strategic design and operational plans for each IAP area under consideration (R. Davis, 2008a).

ISG program team members should also develop alternate action plans using what–if scenarios extending beyond the IAP risk assessment results (R. Davis, 2008a). Contingency Theory suggests there is no single best leadership approach (R. Davis, 2008a; Yukl, 2011). Therefore, consideration and analysis of situational factors can provide more effective leadership (R. Davis, 2008a; Yukl, 2011). Supporting contingency posturing are IAP plan commitments needing appropriate risk treatment for future actions. Specifically, the accepted optimum risk solution can create future problems (R. Davis, 2008a). Consequently, risk assessment situational analysis of assumptions regarding future events may suggest a need for contingency plans providing alternative IAP action plan solutions (R. Davis, 2008a).

Control Objective Selection

Control objective planning is the conduit for assessing and evaluating organizational IAP strengths and weaknesses based on management's entity governance philosophy (R. Davis, 2008a). Control objectives define the expected purpose or result of controls (Davis, 2008a). ISG program control objective selection conveys essentiality to sustaining entity information assets (R. Davis, 2008a). Determining IAP control objectives emulates the establishment of operational and IT objectives (R. Davis, 2008a). Thus, IAP control objective planning allows forecasting future IAP direction and relevant influences, considering entity strengths and weaknesses (R. Davis, 2008a). Managerially accepted IAP control objectives enable policy creation and deployment (R. Davis, 2008a). Performing ISG maturity assessments can help determine where IAP improvements are most needed (e.g., R. Davis, 2017; Yaokumah, 2014; Yaokumah & Brown, 2014).

Control objectives mirror prior premising or planning assumptions generated during development (R. Davis, 2008a). Operational, IT, and IAP control objectives provide the expectations against which deployed IAP control measurements can determine objective achievement (R. Davis, 2008a). Usually, ISG program control objectives rely on IAP control objective planning techniques. From a systems' perspective, the design, deployment, maintenance, and disposal of policies, directives, procedures, standards, and rules are control objective life cycle elements (R. Davis, 2011). Operationally, IAP control objective life cycle elements are available administrative tools to obtain desired results while preventing, detecting, or correcting errors, mistakes, omissions, irregularities, and illegal acts (R. Davis, 2011).

The relationship between managerial requirements and control objectives is bidirectional (R. Davis, 2008a). Information security requirements are convertible into information security control objectives considering the bidirectional linkage between managerial requirements and control objectives (R. Davis, 2008a). Information needs to maintain conformance with all applicable de facto and de jure standards while achieving control objectives. From an ISG perspective, information criteria empower information asset measurement. ISG manager-leaders should establish overall and detailed IAP objectives enabling congruency with operational and IT control objectives (R. Davis, 2017).

Information criteria due diligence by ISG manager-leaders usually permits operational and IT control objective achievement (R. Davis, 2008a).

Management's adopted high-level control objectives indicate the operational requirements for information and IT affected by IAP deployments (R. Davis, 2008a). Various overall and detailed cybersecurity control objectives have received inscription by for-profit and not-for-profit entities to establish foundational IAP control objectives (R. Davis, 2008a). Potential IAP control objective development can occur using the Delphi Technique, Strengths–Weaknesses–Opportunities–Threats Analysis, The Four Disciplines of Security Management: An Information Security Reference Model, and Control Objectives for Information and Related Technology framework (R. Davis, 2008a). However, selected IAP control objectives should reflect prescribed undertakings designed to ensure effective and efficient processes that deliver legally compliant information confidentiality, integrity, and availability (R. Davis, 2008a).

As depicted in Figure 3.8, when designing an ISG program, control objective selections are derivable from the IAP risk assessment (R. Davis, 2008a). After the adoption of control

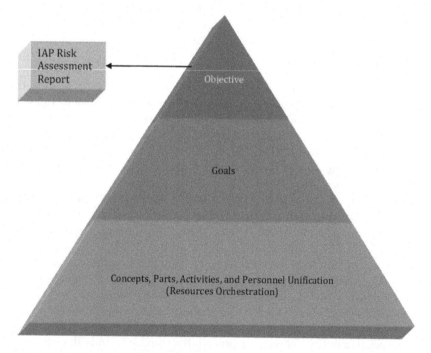

Figure 3.8 Top-down IAP Controls-Based Approach.

Note: Adapted from *Ensuring Information Assets Protection* by R. E. Davis, 2009, Lulu. Copyright 2009 by Robert E. Davis. Adapted with permission.

objectives, management should determine control goals. Next, management should connect (or interrelate) concepts, parts, activities, and personnel allowing unified operations for achieving established control objectives and goals (R. Davis, 2008a). Entity manager-leaders typically enable processes using control objectives designed to comply with external and internal operational requirements (R. Davis, 2008a).

Resource orchestration typically requires management to deploy policies, procedures, and standards for processes (R. Davis, 2008a). Circumstantially, directive and rule deployments occur to relay unified operations' intentions while performance measures set task diligence expectations (R. Davis, 2008a). Control objectives and goal transformations into unified operations with integrated operational IAP policies, directives, procedures, standards, measures, and rules are processes generally reflecting appropriately designed IAP controls (R. Davis, 2008a).

Control Goal Selection

Activity goals can drive efficient operational processes, with detrimental IAP consequences (R. Davis, 2008a). Consequently, when developing the ISG program guiding principles, management should consider compliance requirements and security standards before adopting goals (R. Davis, 2008a). ISG program goals are obtainable from an adopted security framework or designable by management based on approved IAP control objectives (R. Davis, 2008a). However, IAP control goals need to align with the entity and IT objectives (Brotby, 2006; R. Davis, 2008a).

Control goal achievement measurements need setting when a control goal comes under consideration for adoption (R. Davis, 2008a). IAP control goal accomplishment indicators attempt to define activities that measure IAP control goal success, assisting in achieving one or more objectives (R. Davis, 2008a). Adaptively, IAP Key Goal Indicators convey critical activity measurements for assessing control goal achievements (R. Davis, 2008a). IAP control goal prioritization can determine the selection of Key Goal Indicators (Brotby, 2006; R. Davis, 2008a).

Organizing

ISG plan development generally requires structural organization (R. Davis, 2008a). The organization of ISG occurs to prevent chaos (R. Davis, 2008a) through identification and classification for functionalization. ISG organizing is designing and structuring systems, processes (R. Davis, 2008a), activities, and roles to accomplish adopted objectives or goals. Consequently, structuring permits coordinating and integrating processes and activities into a cohesive whole, moving toward objective achievement (R. Davis, 2008a). Structuring also enables activity segmentation into tasks, each with task objectives and goals (R. Davis, 2008a). Moreover, ISG requires the appropriate assignment of roles to achieve program objectives and goals (R. Davis, 2008a).

Cybernetics control theory illuminates the role of organizational structure in information governance (Boyson, 2014; R. Davis, 2017). Information is definable as a quasiphysical concept connected to an organizational degree in a system (Boyson, 2014; R. Davis, 2017). From the systems' perspective, ISG structures are the results of process (Misangyi & Acharya, 2014; R. Davis, 2017). Structures deployed by an ISG system allot responsibilities and rights within the structures and necessitate assurance that manager-leaders are operating effectively and expectantly within the defined structures (R. Davis, 2017; Singh et al., 2013; Too & Weaver, 2014). A manager-leader's role is to administrate within the defined ISG system framework (R. Davis, 2017; Too & Weaver, 2014). Thus, ISG reflects the system through which an entity directs and controls information security activities (Kushwaha, 2016; R. Davis, 2017; Williams et al., 2013).

ISG-designed tasks and deployed technology affect organizational structures (Guadalupe et al., 2014; Hitt & Brynjolfsson, 1997; Meyer & Rowan, 1977; R. Davis, 2017; Sor, 2004). Thus, information security is structural and technical (Boyson, 2014; R. Davis, 2017). Information security solutions may require development or acquisitions to realize an ISG strategy (R. Davis, 2012a). An ISG program necessitates alignment of entity functions, horizontally and vertically, considering authority–activity relationships and information system ownerships (R. Davis, 2008a). Entities typically use Simple, Bureaucratic, Professional, or Divisional organizational structures (Mukherji, 2002; R. Davis, 2017; Steiger et al., 2014). In contrast, where bureaucracy, complexity, and centralization are excessively confining, the Adhocracy organizational structure supports innovating and operating to overcome environmental circumstances (Mukherji, 2002; R. Davis, 2017; Steiger et al., 2014). Consequently, less traditional entities should rely on informal organizational structures strengthened through boundary spanning and alliance-building managerial techniques.

Individual intellectual capacity and reasoning power limitations are general inducements for a chief information security officer to request group consultations with subject matter experts (R. Davis, 2008a) and the ISG program team members. Consequently, a management advisory or steering committee formation can determine risks, objectives, and goals for the ISG program (R. Davis, 2008a). Organizationally diversified representation should exist within the ISG risk assessment group to ensure relevant items come under consideration and receive appropriate treatment, without hindering productivity (R. Davis, 2008a).

Orchestrating

The organizing process transforms the IAP action plan into controllable areas and includes activities grouping based on efficient usage of available resources. People, information, processes, and infrastructure are ISG resource classifications requiring appropriate management (De Haes et al., 2013; R. Davis, 2008a, 2017). Entrusted manager-leaders primarily pursue objective and goal accomplishment through skillful resource usage (R. Davis, 2008a). Skillful resource use typically includes financial budgeting to determine cost variations from expected expenditures (R. Davis, 2008a). Prescriptively, if the entity's control environment enables superior IAP control analysis, superior information security designs for deployment are feasible (R. Davis, 2008a).

ISG administration requires employing available personnel considering the external and internal environments (R. Davis, 2008a). Several relationships are usually present in an entity's organizational structure that can integrate resources based on roles (R. Davis, 2008a). Executive team structure can be a pivotal organizational design choice (Guadalupe et al., 2014). Nonetheless, ISG program team membership selection is critical to the assessment process of the effectiveness of goals and objectives (R. Davis, 2008a). ISG program team members assisting in determining risks, control objectives, and control goals can be the same individuals (R. Davis, 2008a). However, the entity ISG program committee membership should include representatives from:

- information security,
- IT operations,
- network infrastructure,
- systems programming,

- application programming,
- database administration,
- systems development, and
- information asset ownership (R. Davis, 2008a).

Entity employees benefit from knowledge sharing and knowledge application (Findikli et al., 2015; R. Davis, 2017). However, organizational structures have a slightly weaker effect on establishing security knowledge sharing in entities (Flores et al., 2014; R. Davis, 2017). Prominently, researchers found that business-based information security management had no significant direct effect on security knowledge sharing (R. Davis, 2017). Moreover, the knowledge barrier prevents efficient communication between information security manager-leaders and business manager-leaders (R. Davis, 2017). The business manager-leaders may internalize the words in an information security discussion yet have no real technical understanding (Lopez, 2012; R. Davis, 2017). As a remedy to the knowledge-sharing challenges, entity manager-leaders can apply Beer's organizational cybernetics framework to ensure a viable governance structure (Arif, 2016) for efficient communication between information security manager-leaders and business manager-leaders (R. Davis, 2017).

The ISG manager-leader needs to prepare and administrate an ISG program designed to inform employees regarding necessary IAP (R. Davis, 2008a). Designing and structuring behaviors are interdependent and multi-dimensional tasks demanding an understanding of managerial principles and practices (R. Davis, 2008a). Introductory IAP training attendance should be mandatory for entity personnel to reduce intentional and unintentional information security risks (R. Davis, 2008a). For newly recruited entity personnel, through coordination with the entity's human resource department, the formal orientation program should minimally include distributing or referencing the IAP policies and related procedures to reduce behavioral risks (R. Davis, 2008a). Subsequently, continuing IAP training needs to occur periodically to sustain tolerable risk levels (R. Davis, 2008a). Additionally, employee promotions, transfers, or terminations necessitate change notification submission to the information security function to increase, decrease, or remove information asset access authorizations (R. Davis, 2008a).

Organizational structures are viewable as organizational processes instead of managerial reporting arrangements (Arif, 2016). ISG manager-leaders should evaluate which practice deployments correlate with ISG effectiveness (R. Davis, 2017). Information security breaches lead to additional costs and significantly affect the entity's reputation (Safa et al., 2016; R. Davis, 2017). ISG manager-leaders should fully implement domain processes to address the challenges for preventing and deterring information security breaches (R. Davis, 2017). ISG manager-leaders should also ensure that selected domain processes are transparent for sharing with stakeholders (R. Davis, 2017). With reliable knowledge acquisition through domain processes, entity manager-leaders can deploy measures that can significantly improve an ISG program. Entity manager-leaders and other stakeholders may use the constructed domain processes as an analytical tool to predict ISG effectiveness realization.

Technologically, an ISG program should address protection requirement integration during information asset development projects (R. Davis, 2008a). Commonly, large IT development projects include the conceptual description, functional requirements and specifications, technical requirements and specifications, design, coding, tests, and implementation (R. Davis, 2020). An ISG program should have security professionals participating in the design, acquisition, testing, and maintenance of IT development projects to ensure that using the Safeguarding-by-Design model, protections function as intended, and protection features resist compromise during maintenance (R. Davis, 2008a). The inscription of cybersecurity principles and strategies should take place during conceptual description development. Functional specifications, testing, and implementation calls for determining IAP requirements, operational verification of each IAP requirement, and procedures for integrating existing security countermeasures, respectively (R. Davis, 2008a).

Directing

Organizational directing is the managerial function of regulating the activities or action courses of entity personnel. Organizational directing by management should enable employees to contribute effectively and efficiently toward accomplishing objectives and goals (R. Davis, 2008a). Managerial authority delegation provides the right to direct and exact performance from others, including the right to prescribe the means and methods for work performance (R. Davis, 2008a). Officially accepted managerial authority implies granted power (R. Davis, 2008a). Power enables edict and command enforcement (R. Davis, 2008a). A managerial obligation is to administrate assigned or assumed programs, systems, activities, or tasks without compromising fiduciary expectations (R. Davis, 2008a). Classically, a formally derived fiduciary obligation from managerial delegation is inherent in most entity positions (R. Davis, 2008a).

Communication can have a positive relationship with organizational performance (Posthuma et al., 2013). A primary element of directing employees is the communication strategies and approaches used within the entity (Hart, 2016). Depending on an entity's technological advancement, employer expectations are conveyable and receivable through auditory, visual, and sensation activities that enable current or future processing for a decisional application (Chen et al., 2012; R. Davis, 2008a). When directing activities, conveyed message effectiveness is only measurable when the sender perceives a change in the receiver(s)'s behavior (Chen et al., 2012; R. Davis, 2008a).

Directing communication effectiveness is determinable by the sender by observing a message's effect on the receiver and seeking receiver feedback (R. Davis, 2008a). There is a sender's obligation to solicit the receiver's feedback to ensure that the communication process is complete (R. Davis, 2008a). Conversely, the receiver(s) should supply feedback to the sender (R. Davis, 2008a) to avoid conveyed message misunderstanding. The importance of feedback in probing communication process effectiveness illuminates asynchronous memorandum issuance limitations (R. Davis, 2008a).

The entity oversight committee or executive management defines directive settings at the topmost entity managerial level (Edwards, 2013). Next, senior management transforms directives into entity policies and standards at the middle entity managerial level (Edwards, 2013). The entity policies and standards serve as the baselines for execution and control (Edwards, 2013). Subsequently, junior management transforms entity policies and standards into procedures for ensuring expected execution at the lower entity managerial level (Edwards, 2013). The topmost, middle, and lower entity managerial levels are viewable as strategic, tactical, and operational IAP management layers, respectively (Edwards, 2013; Yaokumah, 2015). Notably, entity employee conformance depends upon the ISG structure, management commitment, IAP objectives and intentions, IAP processes, and guidelines concerning why and how individuals can demonstrate IAP expectation adherence (Edwards, 2013).

Principles are general statements that convey guiding values or philosophies (Posthuma et al., 2013). Entity principles should reflect mission, vision, and value statements

(Posthuma et al., 2013). Typically referenced as guiding principles, the managerial intent of mission, vision, and value statements is provisioning rational direction for lower organizational level personnel (Posthuma et al., 2013). Organizational directing starts at the strategic level, where executive manager-leaders indicate the significance of information assets and the assistance information assets provided for fulfilling the entity's strategic vision (Coertze & Von Solms, 2013). In directing ISG action plans, there are nine principles for creating an IAP culture (Barton et al., 2016). The IAP culture principles are (a) awareness, (b) responsibility, (c) response, (d) ethics, (e) participation, (f) risk assessment, (g) security design and deployment, (h) security management, and (i) reassessment (Barton et al., 2016).

Controlling

Potential exposures presented by resource-users include perpetration of irregularities and illegal acts (R. Davis, 2008a). Management's control methods over compliance requirements can ensure the deployment of appropriate measures to ascertain whether the entity's personnel understand the implemented governance practices and employees are following governance processes as intended (R. Davis, 2008b). Legal compliance procedures for maintaining ethical behavior should be set by middle management and promoted through exemplary behavior (R. Davis, 2008a, 2008b).

Identifying control requirements enabling compliance with laws and regulations, policies, directives, and best practices is an ISG program management responsibility (R. Davis, 2008a). Consequently, the chief information security officer or a designated ISG program manager should determine the

- nature of controls,
- type of controls,
- applicable standards,
- performance measurements,
- performance comparisons,
- evaluation methods,
- correction methods, and
- control techniques (R. Davis, 2008a).

Control activities help ensure the carrying out of management directives. When contributing to controlling an entity, manager-leaders can deploy organization, policies, procedures, personnel, accounting, budgeting, reporting, and control reviews (R. Davis, 2010, 2020). Nevertheless, selected control activities usually receive support by using information assets to help achieve entity objectives and goals (R. Davis, 2008a). Specifically, entity systems, processes, activities, and tasks typically require digitally encoded information to meet organizational objectives. Entity manager-leaders need to ensure interdependence between strategic planning and IAP deployments (R. Davis, 2020). IAP must align with and enable the entity employees to apply informational sources fully. Thereby, through appropriate IAP, manager-leaders can maximize benefits, capitalize on opportunities, and gain a competitive advantage for the entity (R. Davis, 2008a).

In technology-driven entity environments, how well manager-leaders administrate system changes is proportional to triumphant delivery on operational objectives (R. Davis, 2008a). Contextually, IT changes are inevitable and necessary to remain operationally viable (R. Davis, 2008a). Consequently, the ISG program must include monitoring pertinent performance measurements (R. Davis, 2008a). To fulfill the monitoring requirement, information asset performance tracking summary records need to indicate change success rates, such as the percentage of changes deployed without an incident, service outage, or impairment for subsequent comparative analysis (R. Davis, 2008a). Furthermore, IAP change management procedures need to support incident reductions and provide appropriate incident or event responses (R. Davis, 2008a). When an incident occurs within the entity's IAP ambit, organizational personnel need to follow accepted standards for preserving evidence to enable comprehensive activity evaluation (R. Davis, 2008a).

Innovative technology adoption can raise security threats (Chou, 2015) and present challenges to manager-leaders that demand a shift in operational procedures, culture, or mindset (Catinean & Cândea, 2013). As technological innovations extend social influence, ethical issues expand for entity employees (Stahl et al., 2014). "In response, a managerial moral assessment concerning what is sound and unsound about new devices (or methods that may emerge; Stahl et al., 2014), and what is appropriate and inappropriate IT options use become imperative (Stahl et al., 2016)" (R. Davis, 2017, p. 55).

A trustworthy record furnishes existence proof (Duranti, 2010). When sought, record content can recreate or validate an existing state, regardless of applied medium or defined attributes (Duranti, 2010). Each entity record created or received should be in pursuance of sustaining activity accountability or compliance with statutory responsibilities (R. Davis, 2010). Records can exist as tangible items, such as paper documents, or intangible items, such as digitally encoded files (Duranti, 2010; R. Davis, 2008a). Practices are the specific methods and procedures that the organization adopts to implement an entity's principles and policies (Posthuma et al., 2013). Thus, record management is definable as the life cycle practices for administrating entity data groups. Characteristically, record management practices address identifying, classifying, prioritizing, preserving, securing, archiving, tracking, retrieving, and destroying data groups.

When using a technological solution, record management systems store, process, and retrieve data sets. Additionally, a well-designed record management system aids in protecting an entity from unauthorized data set manipulation, demonstrates compliance with applicable laws and regulations, and increases organizational efficiency by promoting the disposition of outdated or reclassified items. Commonly, IT application files are a repository of related records, with each record representing related data (R. Davis, 2010). Given the indicated context, the replacement of paper documents with electronic records can significantly affect how an entity conducts affairs and organizational structuring. Specifically, management may reduce or relinquish several traditional processes for paper-based systems with electronic record workflow deployment. Likewise, the design and operationalization of new tasks within the automated processes must ensure encoded data resist altercation, loss, or erasure.

References

Arif, S. (2016). Leadership for change: Proposed organizational development by incorporating systems thinking and quality tools. *Business Process Management Journal*, 22, 939–956. https://doi.org/10.1108/BPMJ-01-2016-0025

Barton, K. A. (2014). *Information system security commitment: A study of external influences on senior management* (Publication No. 3666132) [Dissertation, Nova Southeastern University]. ProQuest Dissertations Publishing.

Barton, K. A., Tejay, G., Lane, M., & Terrell, S. (2016). Information system security commitment: A study of external influences on senior management. *Computers & Security*, 59, 9–25. https://doi.org/10.1016/j.cose.2016.02.007

Boyson, S. (2014). Cyber supply chain risk management: Revolutionizing the strategic control of critical IT systems. *Technovation, 34*, 342–353. http://doi.org/10.1016/j.technovation.2014.02.001

Brotby, K. W. (2006). *Information security governance: Guidance for boards of directors and executive management* (2nd ed.). IT Governance Institute.

Catinean, I., & Cândea, D. (2013). Characteristics of the cloud computing model as a disruptive innovation. *Review of International Comparative Management, 14*, 783–803. www.rmci.ase.ro

Chen, Y., Ramamurthy, K., & Wen, K. (2012). Organizations' information security policy compliance: Stick or carrot approach? *Journal of Management Information Systems, 29*(3), 157–188. https://doi.org/10.2753/MIS0742-1222290305

Chou, D. C. (2015). Cloud computing: A value creation model. *Computer Standards & Interfaces, 38*, 72–77. https://doi.org/10.1016/j.csi.2014.10.001

Christ, T. W. (2013). The worldview matrix as a strategy when designing mixed methods research. *International Journal of Multiple Research Approaches, 7*, 110–118. https://doi.org/10.5172/mra.2013.7.1.110

Coertze, J., & Von Solms, R. (2013). A model for information security governance in developing countries. In K. Jonas, I. A. Rai, & M. Tchuente (Eds.), *E-infrastructure and e-services for developing countries* (pp. 279–288). Lecture Notes of the Institute for Computer Sciences, Social Informatics and Telecommunications Engineering, Vol. 119. https://doi.org/10.1007/978-3-642-41178-6_29

Davis, K. (2016). A method to measure success dimensions relating to individual stakeholder groups. *International Journal of Project Management, 34*, 480–493. https://doi.org/10.1016/j.ijproman.2015.12.009

Davis, R. E. (2006). *IT auditing: IT governance*. Pleier.

Davis, R. E. (2008a). *IT auditing: Assuring information assets protection*. Pleier.

Davis, R. E. (2008b). *IT auditing: IT service delivery and support*. Pleier.

Davis, R. E. (2009). *Ensuring information assets protection*. Lulu.

Davis, R. E. (2010). *IT auditing: An adaptive system*. www.amazon.com

Davis, R. E. (2011). *Assuring IT governance*. www.amazon.com

Davis, R. E. (2012a). *Assuring information security*. www.amazon.com

Davis, R. E. (2012b). The case for continuous auditing of management information systems. In J. Oringel (Ed.), *Effective auditing for corporates: Key developments in practice and procedures* (pp. 209–217). Bloomsbury Information.

Davis, R. E. (2017). *Relationship between corporate governance and information security governance effectiveness in United States corporations* (Publication No. 10603383) [Doctoral Study, Walden University]. ProQuest Dissertations Publishing.

Davis, R. E. (2020). *IT auditing using a system perspective*. IGI Global.

De Haes, S., van Grembergen, W., & Debreceny, R. S. (2013). COBIT 5 and enterprise governance of information technology: Building blocks and research opportunities. *Journal of Information Systems, 27*(1), 307–324. https://doi.org/10.2308/isys-50422

Dellis, A., Skolarikos, A., & Papatsoris, A. G. (2014). Why should I do research? Is it a waste of time? *Arab Journal of Urology, 12*(1), 68–70. https://doi.org/10.1016/j.aju.2013.08.007

Derakhshandeh, A., & Gholami, R. (2012). A relationship between leadership style and perceived organizational effectiveness by directors and managers in organizations. *Management Science Letters, 2*(3), 845–850. https://doi.org/10.5267/j.msl.2011.12.099

Duranti, L. (2010). Concepts and principles for the management of electronic records, or records management theory is archival diplomatics. *Records Management Journal, 20*(1), 78–95. https://doi.org/10.1108/09565691011039852

Edwards, C. K. (2013). *A framework for the governance of information security* (Publication No. 3607548) [Dissertation, Nova Southeastern University]. ProQuest Dissertations Publishing.

Farahmand, F., Navathe, S. B., Sharp, G. P., & Enslow, P. H. (2005). A management perspective on risk of security threats to information systems. *Information Technology and Management, 6*(2–3), 203–225. https://doi.org/10.1007/s10799-005-5880-5

Fenz, S., Heurix, J., Neubauer, T., & Pechstein, F. (2014). Current challenges in information security risk management. *Information Management & Computer Security, 22*, 410–430. https://doi.org/10.1108/IMCS-07-2013-0053

Findikli, M., Yozgat, U., & Rofcanin, Y. (2015). Examining organizational innovation and knowledge management capacity: The central role of strategic human resources practices (SHRPs). *Procedia-Social and Behavioral Sciences*, *181*, 377–387. https://doi.org/10.1016/j.sbspro.2015.04.900

Flores, W. R., Antonsen, E., & Ekstedt, M. (2014). Information security knowledge sharing in organizations: Investigating the effect of behavioral information security governance and national culture. *Computers & Security*, *43*, 90–110. https://doi.org/10.1016/j.cose.2014.03.004

Garba, A. B., Armarego, J., Murray, D., & Kenworthy, W. (2015). Review of the information security and privacy challenges in bring your own device (BYOD) environments. *Journal of Information Privacy and Security*, *11*, 38–54. https://doi.org/10.1080/15536548.2015.1010985

Guadalupe, M., Li, H., & Wulf, J. (2014). Who lives in the C-suite? Organizational structure and the division of labor in top management. *Management Science*, *60*, 824–844. https://doi.org/10.1287/mnsc.2013.1795

Hart, A. J. (2016). *Exploring the influence of management communication behaviors on employee engagement* (Publication No. 10056411) [Doctoral Study, Walden University]. ProQuest Dissertations Publishing.

Hitt, L. M., & Brynjolfsson, E. (1997). Information technology and internal firm organization: An exploratory analysis. *Journal of Management Information Systems*, *14*(2), 81–101. https://doi.org/10.1080/07421222.1997.11518166

Huang, D. L., Rau, P. L. P., & Salvendy, G. (2007). A survey of factors influencing people's perception of information security. In J. A. Jacko (Ed.), *Human-computer interaction* (pp. 906–915). Lecture Notes in Computer Science, Vol. 4553. https://doi.org/10.1007/978-3-540-73111-5_100

ISO Technical Management Board Working Group. (2009). Risk assessment. *ISO/IEC Guide 73, Risk Management-Vocabulary*. www.iso.org/obp/ui/#iso:std:iso:guide:73:ed-1:v1:en

Kim, S. H., Yang, K. H., & Park, S. (2014). An integrative behavioral model of information security policy compliance. *The Scientific World Journal*, *2014*, 1–12. https://doi.org/10.1155/2014/463870

Kushwaha, P. (2016). Amalgamation of the information security management system with business-paradigm shift. *International Journal of Computer Science and Information Security*, *14*(1), 105–111. https://sites.google.com/site/ijcsis

Lamba, A. (2014). Cyber attack prevention using VAPT tools (vulnerability assessment & penetration testing). *Cikitusi Journal for Multidisciplinary Research*, *1*(2), 64–71. www.cikitusi.com

Li, J., Duan, Q. Y., Gong, W., Ye, A., Dai, Y., Miao, C., . . . Sun, Y. (2013). Assessing parameter importance of the common land model based on qualitative and quantitative sensitivity analysis. *Hydrology and Earth System Sciences*, *17*(8), 3279–3293. https://doi.org/10.5194/hess-17-3279-2013

Lopez, R. H. (2012). *Information data security specialists' and business leaders' experiences regarding communication challenges* (Publication No. 3503982) [Doctoral Study, Walden University]. ProQuest Dissertations Publishing.

Luecke, R. (2005). *Harvard business essentials: Strategy: Create and implement the best strategy for your business*. Harvard Business School.

Magdaraog, Jr., G. A. (2014). Warning signs in the workplace: An analysis of risk factors in employee fraud. *The Carrington Rand Journal of Social Sciences*, *1*(1), 73–82. www.carringtonrand.com

Mayoh, J., & Onwuegbuzie, A. J. (2015). Toward a conceptualization of mixed methods phenomenological research. *Journal of Mixed Methods Research*, *9*, 91–107. https://doi.org/10.1177/1558689813505358

McCusker, K., & Gunaydin, S. (2015). Research using qualitative, quantitative or mixed methods and choice based on the research. *Perfusion*, *30*, 537–542. https://doi.org/10.1177/0267659114559116

Meyer, J. W., & Rowan, B. (1977). Institutionalized organizations: Formal structure as myth and ceremony. *American Journal of Sociology*, *83*(2), 340–363. https://doi.org/10.1086/226550

Misangyi, V. F., & Acharya, A. G. (2014). Substitutes or complements? A configurational examination of corporate governance mechanisms. *Academy of Management Journal*, *57*(6), 1681–1705. https://doi.org/10.5465/amj.2012.0728

Mukherji, A. (2002). The evolution of information systems: Their impact on organizations and structures. *Management Decision*, *40*(5), 497–507. https://doi.org/10.1108/00251740210430498

Nazareth, D. L., & Choi, J. (2015). A system dynamics model for information security management. *Information & Management*, *52*, 123–134. https://doi.org/10.1016/j.im.2014.10.009

Nicho, M. (2018). A process model for implementing information systems security governance. *Information and Computer Security*, *26*(1), 10–38. https://doi.org/10.1108/ICS-07-2016-0061

Nwekeaku, C. (2013). University leadership and management of research for national transformation of Nigeria. *Journal of Education and Practice*, *4*(22), 187–193. www.iiste.org/Journals/index.php/JEP

Posthuma, R. A., Campion, M. C., Masimova, M., & Campion, M. A. (2013). A high performance work practices taxonomy: Integrating the literature and directing future research. *Journal of Management*, *39*(5), 1184–1220. https://doi.org/10.1177/0149206313478184

Raelin, J. D., & Bondy, K. (2013). Putting the good back in good corporate governance: The presence and problems of double-layered agency theory. *Corporate Governance: An International Review*, *21*, 420–435. https://doi.org/10.1111/corg.12038

Rubino, M., & Vitolla, F. (2014). Corporate governance and the information system: How a framework for IT governance supports ERM. *Corporate Governance: The International Journal of Business in Society*, *14*, 320–338. https://doi.org/10.1108/CG-06-2013-0067

Safa, N. S., Von Solms, R., & Furnell, S. (2016). Information security policy compliance model in organizations. *Computers & Security*, *56*, 70–82. https://doi.org/10.1016/j.cose.2015.10.006

Siddiqui, N., & Fitzgerald, J. A. (2014). Elaborated integration of qualitative and quantitative perspectives in mixed methods research: A profound enquiry into the nursing practice environment. *International Journal of Multiple Research Approaches*, *8*, 137–147. https://doi.org/10.5172/mra.2014.8.2.137

Singh, A. N., Picot, A., Kranz, J., Gupta, M. P., & Ojha, A. (2013). Information security management (ISM) practices: Lessons from select cases from India and Germany. *Global Journal of Flexible Systems Management*, *14*, 225–239. https://doi.org/10.1007/s40171-013-0047-4

Sor, R. (2004). Information technology and organisational structure: Vindicating theories from the past. *Management Decision*, *42*(2), 316–329. https://doi.org/10.1108/00251740410513854

Srivastava, H., & Kumar, S. A. (2015). Control framework for secure cloud computing. *Journal of Information Security*, *6*, 12–23. https://doi.org/10.4236/jis.2015.61002

Stahl, B. C., Eden, G., Jirotka, M., & Coeckelbergh, M. (2014). From computer ethics to responsible research and innovation in ICT: The transition of reference discourses informing ethics-related research in information systems. *Information & Management*, *51*, 810–818. https://doi.org/10.1016/j.im.2014.01.001

Steiger, J. S., Hammou, K. A., & Galib, M. H. (2014). An examination of the influence of organizational structure types and management levels on knowledge management practices in organizations. *International Journal of Business and Management*, *9*(6), 43–57. https://doi.org/10.5539/ijbm.v9n6p43

Syamsuddin, I. (2013). Multicriteria evaluation and sensitivity analysis on information security. *International Journal of Computer Applications*, *69*(24), 22–25. https://doi.org/10.5120/12120-8242

Tarafdar, M., D'Arcy, J., Turel, O., & Gupta, A. (2015). The dark side of information technology. *MIT Sloan Management Review*, *56*(2), 61–70. http://sloanreview.mit.edu

Too, E. G., & Weaver, P. (2014). The management of project management: A conceptual framework for project governance. *International Journal of Project Management*, *32*, 1382–1394. https://doi.org/10.1016/j.ijproman.2013.07.006

Tsohou, A., Karyda, M., & Kokolakis, S. (2015). Analyzing the role of cognitive and cultural biases in the internalization of information security policies: Recommendations for information security awareness programs. *Computers & Security*, *52*, 128–141. https://doi.org/10.1016/j.cose.2015.04.006

Venkatesh, V., Brown, S. A., & Bala, H. (2013). Bridging the qualitative-quantitative divide: Guidelines for conducting mixed methods research in information systems. *MIS Quarterly*, *37*, 21–54. www.misq.org

Wiley, A., McCormac, A., & Calic, D. (2020). More than the individual: Examining the relationship between culture and information security awareness. *Computers & Security*, 88, 1–8. https://doi.org/10.1016/j.cose.2019.101640

Williams, S. P., Hardy, C. A., & Holgate, J. A. (2013). Information security governance practices in critical infrastructure organizations: A socio-technical and institutional logic perspective. *Electronic Markets*, 23, 341–354. https://doi.org/10.1007/s12525-013-0137-3

Yaokumah, W. (2013). *Evaluating the effectiveness of information security governance practices in developing nations: A case of Ghana* (Publication No. 3557634) [Dissertation, Capella University]. ProQuest Dissertations Publishing.

Yaokumah, W. (2014). Information security governance implementation within Ghanaian industry sectors: An empirical study. *Information Management & Computer Security*, 22, 235–250. https://doi.org/10.1108/IMCS-06-2013-0044

Yaokumah, W. (2015). Evaluating the effectiveness of information security governance practices in developing nations: A case of Ghana. In *Standards and standardization: Concepts, methodologies, tools, and applications* (pp. 1317–1333). IGI Global. https://doi.org/10.4018/978-1-4666-8111-8.ch062

Yaokumah, W., & Brown, S. (2014). An empirical examination of the relationship between information security/business strategic alignment and information security governance domain areas. *Journal of Business Systems, Governance & Ethics*, 9(2), 50–65. https://doi.org/10.15209/jbsge.v9i2.718

Yilmaz, K. (2013). Comparison of quantitative and qualitative research traditions: Epistemological, theoretical, and methodological differences. *European Journal of Education*, 48, 311–325. https://doi.org/10.1111/ejed.12014

Yukl, G. (2011). Contingency theories of effective leadership. In A. Bryman, D. Collinson, K. Grint, B. Jackson, & M. Uhl-Bien (Eds.), *The SAGE handbook of leadership* (pp. 286–298). Sage.

Zhao, X., Xue, L., & Whinston, A. B. (2013). Managing interdependent information security risks: Cyberinsurance, managed security services, and risk pooling arrangements. *Journal of Management Information Systems*, 30(1), 123–152. https://doi.org/10.2753/MIS0742-1222300104

Recommended Reading

Farnan, O. J., & Nurse, J. R. (2015). Exploring a controls-based assessment of infrastructure vulnerability. In C. Lambrinoudakis, & A. Gabillon (Eds.), *International conference on risks and security of internet and systems* (pp. 144–159). Lecture Notes in Computer Science, Vol. 9572. https://doi.org/10.1007/978-3-319-31811-0_9

Greco, S., Matarazzo, B., & Słowiński, R. (2016). Decision rule approach. In S. Greco, M. Ehrgott, & J. Figueira (Eds.), *Multiple criteria decision analysis* (pp. 497–552). https://doi.org/10.1007/978-1-4939-3094-4_13

Huff, A. S., & Reger, R. K. (1987). A review of strategic process research. *Journal of Management*, 13(2), 211–236. https://doi.org/10.1177/014920638701300203

Lutsenko, I., Fomovskaya, E., Vihrova, E., & Serdiuk, O. (2016). Development of system operations models hierarchy on the aggregating sign of system mechanisms. *Eastern-European Journal of Enterprise Technologies*, 3(2), 39–46. https://doi.org/10.15587/1729-4061.2016.71494

Neely, M. P., & Cook, J. S. (2011). Fifteen years of data and information quality literature: Developing a research agenda for accounting. *Journal of Information Systems*, 25(1), 79–108. https://doi.org/10.2308/jis.2011.25.1.79

Information Protection Classifications with Criteria and Definitions

Information Criteria Classifications and Definitions

Criteria	Classification	Definition
Confidentiality (Sensitivity)	Top Secret	Item could cause grave harm to national security.
	Secret	Item could cause serious damage to national security.
	Confidential	Item could moderately affect national security.
	Private	Item could cause serious harm to the entity, customers, or employees.
	Sensitive	Item could cause moderate harm to the entity, customers, or employees.
	Internal	Item should not extend beyond the entity's business perimeter.
	External	Item protection and handling requirements are provided by an outside entity.
	Public	Item will not harm the entity or employee(s).
	Unclassified	Information is not sensitive or restricted.
Integrity (Criticality)	Financial	Item usage in reporting operational results.
	Statistical	Item provides the means to quantitatively assess a defined population.
	Commentary	Item provides additional or supplementary information regarding an entity activity.
Availability (Impact)	Critical	Item restoration must occur as soon as possible to sustain a crucial process.
	Essential	Item restoration must occur as soon as required resources are utilizable.
	Desirable	Item suspension for the duration of an emergency is acceptable.
	Necessary	Item restoration must occur as soon as the entity returns to a normal processing environment.

Chapter 4

Security Governance Processes

Abstract

ISG-expected outcomes could guide managerial actions enabling entity-wide framework integration and transparency. At the Governance Tree tier-four level, management commonly needs ISG that enables strategic alignment, intrinsic value delivery, adaptive risk management, judicious resource allotments, and accurate performance measurement to accomplish protection expectations. Generally, management's attitude regarding ISSM, clearly defining policies and principles to ensure proper practices, communicating practices to internal and external parties, and establishing appropriate systems to achieve objectives affecting information confidentiality, integrity, and availability demonstrates ISG commitment levels. Chapter 4 conveys Governance Tree tier-five level activities supporting Governance Tree tier-four processes for effectual ISG.

Introduction

As the imperative to manage organizational operations to meet stakeholder expectations for strategic alignment, value delivery, risk management, resource management, and performance measurement drives corporate governance, so has stakeholders focused on ISG achieving similar accountabilities (Davis, 2017; Yaokumah & Brown, 2014). Theories help conceptualize structures and objects that shape activities (Davis, 2017; Imenda, 2014; Scharff, 2013; Zachariadis et al., 2013). Researchers use a theoretical framework to synthesize and integrate cogitations when describing, explicating, or predicting a phenomenon under study, as well as guiding an investigation (Davis, 2017; Imenda, 2014). Consequently, ISG construction can occur through frameworks, standards, and policy definitions, where appropriate strategy and security policy require contextual deployment to protect effactually against potential risks (Davis, 2017; Silic & Back, 2014).

Effective ISG necessitates the open engagement of and support from entity executives and senior manager-leaders (Davis, 2008a). Generally, management's attitude regarding ISSM, clearly defining policies and principles to ensure proper practices, communicating practices to internal and external parties, and establishing appropriate systems to achieve objectives affecting information confidentiality, integrity, and availability demonstrates ISG commitment levels (Davis, 2008a). Active participation by those charged with governance is usually indispensable to driving employee IAP due diligence (Davis, 2008a). Upon adopting active participation in governance, executive management's positive security service attitude conveys open support for effectual ISG (Davis, 2008a).

Thorough security requirement knowledge, risk management practices, and sub-categorical risk assessment techniques are central process elements that permit sustaining an ISG program (Davis, 2008a). Developing an organizationally adjusted ISG structure is an undertaking requiring an in-depth understanding of the entity's external and internal environments (Davis, 2008a). An entity's mission and operating environment considerations are imperative when deploying an effective ISG program (Davis, 2008a). Typically, the security confidentiality, integrity, and availability model descriptors are employable as generally accepted information security principles aiding in evaluating administrative practices (Davis, 2008a).

Within the cybersecurity practice domain, assigned responsibilities are requirements to complete program management risk assessments that enable conceiving risk mitigation strategies and controls (Davis, 2008a). Manager-leaders must furnish expectation guidance to facilitate the risk assessment process (Davis, 2008a). Consequently, senior manager-leaders should suggest or provide acceptable documentation formats for completing minimum baseline or current security compliance requirements (Davis, 2008a). Moreover, due care of information assets dictates consistent resource administration considering an entity's ability to deliver results or value at an affordable cost, within an acceptable risk level (Davis, 2008a). Ascertaining an acceptable resource risk level has a prerequisite of organizational risk analyses redressing foreseeable threats, opportunities, and vulnerabilities (Davis, 2008a). Contextually, risk management principles and practices are significant drivers for ISG safeguarding processes, activities, and tasks (Davis, 2008a).

Information security is typically a program enabling and optimizing cybersecurity services to satisfy organizational requirements while simultaneously providing strategic and tactical cybersecurity infrastructure administration that complies with applicable laws and regulations (Davis, 2008a). Cascading from the risk management goal of appropriately addressing threats, opportunities, and weaknesses, a primary security risk assessment objective is to provide recommendations that maximize confidentiality, integrity, and availability protection reflective of the operating environment, while sustaining usability and functionality (Davis, 2008a). In this chapter, the author discusses framed processes for achieving an organizationally adjusted ISG program.

Framing Information Security Governance

As Chapter 1 on security governance suggested, an ISG program's overall objective is provisioning assurance that information assets receive appropriate protection levels commensurate with the valuation or the risk an information asset compromise poses to the entity. Governance Tree tier-level equality indicates sharing similar structural perceptions (Davis, 2008a). ISG expected outcomes could guide managerial actions enabling entity-wide framework integration and transparency (Davis, 2008a). As depicted in Figure 4.1, at the Governance Tree tier-four level, management commonly needs ISG that enables strategic alignment, intrinsic value delivery, adaptive risk management, judicious resource allotments, and accurate performance measurement to accomplish protection expectations (Davis, 2008a, 2017; Mohare & Lanjewar, 2012). In addressing information security issues, management can apply:

- Strategic alignment centering on ensuring entity, IT, and information security plan linkage; defining, maintaining, and validating the information security value proposition; and information security operational congruence with the entity and IT operations (Davis, 2008a, 2017). Entity manager-leaders should enhance strategic alignment attributes to achieve effectual ISG (Davis, 2017; Yaokumah & Brown, 2014). Effective strategic alignment must be dynamic, sharable, and malleable (Yaokumah & Brown, 2014) to meet entity, IT, and information security environment changes (Davis, 2008a).

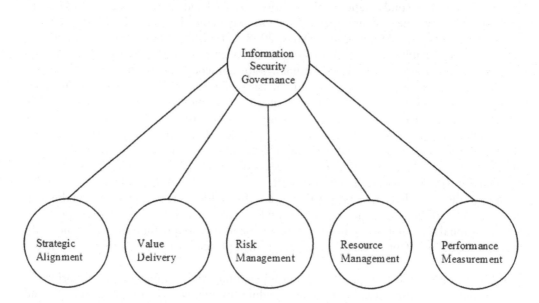

Figure 4.1 Governance Tree: Third and Fourth Tier Structural View: Information Security Governance.

Note: Adapted from *IT Auditing: Assuring Information Assets Protection* by R. E. Davis, 2008a, Pleier. Copyright 2008 by Robert E. Davis. Adapted with permission.

- Value delivery that executes the information security value proposition throughout the delivery cycle, ensuring information security delivers benefits against the adopted entity strategy, concentrates on optimizing costs and proves intrinsic information security value (Davis, 2008a, 2017). Effectual ISG value delivery practices recognize different investment categories that must be asymmetrically evaluated and managed (Yaokumah & Brown, 2014).
- Risk management principles, processes, and approaches using a systematic application (Davis, 2017; Rasheed et al., 2015). Consequently, organizational risk management necessitates information security risk awareness by senior officials, a clear understanding of the entity's appetite for information security risks, requirements to accomplish information security compliance, transparency regarding significant information security risks, and embedding internal risk management responsibilities (Davis, 2008a).
- Resource management reflecting the intention for optimal investment in and the proper administration of information security resources (Davis, 2008a, 2017; Mohare & Lanjewar, 2012; Yaokumah, 2013). Resource management focus areas are information security knowledge and infrastructure processing efficiency (Davis, 2008a).
- Performance measurement practices to ensure organizational objective achievement through quantifying, monitoring, and reporting information security systems, processes, and related activities (Davis, 2017; IT Governance Institute, 2008). Minimally, performance measurement administrators track and monitor information security strategy implementations, information security project completions, information security resource utilization, information security process performance, and information security service delivery (Davis, 2008a).

Governance Tree tier-four framework nodes provide the basis for developing a cost-effective information security program that supports entity objectives and enables an acceptable predictability level for operations by limiting adverse events (Davis, 2008a). However, the Governance Tree ISG framework can intermix with other available information security-related practices (Davis, 2008a) such as ISO 27000. Furthermore, the ISG outcomes are flexible enough for alignment with most entity-level frameworks (Davis, 2008a).

Tier Four Strategic Alignment

Information security manager-leader strategic alignment operationalization includes congruence, connection, and participation abstractions (Schobel & Denford, 2013). A manager-leader's selected tactics misaligned with the adopted entity focal strategy can prevent objective performance realization (Davis, 2017; Hardcopf et al., 2017). When linked to entity-level governance, ISG is the most fitting path to acquire control of information security processes and ensure alignment with organizational strategies (Davis, 2017; Rebollo et al., 2015). ISG strategic alignment between operational units, the information security function, and strategies establishment occurs when strategic management ensures that the information security strategies are congruent with organizational strategies (Davis, 2017; Yaokumah & Brown, 2014). For effective strategic alignment, the entity-level strategies should encompass critical information security capabilities, future security requirements, people, and information assets that are deployable to meet organizational needs (Davis, 2017; Yaokumah & Brown, 2014). Whereby, strategic alignment must exhibit mutability, commitment, and adaptability attributes (Davis, 2017; Yaokumah & Brown, 2014). The strategic alignment attributes help meet changing operational and security environments (Davis, 2017; Yaokumah & Brown, 2014).

Effectual ISG realization can occur through sound corporate governance (Yaokumah & Brown, 2014). Three strategy levels' manager-leaders typically consider within an organization concerning for-profit entity alignment: corporate, business, and functional (Alsudiri et al., 2013; Davis, 2017). The relationship between corporate governance, IT governance, and ISG vary in academic literature (Davis, 2017; Williams et al., 2013). Figure 4.2 depicts

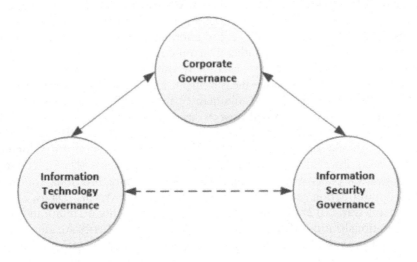

Figure 4.2 Functional Corporate Governance, Information Technology Governance, and Information Security Governance Strategic Alignments.

Note: Adapted from *IT Auditing: Assuring Information Assets Protection* by R. E. Davis, 2008a, Pleier. Copyright 2008 by Robert E. Davis. Adapted with permission.

corporate, IT, and information security functional strategic alignment. A corporation's information security and IT functions should align with the organizational vision, mission, values, objectives, and strategies for effective practices (Alsudiri et al., 2013; Davis, 2011, 2017).

Nodal structural connectivity imposes ISG alignment with entity-level governance requirements (Davis, 2008a, 2017; Yaokumah, 2013). Hierarchical node connectivity establishment often transpires when standard attribute sharing occurs in parent–child data relationships, for example (Davis, 2011, 2017; Kearney & Kruger, 2013). In contrast, vertical node equality defines similar data-sharing perceptions (Davis, 2011, 2017). Corporate executive manager-leaders provide the foundation for creating legitimate governance structures (Abraham, 2012) that allow organizational sharing relationships (Davis, 2017). Information security nodal connectivity enables developing and sustaining information systems strategically aligned with the entity's goals and objectives (Davis, 2008a). ISG's strategic alignment with IT governance activities is also necessary for maintaining information security congruency with entity governance (Davis, 2008a, 2017).

ISG should reflect good entity governance (Davis, 2017; Yaokumah & Brown, 2014). By which, information security processes should portray good ISG (Davis, 2017). Conversely, consistently applied ISG can improve entity governance (Davis, 2011, 2017). Monitoring and reporting enable information security alignment with operational processes and requirements, consequently strengthening the governance bidirectional entity information security relationships (Davis, 2011, 2017; Kwon et al., 2013). Organizational IT manager-leaders ensure strategic alignment when appropriate control deployments occur under an effective ISG program (Davis, 2011, 2017; Mohare & Lanjewar, 2012).

Information security risk management, performance measurement, resource management, and value delivery practices are strategic alignment predictor variables (Davis, 2017; Yaokumah, 2013; Yaokumah & Brown, 2014). Organizational risk management, resource management, performance measurement, and value delivery practices positively correlate to effective ISG strategic alignment (Davis, 2017; Yaokumah, 2013; Yaokumah & Brown, 2014). In other words, the integration of information security predictor variables can generate ISG success (Davis, 2017; Yaokumah, 2013; Yaokumah & Brown, 2014). However, IT governance structures, processes, and relational mechanisms also apply to ISG efficacy achievement (Davis, 2017; Yaokumah, 2013). Additionally, entity information systems personnel can perceive security strategy as driven bottom-up rather than top-down (Ahmad et al., 2014; Davis, 2017).

Effectual ISG strategic alignment substantially enhances an entity's risk management, resource management, performance measurement, and value delivery processes (Davis, 2017; Mohare & Lanjewar, 2012; Yaokumah & Brown, 2014). A cross-organizational committee of manager-leaders should exist to develop, deploy, and monitor the entity and ISG strategic plans for objectives and goals synchronization (Davis, 2011, 2017). The IAP service strategy should address opportunity identification for service development that unilaterally meets internal and external customer requirements (Davis, 2008b). Once approval of strategic plans occurs, manager-leaders must ensure directional transformation into the right information security service and support deployments (Davis, 2011, 2017; Mohare & Lanjewar, 2012). Activity alignment and adaptability orientations are complementary operationalizations (Davis, 2017; Hodgkinson et al., 2014). An adopted strategic objective can be providing optimal value to customers, and appropriate information security realization can create a service advantage (Davis, 2011, 2017), though achieving the optimal customer value objective through appropriate information security realization is not riskless (Davis, 2011, 2017; Hashizume et al., 2013; Rebollo et al., 2015).

Depending on the entity's manager-leaders, there may be a lack of knowledge and an ad-hoc approach to information security strategy development (Ahmad et al., 2014; Davis, 2017). When ISG misalignment to entity-level governance and IT governance occurs,

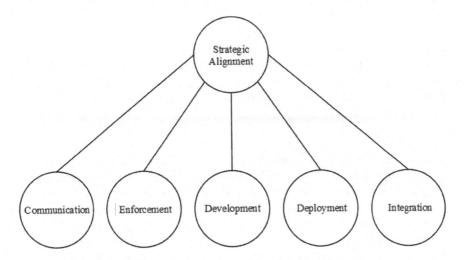

Figure 4.3 Governance Tree – Fourth and Fifth Tier Structural View: Strategic Alignment.

Note: Adapted from *Assuring IT Governance* by R. E. Davis, 2011, Amazon.com. Copyright 2011 by Robert E. Davis. Adapted with permission.

financial, legal, reputational, and operational risks can escalate beyond demarcated tolerance levels (Davis, 2008a, 2017; Yaokumah, 2014). A functional entity's very existence might depend on how well IT manager-leaders safeguard information assets used in achieving the adopted organizational mission (Bahl & Wali, 2014; D'Arcy et al., 2014; Davis, 2008a, 2017). As depicted in Figure 4.3, at the Governance Tree tier-five level, management needs ISG that enables exceptional communications, rigorous enforcement, appropriate development, reliable deployment, and seamless integration to accomplish protection expectations (Davis, 2011, 2017). Therefore, information security strategic alignment necessitates

- communication among all linked parties based on constructive relationships, common language utilization, and the shared commitment to resolve information security-related issues crucial to successful ISG program structures and processes (Davis, 2008a, 2017),
- active behavioral enforcement occurring through punishment severity, reward significance, and control certainty (Davis, 2017),
- strategy design development occurring in top-down sequential order—whether manager-leaders apply a formal or informal strategic planning system (Davis, 2011, 2017).
- information security manager-leaders assessing and ensuring the quality of protection mechanism deployments (Davis, 2017; Wu et al., 2015), and
- organizational manager-leaders recognize the importance of ISG as an integrative program for successful IT governance and entity-level governance (Davis, 2017; Yaokumah, 2014).

Tier Five Communication

The Direct-Control Cycle Model forms the foundation for strategic alignment communication diffusion. The direct-control cycle is hierarchical, with the direct side flowing from top to bottom, while the control side flows from bottom to top (Yaokumah, 2015). The direct side of the Direct-Control Cycle Model begins from the strategic level, which comprises the entity oversight committee (Yaokumah, 2015), giving directives to the highest executive manager-leader (Davis, 2011). The directives usually reflect external and internal environment factor considerations (Davis, 2008a, 2017; Yaokumah, 2015). The control side of the Direct-Control Cycle Model begins at the operational level, transfers to the tactical level, and then to the strategic level manager-leaders (Yaokumah, 2015). Thus, the control side of the Direct-Control Cycle Model involves entity employees monitoring and reporting controls to higher administrative levels (Yaokumah, 2015).

Tier Five Enforcement

Entity manager-leaders should communicate and enforce consequences for noncompliance with organizational controls (Davis, 2017). Problems can arise as to who enforces controls, how manager-leaders assure the carrying out of intentions, and how much autonomy individuals and groups should have (Davis, 2011, 2017). Information security controls need active monitoring and enforcement, with manager-leaders held accountable for counterproductive workplace behavior (Davis, 2017). Auditor-supplied corrective action information supports enforcement functions necessary to remedy activities found non-compliant with expectations or mandates (Davis, 2008a). In most cases, the confidentiality, integrity, and availability impact levels consider the effects of unauthorized disclosure, modification, or service denial on a responsible entity's ability to sustain internal and external control processes (Davis, 2008a).

Tier Five Development

ISG planning allows forecasting the future organizational direction and relevant influences and deriving a better strategy for accomplishing objectives (Davis, 2008a, 2017). An extensive grasp of the entity's environment, processes, and organizational objectives enables effective information security strategy development (Davis, 2017; Flores et al., 2014). Stakeholder identification and salience application can help determine general classes relevant to strategy development (Davis, 2017; Tashman & Raelin, 2013). Like entity-level strategic planning, the ISG planning process translates strategy into measurable tactical and operational plans and retranslating operational plans into policies, procedures, directives, standards, and rules (C. Edwards, 2013; Davis, 2008a, 2017).

Tier Five Deployment

Exercising effective entity-level governance throughout an organizational formation requires the top-level oversight committee and management team understand what to expect from programs, systems, and processes (Davis, 2008a, 2017). Entity manager-leaders should continually seek confirmation that information security delivers reliable services supporting the organization's strategic design for accomplishing adopted objectives (Davis, 2011, 2017). Implemented security strategies to protect information systems can use preventive strategies to maintain technological service availability (Ahmad et al., 2014; Davis, 2017). As a preventive strategy, though policies are necessary for communicating expected behavior, determining the effectiveness of adopted information security objectives is even more critical (Davis, 2017). Without effectual ISG deployment, the Information Security Office often does not participate in the decision-making and approval-authorization process for information assets (Davis, 2011, 2017).

Tier Five Integration

The Governance, Risk Management, and Compliance Model link interactive elements of all entity ISG domains (Yaokumah, 2015). The Governance, Risk Management, and Compliance Model conceptualize people, processes, and technology that consist of security drivers, security management, and stakeholders interacting to administrate entity information security (Yaokumah, 2015). The security driver construct includes laws and regulations that entities must comply with, operational objectives, and emerging security threats (Yaokumah, 2015). Security management encompasses policy development, processes, and security metric frameworks (Yaokumah, 2015). Entity stakeholders are driven by organizational environment requirements when developing the security policy framework (Yaokumah, 2015). The policy framework forms the basis for activities under the process framework (Yaokumah, 2015). After that, activity measurement and report generation occur for submission to the stakeholders using metrics (Yaokumah, 2015). Nonetheless, internal systems integration positively moderates the relationship between inter-functional coordination and an entity's customer-responding capability (Roberts & Grover, 2012).

Tier Four Value Delivery

The stakeholder perspective promotes a value-laden approach to entity-level governance instead of other unilateral views (Abraham, 2012; Davis, 2017). Stakeholder-derived value is from the relevance and quality of services and products (Davis, 2017; Harrison & Wicks, 2013). Ascertaining the degree that manager-leaders should prioritize competing stakeholder claims can occur through organizational and societal level stakeholder legitimacy, power, and urgency assessments (Davis, 2017; Tashman & Raelin, 2013). Given the identification of stakeholders and perceived salience, strategic correlation occurs by satisfying the entity stakeholders' value and determining valued outcomes (Davis, 2017). Administrative practices ensure efficient and effective stakeholder value delivery through good governance (Davis, 2017; Mishra & Mohanty, 2014). Investors prefer to deal with entities that have acceptable and credible governance practices (Davis, 2017; Mishra & Mohanty, 2014).

Societies and stakeholders assert that entities should be accountable for supporting social and environmental sustainability efforts in a financially responsible manner (Davis, 2017; Glavas & Mish, 2015). Managerial conceptual congruence nourished the Triple Bottom Line (Davis, 2017; Glavas & Mish, 2015) as a worthy endeavor (Slaper & Hall, 2011). Managers frequently used the Triple Bottom Line approach to describe entity social responsibility activities (Davis, 2017; Nalband & Kelabi, 2014). The Triple Bottom Line approach places value on financial returns, human resources, and physical environment considering fair practices benefiting labor, the community, and the greater common good (Davis, 2017; Sharma & Khanna, 2014; Slaper & Hall, 2011).

Program management can reflect entity value creation beyond project portfolio performance (Davis, 2017; Rijke et al., 2014). Value creation and subsequent value appropriation occur through effective and efficient value management (Davis, 2017). Creating value for sustainable solutions means increasing the entity's value propositions and remediating unsustainable practices affecting social and ecological systems (Davis, 2017). The stakeholder model aligns with sustainable development (Davis, 2017; Miles, 2012). However, heterogeneity in defining stakeholders has induced confusion and inadvertent nonachievements in addressing stakeholder expectations and furnishing optimal value delivery (Davis, 2017; Gil-Lafuente & Paula, 2013).

Creating optimized value for stakeholders is the responsibility of manager-leaders (Davis, 2017; Tashman & Raelin, 2013). As common program success factors, value delivery practices must engage all stakeholders and assign accountability to deliver expected capabilities and benefit realization (Davis, 2011, 2017; Rijke et al., 2014; Yaokumah & Brown, 2014). ISG value delivery is a strategic alignment function of information security strategies and organizational objectives (Davis, 2017; Mohare & Lanjewar, 2012; Yaokumah & Brown, 2014). The general strategic alignment model explicates the value generated from congruence within an entity (Flores et al., 2014). Managed value delivery defines and monitors significant metrics and responds swiftly to any changes or deviations and provides continuous activity monitoring, evaluation, and improvement (Davis, 2011, 2017; Rijke et al., 2014).

Primary information security value occurs if deployed IAP helps meet entity objectives for information systems (Davis, 2011, 2017; Pérez-Méndez & Machado-Cabezas, 2015). Information security services can create value (Liang-Chuan & Liang-Hong, 2015), assisting in overall ISG value delivery (Davis, 2017). For most entities, information security's value generation occurs when requested information delivery transpires within the expected budget and timeframe while fulfilling functionality requirements (Davis, 2011, 2017). Communicating identified data transparently within the budget and timeframe, and enabling organizational personnel to carry out their duties, demonstrates information security value realization (Davis, 2011, 2017). Nonetheless, nonfinancial considerations can also determine delivery value – such as information presentation usefulness (Davis, 2017; Hughes et al., 2013).

Essential management practices can ensure value delivery efficacy (Davis, 2011, 2017; Yaokumah & Brown, 2014). "As with links in a metal chain hoisting precious cargo, manager-leaders must provide appropriate ISG tensile strength for the organizational environment to achieve [entity] objectives (Davis, 2011)" (Davis, 2017). Considering that acquiring and maintaining ISG resources have costs, IAP must produce expected benefits from deployment until retirement to justify expenditures (Davis, 2011, 2017). Unfortunately, entity and contracted third-party IAP providers tend to promise too much without effective governance, while the IT end-user community assumes too much (Davis, 2011, 2017). If the expectation circumstance exists, there is the potential for bilateral misunderstandings, resource mismanagement, poor performance, or outcome misalignment that invariably reduce ISG value delivery (Davis, 2011, 2017).

Entity-level business models reflect interrelated activity sets, enabling value creation, value delivery, and value appropriation (Davis, 2017; Lambert & Davidson, 2013). Business operations commonly rely on successful supply chain management to satisfy product and service demands (Davis, 2017; Saber et al., 2014). Cybersecurity issues necessitate appropriate responses to maintain an acceptable cyber-resilience level for supply chains (Boyes, 2015; Davis, 2017). Information security manager-leaders can resolve supply chain cyber-resilience issues considering the nature of threats, vulnerabilities, and cybersecurity attributes (Boyes, 2015; Davis, 2017). Typically, information security initiatives positively associate with supply chain operations that, in turn, positively influence supply chain performance (Davis, 2017; Sindhuja, 2014).

Arguably, IT systems, processes, activities, and tasks represent the dominant support structure for information and communication configurations (Davis, 2011, 2017; Sun & Bhattacherjee, 2014). Organizational manager-leaders generally aspire to use technology to integrate information, achieve process efficiencies, and transform service delivery into an effective paragon (Davis, 2011, 2017). However, most manager-leaders realize that emphasizing technologies and entity-centric solutions will not produce the desired outcomes; a holistic approach is necessary (Davis, 2011, 2017; De Haes et al., 2013). Effectual ISG

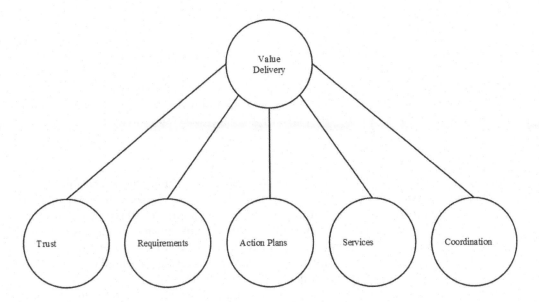

Figure 4.4 Governance Tree – Fourth and Fifth Tier Structural View: Value Delivery.

Note: Adapted from *Assuring IT Governance* by R. E. Davis, 2011, Amazon.com. Copyright 2011 by Robert E. Davis. Adapted with permission.

value delivery practitioners need to recognize that different investment categories require evaluation and administration asymmetrically (Davis, 2017; Yaokumah & Brown, 2014). As depicted in Figure 4.4, at the Governance Tree tier-five level, management needs ISG that enables oversight trust, satisfies requirements, defines appropriate action plans, supports service optimization, and appreciates functionality coordination to accomplish protection expectations (Davis, 2011, 2017). Thus, information security value delivery necessitates

- trustworthy stewards with intrinsic motivation and orientation to serve the collective rather than themselves (Davis, 2017; Glinkowska & Kaczmarek, 2015; Heracleous & Lan, 2012; Pande & Ansari, 2014),
- ensuring defined security requirement installation and maintenance occur within the entity's information asset configurations (Davis, 2009b),
- cost–benefit analysis to examine alternative action plans in determining recommended IAP deployment or determining the degree of most efficient IAP deployment while providing the greatest return for reducing risks (Davis, 2020),
- information security manager-leaders assessing and ensuring the service quality of protection mechanism deployments (Davis, 2017; Wu et al., 2015), and
- coordination through trust and commitment relational bonding affecting behavioral processes that generate collaborative advantages (Chi & Holsapple, 2005).

Tier Five Trust

Trust is a perceptional desire to rely on something or someone for protection (Safa & Von Solms, 2016). Implicit in an aligned definition for effective ISG with entity-level governance is the information security manager-leader's fiduciary relationship with other stakeholders (Yaokumah, 2013). The fiduciary relationship exists because there is usually an inequality in training or knowledge (Brakewood & Poldrack, 2013) between the information security manager-leader and other entity stakeholders (Davis, 2017). Consequently, other entity stakeholders entrust the information security manager-leader to act in their best interest (Davis, 2017). Organizational information asset valuation connection may only represent items with the required criteria for achieving an entity objective (Davis, 2008a). However, an organizational information asset unrelated to objective achievement may compromise objective realization (Davis, 2008a; Zhao et al., 2013).

Tier Five Requirements

Entity IAP personnel need to have information security engineering knowledge when attempting to satisfy combined organizational and security mandates that may include legal, business, functional, user, and nonfunctional requirements (Davis, 2012a). If an entity employee is unavailable for the fulfillment of requirements, hiring an external information security engineer may be necessary to ensure confidentiality, integrity, and availability through control assessment consideration in meeting presented needs. Reflective of the applied development and deployment methodologies, the assigned information security person wears a designer at work hat and puts the IAP operational process puzzle pieces together in an acceptable form, constructed to meet the defined requirements.

Tier Five Action Plans

Corrective IAP action plans commonly reflect recommendations that enable bringing reported conditions to a level aligned with acceptable standards or best practices (Davis, 2010, 2020). As depicted in Figure 4.5, IAP corrective action responses are sub-classifiable as remedial or improvement activities (Davis, 2010, 2020). Remedial

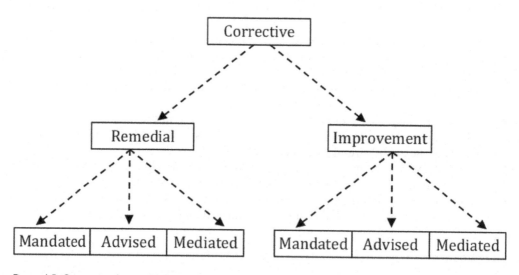

Figure 4.5 Corrective Action Dichotomy.

Note: Adapted from *IT Auditing: An Adaptive System* by R. E. Davis, 2011, Lulu. Copyright 2011 by Robert E. Davis. Adapted with permission.

actions typically address gaps in IAP conditions to minimize unacceptable risks (Davis, 2020). Contrastingly, improvement actions typically address enhancing IAP conditions to minimize unacceptable deviation risks (Davis, 2010, 2020). Cascading, corrective activities for remedial and improvement actions can sub-topically represent refinement to mandated, advised, or mediated classifications (Davis, 2010, 2020). Mandated actions are statutory requirement fulfillment expectations (Davis, 2020). Advised actions are recommendation notifications (Davis, 2010, 2020). Mediated actions are conciliations between the information security manager-leader and other stakeholders (Davis, 2010, 2020).

Tier Five Services

The establishment and functioning of support processes consistent with entity-centric service requirements are necessary to deliver appropriate IAP services (Davis, 2008b). For value delivery, the information security manager-leader must enable the accommodation of information asset management through implementation and control of a database containing details regarding IAP architectural elements used in service provisioning and administration (Davis, 2009b). Moreover, when considering a service action plan, real options include applying formal and informal cost–benefit analysis. A formal cost–benefit analysis should occur when there is a significant cost expectation for an IAP deployment (Davis, 2010, 2020). Informally, the information security manager-leader may elect to address benefits and costs in a "favorable and unfavorable" manner based on professional judgment (Davis, 2010, 2020). Whether the Information Security Office preparer uses a formal or informal cost–benefit analysis for an action plan, the control system, process, activity, or task should be efficient and economical (Davis, 2010, 2020). When an IAP service does not transpire or obtain completion within the expected timeframe, the information security manager-leader should inscribe the reason for rescinding the obligation or why there was a delay in deployment (Davis, 2010, 2020).

Tier Five Coordination

Value chain linkages can lead to competitive advantage through coordination (Porter, 1998). Establishing vertical and horizontal coordination helps build stronger linkages (Goodman & Rousseau, 2004). The coordination of IAP service launches across multiple entities is vital to information security value delivery. An appropriate inter-organizational control environment can enhance coordination effectiveness and efficiency (Davis, 2008a; Mentzer et al., 2007). Concerning coordination, project personnel typically meet, discuss, and select whether to adopt new functionality, live with shortfalls, institute a workaround, or customize an IAP package (Gosain et al., 2005), considering employee trust and commitment. Knowledge management is the coordinating instrument (Darroch, 2005) that can address gaps in functionality between organizational requirements and IAP package provisions (Gosain et al., 2005).

Tier Four Risk Management

Extensive risk exposure can lead to disappointment in attaining organizational management's established objectives for the entity (Badara & Saidin, 2014; Davis, 2017). Risk management has a goal of creating and protecting stakeholder value (Frigo & Anderson, 2011a). In accomplishing the stakeholder goal, risk management practices must integrate a systematic approach to identifying risk and defining the effect on an entity's ability to provide goods or services (Davis, 2008a, 2017; Mohare & Lanjewar, 2012). The institutionalized entity-level risk management framework should be a strategic axial-enabling diverse strategy spoke acceptance (Davis, 2011, 2017; Williams et al., 2013). Entity-level risk management should represent the proactive process by which organizational manager-leaders methodically address activity risks for achieving sustained benefit within each activity and across the affairs portfolio (Davis, 2011, 2017).

An entity's strategic mission and risk management system consideration are necessary for achieving proper organizational performance and conformance equilibrium (Davis, 2011, 2017). Entities must establish a single control definition that serves all organizational units to empower performance and conformance through entity-centric risk management (Davis, 2011, 2017). Entity-level risk management must also provide standards against which organizational unit manager-leaders can assess deployed control systems and determine necessary improvements (Davis, 2011, 2017; Flores et al., 2014). Cascading from the administrative requirements, entities that execute a healthy balance between performance and conformance through appropriate value delivery risk management have the best long-term prospects for thriving in their regulatory environment (Davis, 2011, 2017).

Risk management is not a platitude for demonstrating effective leadership (Boyson, 2014; Davis, 2008a, 2017). The individuals responsible for governance within an entity must provide guidance dedicated to appropriately handling encountered organizational risks (Boyson, 2014; Davis, 2008a, 2017). In particular, the risks associated with information and related technology necessitate comprehensive administration based on a carefully executed impact and likelihood assessment regarding potential adverse event occurrences (Boyson, 2014; Davis, 2008a, 2017). Determining information asset risk magnitudes to ensure appropriate resource allocations addressing threats, opportunities, and vulnerabilities affecting an entity is necessary for realizing effectual ISG (Davis, 2008a, 2017).

Entity-level risk management necessitates information security risk awareness by manager-leaders (Clark & Harrell, 2013; Davis, 2008a, 2017; Mohare & Lanjewar, 2012). Correspondingly, there is a need for a precise understanding of organizational management's appetite for information security risks and information security compliance requirements (Clark & Harrell, 2013; Davis, 2008a, 2017; Mohare & Lanjewar, 2012). There is also a need for transparency regarding significant organizational information security risks and embedding managerial responsibilities (Clark & Harrell, 2013; Davis, 2008a, 2011, 2017; Mohare & Lanjewar, 2012). Common information system security countermeasures reduce risk to information systems and entities when correctly deployed (Barton et al., 2016; Davis, 2017). Deployed managerial processes and IT risk assessments can help determine IAP countermeasure intensity (Davis, 2008a, 2017; Flores et al., 2014; Rubino & Vitolla, 2014). However, an entity can lack formal information security awareness methodologies for systematically identifying audience communication requirements (Davis, 2017; Stewart & Lacey, 2012).

Strategic alignment practices are entity risk management predictors (Davis, 2017; Yaokumah & Brown, 2014). With entity-level risk management alignment, ISG can furnish a framework for evaluating investments in IAP, appropriate resource coverage, and enable objectives achievement (Davis, 2008a, 2017). Information asset managerial due care dictates consistent information security resource administration considering an entity management's ability to deliver results or value at an affordable cost—within an acceptable risk level (Davis, 2008a, 2017; Yaokumah & Brown, 2014). Ascertaining an appropriate resource risk level necessitates reviewing the entity risk analyses addressing foreseeable threats, opportunities, and vulnerabilities (Davis, 2008a, 2017; Mohare & Lanjewar, 2012). Contextually, risk management principles and practices are critical drivers for ISG IAP activities (Davis, 2008a, 2017).

Responsibility for appropriate safeguarding activities must span an entity's total tangible and intangible resources (Davis, 2008a, 2017; Magdaraog, Jr., 2014). Risk management necessitates continuous efforts addressing threats, opportunities, and vulnerabilities (Davis, 2008a, 2017; Mohare & Lanjewar, 2012). However, most entity manager-leaders neglect some information assets' resource security significance (Davis, 2017; Magdaraog, Jr., 2014). Specifically, security managers largely ignore business security risks (Ahmad et al., 2014; Davis, 2017) while sampled supply chain initiatives indicate risk management efforts cluster around internally oriented system developments and core supplier-oriented sourcing (Boyson, 2014; Davis, 2017).

Significant barriers perceivably obstruct risk management implementation or impede risk management proficiency in entity programs (Davis, 2017; Rasheed et al., 2015). Monetary constraints, schedule requirements, unstable organizational environment, lack of executive commitment toward risk, and a deficit of risk-aware culture are the primary barriers impeding risk management deployment (Davis, 2017; Rasheed et al., 2015). Regarding unstable organizational environments, supply chain risk volatility and uncertainty inhibit predicting potential disruptions (Chopra & Sodhi, 2014; Davis, 2017; Kumar et al., 2014).

Concerning contextual constraints, risk management approaches do not explicitly furnish support tools for decision-makers in choosing an appropriate risk versus cost trade-off (Davis, 2017; Deursen et al., 2013; Fenz et al., 2014). However, hacking, incident protection, IT planning and operating, and IT internal control are usable as risk management measures when considering information security countermeasures (Davis, 2017; Kim et al., (2012). Information security efforts should derive from coordination through assessed risks, relevant controls development, and deployment, with implemented effectiveness monitoring of controls (Davis, 2017; Flores et al., 2014).

Entity control systems are governance requirement projections that may contain misconceived control elements because control construction is dependent on the architectural "frame-of-reference" (Davis, 2008a, 2017; Magdaraog, Jr., 2014). Control systems are also entity-centric and may embrace mistaken assumptions regarding required control assurance levels to satisfy stakeholders (Davis, 2008a, 2017; Samad-Khan, 2008). Stemming from managerialism, configured control mechanisms may only minutely affect market inefficiencies and resulting entity governance issues (Davis, 2017; Raelin & Bondy, 2013). Thus, employing risk management-based controls may do little to enhance stakeholder fiduciary confidence in the entity's personnel because manager-leaders typically can override deployed controls (Davis, 2008a, 2017).

Reflective of deploying an appropriate ISG approach, the strategic objectives for undertaking IAP risk management are to provide a framework that enables future activity to occur in a consistent and controlled manner (Davis, 2008a). In totality, an adopted IAP risk management framework should provide the structures, methodologies, procedures, and definitions that an entity has chosen to use for deploying risk management processes (Davis, 2008a). As shown in Figure 4.6, at the Governance Tree tier-five level, entity administrators need ISG that enables strategic, compliance, tactical, environmental, and operational risk management to accomplish protection

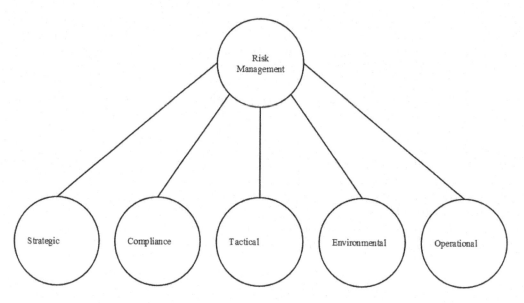

Figure 4.6 Governance Tree – Fourth and Fifth Tier Structural View: Risk Management.

Note: Adapted from *Assuring IT Governance* by R. E. Davis, 2011, Amazon.com. Copyright 2011 by Robert E. Davis. Adapted with permission.

expectations (Davis, 2011, 2017). Consequently, information security risk management necessitates:

- a process for identifying, assessing, managing, and reporting IAP strategic risks that could inhibit an entity's ability to achieve organizational strategies (Frigo & Anderson, 2011b);
- a process for identifying, assessing, managing, and reporting IAP compliance risks resulting from noncompliance with laws, regulations, policies, directives, procedures, standards, or rules (Losiewicz-Dniestrzanska, 2015);
- a process for identifying, assessing, managing, and reporting IAP tactical risks that could inhibit an entity's ability to achieve designed configurations;
- a process for identifying, assessing, managing, and reporting IAP environmental risks created by internal and external events or scenarios that could inhibit an entity's ability to achieve strategic objectives (Frigo & Anderson, 2011a); and
- a process for identifying, assessing, managing, and reporting the IAP operational risks that inhibit an entity's ability to protect information asset deployments (Abdul Rahim et al., 2015; Samad-Khan, 2008).

Tier Five Strategic

Strategic IAP as an administrative decision (Akpinar, 2017; Davis, 2011) refers to "what" the entity selects for a course of action and "why" the entity selects a course of action (Coertze & Von Solms, 2013; Davis, 2008a). Strategic IAP thinking, planning, and actions are foundational to entity management's ability to (a) understand the organizational environment, (b) recognize emerging industry patterns and trends, (c) anticipate issues that can arise within the organizational environment, (d) predict outcomes of planned initiatives and how they might affect the organization's direction, and (e) develop proper fallback plans to mitigate the miscalculation risks. Strategic IAP risk represents a possible loss source, often determined by the activated strategy, adopted objectives, and plan performance. Strategic IAP risk management focuses on internal and external scenarios that will enable the entity to achieve strategic objectives. Strategic IAP risk management needs to account for risks related to shifts in customer IT use, competitive pressures, technological changes, and stakeholders' pressure. Crucial to strategic IAP risk management is administering and measuring as many perceived threats, vulnerabilities, and opportunities as possible.

Tier Five Compliance

Compliance does not ensure information security (Mattsson, 2014). Compliance IAP risk is the possibility that an information security service or product will not enable conformance or performance with applicable laws, regulations, policies, directives, procedures, standards, or rules. Entity personnel that dismisses acting according to applicable (a) government statutes; (b) industry standards; or (c) policies, directives, procedures, standards, or rules can cause undesirable organizational consequences. As the IAP risk first tier, government statute compliance is the most compelling risk consideration, given law or regulation noncompliance can result in a large monetary fine or imprisonment (Davis, 2008a, 2009a). Industry standards are the second tier of compliance risk because applicable industry standard noncompliance can result in the enactment of an entity boycott. Compliance with the entity's policies, directives, procedures, standards, or rules is the third tier of compliance risk addressing adherence to organizational expectations, potentially resulting in employment termination.

Tier Five Tactical

At the tactical IAP decision level, manager-leaders interpret strategic goals into targets and operating criteria (Davis, 2011; J. Edwards et al., 2000). Moreover, tactical IAP risk management refers to "how" the entity's manager-leaders plan to accomplish information security strategies. In other words, tactical IAP risk management refers to how the entity manager-leaders plan to achieve the IAP strategic objectives. Tactical IAP thinking and planning consider the resources available while contemplating the potential challenges, then determining the most effective and efficient way to use orchestrated resources to achieve strategic goals while delivering quality results. Thus, decision-making at the tactical IAP risk level must focus on optimizing information security resources (Anderson & Choobineh, 2008).

Tier Five Environmental

Environmental IAP risk management addresses tangible or intangible items. Nonetheless, the focal consideration is the control environment's risk factors epitomizing entity management's attitude, awareness, and actions (Davis, 2008a). Transitively, if executive manager-leaders intend to maintain the entity-level control environment at an acceptable risk level, so must the ISG program manager-leaders maintain the IAP control environment at an acceptable risk level (Davis, 2008a). Inappropriate IAP environmental controls are significant risks to an entity deploying and using IT (Davis, 2020; Farahmand et al., 2005). Management's attitude toward and awareness of IT capabilities are vital in establishing an entity-wide consciousness of IAP control issues (Davis, 2020). Unfortunately, IAP controls cannot ensure the successful attainment of entity management's mission (Davis, 2020). Bad decisions, poor administration, competition, collusion, and control overrides can still present problems to sustaining effective management of the control environment (Davis, 2020). Determination of environmental IAP risk assessment frequency should occur after assessing risk impacts, compliance history, ethics' failures, and incident likelihoods (Davis, 2008a).

Tier Five Operational

Operational risk is the loss potential from an operational failure (Samad-Khan, 2008). Simultaneously, operational IAP risks are the possibilities of not executing against the ISG strategic plan. However, operational IAP risk management is not just concerned with measurement (Samad-Khan, 2008). Operational IAP risk management uses a robust and systematic process for integrating risk-reward and risk-control information into organizational decisions (Samad-Khan, 2008). Specifically, operational IAP risk management is the activity for making organizational decisions where the assumed risk level net of controls has alignment with the risk and loss tolerance standards of entity stakeholders (Samad-Khan, 2008). Operational IAP risk management enables conducting risk assessments, risk decisions, and risk control deployments (Samad-Khan, 2008).

Tier Four Resource Management

Entity manager-leaders face constant pressure to achieve and maintain a competitive advantage in the marketplace (Cegielski et al., 2013; Davis, 2017). Given the insistence to achieve and maintain a competitive advantage, entity manager-leaders should center on the deployment and combination of inputs rather than opportunity avoidance (Chou, 2015; Davis, 2017). Of consequence is dynamic capabilities viewable as strategic options that give an entity a choice to pursue new directions when opportunities emerge (Cegielski et al., 2013; Davis, 2017). Nonetheless, practitioners and researchers believe that an entity's competitive advantage derived from IT use often is temporary (Cegielski et al., 2013; Davis, 2017). Information systems scholars have also questioned how IT deployment and use can infuse an entity with a competitive advantage (Bharadwaj et al., 2013; Davis, 2017; Drnevich & Croson, 2013; Seddon, 2014).

The information systems resource-based perspective focuses on understanding what resources are most likely to contribute to an entity's competitive advantage (Davis, 2017; Pan et al., 2015). Consequently, "resource orchestration" enables integrating resource management notions and asset orchestration (Cui & Pan, 2015; Davis, 2017; Wang et al., 2012). Resource orchestration furnishes a more precise interpretation of the manager-leaders' role in structuring an organizational resource portfolio, bundling organizational resources into capabilities, and leveraging the organizational capabilities to create value for customers (Cui & Pan, 2015; Davis, 2017; Wang et al., 2012). Typically, administrative IT oversight enhances value when using a resource-based lens (Davis, 2017; Turel & Bart, 2014).

An information security management system reflects a holistic approach to managing information security – confidentiality, integrity, and availability of information and data. Analyzing the phrase "information security management system" can enhance understanding of ISO/IEC 27001 standards. Thus, start with the definition that a system is a group of interconnected elements with a purpose (Davis, 2010, 2020). Next, reflect on processes that modify system elements to achieve system goals (Davis, 2010, 2020). In the end, accept that security systems acquire and preserve a congruous condition. Hence, extrapolated, an information security management system has processes specifically installed to achieve management's organizational objectives through protection measures.

IT architecture refers to technology priorities and choices that allow applications, software, networks, hardware, and data management integration into a cohesive platform (Davis, 2017; Masa'deh, 2013). Digital strategies of orchestrators can have consequences beyond the boundaries of the perceived ecosystems when ecosystems overlap (Davis, 2017; Markus & Loebbecke, 2013). In turn, the cross-boundary industry disruptions can alter value networks to multisided markets (Davis, 2017; Pagani, 2013). Commonly, a disruptive IT generates a response from the entities serving the same market (Carlo et al., 2014; Catinean & Cândea, 2013; Cui & Pan, 2015; Davis, 2017). With the increased global competitiveness, the development of platforms for IT disruptive advantage to obtain organizational differentiation and sustainability is a top strategic issue for entity manager-leaders (Berman & Marshall, 2014; Davis, 2017). Disruptive IT platform modifications can result in radical and pervasive innovations in software development entities across three innovation types: adopted base technologies, produced services, and selected processes (Carlo et al., 2014; Davis, 2017).

There are four ISG resource classifications: people, infrastructure, processes, and information (Davis, 2011, 2017; De Haes et al., 2013), which require orchestration. Organizational resource usage should occur judiciously and productively to achieve entity management's operational objectives while simultaneously executing defined control objectives (Davis, 2011, 2017; De Haes et al., 2013). Control techniques for ISG resource management include relational mechanisms, structures, and processes (Davis, 2017; Schobel & Denford, 2013). Where applied, the prime path to rightsizing ISG controls is supplying diligent subordinates with justified resources needed to achieve the specific ISG IAP goals (Davis, 2011, 2017; De Haes et al., 2013). However, regardless of the control techniques and technological capabilities available, the best possible control means is selecting high-quality employees (Davis, 2011, 2017).

High-quality ISG personnel are critical to sustaining the IT unit's effectiveness and efficiency (Cavusoglu et al., 2013; Davis, 2011, 2017). Moreover, without competent entity IAP personnel to manage or manipulate IT resources, even a superbly designed architecture can become ineffective and inefficient (Davis, 2011; Hashizume et al., 2013) in preventing or deterring an information security breach (Davis, 2017). An entity's human resource practices can assist in ISG resource quality assurance through legal screening processes to assess ISG talent competency and ethics (Davis, 2011, 2017; Guo & Yuan, 2012; Price, 2014). As for deployed information security personnel, ISG manager-leaders can enhance IAP service quality by ensuring relevant education and training (Davis, 2011, 2017; Hashizume et al., 2013; Singh et al., 2013).

At the Governance Tree tier-five level, considering Figure 4.7, management needs ISG that sustains knowledgeable people, security infrastructure, resource orchestration,

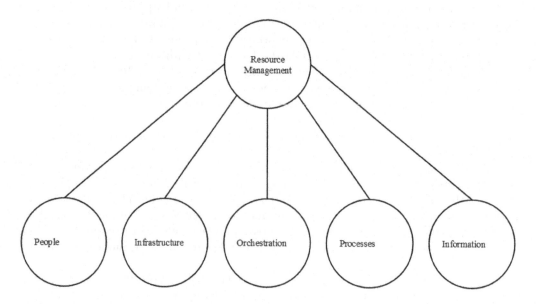

Figure 4.7 Governance Tree – Fourth and Fifth Tier Structural View: Resource Management.

Note: Adapted from *Assuring IT Governance* by R. E. Davis, 2011, Amazon.com. Copyright 2011 by Robert E. Davis. Adapted with permission.

effective processes, and service information to accomplish protection expectations (Davis, 2011, 2017). Hence, information security resource management necessitates:

- knowledge workers that are people well versed in technology deployments, information constructs, and ethical behaviors (Haag & Cummings, 2008),
- security infrastructure practices for the development or acquisition, testing, implementation, maintenance, and disposal of IAP elements (Davis, 2009b),
- resource orchestration that provides a bridge between uncertain environmental factors and security capabilities (Cui & Pan, 2015; Wang et al., 2012),
- processes to effectively provide IAP that minimizes information security risks (Davis, 2008a), and
- service information collection, organization, administration, and dissemination (Haag & Cummings, 2008).

Tier Five People

Knowledge can represent various abstraction levels, including supplying contextual explications of information security intelligence, directing actions to undertake when effecting information security intelligence, designed information security intellectual property, or information security capabilities (Haag & Cummings, 2008). Technology-literate IAP people know how and when to apply technological countermeasures (Haag & Cummings, 2008). In making decisions, informational answers concerning who, what, when, why, where, and how can assist in issue resolution (Haag & Cummings, 2008). Given that supplying IAP extends to social responsibilities, accurate personal and cultural interpretation assessments are necessary to permit appropriate ethical behaviors (Haag & Cummings, 2008).

Tier Five Infrastructure

Infrastructure is the structure beneath a structure (Haag & Cummings, 2008). Thus, cyber-security infrastructure is the structure beneath an IT infrastructure (Haag & Cummings, 2008). Usually, an information security work unit that is responsible for developing and deploying good ISG usually includes resilient security regarding the entity's IT infrastructures and information systems supporting critical functions or operational processes (Davis, 2008a). Specifically, the network infrastructures should have adequate IAP for IT hardware, operating systems, configuration systems, facilities, and support structures (Davis, 2008a). In general, an IAP life cycle covers the phases of needs' determination and demonstration, development, production, use, and disposal or retirement. Consequently, considering common IT infrastructure risks, expressing cybersecurity governance expectations within entity IT control objectives is imperative.

Tier Five Orchestration

Asset orchestration entails administrative searching, selecting, and configuring resources and capabilities that require the ability to match investment decisions with congruent deployment decisions (Tan et al., 2014). Moreover, asset orchestration involves identifying the critical assets and developing a governance system with the means for practical use (Hitt, 2016). Asset orchestration also involves the coordination of co-specialized assets and productive usage (Hitt, 2016). Enabling accommodation of essential IT asset management requirements is implementing and controlling a configuration database containing details regarding IT architecture elements used in provisioning and management of IT services (Davis, 2009b). In ensuring successful IT asset management, relevant inventory management best practice adoption is necessary (Davis, 2009b).

Tier Five Processes

Knowledge of the current and upcoming life cycle phases of information assets is essential for determining the applicable primary information security processes. The adopted processes for coordinating security knowledge-sharing mechanisms influence security knowledge-sharing in entities (Davis, 2017; Flores et al., 2014). Where information security process alignments occur with the accepted IT value definition, service basic principles should deliver appropriate quality, on-time, and within budget, while achieving promised benefits (Davis, 2008b). IT service delivery and support benefits usually translate into a competitive advantage, reduced elapsed time for service request fulfillment, customer satisfaction, reduced customer wait time, and increased employee productivity and profitability (Davis, 2008b).

Tier Five Information

Information and decisions have convergence points when conjoined with the binodal processes conveying entity governance relationships (Davis, 2008a, 2017). Information practice domains include data processing systems design, organization analysis, and advertising effectiveness (Davis, 2008a, 2017). In contrast, decision practice areas encompass organization, learning, cybernetics, and suboptimization disciplines (Davis, 2008a, 2017). On the one hand, application-level information techniques enable classification determination, impact assessments, and technological evaluations (Davis, 2017; Hughes et al., 2013). On the other hand, application-level decision techniques can provide objective determination, interaction assessments, performance estimates, and organizational analysis (Davis, 2008a, 2017).

Tier Four Performance Measurement

ISG strategic alignment occurs when proper deployment monitoring ensures objective achievement under the adopted organizational vision (Davis, 2011, 2017). A monitoring system's essence is feedback information on employees' efficacy (Davis, 2011, 2017; Rebollo et al., 2015). IAP performance feedback reporting regularly addresses measurement, matching, and process regulation (Davis, 2011, 2017; Stewart & Lacey, 2012). The information security countermeasures can be good or bad, precise or imprecise, and formal or informal (Davis, 2011, 2017). Nonetheless, controls have two dominant attributes: performance measurement against a standard and performance remediation (if needed) considering the measure (Davis, 2011, 2017). A thriving control system institutes corrections before process deviations become acute (Davis, 2011, 2017).

ISG-deployed controls require effective performance management (Atoum et al., 2014; Davis, 2017). Controls are the activities and tasks, increasing certainty that organizational plans achieve the desired outcomes (Davis, 2011, 2017). IT dispersion limits the effectiveness of many traditional controls (Davis, 2011, 2017). Nonetheless, an entity's service performance usually is measurable quantitatively or qualitatively (Davis, 2011, 2017). However, selecting the appropriate measurement of monitored performance activities is crucial for effective performance management (Davis, 2011, 2017; Flores et al., 2014).

Performance management control techniques include Balanced Scorecard Analysis, Management by Exception, Management by Objectives, Assurance Reporting, Network Analysis (Davis, 2011, 2017; De Haes et al., 2013), and Budget Analysis (Davis, 2011, 2017; Shaaban & Conrad, 2013). The individuals measuring performance may or may not participate in monitored activities (Davis, 2011, 2017). Nonetheless, behavioral considerations are germane in choosing measurement performers (Crossler et al., 2013; Davis, 2011, 2017; Flores et al., 2014). Furthermore, behavioral factors are germane to what is measured and the standards used for comparative analysis (Crossler et al., 2013; Davis, 2011, 2017; Flores et al., 2014). Measurements should reflect the entity's strategy while furnishing critical data and information about significant processes, systems, and programs (Davis, 2011, 2017; Deursen et al., 2013). Data generated from deployed tracking processes, institutionalized measures, or indicators can receive adaptive evaluation and change to improve organizational goals (Davis, 2011, 2017; Flores et al., 2014).

Performance measurement practice and research necessitate understanding strategic organizational intent is an essential prerequisite for deploying efficient and appropriate monitoring, evaluation (Yaokumah & Brown, 2014), and assessment systems that ensure effective IAP change management (Davis, 2017). Using an IAP maturity model can help manager-leaders identify risk issues (Boyson, 2014; Davis, 2017). Procedurally, an IAP maturity model provides a standard means to inscribe, evaluate, and assess the state of controls (Davis, 2017; De Haes et al., 2013; Looy et al., 2013). Collectively, entity manager-leaders can identify risk issues and rate controls by reviewing an IAP maturity model report (Davis, 2017; De Haes et al., 2013). Some information security manager-leaders suggest that if trained individuals appropriately monitor a correctly configured system, breach risk minimization will prevail (Davis, 2017; Lopez, 2012).

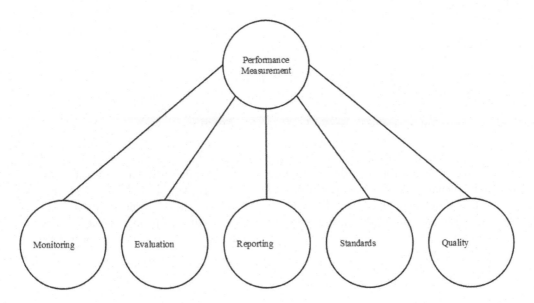

Figure 4.8 Governance Tree – Fourth and Fifth Tier Structural View: Performance Measurement.

Note: Adapted from *Assuring IT Governance* by R. E. Davis, 2011, Amazon.com. Copyright 2011 by Robert E. Davis. Adapted with permission.

IT deployments continue to advance toward a tiered decentralized world of distributed platforms for entering, processing, storing, and retrieving information (Davis, 2008a, 2017). Given the increasing complexity of IT-based systems and networks, there is a mounting information security challenge for service providers and users (Bahl & Wali, 2014; Davis, 2008a, 2017). Stringent mandatory security requirements can cause a shift in outsourcing (Davis, 2017; Sen & Borle, 2015). The greater number of clients an industry-managed security service provider accepts can generate a corresponding increase in system interdependency risk (Davis, 2017; Sen & Borle, 2015). When an entity outsources a process, monitoring can detect contractual risks (Davis, 2011, 2017). For outsourced activities, entity management should have processes to govern the relationship with third-party providers and third-party providers' performance (Boyson, 2014; Davis, 2011, 2017).

At the Governance Tree tier-five level, considering Figure 4.8, management needs ISG that enacts continuous monitoring, continuous evaluation, contextual reporting, ratiocinative standards, and governance quality to accomplish protection expectations (Davis, 2011, 2017). Hence, information security performance measurement necessitates:

- continuous monitoring to address the myriad of managerial, operational, and technical issues that can thwart satisfying an entity's mission (Davis, 2008a);
- continuous evaluation to address the myriad of managerial, operational, and technical issues that can thwart satisfying an entity's mission (Davis, 2008a);
- contextual reporting to ensure alignment with the entity's mission (Davis, 2008a);
- ratiocinative standards institutionalization that conveys minimum performance expectations; and
- ISG quality criteria, validation, and verification processes (Davis, 2009a).

Tier Five Monitoring

Entity manager-leaders typically inscribe policies and procedures for prespecified and routine decisions that form reference terms (Davis, 2012b). The designed policies and procedures provide time for manager-leaders to address nonroutine activities and consider improvements to the deployed control processes by removing the more mundane aspects of daily operations (Davis, 2012b). However, process monitoring is necessary to ensure expected outcomes' achievement for assigned functional responsibilities and irregular activity detection ensue on a timely basis (Davis, 2012b). Though manual performance monitoring can suffice in low-technology situations, automated IAP controls become a necessary part of the IT architecture in most high-technology environments (Davis, 2012b) for ensuring information confidentiality, integrity, and availability. The technology underpinnings to enable an effective continuous monitoring strategy should include several key components: independence from the system that processes the data, the ability to compare data and information across multiple platforms, the ability to process large volumes of data, and prompt notification to management of items that represent IAP control exceptions (Davis, 2012b).

Tier Five Evaluation

IAP countermeasure monitoring completion empowers an information security officer to determine if appropriate IAP control deployments exist for entity systems, processes, activities, and tasks. When an IAP control absence for an entity system, process, activity, or task exists, there is a need for inscription by an assigned information security officer (see the Appendix) that may necessitate control objective development with linked procedures. Where controls exist for an entity system, process, activity, or task, standards need inscription to reduce the possibility of irregular or illegal acts. As a regular action course, the discovery of standard variation requires evaluation and subsequent inscription for remediation or improvement (see the Appendix). As a general control, requiring evaluation inscription contributes to an environment that is conducive to effective ISG.

Tier Five Reporting

The IAP reporting objective determines the appropriate provisioning of information. IT may convey the entity's IAP condition to authorized parties. Reporting information to be complete, current, and timely necessitates authorized reviewer availability and accessibility per specifications and reclamation in a desirable form when necessary (Davis, 2008a, 2020). Reporting information integrity establishes an unimpaired or unmarred content representation for the entire correspondence life cycle (Davis, 2008a, 2020). An IAP evaluation report can identify control gaps and the source of the vulnerabilities. The executive summary of the IAP evaluation report must elaborate on the state of countermeasures. Notably, deficiencies and weaknesses need clear communication to enable applying the management by exception strategy (Davis, 2010). Of the potential vulnerability inscriptions in the IAP evaluation report, identifying significant or material risks is crucial. The IAP evaluation report must also include recommendations to address identified issues (Davis, 2010, 2020).

Tier Five Standards

Information security standards must receive design and deployment ratiocination (Davis, 2008a, 2017; Järveläinen, 2012). Evaluating the current entity information security state requires comparison to de facto and de jure standards for performance measurement (Davis, 2008a, 2017). Standards can reflect specific IAP objectives or goals for comparison against performance (Davis, 2011, 2017). IT manager-leaders need to consider the significance of compliance with standards for achieving effectual ISG (Davis, 2017; Lopez, 2012; Price, 2014). Effectiveness evaluation requires measurement against established IAP standards (Davis, 2008a, 2017), yet standards and audits play disparate roles in interorganizational IT relationships (Davis, 2017; Järveläinen, 2012). The performance measurement extraction point is crucial to an accurate standard comparison assessment. ISG manager-leaders need to establish standards as baselines for gauging quantity, weight, extent, value, or quality (Davis, 2011, 2017).

Tier Five Quality

ISG quality is the extent to which IAP satisfies functionality requirements, capability requirements, or best practices while complying with standards. Robust entity information security is a critical exceptional management model factor (Davis, 2017; Stagliano & Sillup, 2014). Effectual ISG realization can occur by applying sound entity governance (Davis, 2017; Yaokumah & Brown, 2014). Effective ISG sustains personnel, policies, processes, and structures deployed by the entity's oversight committee to direct, inform, manage, and monitor information security activities toward objective achievement (Davis, 2008a, 2017). Strategic design development usually occurs in sequential order—whether manager-leaders have a formal or informal strategic planning system (Davis, 2011, 2017). Regarding design operationalization, ISG practice effectiveness is evident in organizationally framed process domain outcomes (Davis, 2017; Yaokumah, 2014). Entity information security manager-leaders must evaluate and ensure the quality of deployed IAP mechanisms to achieve exceptional ISG performance (Davis, 2017; Wu et al., 2015). Quality is the most likely IAP service measurement.

References

Abdul Rahim, N. F., Haron, H., & Mohamed Zainal, S. R. (2015). Perceived operational risk management and customer complaints in Malaysian conventional banking industry. *Advanced Science Letters*, 21(4), 745–750. https://doi.org/10.1166/asl.2015.5936

Abraham, E. S. (2012). Information technology, an enabler in corporate governance. *Corporate Governance: The International Journal of Business in Society*, 12, 281–291. https://doi.org/10.1108/14720701211234555

Ahmad, A., Maynard, S. B., & Park, S. (2014). Information security strategies: Towards an organizational multi-strategy perspective. *Journal of Intelligent Manufacturing*, 25, 357–370. https://doi.org/10.1007/s10845-012-0683-0

Akpinar, M. (2017). The exercise of power in inter-organisational relationships in response to changes in the institutional environment: Cases from the European automotive industry. *International Journal of Automotive Technology and Management*, 17(1), 51–71. https://doi.org/10.1504/IJATM.2017.082276

Alsudiri, T., Al-Karaghouli, W., & Eldabi, T. (2013). Alignment of large project management process to business strategy: A review and conceptual framework. *Journal of Enterprise Information Management*, 26, 596–615. https://doi.org/10.1108/JEIM-07-2013-0050

Anderson, E. E., & Choobineh, J. (2008). Enterprise information security strategies. *Computers & Security*, 27(1–2), 22–29. https://doi.org/10.1016/j.cose.2008.03.002

Atoum, I., Otoom, A., & Ali, A. A. (2014). A holistic cyber security implementation framework. *Information Management & Computer Security*, 22, 251–264. https://doi.org/10.1108/IMCS-02-2013-0014

Bahl, S., & Wali, O. P. (2014). Perceived significance of information security governance to predict the information security service quality in software service industry. *Information Management & Computer Security*, 22, 2–23. https://doi.org/10.1108/IMCS-01-2013-0002

Badara, M. S., & Saidin, S. Z. (2014). Internal audit effectiveness: Data screening and preliminary analysis. *Asian Social Science*, 10(10), 76–85. https://doi.org/10.5539/ass.v10n10p76

Barton, K. A., Tejay, G., Lane, M., & Terrell, S. (2016). Information system security commitment: A study of external influences on senior management. *Computers & Security*, 59, 9–25. https://doi.org/10.1016/j.cose.2016.02.007

Berman, S., & Marshall, A. (2014). Reinventing the rules of engagement: Three strategies for winning the information technology race. *Strategy & Leadership*, 42, 22–32. https://doi.org/10.1108/SL-05-2014-0036

Bharadwaj, A., El Sawy, O. A., Pavlou, P. A., & Venkatraman, N. (2013). Digital business strategy: Toward a next generation of insights. *MIS Quarterly*, 37, 471–482. www.misq.org

Boyes, H. (2015). Cybersecurity and cyber-resilient supply chains. *Technology Innovation Management Review*, 5(4), 28–34. http://doi.org/10.22215/timreview/888

Boyson, S. (2014). Cyber supply chain risk management: Revolutionizing the strategic control of critical IT systems. *Technovation*, 34, 342–353. http://doi.org/10.1016/j.technovation.2014.02.001

Brakewood, B., & Poldrack, R. A. (2013). The ethics of secondary data analysis: Considering the application of Belmont principles to the sharing of neuroimaging data. *NeuroImage*, 82, 671–676. http://doi.org/10.1016/j.neuroimage.2013.02.040

Carlo, J. L., Gaskin, J., Lyytinen, K., & Rose, G. M. (2014). Early vs. late adoption of radical information technology innovations across software development organizations: An extension of the disruptive information technology innovation model. *Information Systems Journal*, 24, 537–569. http://doi.org/10.1111/isj.v24.6

Catinean, I., & Cândea, D. (2013). Characteristics of the cloud computing model as a disruptive innovation. *Review of International Comparative Management*, 14, 783–803. www.rmci.ase.ro

Cavusoglu, H. (Huseyin), Cavusoglu, H. (Hasan), Son, J. Y., & Benbasat, I. (2013). Institutional pressures in security management: Direct and indirect influences on organizational investment in information security control resources. *Information & Management*, 52, 385–400. http://doi.org/10.1016/j.im.2014.12.004

Cegielski, C. G., Bourrie, D. M., & Hazen, B. T. (2013). Evaluating adoption of emerging IT for corporate IT strategy: Developing a model using a qualitative method. *Information Systems Management*, 30, 235–249. http://doi.org/10.1080/10580530.2013.794632

Chi, L., & Holsapple, C. (2005). Understanding computer-mediated interorganizational collaboration: A model and framework. *Journal of Knowledge Management*, 9(1), 53–75. https://doi.org/10.1108/13673270510582965

Chopra, S., & Sodhi, M. S. (2014). Reducing the risk of supply chain disruptions. *MIT Sloan Management Review*, 55(3), 73–80. http://sloanreview.mit.edu

Chou, D. C. (2015). Cloud computing: A value creation model. *Computer Standards & Interfaces*, 38, 72–77. https://doi.org/10.1016/j.csi.2014.10.001

Clark, M., & Harrell, E. C. (2013). Unlike chess, everyone must continue playing after a cyber-attack. *Journal of Investment Compliance*, 14(4), 5–12. https://doi.org/10.1108/JOIC-10-2013-0034

Coertze, J., & Von Solms, R. (2013). A model for information security governance in developing countries. In K. Jonas, I. A. Rai, & M. Tchuente (Eds.), *E-infrastructure and e-services for developing countries* (pp. 279–288). Lecture Notes of the Institute for Computer Sciences, Social Informatics and Telecommunications Engineering, Vol. 119. https://doi.org/10.1007/978-3-642-41178-6_29

Crossler, R. E., Johnston, A. C., Lowry, P. B., Hu, Q., Warkentin, M., & Baskerville, R. (2013). Future directions for behavioral information security research. *Computers & Security, 32*, 90–101. https://doi.org/10.1016/j.cose.2012.09.010

Cui, M., & Pan, S. L. (2015). Developing focal capabilities for e-commerce adoption: A resource orchestration perspective. *Information & Management, 52*, 200–209. https://doi.org/10.1016/j. im.2014.08.006

D'Arcy, J., Herath, T., & Shoss, M. K. (2014). Understanding employee responses to stressful information security requirements: A coping perspective. *Journal of Management Information Systems, 31*(2), 285–318. https://doi.org/10.2753/MIS0742-1222310210

Davis, R. E. (2008a). *IT auditing: Assuring information assets protection*. Pleier.

Davis, R. E. (2008b). *IT auditing: IT service delivery and support*. Pleier.

Davis, R. E. (2009a). *Assuring IT legal compliance*. www.amazon.com.

Davis, R. E. (2009b). *IT auditing: Systems and infrastructure life cycle management*. Pleier.

Davis, R. E. (2010). *IT auditing: An adaptive system*. www.amazon.com

Davis, R. E. (2011). *Assuring IT governance*. www.amazon.com

Davis, R. E. (2012a). *Assuring information security*. www.amazon.com

Davis, R. E. (2012b). The case for continuous auditing of management information systems. In J. Oringel (Ed.), *Effective auditing for corporates: Key developments in practice and procedures* (pp. 209–217). Bloomsbury Information.

Davis, R. E. (2017). *Relationship between corporate governance and information security governance effectiveness in United States corporations* (Publication No. 10603383) [Doctoral Study, Walden University]. ProQuest Dissertations Publishing.

Davis, R. E. (2020). *IT auditing using a system perspective*. IGI Global.

De Haes, S., Grembergen, W., V., & Debreceny, R. S. (2013). COBIT 5 and enterprise governance of information technology: Building blocks and research opportunities. *Journal of Information Systems, 27*(1), 307–324. https://doi.org/10.2308/isys-50422

Deursen, N. V., Buchanan, W. J., & Duff, A. (2013). Monitoring information security risks within health care. *Computers & Security, 37*, 31–45. https://doi.org/10.1016/j.cose.2013.04.005

Darroch, J. (2005). Knowledge management, innovation and firm performance. *Journal of Knowledge Management, 9*(3), 101–115. https://doi.org/10.1108/13673270510602809

Drnevich, P. L., & Croson, D. C. (2013). Information technology and business-level strategy: Toward an integrated theoretical perspective. *MIS Quarterly, 37*, 483–509. www.misq.org

Edwards, C. K. (2013). *A framework for the governance of information security* (Publication No. 3607548) [Dissertation, Nova Southeastern University]. ProQuest Dissertations Publishing.

Edwards, J. S., Duan, Y., & Robins, P. C. (2000). An analysis of expert systems for business decision making at different levels and in different roles. *European Journal of Information Systems, 9*(1), 36–46. https://doi.org/10.1057/palgrave.ejis.3000344

Farahmand, F., Navathe, S. B., Sharp, G. P., & Enslow, P. H. (2005). A management perspective on risk of security threats to information systems. *Information Technology and Management, 6*(2–3), 203–225. https://doi.org/10.1007/s10799-005-5880-5

Fenz, S., Heurix, J., Neubauer, T., & Pechstein, F. (2014). Current challenges in information security risk management. *Information Management & Computer Security, 22*, 410–430. https://doi. org/10.1108/IMCS-07-2013-0053

Flores, W. R., Antonsen, E., & Ekstedt, M. (2014). Information security knowledge sharing in organizations: Investigating the effect of behavioral information security governance and national culture. *Computers & Security, 43*, 90–110. https://doi.org/10.1016/j.cose.2014.03.004

Frigo, M. L., & Anderson, R. J. (2011a, April). What is strategic risk management? *Strategic Finance, 92*(10). https://sfmagazine.com/

Frigo, M. L., & Anderson, R. J. (2011b). Strategic risk management: A foundation for improving enterprise risk management and governance. *Journal of Corporate Accounting & Finance, 22*(3), 81–88. https://doi.org/10.1002/jcaf.20677

Gil-Lafuente, A., & Paula, L. B. (2013). Algorithm applied in the identification of stakeholders. *Kybernetes, 42*, 674–685. https://doi.org/10.1108/K-04-2013-0073

Glavas, A., & Mish, J. (2015). Resources and capabilities of Triple Bottom Line firms: Going over old or breaking new ground? *Journal of Business Ethics, 127,* 623–642. https://doi.org/10.1007/s10551-014-2067-1

Glinkowska, B., & Kaczmarek, B. (2015). Classical and modern concepts of corporate governance (stewardship theory and agency theory). *Management, 19*(2), 84–92. https://doi.org/10.1515/manment-2015-0015

Goodman, P. S., & Rousseau, D. M. (2004). Organizational change that produces results: The linkage approach. *Academy of Management Executive, 18*(3), 7–19. https://doi.org/10.5465/AME.2004.14776160

Gosain, S., Lee, Z., & Kim, Y. (2005). The management of cross-functional inter-dependencies in ERP implementations: Emergent coordination patterns. *European Journal of Information Systems, 14*(4), 371–387. https://doi.org/10.1057/palgrave.ejis.3000549

Guo, K. H., & Yuan, Y. (2012). The effects of multilevel sanctions on information security violations: A mediating model. *Information & Management, 49,* 320–326. https://doi.org/10.1016/j.im.2012.08.001

Haag, S., & Cummings, M. (2008). *Management information systems for the information age* (Laureate Education, Inc., custom ed.). McGraw-Hill/Irwin.

Harrison, J. S., & Wicks, A. C. (2013). Stakeholder theory, value, and firm performance. *Business Ethics Quarterly, 23,* 97–124. https://doi.org/10.5840/beq20132314

Hashizume, K., Rosado, D. G., Fernández-Medina, E., & Fernandez, E. B. (2013). An analysis of security issues for cloud computing. *Journal of Internet Services and Applications, 4*(1), 1–13. https://doi.org/10.1186/1869-0238-4-5

Hardcopf, R., Gonçalves, P., Linderman, K., & Bendoly, E. (2017). Short-term bias and strategic misalignment in operational solutions: Perceptions, tendencies, and traps. *European Journal of Operational Research, 258*(3), 1004–1021. https://doi.org/10.1016/j.ejor.2016.09.036

Heracleous, L., & Lan, L. L. (2012). Agency theory, institutional sensitivity, and inductive reasoning: Towards a legal perspective. *Journal of Management Studies, 49,* 223–239. https://doi.org/10.1111/j.1467-6486.2011.01009.x

Hitt, M. A. (2016). Asset orchestration. In M. Augier & D. J. Teece (Eds.), *The Palgrave encyclopedia of strategic management* (pp. 1–3). https://doi.org/10.1057/978-1-349-94848-2_457-1

Hodgkinson, I. R., Ravishankar, M. N., & Aitken-Fischer, M. (2014). A resource-advantage perspective on the orchestration of ambidexterity. *The Service Industries Journal, 34,* 1234–1252. https://doi.org/10.1080/02642069.2014.942655

Hughes, D., Bon, J., & Rapp, A. (2013). Gaining and leveraging customer-based competitive intelligence: The pivotal role of social capital and salesperson adaptive selling skills. *Journal of the Academy of Marketing Science, 41,* 91–110. https://doi.org/10.1007/s11747-012-0311-8

Imenda, S. (2014). Is there a conceptual difference between theoretical and conceptual frameworks? *Journal of Social Sciences, 38,* 185–195. www.krepublishers.com

IT Governance Institute. (2008). *Information security governance: Guidance for information security managers.* Author.

Järveläinen, J. (2012). Information security and business continuity management in interorganizational IT relationships. *Information Management & Computer Security, 20,* 332–349. https://doi.org/10.1108/09685221211286511

Kearney, W. D., & Kruger, H. A. (2013). A framework for good corporate governance and organisational learning: An empirical study. *International Journal of Cyber-Security and Digital Forensics, 2,* 36–47. http://sdiwc.net

Kim, A. C., Lee, S. M., & Lee, D. H. (2012). Compliance risk assessment measures of financial information security using system dynamics. *International Journal of Security and Its Applications, 6*(4), 191–200. www.sersc.org

Kumar, S., Himes, K. J., & Kritzer, C. P. (2014). Risk assessment and operational approaches to managing risk in global supply chains. *Journal of Manufacturing Technology Management, 25,* 873–890. https://doi.org/10.1108/JMTM-04-2012-0044

Kwon, J., Ulmer, J. R., & Wang, T. (2013). The association between top management involvement and compensation and information security breaches. *Journal of Information Systems*, 27(1), 219–236. https://doi.org/10.2308/isys-50339

Lambert, S. C., & Davidson, R. A. (2013). Applications of the business model in studies of enterprise success, innovation and classification: An analysis of empirical research from 1996 to 2010. *European Management Journal*, 31, 668–681. https://doi.org/10.1016/j.emj.2012.07.007

Liang-Chuan, W., & Liang-Hong, W. (2015). Improving the global supply chain through service engineering: A services science, management, and engineering-based framework. *Asia Pacific Management Review*, 20, 24–31. https://doi.org/10.1016/j.apmrv.2014.12.002

Looy, A. V., De Backer, M., Poels, G., & Snoeck, M. (2013). Choosing the right business process maturity model. *Information & Management*, 50, 466–488. https://doi.org/10.1016/j.im.2013.06.002

Lopez, R. H. (2012). *Information data security specialists' and business leaders' experiences regarding communication challenges* (Publication No. 3503982) [Doctoral Study, Walden University]. ProQuest Dissertations Publishing.

Losiewicz-Dniestrzanska, E. (2015). Monitoring of compliance risk in the bank. *Procedia Economics and Finance*, 26, 800–805. https://doi.org/10.1016/S2212-5671(15)00846-1

Magdaraog, Jr., G. A. (2014). Warning signs in the workplace: An analysis of risk factors in employee fraud. *The Carrington Rand Journal of Social Sciences*, 1(1), 73–82. www.carringtonrand.com

Markus, M. L., & Loebbecke, C. (2013). Commoditized digital processes and business community platforms: New opportunities and challenges for digital business strategies. *MIS Quarterly*, 37, 649–654. www.misq.org

Masa'deh, R. (2013). The impact of information technology infrastructure flexibility on firm performance: An empirical study of Jordanian public shareholding firms. *Jordan Journal of Business Administration*, 9, 204–224. https://doi.org/10.12816/0002054

Mattsson, U. T. (2014). Bridging the gap between access and security in big data. *ISACA Journal*, 6, 1–5. www.isaca.org/resources/isaca-journal

Mentzer, J. T., Myers, M. B., & Stank, T. P. (Eds.). (2007). *Handbook of global supply chain management*. Sage.

Miles, S. (2012). Stakeholders: Especially contested or just confused? *Journal of Business Ethics*, 108, 285–298. https://doi.org/10.1007/s10551-011-1090-8

Mishra, S., & Mohanty, P. (2014). Corporate governance as a value driver for firm performance: Evidence from India. *Corporate Governance*, 14, 265–280. https://doi.org/10.1108/CG-12-2012-0089

Mohare, R., & Lanjewar, U. (2012). Determinants of business information security. *International Journal of Marketing and Technology*, 2(7), 203–209. www.ijmra.us

Nalband, N. A., & Kelabi, S. L. (2014). Redesigning Carroll's CSR pyramid model. *Journal of Advanced Management Science*, 2, 236–239. https://doi.org/10.12720/joams.2.3.236-239

Pagani, M. (2013). Digital business strategy and value creation: Framing the dynamic cycle of control points. *MIS Quarterly*, 37, 617–632. www.misq.org

Pan, G., Pan, S.-L., & Lim, C.-Y. (2015). Examining how firms leverage IT to achieve firm productivity: RBV and dynamic capabilities perspectives. *Information & Management*, 52, 401–412. https://doi.org/10.1016/j.im.2015.01.001

Pande, S., & Ansari, V. A. (2014). A theoretical framework for corporate governance. *Indian Journal of Corporate Governance*, 7(1), 56–72. https://doi.org/10.1177/0974686220140104

Pérez-Méndez, J. A., & Machado-Cabezas, Á. (2015). Relationship between management information systems and corporate performance. *Spanish Accounting Review*, 18, 32–43. https://doi.org/10.1016/j.rcsar.2014.02.001

Porter, M. E. (1998). *Competitive advantage: Creating and sustaining superior performance*. Free Press.

Price, J. D. (2014). *Reducing the risk of a data breach using effective compliance programs* (Publication No. 3619214) [Doctoral Study, Walden University]. ProQuest Dissertations Publishing.

Raelin, J. D., & Bondy, K. (2013). Putting the good back in good corporate governance: The presence and problems of double-layered agency theory. *Corporate Governance: An International Review, 21*, 420–435. https://doi.org/10.1111/corg.12038

Rasheed, S., ChangFeng, W., & Yaqub, F. (2015). Towards program risk management and perceived risk management barriers. *International Journal of Hybrid Information Technology, 8*, 323–338. https://doi.org/10.14257/ijhit.2015.8.5.35

Rebollo, O., Mellado, D., Fernández-Medina, E., & Mouratidis, H. (2015). Empirical evaluation of a cloud computing information security governance framework. *Information and Software Technology, 58*, 44–57. https://doi.org/10.1016/j.infsof.2014.10.003

Rijke, J., Herk, S. V., Zevenbergen, C., Ashley, R., Hertogh, M., & Heuvelhof, E. T. (2014). Adaptive programme management through a balanced performance/strategy oriented focus. *International Journal of Project Management, 32*, 1197–1209. https://doi.org/10.1016/j.ijproman.2014.01.003

Roberts, N., & Grover, V. (2012). Leveraging information technology infrastructure to facilitate a firm's customer agility and competitive activity: An empirical investigation. *Journal of Management Information System, 28*(4), 231–270. https://doi.org/10.2753/MIS0742-1222280409

Rubino, M., & Vitolla, F. (2014). Corporate governance and the information system: How a framework for IT governance supports ERM. *Corporate Governance: The International Journal of Business in Society, 14*, 320–338. https://doi.org/10.1108/CG-06-2013-0067

Saber, Z., Bahraami, H. R., & Haery, F. A. (2014). Analysis of the impact of supply chain management techniques: A competitive advantage in the market. *International Journal of Academic Research in Economics and Management Sciences, 3*(1), 75–88. https://doi.org/10.6007/IJAREMS/v3-i1/579

Safa, N. S., & Von Solms, R. (2016). An information security knowledge sharing model in organizations. *Computers in Human Behavior, 57*, 442–451. https://doi.org/10.1016/j.chb.2015.12.037

Samad-Khan, A. (2008). Modern operational risk management. *Emphasis, 2*, 26–29. www.stamfordrisk.com/pdf/Modern_Operational_Risk_Management.pdf

Scharff, R. (2013). Being post-positivist . . . or just talking about it? *Foundations of Science, 18*(2), 393–397. https://doi.org/10.1007/s10699-011-9249-4

Schobel, K., & Denford, J. S. (2013). The chief information officer and chief financial officer dyad in the public sector: How an effective relationship impacts individual effectiveness and strategic alignment. *Journal of Information Systems, 27*(1), 261–281. https://doi.org/10.2308/isys-50321

Seddon, P. B. (2014). Implications for strategic IS research of the resource-based theory of the firm: A reflection. *The Journal of Strategic Information Systems, 23*, 257–269. https://doi.org/10.1016/j.jsis.2014.11.001

Sen, R., & Borle, S. (2015). Estimating the contextual risk of data breach: An empirical approach. *Journal of Management Information Systems, 32*, 314–341. https://doi.org/10.1080/07421222.2015.1063315

Shaaban, H., & Conrad, M. (2013). Democracy, culture and information security: A case study in Zanzibar. *Information Management & Computer Security, 21*, 191–201. https://doi.org/10.1108/IMCS-09-2012-0057

Sharma, J. P., & Khanna, S. (2014). Corporate social responsibility, corporate governance and sustainability: Synergies and inter-relationships. *Indian Journal of Corporate Governance, 7*(1), 14–38. https://doi.org/10.1177/0974686220140102

Silic, M., & Back, A. (2014). Information security: Critical review and future directions for research. *Information Management & Computer Security, 22*, 279–308. https://doi.org/10.1108/IMCS-05-2013-0041

Sindhuja, P. N. (2014). Impact of information security initiatives on supply chain performance: An empirical investigation. *Information Management & Computer Security, 22*, 450–473. https://doi.org/10.1108/IMCS-05-2013-0035

Singh, A. N., Picot, A., Kranz, J., Gupta, M. P., & Ojha, A. (2013). Information security management (ISM) practices: Lessons from select cases from India and Germany. *Global Journal of Flexible Systems Management, 14*, 225–239. https://doi.org/10.1007/s40171-013-0047-4

Slaper, T. F., & Hall, T. J. (2011, Spring). The triple bottom line: What is it and how does it work. *Indiana Business Review, 86*(1), 4–8. www.ibrc.indiana.edu/ibr/2011/spring/article2.html

Stagliano, A. J., & Sillup, G. P. (2014). Transparency and risk assessment reporting: A case study sector survey of cybercrime disclosures. *Journal of Business and Economics, 5*, 1134–1140. https://doi.org/10.15341/jbe(2155-7950)/07.05.2014/017

Stewart, G., & Lacey, D. (2012). Death by a thousand facts: Criticising the technocratic approach to information security awareness. *Information Management & Computer Security, 20*(1), 29–38. https://doi.org/10.1108/09685221211219182

Sun, Y., & Bhattacherjee, A. (2014). Looking inside the "IT Black Box": Technological effects on IT usage. *Journal of Computer Information Systems, 54*(2), 1–15. https://doi.org/10.1080/0887 4417.2014.11645681

Tan, F., Pan, S. L., & Zuo, M. (2014). The role of organisational interdependencies and asset orchestration in business integration: A case study of M.Com. *International Journal of Information Management, 34*(6), 780–784. https://doi.org/10.1016/j.ijinfomgt.2014.07.004

Tashman, P., & Raelin, J. (2013). Who and what really matters to the firm: Moving stakeholder salience beyond managerial perceptions. *Business Ethics Quarterly, 23*, 591–616. https://doi.org/10.5840/beq201323441

Turel, O., & Bart, C. (2014). Board-level IT governance and organizational performance. *European Journal of Information Systems, 23*, 223–239. https://doi.org/10.1057/ejis.2012.61

Wang, N., Liang, H., Zhong, W., Xue, Y., & Xiao, J. (2012). Resource structuring or capability building? An empirical study of the business value of information technology. *Journal of Management Information Systems, 29*(2), 325–367. https://doi.org/10.2753/MIS0742-1222290211

Williams, S. P., Hardy, C. A., & Holgate, J. A. (2013). Information security governance practices in critical infrastructure organizations: A socio-technical and institutional logic perspective. *Electronic Markets, 23*, 341–354. https://doi.org/10.1007/s12525-013-0137-3

Wu, S. P. J., Straub, D. W., & Liang, T. P. (2015). How information technology governance mechanisms and strategic alignment influence organizational performance: Insights from a matched survey of business and IT managers. *MIS Quarterly, 39*, 497–518. www.misq.org

Yaokumah, W. (2013). *Evaluating the effectiveness of information security governance practices in developing nations: A case of Ghana* (Publication No. 3557634) [Dissertation, Capella University]. ProQuest Dissertations Publishing.

Yaokumah, W. (2014). Information security governance implementation within Ghanaian industry sectors: An empirical study. *Information Management & Computer Security, 22*, 235–250. https://doi.org/10.1108/IMCS-06-2013-0044

Yaokumah, W. (2015). Evaluating the effectiveness of information security governance practices in developing nations: A case of Ghana. In *Standards and standardization: Concepts, methodologies, tools, and applications* (pp. 1317–1333). https://doi.org/10.4018/978-1-4666-8111-8.ch062

Yaokumah, W., & Brown, S. (2014). An empirical examination of the relationship between information security/business strategic alignment and information security governance domain areas. *Journal of Business Systems, Governance & Ethics, 9*(2), 50–65. https://doi.org/10.15209/jbsge.v9i2.718

Zachariadis, M., Scott, S., & Barrett, M. (2013). Methodological implications of critical realism for mixed-methods research. *MIS Quarterly, 37*, 855–879. www.misq.org

Zhao, X., Xue, L., & Whinston, A. B. (2013). Managing interdependent information security risks: Cyberinsurance, managed security services, and risk pooling arrangements. *Journal of Management Information Systems, 30*(1), 123–152. https://doi.org/10.2753/MIS0742-1222300104

Recommended Reading

Maleh, Y., Zaydi, M., Sahid, A., & Ezzati, A. (2018). Building a maturity framework for information security governance through an empirical study in organizations. In Y. Maleh (Ed.), *Security and privacy management, techniques, and protocols* (pp. 96–127). https://doi.org/10.4018/978-1-5225-5583-4.ch004

Posthumus, S., & Von Solms, R. (2004). A framework for the governance of information security. *Computers & Security, 23*(8), 638–646. https://doi.org/10.1016/j.cose.2004.10.006

Sigauke, J., Mupfiga, P., & Tsokota, T. (2015). An analysis of the information security governance in the state owned enterprises (SOE) in Zimbabwe. *The International Journal of Engineering and Science (IJES)*, 4(12), 49–53. www.theijes.com

Von Solms, B. (2006). Information security: The fourth wave. *Computers & Security*, 25(3), 165–168. https://doi.org/10.1016/j.cose.2006.03.004

Von Solms, R., & Von Solms, B. (2006). Information security governance: A model based on the direct-control cycle. *Computers & Security*, 25(6), 408–412. https://doi.org/10.1016/j.cose.2006.07.005

Control Evaluation Worksheets

Control Evaluation Worksheets 1a: Single Risk Ratings

Security Objective	Confidentiality	Integrity	Availability	Combined Rating

Control Evaluation Worksheets 1b: Single Risk Ratings

Configuration Name	Confidentiality	Integrity	Availability	Combined Rating

Control Evaluation Worksheets 2a: Group Risk Ratings

Security Objective	Information System	Information Type	Combined Rating

Control Evaluation Worksheets 2b: Group Risk Ratings

Configuration Name	Configuration Category	Configuration Type	Combined Rating

Control Evaluation Worksheets 3: Summary Risk Sheet

Category	Explanation
[Title of Risk Item]	
[Type of Risk]	
[Ambit of Risk]	
[Nature of Risk]	
[Stakeholders]	
[Risk Valuation]	
[Risk Tolerance/Appetite Level]	
[Risk Treatment Mechanisms]	
[Potential Action for Remediation/Improvement]	
[Strategy and Policy Development/Deployment]	

Chapter 5

Organizational Employees

Abstract

Stakeholders need to know entity manager-leaders are applying appropriate practices for ensuring that information assets remain protected. Numerous governance failures have resulted from organizational commitment lapses by entity employees. Making ethical decisions often requires a trade-off for entity employees. After a scandal results from perceived ethical misconduct, the proper course of action appears obvious. Entity manager-leaders should consider information asset users and user perceptions as significant factors in providing a secure environment. IT manipulation nonetheless continually enables intentional or unintentional IAP breaches. Through delegation, every entity employee assumes responsibility for maintaining the control system that safeguards information assets. Entity employee IAP education, training, and awareness are critical in reducing the risk of a cybersecurity breach. In Chapter 5, the author discusses responsibility delegation and counterproductive workplace behavior. Chapter 5 also provides IT-incident response team insights, employee development strategies, and an overview of entity IT audit team activities.

Introduction

Statutory accountability supersedes professional requirements (Davis, 2008a). However, information and communication technology can cause societal engineering and organizational dilemmas when statutory accountability exists (Davis, 2008a). Additionally, just because a particular action choice is legal does not ensure ethicality (Davis, 2008a). Perceiving legal compliance as an organizational ethic's goal rather than the starting point can lead to poor IAP administration, with disastrous consequences for employees and the entity (Davis, 2008a). Deep knowledge acquisition by manager-leaders permits effective information security activity coordination (Davis, 2017; Flores et al., 2014). Concerning IAP, the entity information security function should:

- establish processes for provisioning user accounts,
- monitor whether crucial functions are divided among different individuals to disable the necessary authority or access, which could result in irregularities or illegal acts,
- evaluate whether crucial functions are divided among different individuals to disable the necessary authority or access, which could result in irregularities or illegal acts,
- verify user access restrictions to information assets consistent with least privilege principles,
- ensure the review of all entity positions for sensitivity level,
- inscribe procedures for friendly and unfriendly terminations,
- install mechanisms for holding users responsible for their actions, and
- retain signed human resource statements inscribing appropriate employee background screenings for entity positions (Davis, 2008a).

Governments and governmental agencies enact laws and regulations to declare unacceptable conduct or actions. Governments and governmental agencies also enact laws and regulations to provide entity stakeholders confidence that management will perform perceived fiduciary responsibilities (Davis, 2009a). The fiduciary relationship between stakeholders and management typically requires the entity's management to safeguard entrusted assets that generate revenues or pay expenses (Davis, 2009a). In sustaining fiduciary safeguarding, an entity's management needs to provide accurate and complete information about past and current organizational performance and assessments of any confirmed future economic events that may or will affect the entity's financial position or status (Davis, 2009a). Thus, entity governance-related laws and regulations present expectations to refrain from participating in unethical, corrupt, or fraudulent behavior (Davis, 2009a).

The entity's control environment influences counterproductive workplace behaviors and fraudulent workplace behaviors (C. Chen et al., 2012; Davis, 2017; Z. Ahmad & Norhashim, 2008). Communication of workplace behavioral values and standards typically is broadcast to organizational personnel through exemplary actions, policy statements, conduct codes, and training (Davis, 2008a, 2017). Exemplary behavior encompasses trustworthiness, with intrinsic motivation and orientation to serving the collective rather than themselves (Davis, 2017; Glinkowska & Kaczmarek, 2015; Heracleous & Lan, 2012; Pande & Ansari, 2014). Designed and implemented multilevel sanctions can prevent information security policy violations in the workplace (Davis, 2017; Guo & Yuan, 2012). Combined, conduct code and cultural training internalization help influence employee conceptions of appropriate behaviors (Davis, 2017; Vance & Siponen, 2012; Z. Ahmad & Norhashim, 2008).

Without competent individuals to manage or manipulate deployed resources, even a superbly designed ISG program will become ineffective and inefficient (Davis, 2008a). Entity manager-leaders need to establish and maintain information security education, training, and awareness programs for employees (Davis, 2008b). Information security personal and IT users should receive proper IAP training (Davis, 2008a). Relevant training attempts to ensure entity personnel can perform an assigned activity or task (Davis, 2008a) while safeguarding the associated information asset(s). Though training has organizational value, learning barriers can exist (Rida-E-Fiza et al., 2015). This chapter presents many of the positive and negative consequences incurred by having organizational employees.

Responsibility Delegation

Employee decisions are essential to achieving IAP goals (Davis, 2008a). Therefore, manager-leaders must ensure that employees accept and comply with IAP goals (Davis, 2008a). IAP goal congruence influences decisional quality (Davis, 2008a, 2017). Where decision quality is essential and subordinates do not share the same IAP goals, manager-leaders face losing control over activities (Davis, 2008a), resulting in detrimental organizational effects (Davis, 2017). Hence, employee IAP goal incongruence potentially suboptimizes ISG decision quality (Davis, 2008a, 2017). In countering suboptimization, manager-leaders should acquire an in-depth understanding of the environment, organizational objectives, and processes to enable information security services alignment with entity needs (Davis, 2017; Flores et al., 2014).

An effective internal control system reflects a mature control environment, secure information assets, quality improvement processes, and resource monitoring activities (Davis, 2008a). Due to a significant role in supporting operational and financial communications, entity employees must implement and maintain designed controls, whether manual or technological, over digitally encoded information (Davis, 2008a). Information and communication systems should identify, capture, and exchange data in a form and time frame that enables employee performance of assigned responsibilities (Davis, 2008a). In maintaining appropriate workflow control, manager-leaders commonly accomplish separation through segregation-of-functions and segregation-of-duties methodologies to prevent, detect, or deter errors, mistakes, omissions, irregularities, and illegal acts (Davis, 2008a). Nonetheless, authority and access rights to information assets require scrutinization for ensuring congruence and compliance with assigned responsibilities (Davis, 2008a).

Entity structural controls must exist to ensure maintaining appropriate employee authority and access rights. Segregation-of-functions is constructing individual work units to achieve entity management's intentions while simultaneously complying with control principles (Davis, 2008a). In contrast, segregation-of-duties is the delineation of employee responsibility assignments within a defined work unit to achieve entity management's intentions while simultaneously complying with control principles (Davis, 2008a). Entity IAP manager-leaders must establish, enforce, and institutionalize segregation-of-functions and segregation-of-duties (Davis, 2008a).

As a fundamental tenet for obtaining adequate control, segregation-of-functions and segregation-of-duties deployments need to support the entity's policies, procedures, directives, and organizational structure established to inhibit one individual from conducting unauthorized actions or gaining unauthorized access to assets (Davis, 2008a). Segregation-of-functions is a control used to reduce opportunities for someone to perpetuate and conceal errors, mistakes, omissions, irregularities, and illegal acts by separating functional responsibilities (Davis, 2009a). Segregation-of-duties is a control used to reduce opportunities for someone to perpetuate and conceal errors, mistakes, omissions, irregularities, and illegal acts by separating employee responsibilities within a function (Davis, 2009a). Therefore, minimally, cybersecurity employees responsible for assigning information asset privileges need to monitor and evaluate whether duties and functions have appropriate division among different individuals to disable the necessary authority or access, resulting in an undetected irregularity or illegal act (Davis, 2008a).

The appropriate functional responsibility separation requires defining IT and operational user work units considering control context (Davis, 2008a). Applied segregation-of-functions ensures organizational responsibilities do not impinge upon independence or corrupt information system integrity (Davis, 2008a). As a segregation-of-duties baseline, IT user separation should ensure that one person does not control all transaction or event phases (Davis, 2006). Within a function, manager-leaders can achieve adequate segregation-of-duties through origination, entry, processing, verifying, and distribution separation (Davis, 2006). Alternatively, adequate IT segregation-of-duties is achievable through transaction authorization, execution, recording, and asset accountability separation (Davis, 2006).

Management may not be aware of each employee's detailed activities in the entity functions (Davis, 2009b). Therefore, discussions with management will provide limited information to IAP personnel for accurately applying a segregation-of-duties method (Davis, 2009b). Moreover, an entity organization chart usually does not supply employees' activity details (Davis, 2009b). Also, testing user privileges provides information about employee rights within the IT architecture but will not provide complete information about assigned activities (Davis, 2009b).

IT-processing centralization does not relieve entity manager-leaders from separating duties within operational and technical functions (Davis, 2008a). Complete segregation-of-duties within a function is generally more feasible in large rather than small entities (Davis, 2008a). Large entities tend to follow rigid norms and are conducive to high specialization-of-duties, detailed labor division, elaborate administration, and minimal personal interaction (Davis, 2008a). Small entities characteristically have flexible norms; low specialization-of-duties; broad span-of-control, exiguous, and simplistic administration; and extensive personal interaction (Davis, 2008a).

Ensuring access restrictions to information assets consistent with least privilege principles requires suitable system settings, user account vigilance, and administrative support (Davis,

2008a). Permission settings for critical information assets should receive regular evaluations for appropriateness (Davis, 2008a). Regarding user account vigilance, operational information security management must establish procedures for provisioning and de-provisioning privileges (Davis, 2008a). The designed procedures necessitate including an approval process for new account requests, granting the most restrictive privilege set needed for the performance of authorized tasks, and a process for periodically disabling or deleting accounts that are no longer needed to perform job responsibilities (Davis, 2008a).

Specific to IT provisioning, an accepted means to sustain accountability is identification and authentication system integration (Davis, 2008a). Identification and authentication systems contain a family of security controls in the technical class that ensures users are individually access accredited (Davis, 2008a). Security identification is the act or process that permits object recognition by a protected domain through unique credentials use to distinguish access request validity (Davis, 2008a). Subsequent identity verification is the authentication process for affirming that a claimed uniqueness is correct by comparing offered credentials to previous stored IT validators (Davis, 2008a).

Access Controls

Logical access controls are the manual and technological policies, procedures, and organizational structures deployed to safeguard symbolic objects (Davis, 2008a, 2017). Operational logical controls attempt to ensure that only designated users with approved authorization can access an information asset (Davis, 2008a, 2017). Authorization controls furnish the ability to verify credentials granted for permitting resource access (Baltatzis et al., 2012; Davis, 2008a, 2017) and use. Thus, derivatively, IT authorization empowers access assignment and allowed action administration for a given information asset (Baltatzis et al., 2012; Davis, 2008a, 2017).

Network infrastructure facilities are the locations where IT hardware and software reside (Davis, 2008a, 2017). As information assets, network infrastructure facilities require access controls (Davis, 2008a, 2017). Physical access controls are the manual and technological policies, procedures, and organizational structures deployed to safeguard tangible objects (Davis, 2008a; Sloan, 2014). Physical access controls address reducing IT risks, usually by limiting access to the buildings and rooms housing information assets or installing mechanical locks on devices (Davis, 2008a). Consistent with logical access controls, users of an entity's information processing facilities should receive authentication and authorization through administering applicable policies and procedures (Davis, 2008a, 2017).

Enforceable entity IAP policies can describe which types of activities are acceptable and unacceptable (Davis, 2008a). Subsequently, the inscribed policy with behavioral expectations is the basis for information asset availability. An access policy for information assets should mandate risk-based identification schemes, difficult-to-guess passcodes and forbid sharing credentials. Depending on the resource's total assessed risk, the access policy should direct users to present different identification credentials through operationally distinct control processes (Davis, 2008a). Entity employees need to understand IAP responsibilities and prohibited activities (Davis, 2008a). Thus, manager-leaders need to provide resources and training for entity employee comprehension of work responsibilities (Davis, 2008a).

Who the users are and what users can do are intertwined and rooted in the ability to manage the full life cycle of identification and enforce organizational access policies (Davis, 2008a). IAP identity management should address ensuring licit activities with countermeasures reducing the risk of inappropriate users compromising information assets and gaining access to objects provided through technology mediums (Davis, 2008a). An authoritative identification source resolves synonymy, order, and association (Davis, 2008a). Identification data can be a single item or multiple items designated to distinguish an object (Davis, 2008a) uniquely. Generally, differentiating identification characteristics reflect proof-by-possession, proof-by-knowledge, or proof-by-property (Davis, 2008a).

When a user requesting access offers credentials, identity verification transforms to authentication (Davis, 2008a). Authentication is the process used to validate identity information provided by a resource-user (Davis, 2008a). Upon identification acceptance, deployed sentries should employ sufficiently strong authentication, particularly for accessing critical resources (Davis, 2008a).

Authentication merely ensures that the user meets the privilege claim without considering user access rights (Davis, 2008a). In other words, authentication does not provide user access right attestation (Davis, 2008a). However, authentication does address the requirement to identify each user accessing an information asset (Davis, 2008a). Credential authenticity is not assessable unless the access requestor is identifiable (Davis, 2008a). Thus, authentication requires identification (Davis, 2008a). Depending on IAP deployment requirements, individually or in combination, a user's possession, knowledge, or attribute can authenticate accessibility (Davis, 2008a). Theoretically, deployable access authentication mechanisms include:

- password,
- biometric,
- single-use,
- certificate,
- two-factor,
- on-demand,
- multi-factor,
- policy-based, and
- challenge-response (Davis, 2008a).

Security labels can combine several overt and covert features to make reproduction difficult, including holography and encapsulation techniques (Davis, 2008a). Assigned security labels commonly supply authentication, theft reduction, and protection against counterfeit credentials (Davis, 2008a). Regarding provisioning physical authentication mediums, an entity's access control process should clearly define how encoded identification delivery happens for users within the context of promoting appropriate confidentiality, integrity, and availability (Davis, 2008a). Specifically, the process to dispense tokenized authentication attributes to users should employ a different delivery channel than the physical item (Davis, 2008a). With the tokenization of physical items before individual assignment or usage, security management must ensure the identification mechanism remains dormant and protected until the authentication verification enabler reaches the intended owner empowered with activation and usage rights (Davis, 2008a). Security authentication is a distinct integrity subclassification that necessitates periodic substantiation when used to permit access to information assets (Davis, 2008a).

Resource access approval can occur before or after resource authorization (Davis, 2008a). After obtaining authorization, the requestor receives access rights to objects that enable performing defined operations (Davis, 2008a). Authorization controls usually ensure prompt and accurate processing, as well as the output of valid source data and information (Davis, 2008a). To deploy appropriate authorization controls requires the Chief Information Security Officer to establish confidentiality and integrity standards; measure activities against accepted standards; and maintain controls over input, processing, and output of data and information that triggered the access requests (Davis, 2008a). Additionally, the authorization process should include static and adaptive procedures to follow and assure permission accuracy upon a process interruption, modification, or change (Davis, 2008a).

IT devices typically enable access to multiple programs and data files for many contingent users (Davis, 2008a). User access multiplicity exacerbates the possibility of unauthorized events occurring during authorized IT sessions (Davis, 2008a). Foundationally, access management should sustain information confidentiality and integrity (Davis, 2008a). Furthermore, information integrity and confidentiality requirements are enforceable when appropriate access controls are deployed (Davis, 2008a).

Most cybersecurity systems initiate a two-stage access process (Davis, 2008a). The first stage is IT authentication for ensuring a user is whom they claim to be through specific identification (Davis, 2008a). IT authentication provides the requisite trust in a user's digital identity (Davis, 2008a). Circumstantially, before passing informational or transactional data between applications and functions internally or externally, a deployed process should verify proper addressing, origin authenticity, and content probity (Davis, 2008a). Furthermore, IAP procedures should maintain general authenticity and other integrity attributes during transmission or transport (Davis, 2008a). Therefore, minimally, proof-of-wholeness controls should be deployed for transferable information assets (Davis, 2008a).

The second interlocking cybersecurity systems' access process stage is IT authorization (Davis, 2008a). Authorization controls provide the ability to verify credentials granted permission to access resources (Davis, 2008a). Thus, derivatively, IT authorization enables specification and subsequent administration of the allowed actions for a given information asset (Davis, 2008a). Usually, accessing information assets without authorization is a criminally prosecutable offense (Davis, 2008a).

Formal, management sanctioned, entity-centric access authorization action plans – with defined authorization profiles – need devising and deployment to reduce IAP violation risks (Davis, 2008a). Subordinately, an access authorization plan's tactical goal should be restricting accessibility to authorized resource-users, so management's endorsed activities can occur effectively and efficiently. In turn, a key performance indicator should measure unauthorized employee activity (Davis, 2008a).

Authorization constructs are implementable through various manual and automated procedures (Davis, 2008a). Information asset authorization represents allowing accessibility to resources based on identification and authentication, roles and responsibilities, and security level classification. Procedures formalize authorization constructs and enable complete user mapping to devices, programs, and information (Davis, 2008a). Deployable procedures for IT accessibility can encompass:

- User-based Access Control: The User-based Access Control Model, also known as Identity-based Access Control, requires a security administrator to define permissions for each subject, based on solitary needs (Davis, 2008a). The User-based Access Control model is usually implemented by designating general subject groups (Davis, 2008a).
- Rule-based Access Control: The Rule-based Access Control Model design permits objects charged with handling to allow or deny access by inspecting requests, then comparing specific rules in the object with the rights assigned to a given subject (Davis, 2008a). Most of the Rule-based Access Control functionality relies on a security label system, which dynamically composes sets of conditions defined by the IAP policy engine (Davis, 2008a).

- Discretionary Access Control: The Discretionary Access Control Model establishes a permission structure for each authorized subject and enables authorized IT resource owners to specify who can access specific information assets within their defined domains (Davis, 2008a). Thus, each subject must define proper permissions for all subjects requesting access to every object they own (Davis, 2008a).
- Mandatory Access Control: The Mandatory Access Control Model implementation transpires with a technological resource arbitrating the final decision to allow or deny a request to access an object based on the subject's permission level and the object's security level (Davis, 2008a). To enable the automated decision, a cybersecurity administrator must classify objects and ensure classification storage in all objects through security labeling (Davis, 2008a). Once deployed, authorized subjects cannot access objects beyond the authorized permission label (Davis, 2008a). Furthermore, only designated cybersecurity administrators can provision and de-provision subject entitlements and privileges to objects after receiving and clearing an acceptable access approval or disapproval notification (Davis, 2008a).
- Role-based Access Control: The Role-based Access Control Model allows creating privilege groups within the context of the entity's work activities, assigning permissions to the defined roles and mapping appropriate subjects to roles considering individual job responsibilities (Davis, 2008a). Using Role-based Access Control, cybersecurity administrators can restrict access to certain functions while enabling other functions necessary to fulfill assigned tasks (Davis, 2008a).
- Context-based Access Control: The Context-based Access Control Model considers the subjects attempting to access objects, the type of objects accessed, and the circumstances in which access attempts transpire (Davis, 2008a). A Context-based Access Control scheme usually begins with the protection afforded by the User-based Access Control or Role-based Access Control architecture (Davis, 2008a).
- Lattice-based Access Control: The Lattice-based Access Control Model requires assigning access permissions to both subjects and objects (Davis, 2008a). Based on the established labels, subjects can only access objects with security levels less than or equal to the defined authorizations (Davis, 2008a).
- Capability-based Access Control: The Capability-based Access Control Model requires designating objects the subject may access (Davis, 2008a). Access to an object is allowed if the subject requesting access possesses an object authorization (Davis, 2008a). Authorized capabilities reside in a protected tag that identifies objects and specifies operations allowed by the subject possessing assigned entitlements (Davis, 2008a).

Additionally, at the detail-level, IT activities for implementing access authorization include:

- authorization tables that list the resources individuals have permission to access and identify the authorized tasks each user can perform (Davis, 2008a). Checking of tables occurs each time a user desires to use a resource or performs an activity to ensure the user has proper authorization (Davis, 2008a).
- data and information locks provide controls by indicating which users can access assets and for what purpose (Davis, 2008a). Locks are installable on a data item, record, file, or system as a separate field within a record, in a separate table, or an addressing index (Davis, 2008a).

Power Granting

Power granting to entity employees can occur through managerial authority, experience, information access, qualifications, competence, seniority, reputation, or respect (Davis, 2008a, 2017). Where information reliability is in question, employee integrity and corresponding controls are suspect (Davis, 2008a, 2017). Making organizational actors accountable for decision-making procedures is an effective self-serving decision restrictor under moral hazard (Davis, 2017; Pitesa & Thau, 2013). The ultimate responsibility for conveying employee expectations rests with the entity's manager-leaders (Davis, 2008a, 2017). Correspondingly, manager-leaders must ensure that employees accept and comply with IAP goals (Davis, 2008a). Thus, there is a managerial imperative that the deployed ISG program attempts to ensure ethical employee behavior (Davis, 2017). An impactful approach is establishing formal IAP accountability and responsibility within all entity work units (Davis, 2017).

Formal position descriptions should exist for each entity employee, which convey duties, prohibitions, and reporting (Davis, 2008a) expectations. Typically, position description preparation occurs through job analyses (Davis, 2008a). Job analyses comprise systematic procedures constructed from observing workflow and interviewing personnel (Davis, 2008a). Consequently, position descriptions determine what primary tasks assist in achieving organizational goals (Davis, 2008a). Position descriptions should include definitions of technical knowledge, skills, and abilities required for successful performance in the designated functional responsibility (Davis, 2008a). Furthermore, itemized duties should indicate responsibilities assumed during emergencies (Davis, 2008a). Position descriptions are useful for hiring, promoting, and performance evaluation purposes (Davis, 2008a).

Inscribed, current, and readily available employee position descriptions are essential (Davis, 2009b). Communication of specific expectations for job performance outlines work activities (Davis, 2009b). Providing instructions on how to do assigned work and defining authority addresses the managerial and procedural aspects of expected performance (Davis, 2009b). From a control perspective, a position description can establish responsibility and accountability. Where position responsibility and accountability inscription occur, descriptions can ensure that individuals receive appropriate information asset access (Davis, 2009b).

An entity's human resource function is accountable for ensuring the review of all entity positions for assignment sensitivity level relative to security requirements (Davis, 2008a). Individually, an approved position description should match assigned employee duties (Davis, 2008a). A human resource policy for recruiting the most qualified individual reflecting morally acceptable traits from a candidate pool conveys a commitment to competent and trustworthy personnel (Davis, 2008b). Promotions driven by objective periodic performance appraisals support the dedication of advancing qualified individuals to higher responsibility levels within the entity (Davis, 2008b).

Requiring periodic safeguarding responsibility confirmation by employees will not only reinforce security policies but also potentially deter individuals from committing illegal acts and might identify issues before becoming significant (Davis, 2008a). Such confirmations should include statements that the individual understands the entity's expectations, comply with the conduct code, and is not aware of any conduct code violations other than those the individual lists in the response (Davis, 2008a). Although individuals with low integrity and ethical values may not hesitate to sign a false confirmation, most entity employees avoid written misrepresentations due to potential evidentiary utilization during assertion veracity verification (Davis, 2008a). In contrast, honest individuals are more likely to submit information security confirmations and disclose non-compliant behavior (Davis, 2008a). Resultingly, conformation response follow-up activities may reveal significant IAP issues (Davis, 2008a).

Information security service delivery and service support are commonly an organizational activity hive requiring appropriate resource allocations to satisfy administrative agreements and expectations (see Figure 5.1). Delivery of services occurs through the implementation of appropriate systems, processes, activities, and tasks. The responsibility for satisfying the information security mission lies with each member of the Information Security Office. In this context, information security service delivery should provide the best possible service levels to meet entity-centric needs with pervasive controls encompassing (a) service level management, (b) availability management, (c) capacity management, (d) financial management, (e) continuity management, (f) risk management, and (g) service reporting.

Information security manager-leaders should define and develop service level agreements and operating level agreements before configuration item deployments. Configuration management and change management are the primary security service support processes enabling delivery control objective achievement. If properly deployed, other secondary security service support processes can occur through asset management, release management, problem management, incident management, supplier management, and customer relationship management. Typically, within the security service support domain, the

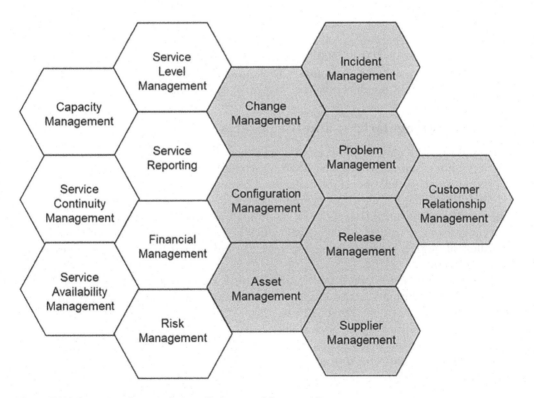

Figure 5.1 Information Security Service Delivery and Support Hive.

Note: Adapted from *IT Auditing: IT service delivery and support* by R. E. Davis, 2008b, Pleier. Copyright 2008 by Robert E. Davis. Adapted with permission.

cybersecurity service desk is a primary sub-process for ensuring a responsive organizational structure. In deploying a cybersecurity service desk, immediate considerations include:

- whether the assigned personnel are physically and emotionally fit to assist or lead a response,
- whether others from whom a response is necessary will be present and able to undertake the roles assigned, and
- whether the assigned personnel will report incidents to senior management.

IT management should pursue serving entity customers through enhanced information asset value. IT is a tool to perform routine processes for most entity users (Davis, 2008b). IT usually pervades all entity organizational structures. Thus, IT enables alternative communication mediums, enhancing teamwork, facilitating better decision-making, and offering business model development opportunities that may lead to value creation and competitive advantages (Davis, 2008b). The information security function is concerned with the adequacy of access controls and service continuity procedures (Davis, 2008b), given the organizational structure.

With manager-leaders increasingly attempting to support every organizational process using IT applications, operational simplicity can proportionally diminish or vanish for employees (Davis, 2008b). Despite transparency provisions through graphical user interfaces, touch screens, color diversity, and help messages, IT complexity can introduce malfunctions or imperfections that may stymie objective achievement (Davis, 2008b). Consequently, incident or problem conditions must be addressed by competent employees if IT is to sustain perceptions as a useful tool for accomplishing entity-centric functionality and reliability objectives (Davis, 2008b). Therefore, management should consider information security service delivery and support foundational components for effective ISG and entity governance that requires periodic IT audit assessments.

Workplace Irregularities and Illegal Acts

Entity stakeholders commonly insist that managers lead subordinates under acceptable practices while sustaining compliance with applicable laws and regulations (Davis, 2008a). Appropriate managerial tone establishment and communications are necessary throughout the entity (Davis, 2008a). The managerial tone includes explicit moral guidance regarding behavioral expectations (Davis, 2008a). As an IAP responsibility, the onus indeed resides with entity manager-leaders to take precautions when employing individuals and to ensure, regardless of motive, reasonable measures prevent individuals from abusing IT resources (Davis, 2008a).

Employees represent a potential limiting factor for an effective ISG program (Davis, 2006, 2008a). As human beings, employees can make mistakes and misunderstand task performance instructions (Davis, 2006, 2008a). Management may also inundate employees with conflicting priorities daily, whereby employees typically focus efforts on items affecting the performance evaluation and positively influencing the reward system (Davis, 2008a). Furthermore, circumstantially, entity personnel may intentionally attempt ISG program circumvention (Davis, 2008a). When confronted with sufficient pressure and a perceived opportunity, some employees will behave unethically or unlawfully rather than accept negative consequences from ethical or lawful behavior (Davis, 2008a) that does not meet performance expectations. However, the threshold at which unethical or unlawful behavior starts varies among individuals (Claycomb et al., 2012; Davis, 2008a).

Due care and due diligence regarding irregularities and illegal acts help ensure IAP alignment with the ISG risk assessment. Often considered the prudent person rule for professionals, discerning employees engage in due care to ensure that they accomplish everything rational to operate an entity using sound, legitimate, and ethical practices (Davis, 2008a). Consequently, prudent persons are diligent in exerting due care (Davis, 2008a). Crucial to sustaining required IAP vigilance is correctly classifying errors, mistakes, omissions, irregularities, and illegal acts (Davis, 2009a, 2020).

As depicted in Figure 5.2, unintentional and intentional acts distinguish characteristics for determining incident classification (Davis, 2009a, 2020; ISACA, 2014). Sub-categorially, an error is the unintentional incorrect task performance (Davis, 2009a, 2020). A mistake is the unintentional misunderstanding of explicated information (Davis, 2009a, 2020). In contrast, an omission is a negligent action associated with pertinent information exclusion that can be unintentional or intentional (Davis, 2009a, 2020).

Intentional and unintentional contemptible conduct perpetration is definable as an irregularity (Davis, 2009a, 2020). However, ISACA (2013) suggests that irregularities are intentional violations of established managerial policies or regulatory mandates. Irregularities can also be deliberate informational misstatements or omissions concerning the entire organization or a system, process, activity, or task, or unintentional illegal acts (Davis, 2009a). Thus, an established management policy or regulatory violation can consist of deliberate informational misstatements or omissions concerning the entity, gross negligence, or unintentional illegal acts (Davis, 2020; ISACA, 2013). Nonetheless, illegal acts are contrary to statutory prescriptions (Davis, 2009a, 2020).

Depending on the geographical location, a workplace irregularity is classifiable as an illegal act (Davis, 2009a). In most democratic governments, the ability to prosecute an illegal act corresponds directly to supporting evidence of the unlawful incident (Davis, 2009a). Perceived workplace illegal acts can receive adjudication in criminal or civil courts of law (Davis, 2009a). Judicially, criminal conviction penalties for illegal workplace acts can include incarceration, fines, and property forfeiture (Davis, 2009a). In comparison, civil conviction sanctions can impose fines and property forfeitures (Davis, 2009a).

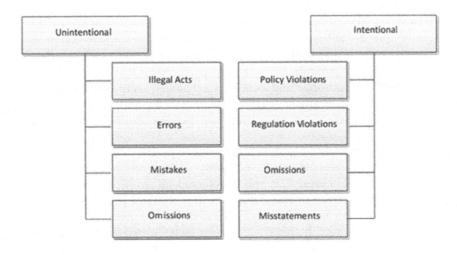

Figure 5.2 Unintentional–Intentional Act Classifications.

Note: Adapted from *IT Auditing: Irregular and Illegal Acts* by R. E. Davis, 2006, Pleier. Copyright 2006 by Robert E. Davis. Adapted with permission.

Table 5.1 Potential Misappropriation of Assets Scenarios

Circumstance	Scenarios
Occupational Opportunities	Employees have access to small and valuable assets, the authority to disburse funds, or noted an application control weakness.
Personal Traits	Employees believe management is unethical or perceives entitlement to information assets.
Situational Pressures	Employees are informed of impending layoffs or must meet the operational goal.

Note: Adapted from *Ensuring Information Assets Protection* by R. E. Davis, 2009, Lulu. Copyright 2009 by Robert E. Davis. Adapted with permission.

Workplace irregularities or illegal acts usually have behavioral warning signs (Davis, 2009a). Therefore, identifying and assessing personnel for workplace behavioral warning signs will help determine the entity's potential irregularities or illegal acts' exposure (Claycomb et al., 2012; Davis, 2009a). As exemplified in Table 5.1, irregularity and illegal act behavioral warning sign categories should include occupational opportunities, personal traits, and situational pressures (Davis, 2009a). Occupational opportunities are circumstances permitting an irregular or illegal activity to occur (Davis, 2009a). Personal traits are the proclivity to commit or rationalize an irregular or illegal act (Davis, 2009a). Situational pressures are stressors internalized by an employee (McGowan et al., 2006), which might influence the decision to commit an irregular or illegal act (Davis, 2009a).

Categorically, counterproductive workplace behavior is intentional conduct contrary to legitimate entity interests (Chernyak-Hai & Tziner, 2014; Claycomb et al., 2012; Davis, 2017; Den Hartog & Belschak, 2012; Zhao et al., 2013). Counterproductive workplace behaviors can take the form of theft, fraud, or sabotage (Den Hartog & Belschak, 2012). In conjunction with economic, technological, and social factors, employees' ethical beliefs link to organizational IT wrongful use (Chatterjee et al., 2015; Davis, 2017).

An uncontrolled entity environment can empower organizational employees to obtain unearned economic rewards (Davis, 2009a). Manager-leaders may deploy an appropriate control system, yet an entity's personnel may perceive control weaknesses existing within the IAP configuration facilitating irregularities or illegal acts for personal profit (Davis, 2009a). An entity's manager-leaders should proactively treat information asset irregular and illegal act risks to minimize opportunity perceptions (Davis, 2009a). Moreover, management needs to authorize and announce scheduled security self-assessments that collectively identify and evaluate legal compliance risks and controls to potentially reduce tactical and operational protection gap perceptions by any entity employee (Davis, 2009a).

Attempted ISG program IAP circumvention comes typically under consideration in contemplating an illegal or irregular act (Davis, 2008a). When considered, potential perpetrators may perceive the ISG program as poorly designed, allowing an illegal or irregular act without circumventing deployed IAP controls (Davis, 2008a). Because of IT's ambit and power, logical access can be an invaluable conduit for the misappropriation of assets (Davis, 2008a). Furthermore, high-tech employees have devised other ingenious ways for asset misappropriations (Davis, 2008a), such as social engineering. If collusion is part of the illegal or irregular act, detection risk for counterproductive workplace behavior expands exponentially (Davis, 2008a, 2010).

Multiple interventions at various levels may be necessary to offset the growing threat of unethical use of information assets (Chatterjee et al., 2015; Davis, 2017). Personal self-sanctions and workgroup sanctions can influence organizational sanctions regarding employee IAP policy violations (Davis, 2017; Guo & Yuan, 2012). Additionally, personal self-sanctions and workgroup sanctions can significantly negatively affect employee intentions to violate IAP policies (Davis, 2017; Guo & Yuan, 2012). However, organizational sanctions can be nonsignificant when personal self-sanctions and workgroup sanctions are inclusive (Davis, 2017; Guo & Yuan, 2012) within the entity.

Manager-leaders should never underestimate insider threats to IAP (Davis, 2008a; Ifinedo, 2014; Posey et al., 2013). Supporting the insider perspective is the acceptance that entity employees with high technical skills and organizational process knowledge pose the greatest threat to safeguarding information assets (Davis, 2008a). Coupled with inadequate countermeasures, employees with access to an entity's internal network could potentially disrupt or corrupt vital services and gain access to unauthorized confidential information (Davis, 2008a). When an entity is seeking success in preventing IAP breaches, policies must minimize the potential for hiring or promoting individuals assessed with a low level of honesty, especially for positions requiring a high level of trust (Davis, 2008a).

Typically, an entity project group or steering committee exists to oversee new system deployments, with authority to make decisions regarding activities affecting implementation (Davis, 2009b). The system project group or steering committee should maintain a carefully planned timetable with procedures to monitor and evaluate information asset deployments. The Information Security Office manager-leader should designate an employee responsible for liaising with entity functions to identify and mitigate any IAP deficiencies or weaknesses associated with new system deployments. Controlled information asset privileges can improve change process performance through assigned roles and responsibilities, needed segregation-of-duties, and current access authorizations.

New or improved information asset documentation represents a critical item for ensuring configuration functionality (Davis, 2009b). Accordingly, up-to-date information asset documentation should be available 2 to 4 weeks before new or improved deployment (Davis, 2009b). Development process documentation provides control over the prevention, detection, and correction of remiss information security countermeasures (Davis, 2009b). Reliable development documentation assists in security breach prevention by establishing a disciplined work environment and improving communications between information asset designers (Davis, 2009b). The existence of a development process audit trail permits information asset vulnerability detection by facilitating supervisory reviews by management, users, technical personnel, and IT auditors (Davis, 2009b). An audit trail also provides evidence of compliance with entity-mandated controls during the development process (Davis, 2009b). Furthermore, documentation of development problems that are detected and subsequently corrected serve to ensure effective issue remediation (Davis, 2009b).

Entity inscription specialists usually write internal documentation (Davis, 2009b). The entity IT function should be responsible for managing various technical documentation types (Davis, 2009b). An assigned IT inscription specialist's responsibilities typically include: preparing and maintaining information about programming, system operations, and user documentation; translating specifications into user documentation; planning, designing, maintaining systems and user support documentation efforts; and providing online help screen content (Davis, 2009b). A data administrator can be a part-time documentation specialist if the assigned responsibilities include maintaining complete, up-to-date documentation about datum and relationships to data records, data files, reports, and business transactions (Davis, 2009b). Additionally, an IT function archivist's responsibility can include development programming, source code, and object code preservation.

Most entity processes benefit from an independent assessment of operational configuration performance (Davis, 2009b). An entity's IT audit function is usually responsible for assuring that programs, program changes, and documentation adhere to established standards (Davis, 2009b). A review of the system configuration protection and outcomes by the IT audit function will provide management with an adequacy assessment and potential recommendations for improvement (Davis, 2009b). Even if the IT audit report provides no recommendations for IAP improvements, a positive opinion is valuable managerial information (Davis, 2009b).

Entity executive manager-leaders can play a proactive role in shaping employee compliance behavior in addition to deterrence-oriented remedies (Hu et al., 2012). As a case in point, executive manager-leader participation in IAP initiatives can have significant direct and indirect influences on employee compliance with IAP policies (Hu et al., 2012). Nonetheless, the effects of executive manager-leader participation and organizational culture on employee behavioral intentions are fully mediated by employee cognitive beliefs regarding compliance with IAP policies (Hu et al., 2012). Therefore, nonexecutive manager-leader participation can strongly affect the entity's organizational culture for employee compliance with IAP policies (Hu et al., 2012).

Governance policies are action courses or methods selected by manager-leaders from alternatives to guide and determine present and future decisions considering the environment (Davis, 2008a, 2017). By which counterproductive workplace behavior is an ISG policy subcategory (Davis, 2017). In designing more effective enforcement, the severity of punishment, the significance of reward, and certainty of control are significant workplace behavioral influences (Davis, 2017). Though rewarding is a plausible IAP strategy (Y. Chen et al., 2012), the effect of reward on IAP policy compliance appears inconclusive (Davis, 2017). Moreover, entities interested in introducing reward enforcement may need to consider intangible rewards such as written or oral commendation to enhance moral standards (Y. Chen et al., 2012).

An entity's personnel decide whether to enforce and comply with policies (Davis, 2006, 2008a; Y. Chen et al., 2012). Psychological and social–organizational factors might encourage or accentuate employee IAP policy compliance (Davis, 2017; Ifinedo, 2014). Workplace social bonding of operational managers and information system professionals generally influences compliance and subjective norms (Ifinedo, 2014). Moreover, compliance and subjective norms can positively affect employee IAP policy compliance (Ifinedo, 2014). Opposingly, blind deployment of routine IAP measures may induce counterproductive workplace behavior (Klein et al., 2015).

IT Incident Response Team

Entity IT should provision secure resource access and intended use within the managerially accepted risk tolerance level. Through delegation, every entity employee assumes responsibility for maintaining the control system that safeguards assets (Davis, 2008a). When instituted with responsibility control, accountability is typically sustainable through applying the check and act steps of the Deming "Plan-Do-Check-Act" management method (Davis, 2008b). Information security managers are typically accountable for responding to intrusions negatively affecting entity information assets (Davis, 2008a). "Thus, security incursions transform information security managers into chief threat firefighters directing resources to extinguish security breach flames" (Davis, 2008a, p. 155). To competently perform the chief threat firefighter service, two critical security incident response elements are necessary: information and organization (Davis, 2008a).

An incident is an event divergent of the standard information asset operations that cause or may cause interruption to or reduction in the agreed-upon quality of service (Davis, 2008b). Whatever the cause, incidents are a common occurrence requiring appropriate resolution to reinstate acceptable information asset operational levels (Davis, 2008b). An entity IT service desk is often the first contact users have when IT services do not perform as anticipated (Davis, 2008b). Since there is a timely corrective action expectation upon incident reporting, employee orientation is critical for maintaining the precipitations of efficient and effective information security service (Davis, 2008b).

Gathering evidence that inappropriate or malicious activity occurred is a control objective for security threat management (Davis, 2008a). Configured controls allowing information security threat management should identify inappropriate or malicious activity within the computing environment (Davis, 2008a). When constructing malicious misuse information asset records, field titling should address incident descriptions such as exploited vulnerability, affected information assets, and attack source (Davis, 2008a). Organizationally, supported by an entity tier-one policy, the ISG program manager-leader should establish a formal IAP structure consisting of

- an Information Security Office that designs, develops, coordinates, and deploys all aspects of entity-wide cybersecurity (Davis, 2008a);
- an ISG Program Committee Representative providing managerial direction regarding cybersecurity and ensuring consistent addressing of cybersecurity as an operational issue (Davis, 2008a); and
- Information Security Officers who manage and coordinate cybersecurity activities within designated work units (Davis, 2008a).

Effectual incident management quickly restores service availability, minimizes service disruptions, and responds to user needs using available resources (Davis, 2008b). Incident management necessitates contingency management (Davis, 2008b). Evidentially, manager-leaders who assign responsibility and delegate authority, considering the work dynamics and the employee available for assignment, practice a contingency management approach (Davis, 2008b). Some employees may react to an incident with unusual behavior. Consequently, appropriate incident management requires establishing links to other internal and external groups (Davis, 2008b). The links to other groups should include law enforcement agencies, response teams, security groups, and the entity's Public Relations Office (Davis, 2008b).

User IT service desk contact can activate incident handling processes dedicated to satisfactory functionality and usability issues resolution (Davis, 2008b). Cybersecurity incidents should be a management concern because information systems are increasingly interconnected through IT (Davis, 2008b). Consequently, cybersecurity incidents can place linked configuration items at risk for information inaccessibility, corruption, or unauthorized disclosure (Davis, 2008b). Significant characteristics of an appropriate IT incident handling capability are

- an understanding of the constituency served;
- a knowledgeable constituency that trusts the incident handling team;
- a means for prompt centralized reporting;
- linkage to other relevant groups; and
- a response team with the necessary knowledge, skills, and abilities (Davis, 2008b).

Cybersecurity incidents are adverse events reflecting inadequate protection or an attempted or threatened breach of a deployed IT countermeasure (Davis, 2008a). Establishing and sustaining a response team that can react swiftly to investigate, contain, mitigate, and remediate incidents are crucial in maintaining IT availability (Davis, 2008a). To a large extent, incident response team proficiency and credibility depend on members' technical skills (Davis, 2008a). Generally, incident response team members need a much broader professional foundation than most IT positions (Davis, 2008a). Expressly, IT incident handling necessitates technoscientific knowledge and experience in several occupational practice domains, including network administration, system administration, system programming, and threat management (Davis, 2008a). Furthermore, at least one incident response team member must qualify as a subject matter expert in applying the entity's preferred computer forensics software (Davis, 2008a).

IT incident handling necessitates leadership to organize, direct, and control an appropriate breach response (Davis, 2008a). Notably, incident response team technical administration is not incident administration (Davis, 2008a). Two important incident response team positions are the manager-leader and deputy manager-leader (Davis, 2008a). Larger entity teams often assign an incident lead as the primary point-of-contact for handling protection breaches (Davis, 2008a). Depending on the magnitude and team size, the incident lead may not perform any incident handling duties, such as evidence acquisition or data analytics (Davis, 2008a). Instead, the incident lead may orchestrate incident handling activities, collect information from incident handlers, provide incident updates to entity manager-leaders, and ensure the meeting of team resource needs (Davis, 2008a). Additionally, an incident response team may require appointing a technical lead (Davis, 2008a). The appointed technical lead must have a robust IT skillset and incident response experience for assuming oversight of and final responsibility for technical work quality (Davis, 2008a).

Inappropriate technical judgment can undermine incident response team credibility or hamper incident resolution (Davis, 2008a). Therefore, assigned individuals must have qualifying knowledge, skills, and abilities for participation in the incident response team (Davis, 2008a). However, the required breadth and depth of technical knowledge and experience for a particular incident can vary, considering the assessed cybersecurity risk (Davis, 2008a). Hence, to appropriately plan, organize, and deploy emergency resources, circumstances can dictate selecting insider and outsider response team members capable of handling incident scenarios (Davis, 2008a).

Full-time IT employees usually have more experiential knowledge regarding the entity's technical environment than managed security service provider personnel (Davis, 2008a). Insider experiential knowledge can help identify false positives and assess information asset target criticality (Davis, 2008a). When the ISG program committee chooses incident response team members from available entity employees, the selected individuals should have a service-orientation and an exceptional understanding of assigned IT (Davis, 2008a). Paramount service-orientation characteristics for incident handling are teamwork and communication skills, while an exceptional IT understanding facilitates providing reliable response recommendations (Davis, 2008a) and committing appropriate actions. Comparatively, as outsiders, managed security service provider personnel may possess more intensive and extensive situational breach knowledge concerning tactics, vulnerabilities, countermeasures, and other issues than entity employees (Davis, 2008a). Managed security service provider personnel may also correlate incidents among clients, which enable novel threat identification and resolution faster than incident response team insiders (Davis, 2008a).

IT incident response work is very demanding (Davis, 2008a). Typically, there is an expectation that the incident response team members will handle an employer protection breach no matter the time or weekday (Davis, 2008a). In combination with performance expectations, incident response team membership can heighten stress (Davis, 2008a). Furthermore, where the entity insiders perform IT incident response handling, with limited administrative or technical assistance from outsiders, employee morale may be negatively affected due to the lack of timely information and providing an appropriate resolution (Davis, 2008a). Thus, selected incident response team candidates may refrain from accepting team membership to avoid potential medical or social repercussions (Davis, 2008a). Consequently, entity manager-leaders may confront recruiting challenges when seeking IT insiders to participate in incident response activities, given a necessary 24-hour and 7-day workweek support commitment (Davis, 2008a).

A Central Incident Response Team handles incidents throughout the entity (Cichonski et al., 2012). The Central Incident Response Team organizational structure can be useful for small entities or localized entities with minimal information asset dispersion (Cichonski et al., 2012). In contrast, where an entity has multiple sites functioning independently, incident management may be more effective when each location maintains a response team (Davis, 2008a). Managerially, the designated Security Operations Center headquarters can host the centralized incident response command center that facilitates standard practices and coordinates activities among dispersed teams (Davis, 2008a). When the manager-leaders deem a centralized incident response command center necessary, processes for logging and monitoring activities at semi-autonomous sites must comply with the entity's policies and applicable legal requirements (Davis, 2008a). Furthermore, site-specific procedures addressing incident handling involving employees should comply with discretion and confidentiality expectations (Davis, 2008a).

Members of the information security function are often the first to recognize that an IAP breach occurred and may perform the initial incident analysis (Davis, 2008a). Cybersecurity incidents can occur through physical security breaches or involve coordinated logical and physical attacks (Davis, 2008a). Communicated threats made against an entity's information asset may not indicate whether logical or physical resources are the attack surface or target (Davis, 2008a). As a result, the IT incident response team may need access to facilities during incident handling (Davis, 2008a).

Physical security for the incident response team's work areas and communication costs should not be remiss during IAP budget preparation (Davis, 2008a). Additionally, there may be a need for participation by information security employees who are not incident response team members during various incident resolution stages (Davis, 2008a). Therefore, close coordination between logical security, physical security, facilities' management, and the incident response team is vital to achieving a holistic IAP approach (Davis, 2008a).

Seeking to preserve electronically encoded evidence implies an incident occurrence requiring extrapolation of facts to prove an irregularity, if not an illegal act (Davis, 2008a). Anticipating potential extrapolation scenarios necessitates information security manager-leaders proactively construct incident response and forensic investigation capabilities considering legal mandates (Cichonski et al., 2012; Davis, 2008a). At rest or in transit, evidence acquisition requires appropriate cybersecurity procedures to ensure non-repudiation (Davis, 2008a). The Chief Information Security Officer must attempt to ensure that measures are in place for preventing destruction, corruption, or unavailability of evidentiary data for forensic investigation (Davis, 2008a). Consequently, procedures addressing the IT infrastructure and processes for incident handling should exist within the entity's cybersecurity documentation (Cichonski et al., 2012; Davis, 2008a).

Extracting transient electronically encoded evidence should follow enacted governmental authorization procedures (Davis, 2008a). Legitimate transient data extraction is commonly known as lawful interception (Davis, 2008a). Lawful interception is the governmentally endorsed legal right to access private communications (Davis, 2008a). Governmental laws or regulations often inscribe the means and authority for conducting lawful interceptions (Davis, 2008a). Applicable governmental statutes include, but are not limited to, the United States Communications Assistance for Law Enforcement Act of 1994, the Dutch Telecommunications Act of 1998, the United Kingdom Regulation of Investigatory Powers of 2000, and Part XI Section 88 of Germany's Telecommunication Act of 2004 (Davis, 2008a).

Most countries require licensed telecommunications operators to provide lawful interception capabilities for capturing target information. However, management needs to ensure that the entity personnel cannot install the lawful interception process (Davis, 2008a). Moreover, the deployed lawful interception process should:

- prevent detection by targeted parties,
- ensure appropriately authorized individuals know about specific interceptions, and
- disable the capability for separate agencies targeting a subject to detect each other during electronic evidence collection (Davis, 2008a).

Lawful interception supports the legal incident evidence extraction process when a network operator or service provider grants the law enforcement officials' accessibility to monitor, review, tag, or capture communications (Davis, 2008a). Lawful interception permits capturing an employee's inbound and outbound data packets to specifically identify delays or inconsistencies in informational treatment (Davis, 2008a). Procedural adherence to lawful interception requirements will ensure legal evidence admissibility (Davis, 2008a) for adjudication.

Cardinally, all potential electronically captured incident evidence needs protection from deletion, contamination, modification, and inaccessibility as soon as possible (Davis, 2008a). When the incident involves data stored in IT, prudent administration dictates informing appropriate parties that evidence attainment will occur through electronic discovery (Davis, 2008a). When informing appropriate parties concerning stored evidence acquisition, the proper notification includes conveying the specific protocols used for preserving electronically encoded evidence and enforceable eradication restrictions for data stored in IT (Davis, 2008a). When feasible, electronically captured evidence needs to maintain stabilization in the environment that existed during the suspect activity (Davis, 2008a).

Conditionally, if someone turns off the target IT during or after an incident, turning the IT on and permitting a computer bootstrap can introduce content changes to files directly or indirectly connected through operating system procedures (Davis, 2008a). Some files interacting with the computer bootstrap process may not be of interest to an investigation (Davis, 2008a). Nevertheless, computer bootstrap configuration modifications can cause previously deleted files containing pertinent information to become irretrievable (Davis, 2008a).

When circumstances will not permit maintaining the embryonic operational state and site until law enforcement authorities arrive or when incident manager-leaders accept legal extraction risks, manager-leader can invoke entity data acquisition procedures for evidence preservation (Davis, 2008a). Data acquisition procedures are tasks for transferring electronically encoded content into a controllable location replicating electronic media types associated with the incident (Davis, 2008a). Upon commitment to using the entity data acquisition course of action, all earmarked hardware media requires protection and the target content during transference to another medium through the approved method (Davis, 2008a). However, capturing volatile data is also critical in situations where evidence integrity can become an issue (Davis, 2008a). Volatile data are transient electronic bits (Davis, 2008a). Therefore, volatile data ceases to exist without appropriate precautions when an IT is shut down (Davis, 2008a). Volatile data capture helps investigators determine the information system state during the incident (Davis, 2008a).

Creating evidential copies through routine backup procedures will only permit replicating specific files (Davis, 2008a). Excluded content in routine backup procedures are files with delete indicators and the designated free space between files (Davis, 2008a). Forensic image obtainment needs to occur using task-oriented software to avoid content limitations inherent with creating evidential copies using routine backup procedures (Davis, 2008a). Appropriate forensic image software replicates an exact working copy of the original media's content (Davis, 2008a). Functionally, applied imaging software for evidential coping should be capable of making an exact replication of every encoded bit contained on the target media (Davis, 2008a). Technologically, media content imaging is achievable without launching the computer's operating system, thereby avoiding tampering allegations, if acquired electronic evidence is for prosecuting criminal misconduct (Davis, 2008a).

Forensic imaging software can capture digitized residual data on targeted recording surfaces (Davis, 2008a). Digitized residual data includes deleted files, fragments of deleted files, and other data still existent within the electronic media's recording surface (Davis, 2008a). Practical forensic imaging replicates a disk surface sector-by-sector as opposed to reproduction file-by-file (Davis, 2008a). Even data commonly considered destroyed can be recoverable from a magnetized surface with appropriate tools (Davis, 2008a). Depending on the product, imaging software can generate a log file of IT parameters such as disk configuration, interface status, and data checksums critical for supportable conclusions regarding an incident (Davis, 2008a).

Functionally reliable forensic imaging practices and software are essential to sustaining evidential continuity (Davis, 2008a). After creating at least two certifiable media images, one replication is insertable as a targeted system substitute for the original IT (Davis, 2008a). The other media image replication is usable for forensic analysis (Davis, 2008a). Once facsimiled, the original media necessitates sealing in a sterilized container, labeled and stored as IAP incident evidence in a secure area until required for judicial proceeding to ensure evidential continuity (Davis, 2008a).

An entity's human resource function employees should inscribe procedures for friendly and unfriendly terminations that address information assets (Davis, 2008a). Disciplinary action or employee counseling procedures should stipulate human resource function involvement when an employee is an incident suspect or is the apparent target of an incident (Davis, 2008a).

Education, Training, and Awareness

Entity employees shape the organizational culture (Khattak et al., 2014). Entity manager-leaders usually find purchasing an IT solution addressing IAP easier than changing a culture (Brotby, 2006; Davis, 2008a). Nonetheless, even the most securable IT solution will not achieve a significant degree of protection if handled by untrained, ill-informed, careless, or indifferent personnel (Brotby, 2006; Davis, 2008a). Depending on the position, becoming an entity employee may only require a standard body of knowledge certification or a few years of experience (Posey et al., 2013). However, for most entities, the hiring emphasis is on acquiring human resources with the expectation that needed organizational learning will occur through handling work-related situations (Johnson, 2017). A well-structured Information Security Office, staffed with suitable individuals, forms the foundation for deploying appropriate IAP and is a critical element for high-quality IT performance (Davis, 2008a). When supporting security responsibility awareness, manager-leaders must clearly articulate that all employees will be held accountable to act within the entity's conduct code and policies if granted information asset access (Davis, 2008a; Siponen et al., 2014).

Entity human resource recruitment efforts should apply professional due care and due diligence hiring practices (Khattak et al., 2014) that render reasonable certainty that a potential employee's competency, reliability, and integrity align with the position's responsibilities (Davis, 2008a). Furthermore, at the activity level, an entity's standard human resource practices should consistently demonstrate recruiting the most qualified individuals, emphasizing the necessary education, training, prior work experience, past accomplishments, and behavioral inclinations (Davis, 2008a). Upon successful recruitment, a signed human resource statement acknowledging appropriate background screening for the individual's assigned position needs safekeeping to permit due care and due diligence verification (Davis, 2008a).

Highly skilled and knowledgeable employees are successful entity conduits (Salas et al., 2015). Employee development strategies are necessary to obtain or sustain entity industry competitiveness (Khattak et al., 2014). Creating a professional development program is a long-term process (Azeem & Mubeen, 2013) and necessitates authorization from entity manager-leaders (Shi et al., 2011; as cited in Johnson, 2017). Professional development program implementation can be critical to entity employee success (Azeem & Mubeen, 2013). Training programs are crucial to employee development and workplace productivity (Anthony & Weide, 2015). Entity employees develop reflective of the content received and knowledge applicability. Requiring training program attendance is one approach to ensuring that employees know the current entity environment (Azeem & Mubeen, 2013).

Training is a significant undertaking for an entity's human resource function (Rob et al., 2016; as cited in Johnson, 2017). In achieving a competitive advantage, training may be a necessary approach to attaining strategic objectives (Niazi, 2011). Entity manager-leaders must understand the importance training has when undertaking activities and tasks (Niazi, 2011). Training is advantageous in enhancing the efficacy of entity employees (Azeem & Mubeen, 2013). Enhancing employee performance levels through training can provide more agile workers in a competitive environment. Entity-specific training can equip employees for facing current and future industry challenges (Niazi, 2011). Consequently, organizational learners enable obtaining a competitive advantage for the entity (Niazi, 2011).

Training is beneficial to organizational performance (Salas et al., 2015). Entity continuity depends on employee performance (Elnaga & Imran, 2013). ISG manager-leaders can enrich service quality by securing superior education and training (Davis, 2011, 2017; Hashizume et al., 2013; Singh et al., 2013). Effective training programs lead to superior return-on-employee-investment (Elnaga & Imran, 2013). Training is a critical element in supplying entity employees with the aptitude, competencies, and knowledge necessary to perform intricate tasks (Moone et al., 2014; as cited in Johnson, 2017). Without training programs in place, entity employees are susceptible to errors, mistakes, and omissions that could result in an IAP breach (Olusegun & Ithnin, 2013). A human resource function's responsibility is to identify training needs and design suitable programs (Azeem & Mubeen,

2013). Options for IAP learning are (a) nonacademic, (b) self-reliance, (c) on-the-job, and (d) academic (Davis, 2005).

Nonacademic instruction is typically procedure-oriented (Davis, 2005). Usage of equipment or software is procedure-oriented (Davis, 2005). Therefore, entity personnel interacting with information assets should receive nonacademic instruction. On-the-job and self-reliance learning usually provide supplemental training for specific equipment and software (Davis, 2005). Relying on unsupervised experiential learning can lead to an assigned employee-confronting issues that the self-reliant individual cannot resolve (Posey et al., 2013) or applying an inappropriate solution. When providing on-the-job learning, manager-leaders should assign newly hired employees with an experienced professional to supply knowledge transfers before unsupervised task assignments (Johnson, 2017). Moreover, academic instruction usually provides problem-oriented supplemental learning (Davis, 2005; Konings & Vanormelingen, 2015).

Information asset users should receive training adequately and appropriately (Davis, 2008a). The most appropriate learning environment for entity employees depends on the knowledge, skills, and ability training requirements (Elnaga & Imran, 2013). There are two locational categories for employee learning: on-site or off-site (Antonioli & Della Torre, 2015; as cited in Johnson, 2017). On-site learning transpires in the workplace, where trainees typically have access to useful tools and materials when the training session is over (Johnson, 2017). On-site training is practical for vocational positions. Entities use nonacademic instruction in the workplace to improve employee performance (Khan, 2012). Alternatively, off-site learning is training that occurs away from the entity's work environment. An advantage of off-site learning is a reduction in possible training distractions (Johnson, 2017). Off-site training is instrumental when the manager-leader seeks to instill academic concepts and ideas in employees to improve performance (Konings & Vanormelingen, 2015).

IAP training provides control (Beebe et al., 2014; Davis, 2008a). Relevant training attempts to ensure personnel preparation to perform assigned tasks given the environment (Davis, 2008a). Moreover, providing employee IAP training can reduce mishaps rooted in inexperience (Johnson, 2017). Training involves evaluating and refining an employee's skills and improving known weaknesses (Azeem & Mubeen, 2013). Usually, training is more procedure-oriented than problem-oriented, where the learner may have experience with the subject matter (Davis, 2005). Training is short-range instruction in the precise actions necessary to perform a task (Azeem & Mubeen, 2013; Davis, 2005). The training environment should align with the instruction objective (Azeem & Mubeen, 2013; Davis, 2005). IAP training attempts to improve employee performance through knowledge attainment, skills enhancement, attitudinal adjustment, and behavioral conformance (Abawajy, 2014; Azeem & Mubeen, 2013; Khan, 2012).

Without well-trained IT users, entities are more susceptible to outsider IAP breaches (Stern, 2017). For accomplishing cybersecurity expectations, the ISG program should include position descriptions, periodically reassessing the adequacy of individual skills, annual training requirements, and professional development programs. Moreover, the ISG program should include monitoring employee training and professional development accomplishments. Entity management should ensure that employees have the knowledge, skills, and abilities to carry out cybersecurity responsibilities.

Appropriate ISG management requires employing available resources considering the external and internal environments (Davis, 2008a). Hiring and retaining high-quality IAP personnel is critical to optimizing and sustaining ISG (Davis, 2008a). Entity human resource practices can help ensure resource quality through legal screening processes to assess information security talent competency and ethics (Davis, 2008a, 2011, 2017; Guo & Yuan, 2012; Price, 2014). The entity's human resource function needs to establish security education and training (Siponen et al., 2014). Information security manager-leaders can enhance service quality by ensuring superior employee education and training (Davis, 2008a). Without competent individuals to manage or manipulate resources, even a superbly designed information security program will become ineffective and inefficient (Davis, 2008a). Education and training can integrate solvable simulations to learn effective IAP countermeasures (Hendrix et al., 2016).

Security training can help protect organizational information that can become organizational knowledge (A. Ahmad et al., 2014). Most manager-leaders understand the costs and benefits security training can have on an entity. The training requirements manager-leaders place on security professionals do not always reflect potential work situations (Mierke, 2014; as cited in Johnson, 2017). Nevertheless, training acceptance is a security employment requisite (Amankwa et al., 2014; as cited in Johnson, 2017). Without proper security training, entity information assets are vulnerable to protection breaches (Davis, 2008a). Entity IAP professionals completing requisite training may enable the Information Security Office to garner the benefits of enhanced capabilities with a lower employee turnover rate that can result in fewer successful IAP attacks (Johnson, 2017).

Common training issues among information security manager-leaders is expense and time away from work duties (Swarnalatha & Prasanna, 2013; as cited in Johnson, 2017). When up-to-date organizational supported training is remiss, information security professionals may accept new employment opportunities. Alternatively, after the entity manager-leaders invest in training staff members, the trained individuals may leave and join a competitor (Swarnalatha & Prasanna, 2013; as cited in Johnson, 2017). Information security staff turnover, especially the movement of exceedingly knowledgeable individuals between competing entities, represents crucial allusions from a competitiveness perspective (A. Ahmad et al., 2014). In overcoming potential workforce reduction risks, manager-leaders need to understand and address the effect of training expectations on employee loyalty in avoiding knowledge leakage.

Having an IT training plan is essential for most entities (Elnaga & Imran, 2013). Information security manager-leaders have a significant role in developing cybersecurity professionals to protect information assets. Inherent risks of IT architectures require highly skilled Information Security Office employees to administer and protect entity networks (Gupta et al., 2016). Entity manager-leaders need to provide continual training to ensure that Information Security Office personnel remain knowledgeable regarding threats, vulnerabilities, and risk-levels associated with the supported information assets (Johnson, 2017). Senior Information Security Office personnel can help junior employees acquire needed skills with continuous training on specific IAP tasks (Shi et al., 2011; as cited in Johnson, 2017).

Cyber cracker groups, criminal organizations, and espionage units use IT capabilities to identify, target, and attack selected entities (Lagazio et al., 2014), typically motivated by financial, personal, or political factors (Arief & Adzmi, 2015; Davis, 2017). Cyber theft, vandalism, trespass, and espionage are a few ever-present entity IAP threats (Mukati & Ali, 2014). Entity manager-leaders must notify employees concerning the need to sustain IAP vigilance (Siponen et al., 2014). Relevant and consistent content are critical success factors in provisioning information security awareness (Safa et al., 2015). The vigilance notification content must convey IAP threats represent plausible insider and outsider activities that can cause grave repercussions to organizational information resources (Siponen et al., 2014).

IAP training policies that communicate prospective roles and responsibilities with pre-requisite educational attainment illustrate expected performance and behavior levels (Davis, 2008b). In contrast, informal IAP awareness attempts may not improve employee attitudes. Entity employees lacking proper attitudes regarding organizational IAP and related expectations could benefit from regular orientation and education (Ifinedo, 2014). Management should also strive to provide regular in-house security awareness sessions, campaigns, and training to positively influence the normative beliefs and, eventually, entity employees' attitudes regarding IAP issues and concerns (Ifinedo, 2014).

Awareness programs should be an integral part of an entity's culture (Safa et al., 2015). Information security awareness is a dynamic process that consequently neces-sitates updating (Safa et al., 2015). Security awareness and accountability expansion throughout an entity are typically necessary (Johnson, 2017). Greater illegal acts aware-ness and appropriate attention to IAP measures are the first two steps to solving the counterproductive workplace behavior issue (Davis, 2008a). There is also a need to provide facilitating conditions, such as broad exposure to emerging security technolo-gies and appropriate incentives to encourage self-reliance to develop or improve the necessary skills and knowledge required to help safeguard organizational information assets (Ifinedo, 2014).

Information security awareness combined with potential cyberattack method updates plays a vital role in reducing IAP breach risks (Safa et al., 2015). For new system deployments, ISG can only be effective if those influencing IT project decisions are adequately informed. IAP project management policies, procedures, rules, and indi-vidual responsibilities need distribution to all affected parties. Furthermore, the risk awareness program should require participating system development employees to periodically sign a statement acknowledging IAP awareness and accepting responsibil-ity for IAP.

Lack of understanding regarding the underlying network topologies and multiple access points enables vulnerabilities to develop and exist unnoticed until an IAP incident occurs. An entity's training environment should permit tailoring IAP expectations to cybersecurity objectives. Training Information Security Office personnel before an entity IT application conversion assists in cybersecurity functionality verification and maintenance. Additional-ly, training Information Security Office personnel before new or improved cybersecurity deployment aids in ensuring an understanding of IAP features. The training of entity per-sonnel regarding IAP features should occur after completing all cybersecurity development activities but before IAP testing for determining vulnerabilities established by changes in configuration or functionality. Understanding the finalized new or improved IAP function-ality reduces response times and increases capability awareness for information security support providers. Learning new hardware or software functionality is procedure-oriented. Therefore, employees should receive nonacademic IAP instructions.

In most circumstances, the information asset development phase includes user testing because programs or equipment are assessable for meeting design requirements. As a mini-mum requirement, new cybersecurity hardware and software testing should occur over 4 weeks before owner acceptance. User acceptance tests are likely to identify operational deployment weaknesses. Once identified, technological designs and related supporting activities, such as training, require revisions to address confirmed weaknesses. Otherwise, cybersecurity test benefits are marginal.

Entities should establish formal security incident response mechanisms and ensure that IT users know established reporting arrangements (Davis, 2008b). Most incident preven-tion efforts focused on physical security while minimizing cybersecurity importance

(Hendrix et al., 2016). The need to reduce the risk and the cost of cybercrimes is clear (Hendrix et al., 2016). A means to achieve incident reductions is training entity employees using available tools (Abawajy, 2014) and ensuring entity employee awareness of current prevention measures (Hendrix et al., 2016).

Prescriptively, education and training are resource knowledge multipliers that can reduce occupational stress associated with responding to an incident (Davis, 2008a). In other words, the more organizational users and IT employees know about detecting, responding, then reporting an incident, the less likely incident response member burnout will occur during actual emergencies (Davis, 2008a). Incident handling education and training are achievable through various instructional platforms, including workshops, seminars, webinars, newsletters, posters, and stickers (Davis, 2008a). As part of breach response training, manager-leaders should enable regular incident team exercises (Hendrix et al., 2016), so members can gain situational experience and improve occupational performance (Davis, 2008a).

IT Audit Team

Various frameworks are available to aid management in deploying governance within an entity. These frameworks include the Committee of Sponsoring Organizations of the Treadway Commission's Internal Control-Integrated Framework (COSO Report), the Organization for Economic Cooperation and Development's Principles of Corporate Governance, and the Report of the Committee on Financial Aspects of Corporate Governance (Cadbury Report). Moreover, available frameworks include The Institute of Internal Auditors' Systems Auditability and Control (SAC) framework, the ISACA Control Objectives for Information and Related Technology (COBIT) framework, and the ISO/IEC's Corporate governance of information technology (Information Technology Governance Standard).

- **COSO Report:** The COSO Report is a leading framework for designing, implementing, and conducting internal control and assessing internal control effectiveness. The COSO Report's internal control system consists of the control environment, risk assessment, information and communication, monitoring, and control activities. The reasoning for the COSO Report include

  - business and operating environments have changed dramatically, becoming increasingly sophisticated, technology-driven, and global;
  - large-scale governance and internal control breakdown occurrences;
  - stakeholders are more engaged, seeking transparency and accountability; and
  - increased expectations for risk assessments at all levels of the organization.

- **Principles of Corporate Governance:** The Principles of Corporate Governance is a recommendation set for enhancing priority areas such as remuneration, risk management, board practices, and shareholder rights. The Principles of Corporate Governance provide a globally recognized benchmark for assessing and improving corporate governance.

- **Report of the Committee on Financial Aspects of Corporate Governance:** The Report of the Committee on Financial Aspects of Corporate Governance recommendation is set for the arrangement of company boards and accounting systems to mitigate corporate governance risks and failures. The final report covers financial, auditing, and corporate governance matters and makes three primary recommendations:

- the Chief Executive Officer and Chairman of companies should be separate individuals;
- boards should have at least three nonexecutive directors, two of whom should have no financial or personal ties to executives; and
- each board should have an audit committee composed of nonexecutive directors.

- **SAC:** Three types of controls, preventive, detective, and corrective, should be evaluated while performing an IT audit. Contrastingly, if management has implemented SAC, instead of the COBIT framework, for controlling IT, the entity is acquainted with control classifications of preventive, detective, and corrective; discretionary and nondiscretionary; voluntary and mandated; manual and automated; and application and general controls. When evaluating financial statement internal controls, an IT auditor is obligated to determine financial controls' effectiveness.
- **COBIT:** COBIT 2019 covers the lifecycle of governance, strategic, and tactical management within the IT domain. COBIT 2019 is a Business Framework for the Governance and Management of Enterprise IT. ISACA developed COBIT in 1996. They published the sixth edition during the Winter of 2018. COBIT 2019 is accepted globally as a toolset that ensures that IT is working effectively. COBIT 2019 provides a common language to communicate goals, objectives, and expected results to all stakeholders. COBIT 2019 is based on and integrates industry standards and acceptable practices for:

  - strategic alignment of IT with enterprise goals,
  - value delivery of services and new projects,
  - risk management,
  - resource management, and
  - performance measurement.

- **Information Technology Governance Standard:** IT governance is the system by which IT current and future use receive direction and control. Corporate governance of IT involves evaluating and directing use to support the entity and monitoring use to achieve objectives. The Information Technology Governance Standard includes the strategy and policies for using IT within an entity. The Information Technology Governance Standard framework comprises definitions, principles, and a model. The Information Technology Governance Standard framework sets out six principles for good corporate governance of IT that encompasses:

  - responsibility,
  - strategy,
  - acquisition,
  - performance,
  - conformance, and
  - human behavior.

The COSO and Cadbury report, as well as Principles of Corporate Governance, focus on entity-level governance frameworks, whereas, SAC, COBIT, and IT Governance Standard provide structures designed for IT governance that permit ISG application.

Planning Activities

Typically, the in-charge IT auditor is responsible for inscribing audit objectives. Business objectives are general statements of the organization's direction. To help define the ambit and effectively perform an IT audit, the IT auditor should understand the entity's mission and information processing. Materiality establishes audit nature, timing, and extent. IT auditors should consider the level of complexity and detail appropriate for the firm audited when selecting an audit risk assessment methodology. The risk assessment method applied to the control framework is a crucial component for preparing focused audit plans. A well-planned, properly structured audit program is essential to evaluate risk management practices, control systems, and compliance with policies concerning IT-related risks at institutions of every size and complexity. IT auditors have the right to prepare, submit, and expect inscribed approval of an engagement letter specifying the audit: ambit, objective, and terms of reference. By selecting the right approach, IT auditors can use an opening conference to establish a positive relationship with the client and ensure participants benefit from the plan presentation. An IT auditor should consider planning incomplete until engagement letter issuance. There is a professional responsibility to convey agreed responsibility, accountability, and authority for the assignment, even when an audit charter exists.

Study and Evaluation Activities

To determine whether control weaknesses exist, an IT auditor generally performs, among other procedures, inquiries, and observations, to study and evaluate controls. Audit procedures should exceed the predetermined quantitative or qualitative design materiality threshold. Determination of the entity's control objectives is dependent on selected methodologies, such as COSO, Strengths – Weaknesses – Opportunities – Threats, or COBIT frameworks. As an action course, the discovery of standard variation requires IT auditor evaluation and subsequent finding form recording. IT auditor working papers should be sufficient, complete, and support audit conclusions. Audit evidence should be easy to perceive, such that a reasonable person would be able to support IT auditor conclusions concerning the audit subject. After performing the study and evaluation of controls, an IT auditor's reassessment may dictate risk reallocation. Additional audit program test procedures may be necessary after studying and evaluating the audit area.

Testing Activities

Audit testing objective determination frequently occurs in the preceding audit phases: Planning as well as Study and Evaluation of Controls. Audit test materiality influences the audit testing nature, timing, and extent. In designing tests, the IT auditor must choose between statistical and nonstatistical testing methodologies. Compliance and substantive testing may take the form of inquiry, observation, inspection, or re-performance. The auditable unit sample size represents sampling risk, acceptable error rate, and the expected extent of errors in the population. Sampling method selection reflects whether audit area statistical inferences are going to occur concerning the population examined. When conducting tests, the collection of sufficient evidential matter required for the alignment with the generally accepted standard of audit fieldwork affects the IT auditor regarding the type of evidence to be collected and the means of acquisition. An IT auditor should consider whether errors in the population might exceed the tolerable error in evaluating results. Audit testing documentation should provide sufficient detail clearly describing testing objectives and sampling processes used. In reassessing risk, the professional IT auditor ensures an audit area's audit risks correlate to all audit objectives.

Reporting Activities

Foundationally, the costs of implementing a management control system with control techniques should never equal or exceed the benefits derived from projected risk reductions unless a law or regulation mandates the control technique. The audit report materiality affects the reporting nature, timing, and extent. If the audit results exceed the initial tolerable rate, an IT auditor must conclude that reporting nature, timing, and extent requires additional comparative analysis or adjustment to audit assurance. During the analysis of the findings, cost–benefit analysis refers to techniques used to examine alternative corrective actions in determining the recommended deployment or determining the most efficient implementation degree while providing the highest return for reducing associated risks.

Audit working paper retention should be thoroughly inscribed and reflect compliance with pertinent laws and regulations. Evaluation of audit evidence persuasiveness is judged based on conditions, such as provider independence and supporting qualifications. After considering associated materiality, audit assurance, and cost–benefit, completing the finding form review and assessment prepares the IT auditor for drafting a report stating an opinion based on conclusions drawn from obtained evidence. If a sequent event does occur, factors affecting the IT auditor's cost–benefit analysis, risk assessments, and materiality, an appraisal should occur for determining audit report effect.

Audit reports should receive a proof-reading and any required editing before distribution to intended recipients. The closing conference provides an opportunity to present the audit process, discuss any concerns, and modify the audit report presentation. If an IT audit report is to be objective, constructive, and gain client acceptance, it should include the client's views regarding the audit conclusions and recommendations. The final audit report should identify gaps in controls and the source of the vulnerabilities. Audit report distribution timeliness should be a significant IT auditor priority.

Follow-Up Activities

Regardless of the method used, the best practice is to include in the final report the intended action and specific time frame for resolution so that auditors can schedule follow-up activities accordingly. At the reporting process conclusion, an IT auditor should have updated the audit function's follow-up database with client management responses to identified potential control improvements as well as estimates for recommendation completion or deployment dates. As a part of the engagement's follow-up activities, an IT auditor should evaluate whether unimplemented findings are still relevant or have a greater significance. Strategic and tactical managers should know: Who performs follow-up procedures for audits in their organization?

References

Abawajy, J. (2014). User preference of cybersecurity awareness delivery methods. *Behaviour & Information Technology, 33*, 236–247. https://doi.org/10.1080/0144929X.2012.708787

Ahmad, A., Bosua, R., & Scheepers, R. (2014). Protecting organizational competitive advantage: A knowledge leakage perspective. *Computers & Security, 42*, 27–39. https://doi.org/10.1016/j.cose.2014.01.001

Ahmad, Z., & Norhashim, M. (2008). The control environment, employee fraud and counterproductive workplace behaviour: An empirical analysis. *Communications of the IBIMA, 3*, 145–155. www.ibimapublishing.com/

Anthony, P. J., & Weide, J. (2015). Motivation and career-development training programs: Use of regulatory focus to determine program effectiveness. *Higher Learning Research Communications*, 5(2), 24–33. https://doi.org/10.18870/hlrc.v5i2.214

Arief, B., & Adzmi, M. A. B. (2015). Understanding cybercrime from its stakeholders' perspectives: Part 2: Defenders and victims. *IEEE Security & Privacy*, 13(2), 84–88. https://doi.org/10.1109/MSP.2015.44

Azeem, M. A., & Mubeen, S. A. (2013). Training and development of non executives in tourism sector: A study of APTDC, India. *International Journal of Management, IT and Engineering*, 3(6), 395–414. www.ijmra.us/itjournal.php

Baltatzis, D., Ilioudis, C., & Pangalos, G. (2012). A role engineering framework to support dynamic authorizations in collaborative environments. *Information Security Journal: A Global Perspective*, 21, 12–27. https://doi.org/10.1080/19393555.2011.624161

Beebe, N. L., Young, D. K., & Chang, F. R. (2014). Framing information security budget requests to influence investment decisions. *Communications of the Association for Information Systems*, 35(7), 134–144. https://doi.org/10.17705/1CAIS.03507

Brotby, K. W. (2006). *Information security governance: Guidance for boards of directors and executive management* (2nd ed.). IT Governance Institute.

Chatterjee, S., Sarker, S., & Valacich, J. S. (2015). The behavioral roots of information systems security: Exploring key factors related to unethical IT use. *Journal of Management Information Systems*, 31(4), 49–87. https://doi.org/10.1080/07421222.2014.1001257

Chen, C. X., Lu, H., & Sougiannis, T. (2012). The agency problem, corporate governance, and the asymmetrical behavior of selling, general, and administrative costs. *Contemporary Accounting Research*, 29(1), 252–282. https://doi.org/10.1111/j.1911-3846.2011.01094.x

Chen, Y., Ramamurthy, K., & Wen, K. (2012). Organizations' information security policy compliance: Stick or carrot approach? *Journal of Management Information Systems*, 29(3), 157–188. https://doi.org/10.2753/MIS0742-1222290305

Chernyak-Hai, L., & Tziner, A. (2014). Relationships between counterproductive work behavior, perceived justice and climate, occupational status, and leader-member exchange. *Journal of Work and Organizational Psychology*, 30, 1–12. https://doi.org/10.5093/tr2014a1

Cichonski, P., Millar, T., Grance, T., & Scarfone, K. (2012). *Computer security incident handling guide: Recommendations of the National Institute of Standards and Technology* (NIST Special Publication 800–61, Rev. 2). https://dx.doi.org/10.6028/NIST.SP.800-61r2

Claycomb, W. R., Huth, C. L., Flynn, L., Mcintire, D. M., & Lewellen, T. B. (2012). Chronological examination of insider threat sabotage: Preliminary observations. *Journal of Wireless Mobile Networks, Ubiquitous Computing, and Dependable Applications*, 3(4), 4–20. https://doi.org/10.22667/JOWUA.2012.12.31.004

Davis, R. E. (2005). *IT auditing: An adaptive process*. Pleier.

Davis, R. E. (2006). *IT auditing: Irregular and illegal acts*. Pleier.

Davis, R. E. (2008a). *IT auditing: Assuring information assets protection*. Pleier.

Davis, R. E. (2008b). *IT auditing: IT service delivery and support*. Pleier.

Davis, R. E. (2009a). *Assuring IT legal compliance*. www.amazon.com

Davis, R. E. (2009b). *IT auditing: Systems and infrastructure life cycle management*. Pleier.

Davis, R. E. (2010). *IT auditing: An adaptive system*. www.amazon.com

Davis, R. E. (2011). *Assuring IT governance*. www.amazon.com

Davis, R. E. (2017). *Relationship between corporate governance and information security governance effectiveness in United States corporations* (Publication No. 10603383) [Doctoral Study, Walden University]. ProQuest Dissertations Publishing.

Davis, R. E. (2020). *IT auditing using a system perspective*. IGI Global.

Den Hartog, D. N., & Belschak, F. D. (2012). Work engagement and Machiavellianism in the ethical leadership process. *Journal of Business Ethics*, 107(1), 35–47. https://doi.org/10.1007/s10551-012-1296-4

Elnaga, A., & Imran, A. (2013). The effect of training on employee performance. *European Journal of Business and Management*, 5(4), 137–147. https://iiste.org/Journals/index.php/EJBM

Flores, W. R., Antonsen, E., & Ekstedt, M. (2014). Information security knowledge sharing in organizations: Investigating the effect of behavioral information security governance and national culture. *Computers & Security*, *43*, 90–110. https://doi.org/10.1016/j.cose.2014.03.004

Glinkowska, B., & Kaczmarek, B. (2015). Classical and modern concepts of corporate governance (stewardship theory and agency theory). *Management*, *19*(2), 84–92. https://doi.org/10.1515/manment-2015-0015

Guo, K. H., & Yuan, Y. (2012). The effects of multilevel sanctions on information security violations: A mediating model. *Information & Management*, *49*, 320–326. https://doi.org/10.1016/j.im.2012.08.001

Gupta, S., Chaudhari, B. S., & Chakrabarty, B. (2016). Vulnerable network analysis using war driving and security intelligence. In H. S. Saini, R. K. Singh, & K. S. Reddy (Eds.), *Lecture notes in networks and systems, Vol. 7: Innovations in electronics and communication engineering* (pp. 465–471). https://doi.org/10.1007/978-981-10-3812-9_49

Hashizume, K., Rosado, D. G., Fernández-Medina, E., & Fernandez, E. B. (2013). An analysis of security issues for cloud computing. *Journal of Internet Services and Applications*, *4*(1), 1–13. https://doi.org/10.1186/1869-0238-4-5

Hendrix, M., AlSherbaz, A., & Victoria, B. (2016). Game based cyber security training: Are serious games suitable for cyber security training? *International Journal of Serious Games*, *3*(1), 53–61. https://doi.org/10.17083/ijsg.v3i1.107

Heracleous, L., & Lan, L. L. (2012). Agency theory, institutional sensitivity, and inductive reasoning: Towards a legal perspective. *Journal of Management Studies*, *49*, 223–239. https://doi.org/10.1111/j.1467-6486.2011.01009.x

Hu, Q., Dinev, T., Hart, P., & Cooke, D. (2012). Managing employee compliance with information security policies: The critical role of top management and organizational culture. *Decision Sciences*, *43*, 615–660. https://doi.org/10.1111/j.1540-5915.2012.00361.x

Ifinedo, P. (2014). Information systems security policy compliance: An empirical study of the effects of socialisation, influence, and cognition. *Information & Management*, *51*(1), 69–79. https://doi.org/10.1016/j.im.2013.10.001

ISACA. (2013). IS audit and assurance standard 1207 irregularity and illegal acts. *ITAF: Information Technology Assurance Framework*. www.isaca.org/resources/frameworks-standards-and-models

ISACA. (2014). IS audit and assurance guideline 2207 irregularity and illegal acts. *ITAF: Information Technology Assurance Framework*. www.isaca.org/resources/frameworks-standards-and-models

Johnson, K. T. (2017). *The training deficiency in corporate America: Training security professionals to protect sensitive information* (Publication No. 10624471) [Doctoral Study, Walden University]. ProQuest Dissertations Publishing.

Khan, M. I. (2012). The impact of training and motivation on performance of employees. *Business Review*, *7*(2), 84–95. https://businessreview.iba.edu.pk/

Khattak, A. N., Rehman, S., & Rehman, C. A. (2014). Realistic job preview (RJP): It's efficiency in recruitment in pharmaceutical industry of Pakistan. *Abasyn Journal of Social Sciences*, *7*(1), 64–77. http://ajss.abasyn.edu.pk/

Klein, L., Biesenthal, C., & Dehlin, E. (2015). Improvisation in project management: A praxeology. *International Journal of Project Management*, *33*, 267–277. https://doi.org/10.1016/j.ijproman.2014.01.011

Konings, J., & Vanormelingen, S. (2015). The impact of training on productivity and wages: Firm-level evidence. *The Review of Economics and Statistics*, *97*(2), 485–497. https://doi.org/10.1162/REST_a_00460

Lagazio, M., Sherif, N., & Cushman, M. (2014). A multilevel approach to understanding the impact of cyber crime on the financial sector. *Computers & Security*, *45*, 58–74. https://doi.org/10.1016/j.cose.2014.05.006

McGowan, J., Gardner, D., & Fletcher, R. (2006). Positive and negative affective outcomes of occupational stress. *New Zealand Journal of Psychology*, *35*(2), 92–98. www.psychology.org.nz

Mukati, M. A., & Ali, S. M. (2014). The vulnerability of cyber security and strategy to conquer the potential threats on business applications. *Journal of Independent Studies and Research, 12*(1), 56–62. https://szabist.edu.pk/journals-jisr/

Niazi, A. S. (2011). Training and development strategy and its role in organizational performance. *Journal of Public Administration and Governance, 1*(2), 42–57. https://doi.org/10.5296/jpag.v1i2.862

Olusegun, O. J., & Ithnin, N. B. (2013). People are the answer to security: Establishing a sustainable information security awareness training (ISAT) program in organization. *International Journal of Computer Science and Information Security, 11*(8), 57–64. https://publons.com/journal/30902/international-journal-of-computer-science-and-info/

Pande, S., & Ansari, V. A. (2014). A theoretical framework for corporate governance. *Indian Journal of Corporate Governance, 7*(1), 56–72. https://doi.org/10.1177/0974686220140104

Pitesa, M., & Thau, S. (2013). Masters of the universe: How power and accountability influence self-serving decisions under moral hazard. *Journal of Applied Psychology, 98*, 550–558. https://doi.org/10.1037/a0031697

Posey, C., Roberts, T., Lowry, P. B., Bennett, B., & Courtney, J. (2013). Insiders' protection of organizational information assets: Development of a systematics based taxonomy and theory of diversity for protection-motivated behaviors. *MIS Quarterly, 37*(4). www.misq.org/

Price, J. D. (2014). *Reducing the risk of a data breach using effective compliance programs* (Publication No. 3619214) [Doctoral Study, Walden University]. ProQuest Dissertations Publishing.

Rida-E-Fiza, S., Farooq, M., & Mirza, F. I. (2015). Barriers in employee effective training and learning. *Mediterranean Journal of Social Sciences, 6*(3 S2), 240–250. https://doi.org/10.5901/mjss.2015.v6n3s2p240

Safa, N. S., Sookhak, M., Von Solms, R., Furnell, S., Ghani, N. A., & Herawan, T. (2015). Information security conscious care behaviour formation in organizations. *Computers & Security, 53*, 65–78. https://doi.org/10.1016/j.cose.2015.05.012

Salas, E., Shuffler, M. L., Thayer, A. L., Bedwell, W. L., & Lazzara, E. H. (2015). Understanding and improving teamwork in organizations: A scientifically based practical guide. *Human Resource Management, 54*(4), 599–622. https://doi.org/10.1002/hrm.21628

Singh, A. N., Picot, A., Kranz, J., Gupta, M. P., & Ojha, A. (2013). Information security management (ISM) practices: Lessons from select cases from India and Germany. *Global Journal of Flexible Systems Management, 14*, 225–239. https://doi.org/10.1007/s40171-013-0047-4

Siponen, M., Mahmood, M. A., & Pahnila, S. (2014). Employees' adherence to information security policies: An exploratory field study. *Information & Management, 51*(2), 217–224. https://doi.org/10.1016/j.im.2013.08.006

Sloan, P. (2014). The reasonable information security program. *Richmond Journal of Law & Technology, 21*(1), 1–92. https://jolt.richmond.edu/

Stern, G. (2017). Getting with the program to beef up cybersecurity. *Biomedical Instrumentation & Technology, 51*(1), 70–75. https://doi.org/10.2345/0899-8205-51.1.70

Vance, A., & Siponen, M. T. (2012). IS security policy violations: A rational choice perspective. *Journal of Organizational and End User Computing, 24*(1), 21–41. https://doi.org/10.4018/joeuc.2012010102

Zhao, H., Peng, Z., & Sheard, G. (2013). Workplace ostracism and hospitality employees' counterproductive work behaviors: The joint moderating effects of proactive personality and political skill. *International Journal of Hospitality Management, 33*, 219–227. https://doi.org/10.1016/j.ijhm.2012.08.006

Recommended Reading

Gai, K., Qiu, M., & Sun, X. (2018). A survey on FinTech. *Journal of Network and Computer Applications, 103*, 262–273. https://doi.org/10.1016/j.jnca.2017.10.011

Guo, Y., & Wang, C. (2020). The impact mechanisms of psychological learning climate on employees' innovative use of information systems. *Journal of Global Information Management (JGIM), 28*(2), 52–72. https://doi.org/10.4018/JGIM.2020040103

Ofori, K. S., Anyigba, H., Ampong, G. O. A., Omoregie, O. K., Nyamadi, M., & Fianu, E. (2020). Factors influencing information security policy compliance behavior. In W. Yaokumah, M. Rajarajan, J. D. Abdulai, I. Wiafe, & F. A. Katsriku (Eds.), *Modern theories and practices for cyber ethics and security compliance* (pp. 152–171). https://doi.org/10.4018/978-1-7998-3149-5.ch010

Singleton, T., & Flesher, D. L. (2003). A 25-year retrospective on the IIA's SAC projects. *Managerial Auditing Journal, 18*(1), 39–53. https://doi.org/10.1108/02686900310454237

Stoel, M. D., & Havelka, D. (2020). Information technology audit quality: An investigation of the impact of individual and organizational factors. *Journal of Information Systems*. https://doi.org/10.2308/isys-18-043

Chapter 6

External Organizational Actors

Abstract

Organizational formations face constant pressure to achieve and maintain a competitive edge in the marketplace. Capabilities logic reflects the general premise that one firm can outperform another if it has a superior ability to develop, use, and protect the essential platform competencies and resources. Nonetheless, if an entity discovers the necessary resources and capabilities are unavailable during the planning phase, outsourcing the operational or IT function may be a viable course of action to pursue. Correspondingly, information security is a management issue that requires an end-to-end view of organizational processes. Chapter 6 discusses supply chain partners and managed service providers considering IAP risks. Chapter 6 also presents critical service provider audit issues.

Introduction

Supply chain management (SCM) and IT management have garnered attention from practitioners and researchers (H. Zhou & Benton, 2007). As IT evolves, entities tend to integrate organizational structures (H. Zhou & Benton, 2007). Increased IT use introduces several cybersecurity risks affecting supply chain cyber-resilience (Boyes, 2015). Therefore, there is a need for collaboration security between supply chain partners (Zeng et al., 2012). Effective supply chain practice integration with effective information sharing becomes crucial for bettering supply chain performance (H. Zhou & Benton, 2007). Supply chain practice centers on item movement, while information sharing centers on information flow (H. Zhou & Benton, 2007). Management's technological investment in the supply chain may reflect business processes' outsourcing (Beasley et al., 2004). However, only when management teams emphasize technology investment and choose the appropriate information to share can an entity achieve effective organizational performance (H. Zhou & Benton, 2007).

Security-related situations ensnaring deployed information assets have recast the way employees conduct operational activities with consumers and other stakeholders (Davis, 2017; Srivastava & Kumar, 2015). Data processing timing can be an IT differentiator (Davis, 2010, 2020). Two types of timing classifications usable for IT processing are batch and real-time configurations (Davis, 2010, 2020). A batch architecture collects records into groups before processing (Davis, 2010, 2020). A real-time architecture processes a record immediately upon submission (Davis, 2010, 2020). Furthermore, an architectural differentiation may occur by IT physical location (Davis, 2010, 2020). The significant categories using physical location criterion are in-house and third-party IT classification (Davis, 2010, 2020). An in-house architecture has computer hardware, software, and personnel physically located on the entity's premises (Davis, 2010, 2020). A third-party architecture provides services where the primary IT hardware or software belongs to an independent entity (Davis, 2010, 2020).

All types of business processes are potential outsource candidates (Beasley et al., 2004). The Internet enables entities to outsource entire business processes and professional staff traditionally in-sourced, such as SCM (Beasley et al., 2004). As entities confront the financial risks of increasing labor and other process costs, manager-leaders may decide to outsource portions of labor-intensive activities to lower costs (Beasley et al., 2004). The entity functions outsourced is commonly dependent on the organizational core competencies and stakeholder expectations (Gottschalk & Solli-Saether, 2005).

Service-level management defines, negotiates, controls, reports, and monitors agreed-upon service levels within predefined standard service parameters (Davis, 2008b). Service level management processes should have objectives, goals, activities, and tasks (Davis, 2008b). Usually, effective IT service delivery is appropriate when system issues receive swift redress to the user's satisfaction (Davis, 2008b). An entity's ability to sustain appropriate IT service is heavily dependent on building service commitments and managing service levels (Davis, 2008b).

Support by the IT auditor's service user entity is crucial when examining service provider controls (Davis, 2005, 2010, 2020). Consequently, the service user's Chief Audit Executive has a responsibility to ensure that the audit charter includes specific rights for service provider engagement auditors (Davis, 2020). Auditing another entity's control system can be a restrictive proposition (Davis, 2005, 2010, 2020), especially when the auditee is uncooperative. In resolving any audit misconceptions, the IT audit team members should receive instructions to convey audit standards to appropriate outsource personnel (Davis, 2005, 2010, 2020). This chapter motivates the need to integrate information security into external organizational actors by participating in interorganizational projects. This chapter further proposes supply chain partners and managed service provider risks and presents critical service provider audit issues.

Supply Chain Partners

SCM typically uses a multidisciplinary system that integrates strategic management, marketing, and organizational behavior (Vries & Huijsman, 2011). Effective and efficient SCM is critical for entity survival and success (Liao & Hong, 2007). A supply chain is definable as two or more parties linked by material, informational, and financial resource flows (Webster, 2005; as cited by Sidorova & Isik, 2010). An entity's supply chain strategy refers to the envisioned means for objective achievement (Qrunfleh & Tarafdar, 2013). When implemented, an entity's supply chain strategy reflects the envisioned commodity pipeline structure (Simon et al., 2015). A supply chain process success or failure experienced by entity manager-leaders reflects performance measured by deployment effectiveness and efficiency (Mentzer et al., 2007). Thus, there may be SCM challenges that require solutions.

SCM involves integration, coordination, and collaboration across entities and throughout the value chain for added stakeholder value creation (Simon et al., 2015). Entities' design and deploy supply chain process integrations to achieve specific objectives while simultaneously inscribing perceived best-practice solutions for reducing the risk of inappropriate responses to environmental conditions (Davis, 2012; Mentzer et al., 2007). Entities that pursue coordinating standard processes and IT infrastructure development can advance the operational vision and intentions (Themistocleous & Corbitt, 2006). Supply chain collaboration efficacy relies upon two factors: internal and external operations' integration and efforts' alignment to geographical dispersion, demand pattern, and item characteristics (Holweg et al., 2005). For activities, SCM identifies, quantifies, assesses, and manages the flow of commodities through value chains with the common goals of lessening waste and maximizing resource efficiency (Vries & Huijsman, 2011). Implementing appropriate practices that support and execute supply chain strategies can enhance supply chain responsiveness and entity performance (Qrunfleh & Tarafdar, 2013).

Reducing waste to produce cost leadership is the essential lean approach focal (Qrunfleh & Tarafdar, 2013). Whereby, supply relationship management is a principle lean production component (Qrunfleh & Tarafdar, 2013). Regarding production, lean manufacturing necessitates buyer–supplier relationships generating exceptional learning motivation and trust (Simpson & Power, 2005). In securing and preserving lean manufacturing benefits, lean supply chain deployments should reflect high information sharing levels, supplier rapid performance improvements, and low transaction costs (Qrunfleh & Tarafdar, 2013). Consequently, a lean supply methodology construct is suppliers actively participating in eliminating all waste (Simpson & Power, 2005) within the commodity pipeline. Nevertheless, an entity that focuses only on waste elimination without considering appropriate resource deployments will not achieve supply chain benefits in terms of responsiveness (Qrunfleh & Tarafdar, 2013).

SCM strategies commonly involve interorganizational and inter-functional integration, coordination, and collaboration throughout the supply links (Qrunfleh & Tarafdar, 2013). As a case in point, allowing alignment flexibility to create differentiation through service levels is the principal agile supply chain approach objective (Qi et al., 2011). Central agile administration elements are physical network alignment to address market and competition requirements, reconfiguration processes, and resolve behavioral and relationship issues (Ismail & Sharifi, 2006). Therefore, agile methodology deployments require buyer–supplier relationships generating exceptional coordination and trust (Ismail & Sharifi, 2006). Nonetheless, interorganizational and inter-functional coordination is the primary challenge of eliminating employee behavioral isolationism (Mentzer et al., 2007).

Delivery, cost, and quality typically drive supplier relationships (Qrunfleh & Tarafdar, 2013; Roh et al., 2014; Simpson & Power, 2005). However, the entity's manager-leaders can adopt broader logistic objectives than timely delivery (Dey et al., 2011; Zhu et al., 2012), cost minimization, and high quality. Additional governance objectives may encompass waste reduction, environmental innovation, or social responsibility (Zhu et al., 2012). Nonetheless, the achievement of supply chain objectives requires forming and sustaining supplier relationships through collaboration or compliance (Harms et al., 2013). Collaboration permits accomplishing supply objectives through trust, whereas compliance achievement occurs using administrative power (Harms et al., 2013).

IT is accelerating the shift in power from producers to customers (Li & Lin, 2006). Customer-driven value chains require, among other characteristics, integrated channels, flexible processes and infrastructures, and integrated suppliers (Themistocleous & Corbitt, 2006). Of the value chain attributes, process flexibility is a core construct for customer-driven SCM (Themistocleous & Corbitt, 2006). Notably, gains are achievable when entities jointly integrate and automate processes at the intra-organizational and interorganizational levels (Senge et al., 2008; Themistocleous & Corbitt, 2006). Thus, by extension, an integrated information security framework that considers intra-organizational and interorganizational activities and processes can strengthen the supply chain (Sindhuja, 2014). Moreover, a cyber supply chain framework can help determine risk governance, system integration, and operations' initiative coverage (Boyson, 2014). Information access control, information partitioning, legal information sharing, and partner trust management are SCM issues. There are four problem solutions: cybersecurity and privacy technologies, inscription classification and risk management, contract management, and partner relationship management (Zeng et al., 2012).

Information Sharing

Intra-organizational and interorganizational process integration alignment is imperative under most operational environment conditions. Where adopted, interorganizational (i.e., supply chain) and intra-organizational (i.e., business processes) strategies need to reflect connectivity and rational selection (Cagliano et al., 2006). Thereby, information flow integrations are a prerequisite to aligning and streamlining processes (Cagliano et al., 2006), whereas the integration of commodity flows lessens waste and improves interorganizational processing efficiency (Cagliano et al., 2006, p. 286). Entities that coordinate the development of standard business processes and IT infrastructure can advance operational visioning and intentions (Themistocleous & Corbitt, 2006). In a rapidly changing entity environment, business process integrations necessitate supporting adaptable and manageable IT infrastructures to gain competitive advantages (Themistocleous & Corbitt, 2006, p. 434).

Process integration design enabling information sharing among business partners is an essential ingredient for successful SCM (Kwon & Suh, 2006; McAdam & McCormack, 2001). Supply chain process integration inhibits information task duplication while offering the advantage of expeditious product and service accessibility (McAdam & McCormack, 2001; Y. Malhotra, 2000). There is an expectation that organizational knowledge repositories will serve as information extraction enablers for customers and suppliers (Y. Malhotra, 2000, 2005). However, the information exchange level acquires a negative influence when supplier abundance exists (Cagliano et al., 2006). Moreover, the entity's place within the supply chain has a meaningful effect on information sharing adoption (Cagliano et al., 2006).

As an intra-organizational and interorganizational structure modifier, process integration represents resource aggregations, disassociations, and collaborations enabling value-added delivery of products and services to customers (Haag & Cummings, 2008; Mentzer et al., 2007). Entities typically design and deploy supply chain process integration for achieving specific objectives, while simultaneously inscribing best-practice solutions to reduce the risk of inappropriate responses to environmental conditions (Davis, 2012; Mentzer et al., 2007). Creating value from intellectual and knowledge-based assets often encompasses systematizing what employees, partners, and customers know and then sharing the resulting information to devise or engage best practices (Davis, 2012). Consequently, business process integration should reflect a balanced approach considering organizational methods and techniques, structure, and people, as well as systems and data for producing optimal results (Davis, 2012; Mentzer et al., 2007).

Information sharing and mutual commitment to performance improvements are necessary for collaboration and compliance approaches, while appropriately managing safeguards that prevent opportunism (Connelly et al., 2013). Information sharing refers to how critical and proprietary information is communicated to supply chain partners (Li & Lin, 2006). Commitment is an enduring desire to maintain a valued relationship (Li & Lin, 2006). Mutual commitment incorporates each party's intention and expectation of relationship continuity and willingness to invest resources in SCM (Li & Lin, 2006). Thus, mutual commitment refers to buyer and supplier willingness to exert effort on behalf of the relationship (Li & Lin, 2006).

Information sharing enhances coordination between supply chain processes to enable material flow and reduce inventory costs (Li & Lin, 2006). Information sharing leads to high supply chain integration levels by enabling entities to make reliable deliveries and swift market introductions (Li & Lin, 2006). Quality information sharing contributes positively to customer satisfaction and partnership caliber (Li & Lin, 2006). Information sharing affects the supply chain performance in total cost and service level (Li & Lin, 2006). Specifically, a higher level of information sharing affiliates with a lower total cost, a higher order fulfillment rate, and a shorter order cycle time (Li & Lin, 2006). While information sharing is consequential, the effect of supply chain performance depends on what, when, how, and with whom information sharing occurs (Li & Lin, 2006).

Scholars and practitioners endorse the criticality of designing and deploying supply chain process integrations permitting information sharing between various designated individuals (Kwon & Suh, 2006; McAdam & McCormack, 2001; Y. Malhotra, 2000). Information sharing positively influences supply chain partner trust and shared vision (Li & Lin, 2006). However, customer uncertainty, technology uncertainty, supply chain partner commitment, and IT enablers do not affect information sharing (Li & Lin, 2006).

Knowledge Sharing

Information defines knowledge for decision-making. Managerial work typically includes acquiring and applying knowledge (Hamel, 2006). Knowledge management transforms administrative principles into everyday practices (Hamel, 2006). Knowledge management is an asset (Ramírez et al., 2012). Knowledge management positively correlates with business innovation (Ramírez et al., 2012). Effective knowledge management supporting innovation management has become an organizational necessity (Tseng et al., 2013). Accordingly, manager-leaders should consider codifying what employees, partners, or customers know (Laszlo & Laszlo, 2002) within knowledge management systems.

Effectual knowledge protection technologies are valuable defense mechanisms for combating inappropriate and malicious behavior (Claycomb et al., 2012). Moreover, the interaction between new management tools and the information systems strategic approach positively affects profitability (Pérez-Méndez & Machado-Cabezas, 2015). Investment in new information systems and new management tools' coupling must occur with a transparent sense of strategy (Pérez-Méndez & Machado-Cabezas, 2015). Therefore, supply chain managers and information security personnel should identify and evaluate potential IAP systems and configuration management tools to ensure organizational network infrastructures maintain knowledge integrity and availability consistent with the adopted security strategy.

IT facilitates organizational learning by enabling knowledge sharing (Kim et al., 2013). The effects of knowledge sharing on innovation can occur through two forms: knowledge donating and knowledge collection (Kamasak & Bulutlar, 2010). Knowledge collection can significantly affect all types of innovation and ambidexterity, while knowledge donations that occur internally and externally may not affect exploratory innovation (Kamasak & Bulutlar, 2010). Knowledge sharing is a knowledge management element (Ramírez et al., 2012). Knowledge management enhanced by technology is an essential component of strategic planning (Routley et al., 2013) for innovations. Thus, knowledge management can include an information system implementation enabling knowledge creation, capturing, and sharing processes (Krogh, 2012) that require appropriate IAP.

Knowledge Creation Processes

There can be a positive correlation between providing specific information regarding the type of knowledge participants should share and the level of knowledge integration process actions (A. Malhotra & Majchrzak, 2014). Explicit knowledge integration occurs when provisioning instructions can generate higher-rated solutions (A. Malhotra & Majchrzak, 2014). Crowds can often create solutions through instinctive discussions (A. Malhotra & Majchrzak, 2014). However, the furnished answers may not be obvious but instead buried in discussion threads (A. Malhotra & Majchrzak, 2014). Additionally, crowd participants tend to cluster into distinct groups of knowledge integration actors, and knowledge integration may depend upon the involved sub-crowds (A. Malhotra & Majchrzak, 2014).

Entities with knowledge base depth develop radical innovations through external market knowledge acquisition (K. Zhou & Li, 2012). In supporting small and medium entities, an advanced conceptual framework is designable when using a predictive crowd to assess disruptive innovation ideas (Peisl et al., 2014). A predictive crowd can remove barriers to adopting disruptive ideas by small and medium entities when attempting evaluation (Peisl et al., 2014). Crowd knowledge transfer requires no tangible monetary reward, but instead, intangible benefits such as recognition and a sense of accomplishment may induce participation (Peisl et al., 2014).

Knowledge Capture Processes

Typically, the accomplishment of knowledge sharing occurs through a knowledge management system. There are several ways to populate a knowledge management database (Davis, 2012). One approach is to review the subject matter literature and extract applicable axioms, definitions, and rules (Davis, 2012). Another approach for acquiring information is to ask subject matter experts to explain their cognitive processes and methods for solving problem scenarios (Davis, 2012). The conveyed information then receives verbal protocol analysis (Davis, 2012). Last, a crowd-sharing initiative could effectively integrate knowledge to create competitive and innovative solutions (A. Malhotra & Majchrzak, 2014).

Combinational knowledge acquisitions make human-based knowledge management systems valuable organizational technology (Davis, 2012). Literary knowledge acquisition is beneficial for learning and referent situations because response paths are direct (Davis, 2012). Nonetheless, queries presented to a knowledge management system can lead to fallacious outcomes (Davis, 2012). Human experts can enrich the information procured from literary resources and possibly provide unpublished experiences that improve the decision process paths (Davis, 2012). Manager-leaders embrace crowd knowledge for ideation, idea selection, and innovation to improve operational performance and increase entity competitiveness (A. Malhotra & Majchrzak, 2014; Peisl et al., 2014).

Knowledge Sharing Processes

Entities with a broad knowledge base can achieve radical innovation through internal knowledge sharing (K. Zhou & Li, 2012). Knowledge communities can ensure intergenerational knowledge transfer (Kuyken, 2012). Formed communities can share tacit and explicit knowledge and foster creation and innovation (Laszlo & Laszlo, 2002). The ubiquitous nature of technology has accelerated the growth of open innovation through external knowledge sharing. Creativity and knowledge sharing are relevant to innovation and competitive advantage (Kuyken, 2012; Semler, 2000; Zhen et al., 2011). Manager-leaders who seek to administrate innovation must ensure that personal repositories of knowledge are accessible and available for collaborative efforts (K. Zhou & Li, 2012). Knowledge sharing affects innovation performance, and accidental knowledge leakage moderates relationships (Ritala et al., 2013). Consequently, entities must balance the risks between knowledge sharing and governance mechanisms (Yang, 2011).

Knowledge sharing is vital for enhancing the innovation capability of entities (Sáenz et al., 2009). In correspondence, design, action, participatory conversations, and learning characterized evolutionary learning communities (Laszlo & Laszlo, 2002). Nevertheless, depending on the innovation capability dimension under review and the technology intensity, the type of knowledge sharing can vary (Sáenz et al., 2009). Moreover, there are primary challenges to innovation from the focus on informal knowledge sharing robustness as a path for innovation (Taminiau et al., 2009). Innovation is relative (Taminiau et al., 2009). A potential beneficial approach to stimulating innovation is to increase the amount of informal knowledge exchange opportunities between actors (Taminiau et al., 2009).

Supply Chain Logistics

Supply chain logistics-related issues can potentially manifest through distinct root causes when seeking to improve SCM, such as misaligned procurement (Thomas & Barton, 2007), extended lead time, bullwhip effect, or whipsaw effect. Misaligned procurement refers to necessary unsecured vendor components and having no alternative suppliers, product shipments, contracted services provisions, or solution deliveries (United States Securities and Exchange Commission, 2014). Extended lead time is the differential in physical versus promised delivery (Christopher et al., 2006). The bullwhip effect reflects the unpredictable or nontransparent demand patterns causing artificial demand amplification and distortion (Lee, 2004). Whipsaw effect in the supply chain represents customer purchase order changing where the sales process does not resolve the adjustment decision (Bayle-Cordier et al., 2015). Any of the mentioned supply chain logistics circumstances can influence the customer value proposition and value appropriation.

Alignment, assessment, contracting, management, and controls have emerged as significant supply chain issues that necessitate administrative consideration (Wisma, 2008). Specifically, manufacturers should contemplate learning style congruency between the entity and the suppliers (Azadegan et al., 2008). Whether strategic or tactical, entity manager-leaders should examine supply chain action alignment with organizational strategies (Cassivi et al., 2008). Buyers should consider conducting a detailed supplier assessment before project commencement (Handfield & Lawson, 2007). Entity manager-leaders must determine whether relational innovations need attention when developing acceptable collaboration means (Cassivi et al., 2008; Soosay et al., 2008). Moreover, entity manager-leaders must consider selectively applying supply chain integration (Parker et al., 2008) considering information security issues.

Entities strive to add value to supply chains by developing and deploying information systems that combine the best parts of various IT data sources and systems (Ketchen et al., 2008). Resultantly, the prevailing supply chain systems furnish information reliably and activity initiation capabilities to all members of the supply chain (Ketchen et al., 2008). An integrated information system enables high collaboration and swift deployment of goods and services (Ketchen et al., 2008). Nevertheless, evaluating system changes and maintenance are critical security service elements contributing to supply chain delivery value (Davis, 2008a; Mentzer et al., 2007). Moreover, due to geographic decentralization, information security risks rise to a higher level. IT decentralization unquestionably heightens the need for effective and efficient network security (Davis, 2008a; Mentzer et al., 2007).

An opportunity-oriented or risk-oriented strategic approach is supplier management options. The opportunity-oriented strategy focuses on SCM occasions for developing sustainable commodities and innovativeness (Harms et al., 2013). Contrastingly, the risk-oriented strategy is reactive to administrative pressure from stakeholders and focuses on SCM risk avoidance (Harms et al., 2013). Stakeholders have placed pressure on manager-leaders to engage in risk management activities in supply chains (Cantor et al., 2014; Davis, 2017). In response, supply chain managers should examine supply chain network technologies to assess configuration vulnerabilities (Boyes, 2015; Davis, 2017) and request consultations with entity information security personnel. Employees responsible for governance within an entity must, without reservation, provide guidance dedicated to appropriately handling supply chain risks (Boyson, 2014).

Altering the supply chain structure based on a risk-oriented strategy often demands cultural changes (Harms et al., 2013). If an entity intends to participate in evolving markets, acceptance of supply chain network redesign by manager-leaders is essential for ensuring effectiveness and efficiency (Groznik & Trkman, 2012; Liao & Hong, 2007). Interorganizational learning might enhance if manager-leaders pay attention to such characteristics as absorptive capacity (Azadegan et al., 2008). Also, entity manager-leaders should refrain from performing or authorizing knowledge sharing across the supply chain unless they are confident about protection mechanisms (Davis, 2017; Manzouri et al., 2013). Technologically, entity manager-leaders may find Active Directory Federation Service the best method to secure information across supply chain partners (Davis, 2017; Manzouri et al., 2013). However, purely technical solutions are unlikely to address the span of potential supply chain IAP threats and vulnerabilities (Boyes, 2015).

The globalization of an entity's supply chains compounds logistics coordination issues connected to three domains: time, distance, and replenishment level (Christopher & Towill, 2002; Sainathuni et al., 2014). Shared intentions identified in a global supply chain strategy formulation drive the performance measures for linked entity capabilities (Mentzer et al., 2007). Global SCM should address information systems security issues regarding integration (Cegielski et al., 2012), coordination (Boyson, 2014), and collaboration (Zeng et al., 2012). Effective global SCM represents a sequence of linked relationships among firms jointly pursuing and mutually sharing information, uncertainties, and benefits for inducing a competitive advantage (Mentzer et al., 2001). Efficient global SCM conveys operating assets and inventory use with higher productivity, enabling fixed assets and funded labor reductions (Mentzer et al., 2007).

Managed Service Providers

Information security is a management issue that requires an end-to-end view of the business processes (Dutta & McCrohan, 2002; as cited by Patnayakuni & Patnayakuni, 2014). Through outsourcing, the organization's management can remove business processes and IT, separately or jointly, from within the entity to a managed service provider (Davis, 2020; Mentzer et al., 2007). There is a difference between business process outsourcing and singular IT outsourcing (Cascarino, 2012; Davis, 2020). Business process outsourcing involves functional transference that may depend on IT (Cascarino, 2012; Davis, 2020). Whereas, singularly, there are many IT service models in the context of cloud computing that can meet an entity's needs (Cătinean & Cândea, 2013; Davis, 2020).

Outsourcing transcends technology and payroll processing by including software applications through the application service provider model and managed service provider systems whereby vendors host and maintain an entity's software through the vendor's off-site configuration or manage the entity hardware and software networks at the organizational site (Beasley et al., 2004). There are no definitive functions an entity can or should outsource (Wisma, 2008). The level of knowledge sharing is a determinant of the structure and governance mechanisms that evolve in IT outsourcing collaborations (Yang, 2011). As part of entity governance, ISG can drive information security service quality. ISG, in an IT outsourcing entity providing software services, has a highly significant and predictable effect on information security service quality (Bahl & Wali, 2014). There is a positive relationship between elements of ISG and information security service quality (Bahl & Wali, 2014).

Critical Success Factors represent identified issue undertakings for objective achievement (Davis, 2011). Managerially, Critical Success Factors' comparative analysis, monitoring, with appropriate adjustments, can ensure successful activity performance (Davis, 2011). Regarding IT, the critical success factors upon deciding to outsource IT functions encompass (a) vendor behavior control, (b) core competence management, (c) vendor resource exploitation, (d) transaction cost reduction, (e) contract completeness, (f) production cost reduction, (g) allegiance exploitation, (i) relationship exploitation, (j) social exchange exploitation, (k) labor demarcation, and (11) stakeholder management (Gottschalk & Solli-Saether, 2005). Of the 11 listed IT outsourcing constructs, core competence management, stakeholder management, and production cost reduction represent the highest-ranking considerations for success (Gottschalk & Solli-Saether, 2005).

Initiation, planning, development, implementation, and operational costs are subcategories of total IT project cost, whether manual or automated. Conversely, benefits are products or improvements resulting from a suggested project and beneficial to the entity. During sourcing analysis, cost–benefit analysis refers to techniques used to examine alternative actions in determining the recommended deployment or determining the most efficient deployment degree while providing the greatest return for reducing associated risks. In other words, sourcing cost–benefit analysis compares possible action cost against the potential resulting loss if management does not undertake an action.

Entity manager-leaders should employ formal cost–benefit analysis when considering outsourcing projects. Generally, a formal cost–benefit analysis should occur when there is a significant cash outlay estimate for the recommended project. Specifically, formal cost–benefit analysis preparation and examination should occur when contemplating systems and infrastructure outsourcing. In the final analysis, the recommended system or infrastructure should be efficient and effective.

Entity manager-leaders can establish an outsourcing platform for IT processing through block time, remote batch, timesharing, or service bureau agreements (Davis, 2010, 2020). Time rental processing by one entity of another entity IT for use by the renter's personnel is block time usage (Davis, 2010, 2020). Cluster mode processing with the entity maintaining minimal input and output hardware is remote batch usage (Davis, 2010, 2020). Timesharing appears as if a particular entity is the sole IT processing user, though multiple customers use the same resources (Davis, 2010, 2020). A service bureau exists when the renter entity leases a wide range of IT-processing capabilities (Davis, 2010, 2020).

The technical development feasibility report helps management determine whether to implement new or improved IT. During feasibility report evaluation of alternative systems or infrastructure configurations, manager-leaders should consider the feasibility of outsourcing. Specifically, if an entity discovers the necessary resources and capabilities are unavailable during the configuration planning phase, outsourcing the necessary functionality may be a viable course of action to pursue (Haag & Cummings, 2008).

As depicted in Figure 6.1, outsourcing involves conveying to a third party what the entity manager-leaders need (Haag & Cummings, 2008) to fulfill imposed expectations (Gottschalk & Solli-Saether, 2005). The desire of entity manager-leaders is essentially the logical requirements for a proposed configuration (Haag & Cummings, 2008). Consequently, the entity manager-leaders ensure an inscription of the logical requirements by developing a proposal request (Haag & Cummings, 2008). A Request for Proposal is a formal document that an entity's management sends to a vendor inviting the vendor to submit a bid (Haag & Cummings, 2008) for hardware, software, services, or any

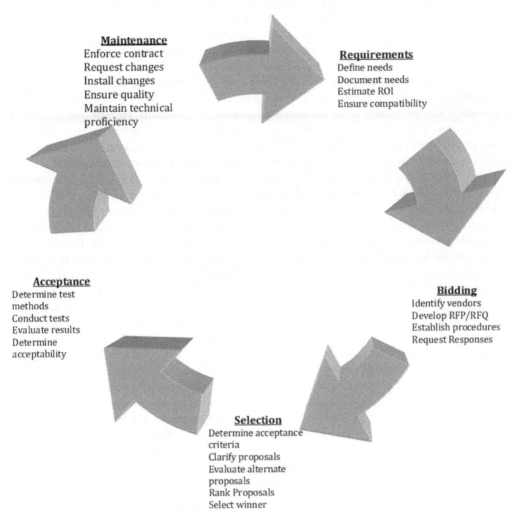

Figure 6.1 Vendor Contracting Life Cycle.

Note: ROI, return on investment; RFP, request for proposal; RFQ, request for quotation. Adapted from *IT Auditing: Systems and Infrastructure Life Cycle Management* by R. E. Davis, 2009b, Pleier. Copyright 2009 by Robert E. Davis. Adapted with permission.

combination of the three (Davis, 2009b). An entity typically issues the request for proposal or request for quotation to assess competing bids when acquiring planned services (Davis, 2009b; Haag & Cummings, 2008).

The outsourcing bidding phase identifies vendors, establishes bidding procedures, and provides vendors with an opportunity to bid on satisfying contract requirements (Davis, 2006; El Wardani et al., 2006). Sole source contracting restricts competition to one vendor (Davis, 2006). Typically, Sole-source Contracts can be more quickly negotiated than a typical competitive contract but are often replete with suspicion (Cohen & Eimicke, 2011). The common suspicion is that the entity's management used irregular or illegal acts to exclude competitors. Nonetheless, Sole-source Contracts can offer crucial savings

(El Wardani et al., 2006) and advantages for the customer and vendor. Alternatively, through cost–benefit analysis, Competitive Bidding, Open-ended Contract, and Preferred Product Agreements commonly reduce the opportunity to commit an illegal act (Davis, 2006). Additionally, the contract selector's potential to negotiate remuneration from a vendor increases (Davis, 2006).

Usually, within a competitive and changing entity environment, manager-leaders have heightened expectations regarding IT service delivery (Davis, 2008b; Năstase et al., 2009). Manager-leaders typically insist on increased quality, functionality, ease of use, decreased delivery time, and continuously improving service levels – with multilateral cost containment or abatement (Davis, 2008b). For IT service delivery personnel, organizational expectations generally translate into providing appropriate service level management (Davis, 2008b). Service level management is typically the primary IT managerial area that ensures that promised services are delivered when and where expected at agreed-upon cost (Davis, 2008b). Consequently, service level management processes should have objectives, goals, and procedures. Customers and resource suppliers need identification and administration to enable service level management (Davis, 2008b; Năstase et al., 2009). Descriptively, sound service level management necessitates clear interfaces and specification of services defined with customers (i.e., service level requirements; Davis, 2008b; Năstase et al., 2009).

Service level management enables quality-of-service monitoring and administration through Key Performance Indicators (Davis, 2008b). Assisting quality-of-service monitoring and administration processes are the service quality plan (Davis, 2008b). Quality of service Key Performance Indicators can range from generic availability and usage statistics to entity-centric per-interaction indicators (Davis, 2008b). Effectual service level management requires identifying potential problems – such as gradual performance degradation (see Table 6.1) – and alerts creation enabling downtime risk minimization (Davis, 2008b). Consequently, service level management practices should include comparing actual performance to pre-defined expectations, determining appropriate actions, and generating expressive reports to permit service improvements (Davis, 2008b).

Table 6.1 Potential Configuration Performance Indicators

Server Performance	Network Performance
CPU Utilization	Buffer Misses
CPU Imbalance	Buffer Utilization
Disk I/O Faults	CPU Utilization
File Cache Misses	Line Utilization
Paging	Discovered Faults
Swapping	Discards
Virtual Memory Utilization	Latency
Physical Memory Utilization	Hardware Errors
Allocation Failures	Software Errors
System Partition Utilization	Packet Losses
User Partition Utilization	Frames Delivered[a]

Note: CPU, central processing unit; I/O, input or output.

a Assumes a frame relay-based network deployment for the IT configuration.
  Adapted from *IT Auditing: IT Service Delivery and Support* by R. E. Davis, 2008b, Pleier. Copyright 2008 by Robert E. Davis. Adapted with permission.

Effective problem management requires tracking service performance and inscribing problems encountered (Davis, 2008b). Management's view of a problem's relative importance will largely depend upon situational alignment with prioritized institutional IT objectives and goals (Davis, 2008b). Senior manager-leaders should establish goals regarding data processing and online service availability (Davis, 2008b). Entity management should maintain records on actual performance in meeting service schedules (Davis, 2008b). Efficient and timely solutions for problems need to demonstrate correspondence with a clear priority statement supported by executive manager-leaders (Davis, 2008b). Problems and delays encountered, the reasons for the problems or delays, and the elapsed time for resolution need recording and analysis to identify any recurring pattern or trend (Davis, 2008b). Subsequently, executive manager-leaders should periodically review and compare the service performance achieved with adopted goals and survey entity users to see if organizational needs were met (Davis, 2008b).

Procedurally, significant service level management responsibilities encompass

- Service Quality Plan Alignment: requires instituting quality projections relative to long-range and short-range IT service plans with provisions for timely updating related to service quality projections (Davis, 2008b). Therefore, IT management should develop, resource, and execute a service quality plan that can obtain the quality specified in requirement specifications as well as the entity's quality policies and procedures (Davis, 2008b). Specific issues for IT manager-leaders to consider when developing a service quality plan include specification of quality criteria, validation, and verification processes – including inspection, walkthroughs, and testing (Davis, 2008b).

- Third-Party Contracts: Outsourcing services needs contractual establishment, modification, and termination processes for all vendors (Davis, 2008b). Approved third party agreements need to address underpinning expectations for supporting entity service and support delivery (Davis, 2008b). Minimally, third-party contracting procedures need to cover legal, financial, organizational, documentary, performance, security, intellectual property, as well as termination responsibilities and liabilities – with a requirement for legal advisor review of all procurement contracts and contract changes (Davis, 2008a, 2008b).

- Service Level Agreement Utilization: allows defining, negotiating, and agreeing-on acceptable service levels (Davis, 2008b). Consequently, a service level agreement is a consensus that outlines minimum performance targets for a service and measurement criteria (Davis, 2008b). A service level agreement enables an entity assurance of an expected amount of stability, reliability, and performance for the provided information assets (Davis, 2008b). Furthermore, a service level agreement may complement or be part of policy-based service level management (Davis, 2008b). The standard IT service level agreement is a contractual concurrence, preferably inscribed, between the IT function and vendors stating what each participating party's responsibilities are regarding information assets (Davis, 2008b; Haag & Cummings, 2008).

- Operating Level Agreement Utilization: explains technical delivery of contractual activities optimally supporting the service level agreements with provisions for timely service quality updating (Davis, 2008b). Operational level agreements with vendors facilitate adherence to negotiated service level agreements (Davis, 2008b). An Operating Level Agreement needs to specify technical processes in terms meaningful to the provider (Davis, 2008b). Moreover, the accepted Operating Level Agreement can also support several service level agreements (Davis, 2008b). Operating level agreements should cover IAP expectations that assist the entity's organizational structure in service delivery and support.

- Service Catalogue Registration: necessitates inventorying supported services, describing identified services, and correlating information assets that support services, with provisions for supported services documentation maintenance (Davis, 2008b).
- Service Level Requirements Recording: necessitates defined performance and capacity requirement inscription in a registry (Davis, 2008b).
- Service Level Monitoring: requires providing benchmarking, scorecards, and dashboards (Davis, 2008b). Benchmarking can provide timely adaptation to trends and developments in the entity's environment (Davis, 2008b). Simultaneously, scorecards address achieving satisfactory results for the largest possible stakeholder segments (Davis, 2008b). Whereas dashboards provide the means for responsible manager-leaders to monitor, evaluate, and guide activities considering service delivery objectives (Davis, 2008b). Specifically, defined Key Goal Indicators with associated Key Performance Indicators enable comparative assessments based on observed or inscribed service process activities (Davis, 2008b).
- Service and Support Improvement Program: requires identifying and deploying future vendor enhancements (Davis, 2008b). Within a service improvement program, management can provide the necessary details upon which the service provider can act (Davis, 2008b). Based on the most recent comprehensive risk assessment, information security administrators should provide details of the control issues and the agreed-upon actions for addressing relevant service delivery and support issues (Davis, 2008b). Moreover, a service improvement program must designate individuals responsible for implementing agreed-upon actions and deployment of target dates (Davis, 2008b).

Whether the entity is large, medium, or small, vendor negotiations are essential to ensuring the best value for the money. Outsourcing contracts necessitate active administration. Entity manager-leaders should take the time to understand contracts and the established organizational relationship and any changing business needs. An acquired outsourcing environment understanding can lead to contractual concessions and built-in protection against perceived future issues. Foreseeing potential environment changes means establishing a contract management team that functions as an interface between the entity and the sourcing vendor. Therefore, an information security officer should assess contract management effects on IAP (Năstase et al., 2009).

Most outsourcing relationships require contractual terms establishment, modification, and termination processes that ensure appropriate IAP (Davis, 2008a). Comprehensive ISG requires communicating security policies and security measures to contractually engaged third parties (Davis, 2008a). Approved third party agreements should address underpinning expectations for supporting information security service delivery (Davis, 2008a).

Cloud computing is an automation architecture in which scalable and elastic IT-enabled capabilities permit delivery as a service using Internet technologies (Cătinean & Cândea, 2013). A cloud computing service has differentiation characteristics distinct from traditional hosting (Davis, 2020). First, cloud computing services are sold on demand, typically by block time minutes or hours (Davis, 2020). Second, cloud computing service elasticity allows users to vary service at any given time (Davis, 2020). Third, the entity providing cloud computing manages the active service (Davis, 2020).

Cloud computing architectures can be public or private (Davis, 2020). Public cloud computing enables open service use through a managed service provider (Cătinean & Cândea, 2013; Davis, 2020; Karajeh et al., 2014). Private cloud computing is a proprietary configuration that supplies hosted services to a limited number of individuals (Davis, 2020; Karajeh et al., 2014). When a provider applies public cloud computing resources to deploy private cloud computing, the resulting configuration is virtual private cloud computing (Davis, 2020). Public or private cloud computing goals are to provide secure, scalable access to computing resources and IT services (Davis, 2020).

Cloud computing architectures can also be community or hybrid (Davis, 2020). Community cloud computing exists when several groups or individuals share a cloud service that supports the community's concerns (Cătinean & Cândea, 2013; Davis, 2020; Karajeh et al., 2014). Hybrid cloud computing combines private, community, or public services that remain in the distinct architectures yet are bound together by standardized or proprietary technology enabling data and application portability (Cătinean & Cândea, 2013; Davis, 2020; Karajeh et al., 2014).

Cloud computing delivers hosted services (Davis, 2010, 2020). The categories of service are information, database, storage, process, application, platform, integration, security, management, governance, testing, and infrastructure (Cătinean & Cândea, 2013; Davis, 2020). Of the listed cloud computing services, primary categories are Infrastructure-as-a-Service, Platform-as-a-Service, and Software-as-a-Service (Cătinean & Cândea, 2013; Davis, 2010, 2020; Karajeh et al., 2014), while Business Process-as-a-Service is a secondary category (Cătinean & Cândea, 2013; Davis, 2020).

- Infrastructure-as-a-Service provides on-demand virtual server instances with unique Internet Protocol addressing and storage blocking (Davis, 2020; Mohammad & Ladan, 2012). The provider's application program interface allows customers to start, stop, access, and configure allocated virtual servers and storage (Davis, 2020). In the entity, cloud computing allows an entity to pay for only needed capacity and bring more capacity online as soon as necessary (Davis, 2020). Because the pay-for-what-you-use model for technology resembles electricity, fuel, and water consumption billing patterns, references sometimes name Infrastructure-as-a-Service as utility computing (Davis, 2020).
- Platform-as-a-Service is a set of development tools hosted on the service provider's infrastructure where developers construct applications on the provider's platform over the Internet (Davis, 2020). Platform-as-a-Service providers may use application program interfaces, website portals, or gateway software installed on the customer's technology (Davis, 2020). Some providers will not allow the movement of customer-created software from the supplied platform (Davis, 2020).
- In the Software-as-a-Service cloud computing model, the service provider supplies the hardware infrastructure, the software product and interacts with the user through a front-end portal (Davis, 2020). Software-as-a-Service is an extensive market (Davis, 2020). Services can range from email to inventory control and database processing (Davis, 2020). Because the service provider hosts the application and the data, the end-user can access the service from anywhere (Davis, 2020).
- As a secondary category, Business Process-as-a-Service is the delivery of automated business process outsourcing services sourced from cloud computing and constructed for multi-tenancy (Cătinean & Cândea, 2013; Davis, 2020). Business-Process-as-a-Service allows the consumer to design, manage, and integrate transactional and collaborative activities based on the Software-as-a-Service provided in the underlining layers (Davis, 2020; Mohammad & Ladan, 2012). Like Infrastructure-as-a-Service and Platform-as-a-Service, a Business Process-as-a-Service provider provisions the tools to access and use the resources in the Business Process-as-a-Service layer (Davis,

2020; Mohammad & Ladan, 2012). Consumers typically do not need to access services in the underlying Business Process-as-a-Service layers (Davis, 2020; Mohammad & Ladan, 2012).

Entities may partially or fully delegate IT asset development, service delivery, and service support to a managed service provider (Davis, 2008b, 2009b). Outsourceable IT activities include IT functions such as data center operations, cybersecurity, and application maintenance (Davis, 2008b). Outsourceable IT resources include infrastructure, platforms, and applications (Davis, 2008b, 2009b). Infrastructure integrates diverse software and hardware solutions, each designed to achieve a specific function. Platforms are technologies, products, or services that furnish essential resources to build complementary technologies, products, or services (Hagiu & Yoffie, 2009). Applications superimpose technology to complete a task (Davis, 2005, 2010, 2020). Usually, the responsibility for confirming outsourced activity compliance with contracts, agreements, laws, and regulations resides with the entity (Davis, 2009b; Haag & Cummings, 2008). When a managed service provider is within the assurance ambit, the assigned auditors are accountable for determining whether the managed service provider follows the contracted service's terms of reference.

Several issues arise when developing Security-as-a-Service for cloud infrastructures. In the current environment, the cloud service providers do not generally offer Security-as-a-Service to tenants (Varadharajan & Tupakula, 2014). Hence, tenants need to plan for securing entity virtual machines hosted by the cloud service provider (Varadharajan & Tupakula, 2014). Although tenants can use different security tools such as anti-virus and host-based intrusion detection systems to secure organizational virtual machines, limitations arise because the provided tools reside in the same system as the monitored architecture and are vulnerable to attacks (Varadharajan & Tupakula, 2014). Moreover, some tenants may not be capable of securing organizational virtual machines (Varadharajan & Tupakula, 2014). Therefore, there is a need for the cloud service provider to offer Security-as-a-Service to such tenants (Varadharajan & Tupakula, 2014).

Furthermore, IAP requirements for tenants may vary, and some tenants may opt for more security services from the cloud provider while others may opt for the baseline default security (Varadharajan & Tupakula, 2014). The greater the level of security measures taken up by the tenant from the provider, the greater is the possibility for the cloud provider to get to know more about tenant systems (Varadharajan & Tupakula, 2014). In other words, the Security-as-a-Service mechanisms and tools offered by the cloud provider can gather more information about the operating system and applications running in the organizational virtual machines (Varadharajan & Tupakula, 2014). In turn, the cybersecurity circumstance can lead to more significant privacy concerns for the tenant. Entity management's privacy concerns refer to the cloud provider employees' ability to discover details regarding the services and applications data in a tenant's machine (Varadharajan & Tupakula, 2014).

As a methodical IT development approach, generic short cycle time development has advantages and disadvantages (Baskerville & Pries-Heje, 2004). Short cycle time development advantages take the primary form of release-orientation and parallel development. Primary disadvantages of short cycle time development include ambit and feature creep through IT development prototyping, forgoing proper testing, and remiss documentation (Baskerville & Pries-Heje, 2004; Haag & Cummings, 2008). Given the 11 Critical Success Factors for outsourcing IT development projects, the diffusing of short cycle time development form should not mitigate an outsourcing decision. However, during the evaluation of the alternative system or infrastructure configurations, management can stipulate the required vendor IT deployment form within the request for proposal. Thus, entity manager-leaders can accept or reject outsourcing candidates, considering the inscribed IT development approach.

IT is suitable for offshore outsourcing of projects with transparent requirements as well as specifications and minimal end-user interaction with technical project team members (Haag & Cummings, 2008). Data conversions and system migration activities are conducive to offshore outsourcing (Haag & Cummings, 2008). Under the waterfall methodology, application development and testing phases are potential candidates for offshore outsourcing (Haag & Cummings, 2008). Specifically, the application development and testing phases where end-user interaction is limited, with well-defined tasks, are good candidates for offshore outsourcing (Haag & Cummings, 2008). Most maintenance activities are performable remotely for stable applications, so application maintenance is also an excellent offshore outsourcing candidate. However, there are cultural risks associated with offshoring when outsourcing processes.

Cultural divergence can impede the successful offshoring of IT development. Specifically, human resource practices, laws and regulations, social value systems, organizational edicts, and technology-orientation can result in barriers to successfully offshoring IT development projects (Baskerville & Pries-Heje, 2004). Usually, the responsibility for confirming outsourced activity compliance with contracts, agreements, policies, procedures, laws, and regulations resides with the entity (Davis, 2009b). Therefore, what is required to overcome impediments is cultural assessment, indoctrination, and integration before establishing a contractual agreement between the parties involved in the offshored IT development projects. Specific issues include

- flexibility, constraints (e.g., workforce);
- legal traditions and viewpoints about liabilities (e.g., vague requirements);
- communication and frequent social exchanges for shared values (e.g., customer involvement);
- adherence to established processes; and
- extensive and very characteristic reliance on, and trust in, tools, components, methods, and tailored processes.

The risks associated with onshoring or offshoring outsourcing IT include contract, privacy, security, diminished technical returns, IT expertise loss, hidden costs, ambit, and decision process (Tafti, 2005). IT outsourcing risk treatment can be acceptance, reduction, or transference (Davis, 2008a, 2011). However, elimination is never an IT outsourcing risk option. Appropriate objectives, goals, policies, procedures, standards, and rules are necessary to enable beneficial IT service delivery and support (Davis, 2008b). Specifically, using ISSM standards usually generates benefits when an entity decides to outsource systems, processes, activities, or tasks. Thus, service level agreements between the entity and service vendor will usually generate fewer disputes and lower costs (Davis, 2008b).

Service Provider Audit

IT Service Management extraction, decomposition, analysis, and assessment can provide the key to unlock the knowledge door for understanding an entity's ISG framework. IT delivery as a service to end-users is a critical managerial component that can affect IT effectiveness as an organizational enabler (Davis, 2008b). Potential risks of implementing inadequate IT service and support include

- inefficient services provided to users,
- unclear service processes,
- inefficient communication of service delivery objectives,
- ineffective communication of service delivery objectives,
- lack of common language for IT service delivery,
- lack of common language for IT service support,
- increased vocational adjustment periods,
- inappropriate prioritization to different provided services,
- user dissatisfaction with services provided,
- ineffective services and required resources planning, and
- ineffective services and required resources maintenance (Davis, 2008b).

Hence, IT service delivery and support areas should receive periodic examinations by IT audit to attest foundational vigor. Outsourced service audits necessitate performance, assuming the service provisioning occurs in the service user's own IT environment. Assigned engagement auditors need the right to (a) review the agreement between the service user and the service provider; (b) carry out IT audit work considered necessary regarding outsourced audit areas; and (c) report findings, conclusions, and recommendations to engagement service user management (Davis, 2005, 2010). When the external service provider proves unwilling to co-operate with the IT auditor, the IT auditor should report the matter to the service user's management.

An entity's manager-leaders should have governance processes addressing the relationship with and the performance of third-party providers for outsourced activities (Boyson, 2014; Davis, 2011, 2017, 2020). IT Governance consists of structures, relationships, and processes (Ula et al., 2011). There exists guidance that provides frameworks for deploying IT Governance. The implementation proceeds mainly by mapping IT Governance responsibilities to the entity hierarchy. A choice for an IT Governance framework applicable to service level management includes Control Objectives for Information and Related Technology. The Control Objectives for Information and Related Technology framework partitions control processes into four interactive domains:

- Align, Plan, and Organize;
- Build, Acquire, and Implement;
- Deliver, Service, and Support; and
- Monitor, Evaluate, and Assess (IT Governance Institute, 2018).

As shown in Figure 6.2, the effectiveness of controls operated in the Align, Plan, and Organize and Monitor, Evaluate, and Assess domains influences the effectiveness of controls in the Build, Acquire, and Implement and the Deliver, Service, and Support domains. In other words, improper alignment, planning, organization, monitoring, evaluations, and assessing by management imply that controls for overbuilding, acquisitions, implementations, delivery, service, and support will be inappropriate. Alternatively, appropriate alignment, planning, organization, monitoring, evaluating, and assessing can identify and correct ineffective controls of overbuilding, acquisition, implementation, delivery, service, and support. The Control Objectives for Information and Related Technology framework provides a common language for executive

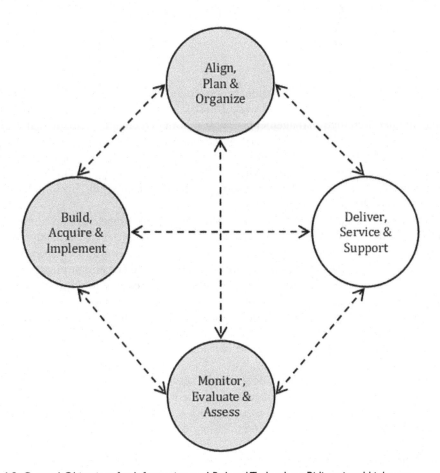

Figure 6.2 Control Objectives for Information and Related Technology Bidirectional Linkages.

Note: Adapted from *IT Auditing: IT Service Delivery and Support* by R. E. Davis, 2008b, Pleier. Copyright 2008 by Robert E. Davis. Adapted with permission.

manager-leaders to communicate objectives, goals, and outcomes with audit, IT, and other professionals (Năstase et al., 2009).

An IT auditor assigned an IT service delivery and support engagement considers performing assurance services based on significant process points established in the Control Objectives for Information and Related Technology framework (Davis, 2008b). Additionally, the engagement IT auditors need to consider applying the ISO/IEC 20000 and ISO/IEC 27000 series of international standards when performing an IT audit (Davis, 2008b). An entity-centric IT service management extraction can transpire from the ISO/IEC standards. An IT auditor will probably find assertion veracity or direct subject matter verification more productive if well-versed in the service delivery and support concepts. The risk-based IT assurance system addressing relevant ISO/IEC 20000, ISO/IEC 27000, and Control Objectives for Information and Related Technology delivery, service, and support areas can assist IT manager-leaders with valuable recommendations reflecting generally accepted IT service management standards. Audit Planning, Study and Evaluation of Controls, Testing and Evaluation of Controls, Reporting, and Follow-up are the processes completed to ensure adequate reporting on the condition of IT-related controls, effectiveness, and efficiency (Davis, 2020).

IT Audit Planning

Primary drivers for IT service management audit planning are verifying delivery and support existence and appropriateness (Davis, 2008b). Service level management, configuration management, change management, operations management, incident management, and problem management are critical outsourced service components when performing an external audit. However, as with other IT audits, the in-charge IT auditor needs to obtain an audit area understanding during engagement planning to comply with ISACA assurance standards and guidelines as well as other applicable attestation, audit, accounting, and IT standards (Davis, 2008b).

IT auditors must clearly define the IT service engagement objectives and ambit (Davis, 2008b). Typically, manager-leaders are interested in IT service delivery and support work performance processes, emphasizing requirements and expectations for ensuring objective achievements (Davis, 2008b). Consequently, IT service delivery and support attestation engagements focus on efficacy and associated processes, intending to improve service performance and process effectiveness (Davis, 2008b). When a managed service provider is within the IT service delivery and support ambit, IT audit is accountable for determining whether appropriate controls exist and are functioning as intended (Davis, 2008b). For outsourced services, the IT auditor should consider such things as

- existence of a formal agreement between the service provider and the service user;
- inclusion of a clause in the outsourcing agreement, which explicitly states that the service provider must meet all legal requirements applying to their activities and comply with acts and regulations concerning the functions undertaken on behalf of the service user;
- stipulation in the outsourcing agreement that activities performed by the service provider is subject to controls and audits as if the contracting entity performed them;
- inclusion of audit access rights in the agreement with the service provider;
- existence of service level agreements with performance monitoring procedures;
- adherence to the service user's security policies;
- adequacy of the service provider's fidelity insurance arrangements; and
- adequacy of the service provider's personnel policies and procedures.

Regarding outsourced services, among other expectations, an IT auditor should obtain and inscribe an understanding of the relationship between the services provided by third parties and the entity's control environment (Davis, 2008b). The in-charge IT auditor should review such items as contracts, service level agreements, policies, and procedures concerning the entity's third-party providers (Davis, 2008b). The in-charge IT auditor should also obtain appropriate expert legal advice (Davis, 2008b). Furthermore, the in-charge IT auditor should review any previous third-party provider audit reports prepared for the entity. Subsequently, the in-charge IT auditor should plan the IT audit work to address the audit objectives relevant to the service provider's environment, taking into account obtained information (Davis, 2008b). In the end, an IT auditor should plan third-party provider audit work to comply with applicable professional audit standards (Davis, 2008b).

The in-charge IT auditor must perform a preliminary control environment assessment corresponding to the audit area under examination to ensure that all significant items will receive appropriate addressing during the IT audit (Davis, 2008b). When evaluating the service provider's control environment, an IT auditor should consider the following elements and activation.

- Communication and enforcement of integrity and ethical values are essential elements that influence the design, administration, and monitoring of controls.
- Commitment to competence is management's consideration of job competency levels and translation into requisite skills and knowledge.
- Participation by those charged with governance for independence from management, experience and stature, the extent of involvement and scrutiny of activities, the information received, the degree to which difficult questions arise and pursued with management, and the interaction with internal and external auditors.
- Management's philosophy and operating style considering management's approach to taking and managing risks and management's attitudes and actions toward financial reporting, information processing, accounting functions and personnel.
- The organizational structures address the operating frameworks within which an entity's activities for achieving objectives are planned, executed, controlled, and reviewed.
- Assignment of authority and responsibility demonstrates how authority and responsibility for operating activities are assigned and how reporting relationships and authorization hierarchies occur.
- The managed service provider's human resource policies and practices for recruitment, orientation, training, evaluating, counseling, promoting, compensating, and remedial actions followed.

Assessing how much control environment risk is associated with a particular entity may be performed using various techniques and tools (Davis, 2008b). For each of the selected audit control environment statements, a compliance value needs a definition, enabling the IT assurance professional to calculate a compliance profile (Davis, 2008b). Therefore, when acquiring an understanding of control environment components, the in-charge IT auditor must consider whether pertinent element deployments exist for the entity and IT (Davis, 2008b). Ordinarily, the in-charge IT auditor obtains relevant control environment audit evidence through a combination of inquiries and other risk assessment procedures (Davis, 2008b). Specific to understanding and defining entity IT control environment risks, the in-charge IT auditor should consider

- previous history,
- performance patterns,
- current IT organizational factors,
- existing IT environment complexity,
- existing IT environment size or ambit,
- planned IT environment complexity,
- planned IT environment size or ambit,
- current IT environment inherent vulnerabilities,
- planned IT environment inherent vulnerabilities, and
- nature of IT initiatives contemplated (Davis, 2008b).

Where service provider's management performs maturity modeling, the in-charge IT auditor should apply analytical procedures on the contents to determine consistency and quality of maturity levels between and within processes, including definitions of maturity model attributes (Davis, 2008b). Audit evidence for the control environment elements may not be available in a documentary form for smaller entities where communication between management and other personnel may be informal yet effective. For example, management's commitment to ethical values and competence implementation is often through the behavior and attitude demonstrated in managing the entity's affairs instead of in an inscribed code of conduct. Consequently, management's attitudes, awareness, and actions are of particular importance in designing a smaller entity's control environment. Additionally, the sole owner-managers often take responsibility for governance where there are no other owners.

Maturity modeling shows the status of the control environment and the establishment of controls in an entity. The entity maturity model also shows controls administration and an awareness of the need to establish better controls, typically ranging from an ad hoc to an optimized level. Maturity modeling provides a high-level guide to help Control Objectives for Information and Related Technology users appreciate requirements for appropriate controls for IT and aids in positioning an entity on the maturity scale. Beneficially, after identifying critical IT processes and controls, maturity modeling enables conveying capability gaps and demonstrating to management needed improvements. After that, entity manager-leaders can devise action plans to bring processes up to the desired capability target level.

The outsourcing of all or selected business processes and IT is a recent phenomenon affecting IT audits (Davis, 2020). The in-charge IT auditor's service audit risk assessments should demonstrate the consideration of the processes under examination (Davis, 2008b). The planning risk assessment can include categories for addressing service level management, configuration management, change management, operations management, performance management, data administration, capacity monitoring, incident management, problem management (Davis, 2008b), and security management. Due to direct activity linkage at the general risk assessment level, IT auditors should consider combining incident management and problem management auditable units if both items are within the assurance ambit (Davis, 2008b). Specific to an IT service audit, the planning risk assessment should include a privacy sub-category within the category for addressing data administration (Davis, 2008b).

IT Audit Study and Evaluation of Controls

An IT auditor controls study produces sufficient audit area documentation demonstrating the comprehensive investigation concerning IT and related manual processes (Davis, 2010). Most organizational processes have control measures assisting in accomplishing control objectives (Davis, 2020). However, even if control measures do not exist, while scrutinizing an audit area for implemented controls, the assigned IT auditors evaluate effectiveness, efficiency, confidentiality, integrity, availability, compliance, or reliability to determine the degree of control objectives achievement (Davis, 2020). Thus, the study and evaluation of controls present an opportunity to assess if management is achieving control objectives (Davis, 2020). Furthermore, if warranted, a preliminary audit risk reassessment and other testing procedures may occur before ending the study and evaluation audit process (Davis, 2020).

Service Level Management

Service level management deployments can flounder because IT management skews service focus toward technology-centric measurements specific to categorized domains (Davis,

2008b). Correctively, the IT service function should provide circumspective insight into service levels that management understands (Davis, 2008b). Objective achievement should reflect the building and measuring of service-based contractual arrangements (Davis, 2008b). Service-based negotiations encourage directed dialog between IT and operational units and promote IT practice unification across configuration items supporting computer applications and organizational processes (Davis, 2008b). Therefore, minimally, the assigned IT auditors can study and evaluate whether

- visible, operationally related IT objectives exist,
- visible, operationally related IT metrics reporting to management,
- definitions of services and associated projects in end-user terms exist,
- service level agreements and contracts creation are monitorable by users,
- users have sought remedies when dissatisfied with the level of service,
- users have the capacity and competence to review the services provided,
- users have the capacity and competence to follow up on the services provided,
- corrective actions' consideration occurred in achieving agreed-upon service levels,
- user requirements appropriately cascade down into configuration item operational requirements,
- services and project portfolios receive collective consideration in enabling setting relative priorities,
- organizational processes that produce information used to monitor compliance with the service level agreements are appropriately controlled, and
- services and project portfolios receive collective consideration in enabling resource allocations on an equitable and achievable basis (Davis, 2008b).

Configuration Management

When examining entity IT services, infrastructure management is administering essential operational components, such as policies, processes, equipment, data, human resources, and external contacts, to enable entity effectiveness (Davis, 2008b). Appropriate configuration management enables management to reduce the risk of requiring back-out procedure enactments due to inadequate preparation or incompatible changes affecting service provider availability and digitized processing integrity (Davis, 2008b). Therefore, the assigned IT auditors can study and evaluate whether the entity IT function and service provider have

- undertaken configuration management planning,
- identified configuration items,
- established a configuration management database,
- established a definitive software library,
- established a definitive hardware store,
- inscribed configuration controls,
- maintained the status of configuration items,
- tracked the status of configuration items,
- reviewed configuration items against configuration management database records, and
- managed configuration item libraries, licenses, and stores (Davis, 2008b).

Change Management

Critical to achieving performance expectations are control procedures for change (Davis, 2008b). Usually, the most critical item to obtain during a change management audit is a complete list of all users with access authorities (Davis, 2008b). Once acquired, an infrastructure access listing with inscribed authorities can help determine the change management security extent and adequacy (Davis, 2008b). An IT auditor should determine whether change controls are adequate to prevent unauthorized hardware or software alterations during software distribution (Davis, 2008b). Specifically, there should be effective procedures for authorization and change control in place (Davis, 2008b). However, even a robust change management protocol may not catch all problems related to a change (Davis, 2008b). During the IT service change management study and evaluation process, an IT auditor can determine whether

- change identification occurs,
- change categorization happens,
- change prioritization occurs,
- emergency change procedures exist,
- impact assessments occur,
- change authorization inscriptions occur,
- release management procedures exist,
- software distribution procedures exist,
- automated tools utilization transpires,
- employees follow configuration management practices,
- operational process redesign is a consideration,
- approval procedures exist to initiate program changes,
- critical checkpoints exist throughout the development process,
- employees follow procedures for emergency software fixes,
- employees follow procedures for temporary software fixes,
- employees follow procedures for new releases,
- change control documentation provides appropriate audit trails, and
- change documentation support software changes (Davis, 2008b).

Service Operations Management

Service operations management invokes regular, day-to-day oversight, and processing activities required for service delivery following agreed-upon service levels (Davis, 2008b). An entity's IT services support unit should manage user expectations through a service desk staffed with competent personnel (Davis, 2008b). Minimally, for IT service desk assurance engagements, an IT auditor should determine if

- service level agreements are measurable,
- users are charged for IT usage,
- meaningful reviews of service level agreement reports occur,
- user management receives the cost scale for IT usage,
- appropriate management levels receive service level agreement reports,
- service desk knowledge databases receive appropriate administration,
- service desk procedures for escalation receive inscription, and
- service desk procedures for obtaining expert help receive adequate inscription (Davis, 2008b).

Table 6.2 Information Criteria-IT Service Problem Matrix

Problem	Operations			Compliance	Security		
	Effectiveness	Efficiency	Reliability	Compliance	Confidentiality	Integrity	Availability
Responsiveness	P		S				P
Throughput		P					S
Economy		P	S				
Accuracy		P		S		P	
Reliability			P	S	P	P	P
Efficiency		P		S			S
Security			S	S	P	P	S
Information	S	S	P	S	S	P	P

Note: P, primary; S, secondary. Adapted from *IT Auditing: IT Service Delivery and Support* by R. E. Davis, 2008b, Pleier. Copyright 2008 by Robert E. Davis. Adapted with permission.

Problem Management

IT audit team members can include the study and evaluation of problem management processes in detail (see Table 6.2) when providing assurance service (Davis, 2008b). The problem management process output typically includes emergency and unplanned change sub-process (Davis, 2008b). When examining management information relevance, timeliness can affect managerial decisions (Davis, 2008b). Therefore, problem information delivery velocity needs assessment for task priority compliance (Davis, 2008b). Consequently, an IT service problem management study and evaluation should include collecting evidence that

- accountability establishment occurs, where specific management receives an assigned problem, and each configuration has a designated problem queue;
- emergency changes receive full inscription before completing item resolution;
- requests associated with user complaints are first inscribed and evaluated before a formal item modification requests submission;
- problem resolutions receive an inscription; and
- authorization to close problem tickets occurs from the manager responsible for the problem resolution or information asset (Davis, 2008b).

Incident Management

Service restoration plans require inscription, communication, and approval (Davis, 2008b). If, after evaluation, audit evidence indicates an incident occurred because of an irregular act that the service user did not receive a report, the assigned IT auditor can recommend a thorough investigation of the subject matter or initiate other appropriate action. With proper authorization, when the incident warrants further investigation, standard audit procedures' performance is necessary to determine irregular act nature, timing, and extent (Davis, 2009a). Standard audit procedures include

- assessing probable complicity level and extent;
- determining knowledge, skills, and disciplines necessary to perform the investigation effectively;

- designing procedures for identifying perpetrators; and
- coordinating activities with appropriate individuals (Davis, 2009a).

IT Audit Testing of Controls

Commonly, IT audit testing foci are auditable unit risks of the audit area (Davis, 2020). IT auditors perform procedures to test control appropriateness and managerial risks for overriding deployed controls, based on assessed risk (Davis, 2009a). IT auditors can also perform tests that reasonably expect to detect material irregularities and weaknesses in controls – which could result in unprevented or undetected material irregularities (Davis, 2009a). Selecting an appropriate technique, method, and tool for conducting audit testing can be challenging (Davis, 2010).

An IT auditor verifies the operating effectiveness of deployed controls (Davis, 2009a). Compliance testing usually is utilized to verify control operating effectiveness (Davis, 2009a). External IT service delivery and support assurance engagements can be general or application control assessments (Davis, 2008b). Consequently, IT auditor controls testing can address performing manual or automated procedures, statistically or nonstatistically (Davis, 2008b). General control testing skews toward an IT auditor performing hardcopy-assisted audit techniques (Davis, 2010, 2020). Conversely, application testing skews toward performing computer-assisted audit techniques (Davis, 2010, 2020). An assigned IT auditor can use publicly available procedures offered by professional associations to perform the required IT service testing (Davis, 2008b).

Unless otherwise dictated by the IT audit risk assessment or audit management, extensive compliance testing is the norm for IT service audits (Davis, 2008b). Usually, there are sufficient manual and automated IT service-related policies, procedures, standards, and rules available to assess the design and operating effectiveness (Davis, 2008b). Evidentially, an IT auditor should consider whether information obtained from the IT service audit planning, study, and testing activities indicates professional due diligence (Davis, 2008b, 2020).

IT Audit Report on Controls

Regarding issuing and agreeing with an external IT service audit report, the in-charge IT auditor should provide reports in an appropriate form to the intended service user recipients upon completion of audit work. An IT auditor should consider discussing the report with the third-party provider before release. However, an IT auditor should not be responsible for issuing the final report to a third-party provider. If the third-party provider receives an audit report copy, the conveyance authorization should ordinarily come from the service user's management. The service provider audit report should specify any restrictions on distribution which the IT auditor or service user management agrees to impose. The IT auditor should also consider including a statement excluding liability to third parties. Where restrictions on the service provider audit exist, the audit report should identify the limitation and explain the restriction effect concerning the assurance engagement.

Procedurally, an IT auditor should bring all evidence-supported recommendations to the attention of the appropriate management level for review and implementation (Davis, 2008b, 2020). However, IT audit report recommendations for IT service delivery and support auditable units are advisory (Davis, 2008b). Therefore, an auditee may dispute findings for technical or grammatical reasons (Davis, 2008b). Furthermore, an auditee may ignore a recommendation considering the risk assessment, cost–benefit analysis, or competing priorities (Davis, 2008b).

When the in-charge IT auditor becomes aware of a hostile reception to an important recommendation, the disputed finding or ignored recommendation should receive the entity's executive manager-leaders and the client's oversight committee's attention (Davis, 2008b). As a managerial decision, the service provider's oversight committee usually has the authority to ensure audit recommendation implementations (Davis, 2008b).

IT Audit Follow-Up

IT auditors should comply with assurance practice follow-up procedures addressing the risks ordinarily associated with IT service delivery and support (Davis, 2008b). Therefore, appropriate follow-up is necessary to ensure corrective action process effectiveness and reestablished confidence in the item or service assessed (Davis, 2008b). Generally accepted audit procedures typically include carrying out sufficient, timely follow-up to verify that management actions address weaknesses promptly (Davis, 2008b, 2020).

After a reasonable elapsed time, an assigned IT auditor should perform follow-up activities that verify corrective action effectiveness in reducing associated risks of inscribed deficiencies and weaknesses. There are several ways to verify a corrective action implementation, including

- reassessing deficient areas,
- assessing new or revised documentation,
- verification during the next scheduled assessment, and
- verification through surveillance.

When considering the effect of previous audits and reviews, the assigned IT auditor should follow-up as if the audit occurred in the service user's environment. Specifically, an IT auditor should request appropriate information from both the service user and the service provider targeting previous relevant findings, conclusions, and recommendations. The assigned IT auditor should determine whether appropriate corrective action implementation occurred promptly by the third-party provider through sufficient procedures.

When verifying corrective action deployment, the crucial IT audit issue is recording appropriate corrective action evidence (Davis, 2008a).

> A solution to an IT audit finding may appear feasible when inscribed but may not be deployable due to various constraints (Davis, 2008). Typically, the failure to adequately identify every root cause for a control weakness will most likely result in a recurrence of the reportable condition (Davis, 2008). (Davis, 2020, p. 248)

References

Azadegan, A., Dooley, K. J., Carter, P. L., & Carter, J. R. (2008). Supplier innovativeness and the role of interorganizational learning in enhancing manufacturer capabilities. *Journal of Supply Chain Management*, 44(4), 14–35. https://doi.org/10.1111/j.1745-493X.2008.00070.x

Bahl, S., & Wali, O. P. (2014). Perceived significance of information security governance to predict the information security service quality in software service industry. *Information Management & Computer Security*, 22(1), 2–23. https://doi.org/10.1108/IMCS-01-2013-0002

Baskerville, R., & Pries-Heje, J. (2004). Short cycle time systems development. *Information Systems Journal*, 14(3), 237–264. https://doi.org/10.1111/j.1365-2575.2004.00171.x

Bayle-Cordier, J., Mirvis, P., & Moingeon, B. (2015). Projecting different identities a longitudinal study of the "whipsaw" effects of changing leadership discourse about the Triple Bottom Line. *The Journal of Applied Behavioral Science, 51*(3), 336–374. https://doi.org/10.1177/0021886314553100

Beasley, M., Bradford, M., & Pagach, D. (2004, July). Outsourcing? at your own risk. *Strategic Finance, 86*(1), 22–29.

Boyes, H. (2015). Cybersecurity and cyber-resilient supply chains. *Technology Innovation Management Review, 5*(4), 28–34. http://timreview.ca

Boyson, S. (2014). Cyber supply chain risk management: Revolutionizing the strategic control of critical IT systems. *Technovation, 34*, 342–353. https://doi.org/10.1016/j.technovation.2014.02.001

Cagliano, R., Caniato, F., & Spina, S. (2006). The linkage between supply chain integration and manufacturing improvement programmes. *International Journal of Operations & Production Management, 26*(3), 282–299. https://doi.org/10.1108/01443570610646201

Cantor, D. E., Blackhurst, J., Pan, M., & Crum, M. (2014). Examining the role of stakeholder pressure and knowledge management on supply chain risk and demand responsiveness. *International Journal of Logistics Management, 25*, 202–223. https://doi.org/10.1016/10.1108/IJLM-10-2012-0111

Cascarino, R. E. (2012). *Auditor's guide to IT auditing* (2nd ed.). John Wiley & Sons.

Cassivi, L., Hadaya, P., Lefebvre, E., & Lefebvre, L. A. (2008). The role of collaboration on process, relational, and product innovations in a supply chain. *International Journal of E-Collaboration, 4*(4), 11–32. https://doi.org/10.4018/jec.2008100102

Cătinean, I., & Cândea, D. (2013). Characteristics of the cloud computing model as a disruptive innovation. *Review of International Comparative Management, 14*, 783–803. www.rmci.ase.ro

Cegielski, C. G., Jones-Farmer, L. A., Wu, Y., & Hazen, B. T. (2012). Adoption of cloud computing technologies in supply chains. *International Journal of Logistics Management, 23*(2), 184–211. https://doi.org/10.1108/09574091211265350

Christopher, M., Peck, H., & Towill, D. (2006). A taxonomy for selecting global supply chain strategies. *The International Journal of Logistics Management, 17*, 277–287. https://doi.org/10.1108/09574090610689998

Christopher, M., & Towill, D. R. (2002). Developing market specific supply chain strategies. *International Journal of Logistics Management, 13*, 1–14. https://doi.org/10.1108/09574090210806324

Claycomb, W. R., Huth, C. L., Flynn, L., Mcintire, D. M., & Lewellen, T. B. (2012). Chronological examination of insider threat sabotage: Preliminary observations. *Journal of Wireless Mobile Networks, Ubiquitous Computing, and Dependable Applications, 3*(4), 4–20. https://doi.org/10.22667/JOWUA.2012.12.31.004

Cohen, S., & Eimicke, W. (2011). Contracting out. In Mark Bevir (Ed.), *The SAGE handbook of governance* (pp. 237–251). SAGE.

Connelly, B. L., Ketchen, D. J., & Hult, G. M. (2013). Global supply chain management: Toward a theoretically driven research agenda. *Global Strategy Journal, 3*(3), 227–243. https://doi.org/10.1111/j.2042-5805.2013.01041.x

Davis, R. E. (2005). *IT auditing: An adaptive process.* Pleier.

Davis, R. E. (2006). *IT auditing: Irregular and illegal acts.* Pleier.

Davis, R. E. (2008a). *IT auditing: Assuring information assets protection.* Pleier.

Davis, R. E. (2008b). *IT auditing: IT service delivery and support.* Pleier.

Davis, R. E. (2009a). *Assuring IT legal compliance.* www.amazon.com

Davis, R. E. (2009b). *IT auditing: Systems and infrastructure life cycle management.* Pleier.

Davis, R. E. (2010). *IT auditing: An adaptive system.* www.amazon.com

Davis, R. E. (2011). *Assuring IT governance.* www.amazon.com

Davis, R. E. (2012). The case for continuous auditing of management information systems. In Joe Oringel (Ed.), *Effective auditing for corporates: Key developments in practice and procedures* (pp. 209–217). Bloomsbury Information.

Davis, R. E. (2017). *Relationship between corporate governance and information security governance effectiveness in United States corporations* (Publication No. 10603383) [Doctoral Study, Walden University]. ProQuest Dissertations Publishing.

Davis, R. E. (2020). *IT auditing using a system perspective*. IGI Global.

Dey, A., LaGuardia, P., & Srinivasan, M. (2011). Building sustainability in logistics operations: A research agenda. *Management Research Review*, 34, 1237–1259. https://doi.org/10.1108/01409171111178774

El Wardani, M. A., Messner, J. I., & Horman, M. J. (2006). Comparing procurement methods for design-build projects. *Journal of Construction Engineering and Management*, 132(3), 230–238. https://doi.org/10.1061/(ASCE)0733-9364(2006)132:3(230)

Gottschalk, P., & Solli-Saether, H. (2005). Critical success factors from IT outsourcing theories: An empirical study. *Industrial Management & Data Systems*, 105(6), 685–702. https://doi.org/10.1108/02635570510606941

Groznik, A., & Trkman, P. (2012). Current issues and challenges of supply chain management. *Ekonomska Istrazivanja*, 25, 1101–1112. https://doi.org/10.1080/1331677X.2012.11517551

Haag, S., & Cummings, M. (2008). *Management information systems for the information age* (Laureate Education, Inc., custom ed.). McGraw-Hill/Irwin.

Hagiu, A., & Yoffie, D. B. (2009). What's your Google strategy? *Harvard Business Review*, 87(4), 74–81. https://hbr.org

Hamel, G. (2006). The why, what, and how of management innovation. *Harvard Business Review*, 84(2), 72–84. https://hbr.org

Handfield, R. B., & Lawson, B. (2007). Integrating suppliers into new product development. *Research Technology Management*, 50(5), 44–51. https://doi.org/10.1080/08956308.2007.11657461

Harms, D., Hansen, E. G., & Schaltegger, S. (2013). Strategies in sustainable supply chain management: An empirical investigation of large German companies. *Corporate Social Responsibility & Environmental Management*, 20, 205–218. https://doi.org/10.1002/csr.1293

Holweg, M., Disney, S., Holmstrom, J., & Smaros, J. (2005). Supply chain collaboration: Making sense of the strategy continuum. *European Journal of Management*, 23, 170–181. https://doi.org/10.1016/j.emj.2005.02.008

Ismail, H. S., & Sharifi, H. (2006). A balanced approach to building agile supply chains. *International Journal of Physical Distribution & Logistics Management*, 36(6), 431–444. https://doi.org/10.1108/09600030610677384

IT Governance Institute. (2018). *COBIT 2019 framework: Introduction and methodology*. ISACA.

Kamasak, R., & Bulutlar, F. (2010). The influence of knowledge sharing on innovation. *European Business Review*, 22(3), 306–317. https://doi.org/10.1108/09555341011040994

Karajeh, H., Maqableh, M., & Masa'deh, R. (2014). Security of cloud computing environment. *Vision 2020: Sustainable Growth, Economic Development, and Global Competitiveness: Proceedings of the 23rd International Business Information Management Association Conference, IBIMA 2014*, 2202–2215. International Business Information Management Association.

Ketchen, D. J., Rebarick, W., Hult, G. T. M., & Meyer, D. (2008). Best value supply chains: A key competitive weapon for the 21st century. *Business Horizons*, 51(3), 235–243. https://doi.org/10.1016/j.bushor.2008.01.012

Kim, J., Lee, K., & Joshi, K. (2013). Globalization of information technology products and services. *Journal of Global Information Technology Management*, 16(3), 1–6. https://doi.org/10.1080/1097198X.2013.10845639

Krogh, G. V. (2012). How does social software change knowledge management? Toward a strategic research agenda. *The Journal of Strategic Information Systems*, 21(2), 154–164. https://doi.org/10.1016/j.jsis.2012.04.003

Kuyken, K. (2012). Knowledge communities: Towards a re-thinking of intergenerational knowledge transfer. *VINE*, 42, 365–381. https://doi.org/10.1108/03055721211267495

Kwon, I.-W. G., & Suh, T. (2006). Factors affecting the level of trust and commitment in supply chain management. *The Journal of Supply Chain Management*, 40(2), 4–14. https://doi.org/10.1111/j.1745-493X.2004.tb00165.x

Laszlo, K., & Laszlo, A. (2002). Evolving knowledge for development: The role of knowledge management in a changing world. *Journal of Knowledge Management*, 6(4), 400–412. https://doi.org/10.1108/13673270210440893

Lee, H. L. (2004). The triple-A supply chain. *Harvard Business Review*, 82(10), 102–112. https://hbr.org

Li, S., & Lin, B. (2006). Accessing information sharing and information quality in supply chain management. *Decision Support Systems*, 42(3), 1641–1656. https://doi.org/10.1016/j.dss.2006.02.011

Liao, K., & Hong, P. (2007). Building global supplier networks: A supplier portfolio entry model. *Journal of Enterprise Information Management*, 20, 511–526. https://doi.org/10.1108/17410390710823671

Malhotra, A., & Majchrzak, A. (2014). Managing crowds in innovation challenges. *California Management Review*, 56(4), 103–123. https://doi.org/10.1525/cmr.2014.56.4.1033

Malhotra, Y. (2000). From information management to knowledge management: Beyond the "hi-tech hidebound" systems. In K. Srikantaiah & M. E. D. Koenig (Eds.), *Knowledge management for the information professional* (pp. 2–15). IGI Global.

Malhotra, Y. (2005). Integrating knowledge management technologies in organizational business processes: Getting real time enterprises to deliver real business performance. *Journal of Knowledge Management*, 9(1), 7–28. https://doi.org/10.1108/13673270510582938

Manzouri, M., Rahman, M. N. A., Nasimi, F., & Arshad, H. (2013). A model for securing sharing information across the supply chain. *American Journal of Applied Sciences*, 10(3), 253–258. https://doi.org/10.3844/ajassp.2013.253.258

McAdam, R., & McCormack, D. (2001). Integrating business processes for global alignment and supply chain management. *Business Process Management Journal*, 7(2), 113–130. https://doi.org/10.1108/14637150110389696

Mentzer, J. T., DeWitt, W., Keebler, J. S., Min, S., Nix, N. W., Smith, C. D., & Zacharia, Z. G. (2001). Defining supply chain management. *Journal of Business Logistics*, 22(2), 1–25. https://doi.org/10.1002/j.2158-1592.2001.tb00001.x

Mentzer, J. T., Myers, M. B., & Stank, T. P. (Eds.). (2007). *Handbook of global supply chain management*. SAGE.

Mohammad, H., & Ladan, T. (2012). Cloud computing uncovered: A research landscape. In A. Hurson & A. Memon (Eds.), *Advances in computers* (pp. 41–85). https://doi.org/10.1016/B978-0-12-396535-6.00002-8

Năstase, P., Năstase, F., & Ionescu, C. (2009). Challenges generated by the implementation of the IT standards CobiT 4.1, ITIL v3 and ISO/IEC 27002 in enterprises. *Journal of Economic Computation & Economic Cybernetics Studies & Research*, 43(3), 5–20. www.ecocyb.ase.ro/

Parker, D. B., Zsidisin, G. A., & Ragatz, G. L. (2008). Timing and the extent of supplier integration in new product development: A contingency approach. *Journal of Supply Chain Management*, 44(1), 71–83. https://doi.org/10.1111/j.1745-493X.2008.00046.x

Patnayakuni, R., & Patnayakuni, N. (2014). Information security in value chains: A governance perspective. *Proceedings of the 20th Americas Conference on Information Systems 20th Americas Conference on Information Systems: Smart Sustainability: The Information Systems Opportunity*, Vol. 3: AMCIS 2014, 1920–1929. Association for Information Systems. https://aisel.aisnet.org/amcis2014/

Peisl, T., Selen, W., Raeside, R., & Albera, T. (2014). Predictive crowding as a concept to support the assessment of disruptive ideas: A conceptual framework. *Journal of New Business Ideas & Trends*, 12(2), 1–13. http://jnbit.org

Pérez-Méndez, J. A., & Machado-Cabezas, Á. (2015). Relationship between management information systems and corporate performance. *Spanish Accounting Review*, 18(1), 32–43. https://doi.org/10.1016/j.rcsar.2014.02.001

Qi, Y., Zhao, X., & Sheu, C. (2011). The impact of competitive strategy and supply chain strategy on business performance: The role of environmental uncertainty. *Decision Sciences*, 42, 371–389. https://doi.org/10.1111/j.1540-5915.2011.00315.x

Qrunfleh, S., & Tarafdar, M. (2013). Lean and agile supply chain strategies and supply chain responsiveness: The role of strategic supplier partnership and postponement. *Supply Chain Management*, 18, 571–582. https://doi.org/10.1108/SCM-01-2013-0015

Ramírez, A. M., Vasauskaite, J., & Kumpikaitė, V. (2012). Role of knowledge management within innovation and performance. *Economics and Management*, *17*(1), 381–389. https://doi.org/10.5755/j01.em.17.1.2293

Ritala, P., Olander, H., Michailova, S., & Husted, K. (2013). Knowledge sharing, knowledge leaking and innovation performance: An empirical study. *Proceedings of the 6th ISPIM Innovation Symposium: Innovating in Global Markets: Challenges for Sustainable Growth*, 1–14. The International Society for Professional Innovation Management.

Roh, J., Hong, P., & Min, H. (2014). Implementation of a responsive supply chain strategy in global complexity: The case of manufacturing firms. *International Journal of Production Economics*, *147*, 198–210. https://doi.org/10.1016/j.ijpe.2013.04.013

Routley, M., Phaal, R., Athanassopoulou, N., & Probert, D. (2013). Mapping experience in organizations: A learning process for strategic technology planning. *Engineering Management Journal*, *25*(1), 35–47. https://doi.org/10.1080/10429247.2013.11431964

Sáenz, J., Aramburu, N., & Rivera, O. (2009). Knowledge sharing and innovation performance. *Journal of Intellectual Capital*, *10*, 22–36. https://doi.org/10.1108/14691930910922879

Sainathuni, B., Parikh, P. J., Zhang, X., & Kong, N. (2014). The warehouse-inventory-transportation problem for supply chains. *European Journal of Operational Research*, *237*, 690–700. https://doi.org/10.1016/j.ejor.2014.02.007

Semler, R. (2000). How we went digital without a strategy. *Harvard Business Review*, *78*(5), 51–58. https://hbr.org

Senge, P., Smith, B., Kruschwitz, N., Laur, J., & Schley, S. (2008). *The necessary revolution: Working together to create a sustainable world*. Broadway Books.

Sidorova, A., & Isik, O. (2010). Business process research: A cross-disciplinary review. *Business Process Management Journal*, *16*(4), 566–597. https://doi.org/10.1108/14637151011065928

Simon, A. T., Serio, L. C. D., Pires, S. R. I., & Martins, G. S. (2015). Evaluating supply chain management: A methodology based on a theoretical model. *Revista de Administração Contemporânea*, *19*(1), 26–44. https://doi.org/10.1590/1982-7849rac20151169

Simpson, D. F., & Power, D. J. (2005). Use the supply relationship to develop lean and green suppliers. *Supply Chain Management*, *10*(1), 60–68. https://doi.org/10.1108/13598540510578388

Sindhuja, P. N. (2014). Impact of information security initiatives on supply chain performance: An empirical investigation. *Information Management & Computer Security*, *22*, 450–473. https://doi.org/10.1108/IMCS-05-2013-0035

Soosay, C. A., Hyland, P. W., & Ferrer, M. (2008). Supply chain collaboration: Capabilities for continuous innovation. *Supply Chain Management*, *13*(2), 160–169. https://doi.org/10.1108/13598540810860994

Srivastava, H., & Kumar, S. A. (2015). Control framework for secure cloud computing. *Journal of Information Security*, *6*, 12–23. https://doi.org/10.4236/jis.2015.61002

Tafti, M. H. A. (2005). Risks factors associated with offshore IT outsourcing. *Industrial Management & Data Systems*, *105*(5), 549–560. https://doi.org/10.1108/02635570510599940

Taminiau, Y., Smit, W., & De Lange, A. (2009). Innovation in management consulting firms through informal knowledge sharing. *Journal of Knowledge Management*, *13*(1), 42–55. https://doi.org/10.1108/13673270910931152

Themistocleous, M., & Corbitt, G. (2006). Is business process integration feasible? *Journal of Enterprise Information Management*, *19*, 434–449. https://doi.org/10.1108/17410390610678340

Thomas, A., & Barton, R. (2007). Integrating local suppliers in a global supply network. *Journal of Manufacturing Technology Management*, *18*, 490–512. https://doi.org/10.1108/17410380710752626

Tseng, C., Wu, Z., & Lin, C. (2013). Corporate governance and innovation ability: Empirical study of Taiwanese electronics manufactures. *International Business Research*, *6*(7), 70–78. https://doi.org/10.5538/ibr.v6n7p70

Ula, M., Ismail, Z., & Sidek, Z. M. (2011). A framework for the governance of information security in banking system. *Journal of Information Assurance & Cyber Security*, *2011*, 1–12. https://doi.org/10.5171/2011.726196

United States Securities and Exchange Commission. (2014). *Form 10-K: NCR Corporation.* www.sec.gov/Archives/edgar/data/70866/000007086613000009/ncr-20121231x10k.htm

Varadharajan, V., & Tupakula, U. (2014). Security as a service model for cloud environment. *IEEE Transactions on Network and Service Management, 11*(1), 60–75. https://doi.org/10.1109/TNSM.2014.041614.120394.

Vries, J., & Huijsman, R. (2011). Supply chain management in health services: An overview. *Supply Chain Management: An International Journal, 16*, 159–165. https://doi.org/10.1108/13598541111127146

Wisma, M. (2008). Global business management: Current trends and practices. *The Journal of Applied Business and Economics, 8*(1), 96–109. www.aebrjournal.org

Yang, D. (2011). How does knowledge sharing and governance mechanism affect innovation capabilities? From the coevolution perspective. *International Business Research, 4*(1), 154–157. https://doi.org/10.5539/ibr.v4n1p154

Zeng, Y., Wang, L., Deng, X., Cao, X., & Khundker, N. (2012). Secure collaboration in global design and supply chain environment: Problem analysis and literature review. *Computers in Industry, 63*, 545–556. https://doi.org/10.1016/j.compind.2012.05.001

Zhen, L., Jiang, Z., & Song, H. (2011). Distributed knowledge sharing for collaborative product development. *International Journal of Production Research, 49*(10), 2959–2976. https://doi.org/10.1080/00207541003705864

Zhou, H., & Benton, Jr., Q. (2007). Supply chain practice and information sharing. *Journal of Operations Management, 25*(6), 1348–1365. https://doi.org/10.1016/j.jom.2007.01.009

Zhou, K. Z., & Li, C. B. (2012). How knowledge affects radical innovation: Knowledge base, market knowledge acquisition, and internal knowledge sharing. *Strategic Management Journal, 33*(9), 1090–1102. https://doi.org/10.1002/smj.1959

Zhu, Q., Sarkis, J., & Lai, K. H. (2012). Green supply chain management innovation diffusion and its relationship to organizational improvement: An ecological modernization perspective. *Journal of Engineering and Technology Management, 29*(1), 168–185. https://doi.org/10.1016/j.jengtecman.2011.09.012

Recommended Reading

Bhalla, A., Sodhi, M. S., & Son, B. G. (2008). Is more IT offshoring better? An exploratory study of western companies offshoring to South East Asia. *Journal of Operations Management, 26*(2), 322–335. https://doi.org/10.1016/j.jom.2007.02.005

Chandel, S., Yang, G., & Chakravarty, S. (2020). RSA-CP-IDABE: A secure framework for multi-user and multi-owner cloud environment. *Information, 11*(8), 382–395. https://doi.org/10.3390/info11080382

Currie, W., & Willcocks, L. P. (2009). Analyzing IT outsourcing decisions: Size, interdependency and risk. In *The practice of outsourcing: From information systems to BPO and offshoring* (pp. 187–212). https://doi.org/10.1057/9780230240841_8

Hamill, J. T., Deckro, R. F., & Kloeber, Jr., J. M. (2005). Evaluating information assurance strategies. *Decision Support Systems, 39*(3), 463–484. https://doi.org/10.1016/j.dss.2003.11.004

Rak, M., Suri, N., Luna, J., Petcu, D., Casola, V., & Villano, U. (2013). Security as a service using an SLA-based approach via SPECS. *2013 IEEE 5th International Conference on Cloud Computing Technology and Science, 2*, 1–6. https://doi.org/10.1109/CloudCom.2013.165

Chapter 7

Information Security Governance Audit

Abstract

Management typically deploys organization, policies, procedures, personnel, accounting, budgeting, reporting, and internal control reviews to control an entity. A control intent is to ensure the achievement of organizational objectives. Conveying the control criticality message across industries is the increasing public and private demands to institutionalize ISG with exceptional program oversight. The typical audit for assuring entity controls applies a risk-based approach. All IT audit team members involved in an ISG assurance engagement can leverage the risk-based approach to justify auditable unit activity selection. The IT audit system's general structure is planning the approach, studying and evaluating controls, testing and evaluating controls, reporting engagement results, and following-up on findings. Assessing ISG is a critical audit service element contributing to an entity's strategic alignment, value delivery, risk management, resource management, and performance measurement. Chapter 7 presents how to apply important IT audit methods from a system perspective when examining ISG managerial processes.

Introduction

Governance supports stakeholder expectations related to management's fiduciary responsibilities. Governance also reflects how an organization achieves the stated mission (Davis, 2011). Specifically, governance is the program by which entities direct and control through managing risk and compliance (Davis, 2011; Yaokumah, 2015). Leadership, stewardship, ethics, security, vision, direction, influence, and values are prominent governance components enabling the flow of stakeholder expectations (Davis, 2008, 2011, 2017; Flores et al., 2014). Usually, the in-charge IT auditor will find the ISG mission statement inscribed within a memorandum or ISG-specific document.

Various respected knowledge leaders, practicing professionals, and professional organizations consider an entity's oversight committee, executive management, internal audit, and external audit as governance cornerstones (Davis, 2011). An entity's manager-leaders should monitor the control environment to ensure performance quality (Davis, 2005, 2010). Typically, the information security function is an entity's subdivision; therefore, the entity's control environment should have replication within the information security control environment (Davis, 2011). Consequently, since information security integration usually occurs in most entity processes, IT audit should be considered an information security-level governance and entity-level governance cornerstone.

Auditors have a general requirement to provide manager-leaders and organizational process owners with assurance and advice regarding designed and deployed entity controls by (a) rendering reasonable assurance that relevant control objectives accomplishment is occurring, (b) identifying where there are significant weaknesses in controls, (c) substantiating the risk associated with control weaknesses, and (d) proffering corrective actions for detected control weaknesses (Davis, 2010). Various institutions enable the design and operation of clear policies and acceptable practices to control information assets (Davis, 2010). Therefore, basing the IT audit system firmly on control objectives removes subjectivity from the audit conclusion, replacing it with authoritative criteria (Davis, 2010).

Control is a well-known management responsibility and audit focus. Control quality monitoring aids in ensuring management fulfills fiduciary responsibilities determined by entity stakeholders concerning the control environment (Davis, 2010, 2020). When properly systematized, the entity-adopted ISG methodology should provide management, and IT auditors, with a series of ISG architecture assessments that enable defining or redefining control usefulness and deployment. Once the auditor assessment results' distribution to appropriate parties occurs, effective interaction between the entity's information security and audit function personnel can begin with a mutual understanding and agreement of roles and objectives.

The IT audit system should be replicable within for-profit and not-for-profit entities (Davis, 2011). However, an entity's audit committee-perceived mandate and mission might affect ISG audit approach variability. Furthermore, the ISG audit approach may vary according to ambit and resources applied. ISG audit evaluation criteria may also fluctuate due to audit objectives. The ISG engagement terms-of-reference should minimally address engagement ambit, reporting lines, and IT audit authority to prevent expectation misinterpretation. Specifically, ISG functional areas and issue definitions, identified highest-organization-level issues' reporting, and auditor information access rights need inscription in the audit charter or engagement letter.

ISG can be an individual audit area examination or an auditable unit examination for every IAP function audit. During the IT audit planning process, all or segments of an entity's ISG related frameworks may become auditable units. Furthermore, ISG audits may cross entity divisional, functional, or departmental demarcations. This chapter presents IT audit planning, studying and evaluating controls, testing and evaluating controls, reporting, and follow-up as processes that drive specific ISG assurance activities.

ISG Audit Planning Process

ISG audits usually have an organizational focus. Organizational-based ISG audits examine deployed frameworks, managerial issues, and departmental activities. However, during organizational-based planning, the IT auditor may discover that a governance framework is remiss. When an entity ISG framework is not operational, the ISG audit planner should use the Control Objectives for Information and related Technology framework to set engagement objectives. Alternatively, an ISG audit may be within the ambit of other IT audit areas. Under this circumstance, a "results-based" IT audit may be appropriate (Davis, 2011). Quantitatively, "results-based" audits can address performance issues using goal and performance indicators as measurement standards (Davis, 2011). Qualitatively, 'results-based' audits can also provide audit area governance knowledge and practices assessments (Davis, 2011). Whatever "results-based" audit measurement standards usage, ISG effectiveness is the primary auditable unit audit objective (Davis, 2011).

Primary drivers for ISG audit planning are verifying governance existence, appropriateness, and strategic alignment. However, as with other IT audits, understanding of a general control environment, information systems, and control procedures should be obtained during engagement planning to ensure compliance with audit standards and guidelines (Davis, 2011). When establishing overall ISG audit objectives, the in-charge IT auditor should consider the following options:

- reporting on the governance system,
- reporting on governance effectiveness,

- financial information inclusion or exclusion, and
- nonfinancial information inclusion or exclusion.

Additionally, other entity assurance efforts and results may need factoring into the ISG audit objectives. Specific to ISG audits, detailed objectives will ordinarily depend upon top-level entity management-adopted control frameworks. Thus, the ISG audit assessment paradigm may reflect performance or compliance expectations.

ISG audit ambit may be affected by the intended audience needs and dissemination levels. The in-charge IT auditor should consider separate and combined auditable unit linkages with other entities and units and, as shown in Figure 7.1, functional processes for determining the audit ambit (Davis, 2011). The in-charge IT auditor should include in the audit ambit relevant processes for planning, organizing, and monitoring the ISG activities. Moreover, the audit ambit should include the control systems for using and protecting the full range of information security resources. Specifically, people, information, processes, and infrastructure are the information security resources that should receive attention within the ISG audit ambit's control systems.

Regarding audit staffing, potential ISG engagement members should have the appropriate seniority and proficiency. When ISG audit objectives involve a wide range of information system functions, assigned IT audit personnel should have extensive organizational knowledge and related processes understanding. The audit personnel selection criteria can

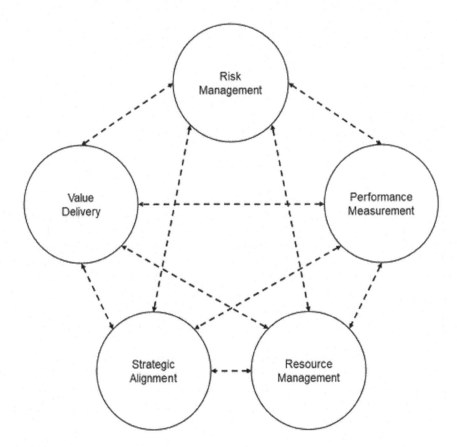

Figure 7.1 Bidirectional Linkages of Auditable Units.

Note: Adapted from *Assuring IT Governance* by R. E. Davis, 2011, Amazon.com. Copyright 2011 by Robert E. Davis. Adapted with permission.

be satisfied through a combination of formal education, relevant certification, and professional experience (Davis, 2011). Upon evaluating potential in-house audit engagement candidates, audit management determines the IT audit function does not have the required skillset; professional service outsourcing may be an option to enable an ISG audit. For example, IT audit staff members may not have the appropriate business, technical, or framework knowledge to promptly perform a scheduled ISG audit. Hence, audit management may consider ISG audit outsourcing to complete the scheduled engagement.

Control Assessment

Usually, entity manager-leaders deploy frameworks that incorporate responsibility, accountability, and authority to ensure ISG effectiveness and control environment appropriateness. Therefore, ISG audit risks are reduceable through understanding the design elements of the deployed frameworks. For example, if an entity has adopted the Information Technology Infrastructure Library (i.e., ITIL) framework, information security service and delivery areas are probably well structured and have appropriate controls to reduce value delivery risk significantly.

When preparing and assessing ISG control environment risks, as previously explained, focal points for consideration are entity management's attitude, awareness, and actions. Assessing how much control environment risk is associated with a particular entity may be performed using various techniques and tools, including Entity Policies – Control Environment Characteristics and Entity Culture – Audit Area Personnel matrices. The Entity Policies – Control Environment Characteristics Matrix, as shown in Appendix A, indicates the list of potential security policies that cross-reference to entity control environment characteristics. Alternatively, as shown in Appendix B, the Entity Culture – Audit Area Personnel Matrix indicates environmental awareness factors cross-referenced to entity personnel qualitative ratings. Managerial strategies to achieve the entity-level objectives for control systems are affected by the control environment's design and operation, information systems, and control procedures (Davis, 2010, 2020).

Control Environment

Entities exist as social organizations with a collective purpose (Davis, 2008, 2020; Mahadeen et al., 2016). Within an entity, internal and external environmental factors influence organizational structures and organizational cultures (Davis, 2008, 2020; Hitt & Brynjolfsson, 1997; Islam et al., 2012; Meyer & Rowan, 1977). Entity environment response immersion with internal strategies requires an adaptive, bidirectional process relying on various information references. Nevertheless, organizational structures exist in two distinct, yet potentially integrated, forms: formal and informal (Davis, 2020; Lucas & Baroudi, 1994; Meyer & Rowan, 1977).

Formal organizational structures commonly reflect a set of constructs associated with regulations, laws, rules, standards, procedures, directives, and policies (Davis, 2020). Informal organizational structures reflect the intermeshing social composition governing employee work behaviors in practice (Davis, 2017, 2020; Flores et al., 2014; Meyer & Rowan, 1977). However, regardless of the entity type, at the control environment foundational level, organizational structures are affected by deployed technology and designed tasks (Davis, 2017, 2020; Guadalupe et al., 2014; Hitt & Brynjolfsson, 1997; Meyer & Rowan, 1977; Sor, 2004). An ISG audit planner must understand the purpose of management's actions concerning the control environment to perform an adequate evaluation of current circumstances or conditions (Davis, 2020).

Critical for a viable ISG audit plan is the IT audit function's organizational status. Specifically, internal IT audit organizational status may become a factor in determining whether to proceed with an ISG audit (Davis, 2011). For instance, management may consider granting the internal IT auditors' access to high-level business documents inappropriate. Accordingly, the audit function's organizational status may require hiring an independent third party to manage and perform the ISG audit. Nonetheless, an ISG audit is documentation intensive and extensive. An ISG audit requires collecting information spanning internal to external repositories. Potential information sources for understanding the governance structure include:

- relevant legislation and regulations;
- policies, procedures, standards, rules, and directives;
- results of previous internal/external audits or reviews;
- organization charts;
- job descriptions;
- key personnel listings;
- process data diagrams and flow charts;
- system data diagrams and flow charts;
- operational memorandums and reports;
- financial memorandums and reports;
- planning reports;
- performance reports;
- recent management meeting reports or minutes;
- deployed control framework manuals;
- risk assessment reports;
- recent management studies or reports; and
- relevant organizational surveys (Davis, 2011).

The in-charge IT auditor should identify and understand general processes enabling ISG structure performance, including the communication channels used for transmitting objective and goals to subordinate levels (i.e., top-down) and transmitting compliance monitoring information (i.e., bottom-up). Internally, entity and ISG-related planning documents, policies, procedures, directives, rules, organization charts, job descriptions, typography maps, and IAP inventory list are usually available to assist in operational structure and design comprehension.

An entity's organizational structure provides the framework within which activities for achieving entity-wide objectives encompass planning, execution, control, and review (Davis, 2011). An entity's manager-leaders develop organizational structures suited to meet perceived needs (Davis, 2011). Entity-centric organizational structure appropriateness is dependent, in part, on size and the nature of activities (Davis, 2020). Furthermore, an effective organizational structure establishment includes deploying proper authority and responsibility with adequate accountability for activities. To enable entity control environment evaluation, the assigned in-charge auditor should obtain ISG structure information, including levels responsible for:

- governing the entity,
- setting strategic direction,
- assessing the performance of the chief executive officer or executive management regarding implementing entity strategies,
- assessing the performance of senior manager-leaders and subordinates who report on deployed strategies,

- determining whether the entity has developed skills required to meet strategic objectives,
- determining whether the entity has developed the technical infrastructure required to meet strategic goals, and
- assessing the entity's capability to sustain current operational goals (Davis, 2011).

Upon ISG audit planner evaluation, a controlled environment means categories can include organization, policies, procedures, personnel, accounting, budgeting, reporting, and internal control reviews for determining the pervasiveness of an entity's control norms (Davis, 2005, 2010, 2020). A formal organizational structure using hierarchical management or preset controls, authority, accountability, and responsibility are generally transparent (Davis, 2020; Quain, 2019). In contrast, authority, accountability, and responsibility are commonly obscure due to the criteria for selecting leadership within an informal organizational structure (Davis, 2020; Quain, 2019). Given that the control environment establishes the organizational tone, the control environment influences employee control consciousness (Mahadeen et al., 2016).

Information Systems

Information systems deployments contain the complete organization, infrastructure, people, and other elements that collect, process, disposition, store, transmit, display, and disseminate useful data (Davis, 2017, 2020; Schryen, 2013). Information systems are built on task configurations enabling data gathering, processing, and arranging for conveyance to accessing users or placement in a storage medium (Davis, 2017, 2020). A primary purpose for entity information systems is accurate, reliable, and timely data dissemination (Davis, 2010, 2020). Information systems and associated technology deployments can provide a competitive advantage and increase control requirements (Davis, 2010, 2020). On the one hand, if properly integrated, among other benefits, IT can provide a competitive advantage through an innovative application (Davis, 2017, 2020; Samson et al., 2005; Soava & Raduteanu, 2014). On the other hand, overly complex information systems using IT can reduce efficiency and effectiveness (Davis, 2020).

Technologies that link information systems can make intra- and inter-organizational communication almost seamless (Davis, 2017, 2020; Farahmand et al., 2005; Guadalupe et al., 2014). IT-based systems, processes, activities, and tasks are essential supporting elements for providing effective and efficient information and communications. Resultingly, the seamless IT network capability has influenced organizational structures (Davis, 2020). Interpretively, an entity's information systems represent the infrastructure to collect data, process transactions, and communicate operational results (Davis, 2010, 2020). In other words, an entity's management information systems represent the aggregation of resources with associated policies and procedures, allowing data processing to generate utilizable information for decision-making (Davis, 2011).

Whether inscribed or not, the in-charge IT auditor should acquire an understanding of the entity's information systems strategies, including

- long-range plans to fulfill the entity's mission and goals,
- short-range plans to fulfill the entity's mission and goals,
- long-range strategies and plans for IT and systems to support entity plans,
- short-range strategies and plans for IT and systems to support entity plans,
- approach to setting the information security strategy,
- approach to developing plans,
- approach to monitoring progress against entity plans,
- approach to change control for information security strategies and plans,

- information security mission statement and agreed objectives and goals for activities, and
- assessments of existing information security activities and systems.

Control Procedures

Controls are procedural and classifiable as preventive, detective, corrective, directive, compensating (Cascarino, 2012), or mitigating measures (Davis, 2008, 2020). Procedures define tasks for accomplishing an activity (Davis, 2010, 2020). A control procedure conveys organizational personnel performance expectations during an undertaken activity or task (Davis, 2020). IAP controls comprise the procedures adopted or devised to furnish management with some degree of comfort regarding the achievement of information security objectives. Thus, IAP control procedures often provide for the safeguarding of organizational information assets. Regardless, an ISG audit planner centers on substantiating control existence in the engagement area that minimizes potential risks (Davis, 2020).

IAP control debacles can lead to financial loss, competitive position reduction, buyer trust elimination, image destruction, or reputation damage. Manager-leaders address the effectiveness of IAP controls for two main reasons. The main reasons are: (a) control weaknesses can lead to undetected material misstatements (Haislip et al., 2016) and (b) ensuring prevention, detection, or correction by organizational employees for perceived potential threats to information (Davis, 2020). Deploying effective IAP control procedures permits more efficient and effective information security management to emerge.

Control procedures should be considered performance processes for accomplishing control objectives and goals (Davis, 2011). Control procedures attempt to assure management's operational intentions occur (Davis, 2011). Like policies, control procedures should provide organizational asset safeguarding expectations and promote effectiveness and efficiency (Davis, 2011).

Audit Risk Assessment

Determination of examinable audit units must occur using a selection method focused on audit area objectives and risks to fulfill ISG audit planner responsibilities. The ISG audit planner performs a risk assessment to ensure that all material audit area items will be addressed adequately during the audit engagement and enable concluding. The audit risk assessment helps identify areas with a relatively high probability of material ISG issues. Applying a risk assessment methodology to the ISG control system is crucial to preparing evidentially supported audit plans. There are various risk assessment methodologies available from which the assigned in-charge IT auditor may choose (Davis, 2010; ISACA, 2013, 2014). Risk assessment methodologies range from simple qualitative classifications to complex quantitative calculations (Davis, 2010; ISACA, 2014).

Specific to an ISG audit, the planning risk assessment should include categories for ISG strategic alignment, value delivery, risk management, performance measurement, performance management, resource management, environmental quality, information quality, legal compliance, fiduciary requirements, and technology requirements. As presented in Appendix C, the in-charge IT auditor should consider itemizing legal compliance under fiduciary requirements and environmental and information quality under quality requirements at the general risk assessment level, while maintaining separate classifications for items at the auditable unit level for working papers (Davis, 2011). Furthermore, performance management and measurement should be combined at the general risk assessment level because performance measurement requires management monitoring and evaluation to provide appropriate governance (Davis, 2011).

ISG Audit Study and Evaluation of Controls

Applying a standard decision-making information classification scheme can help the in-charge IT auditor (Davis, 2011) evaluate entity and ISG frameworks. Different managerial information types are fundamental to decision-making for strategic, tactical, or operational planning levels (see Table 7.1). The decision-making planning level categories reflect the duration and management level involvement. Interval data is the classification for all information classification items and decision-making categories (Davis, 2011). The five-point Likert-like scale is 1 – very low, 2 – low, 3 – moderate, 4 – high, and 5 – very high (Davis, 2011). Very low is when the information strongly disagrees with the parameter mentioned for the item without any mental reservation. Low is when the information does not agree with the item's parameter, yet there is a cognitive reservation element. Moderate is a level at which the information takes a neutral stand between agreement and disagreement with the parameter mentioned for the item. High is a level at which the information agrees with the parameters referred to for the item, yet there is a cognitive reservation element. Very high is a level at which the information strongly agrees with the parameters described for the item without any mental reservation.

Strategic plans inscribe executive managements' assessment concerning long-range plan achievement using available resources (Davis, 2011). External, simulation, and predictive-future information provide very high management assistance in making strategic decisions (Davis, 2011). Regarding sub-categorical external information, competitive actions, customer actions, availability of resources, demographic studies, and government actions are specific information useful in strategic decision-making (Davis, 2011). Thus, to determine strategic plan development reliability, an assigned IT auditor must study and evaluate external, simulation, and long-term predictive-future information to assess entity and ISG strategy viability. The assigned IT auditor must also consider whether top-level manager-leaders initiated the appropriate activities concerning information security and whether appropriate monitoring of activities occurred.

Tactical plans focus on allocating predetermined available resources and reflect mid-level management decisions (Davis, 2011). Descriptive-historical, performance-current, simulation, and short-term predictive information provide high assistance to management in making tactical decisions (Davis, 2011). As a result, to determine tactical plan deployment

Table 7.1 Information Classification – Decision-Making Metrix

Information Classification Items	Decision-making Categories		
	Strategic	Tactical	Operational
External	Very High	Moderate	Very Low
Internal	Moderate	High	Very High
Online	Low	High	Very High
Real-time	Very High	Very High	Very High
Descriptive-Historical	Low	High	Moderate
Performance-Current	Moderate	High	Very High
Predictive-Future	Very High	High	Low
Simulation	Very High	High	Low

Note: Adapted from *Assuring IT Governance* by R. E. Davis, 2011, Amazon.com. Copyright 2011 by Robert E. Davis. Adapted with permission.

integrity, an assigned IT auditor must study and evaluate descriptive-historical information related to tactical issues and attempt to conceive alternative scenarios that may be more appropriate for the entity (Davis, 2011).

Operational plans usually address routine decisions (Davis, 2011). Internal and performance-current information provides very high assistance to management in making operational decisions. Consequently, to determine operational plan effectiveness and efficiency, the assigned IT auditor must study and evaluate internal and performance-current information for objective achievement (Davis, 2011).

A management information system attempts to align data to intended usage (Davis, 2011). As depicted in Figure 7.2, data elements, activity, function operation, and system are the pyramided classifications that delineate information requirements. Graphically, data elements are present at the pyramid's base and systems at the apex (Davis, 2011). Concerning comprehensiveness, starting at the base, the pyramid reflects increasing information summary requirements at each level (Davis, 2011). Concurrently, the information level of detail reflects decreasing summarization starting at the apex (Davis, 2011). Therefore, there is an inverse relationship between the level of detail and comprehensiveness for an entity's management information system (Davis, 2011).

The ISG audit plan may include evaluating top-level management's employed processes for elaborating, communicating, enforcing, and monitoring IAP policies and legal compliance. Specifically, human resource policies and contractual compliance must receive an evaluation by assigned IT auditor. For compliance process assessments within the ISG audit ambit, compliance enforcement activities addressing correcting, notifying, logging, and auditing should receive top-priority status. Sub-categorically, when evaluating IAP policies, directives, standards, and procedures, an IT auditor should determine conformity to applicable laws and regulations.

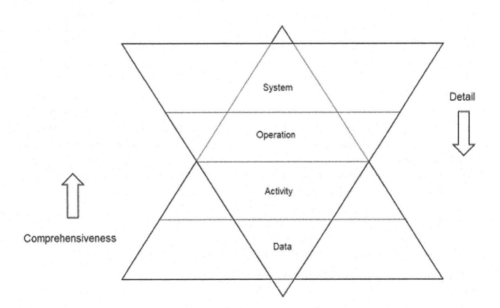

Figure 7.2 Information Summarization Pyramids.

Note: Adapted from *Assuring IT Governance* by R. E. Davis, 2011, Amazon.com. Copyright 2011 by Robert E. Davis. Adapted with permission.

Organizational strategic and support area coverage should come under study and evaluation during an ISG audit. Comprehensively, the assigned IT auditors can examine policies for providing defined strategic planning areas with appropriate expectations (Davis, 2011). Organizational changes, technology evaluation, regulatory requirements, business process re-engineering, and resource management should receive examination for policies' coverage adequacy if addressed in the strategic plan (Davis, 2011). Depending on audit ambit, the IT audit team members may receive directions to study and evaluate inscribed policies for:

- security,
- human resources,
- data ownership,
- end-user computing,
- intellectual property,
- data retention,
- system acquisition,
- system implementation,
- outsourcing,
- independent assurance,
- continuity planning,
- insurance, and
- privacy.

Information Security Strategic Alignment

Since having a sound plan is vital to accomplishing an entity's mission, developing a strategically aligned information and communication plan is vital to achieving entity confidentiality, integrity, and availability objectives. The first ISG audit strategic and tactical study and evaluation step should be reviewing adopted organizational planning processes or methodologies. An entity's ISG should have specific, measurable, and approved objectives. Information security should have a structure that allows systematic conducting of affairs at a departmental level, reflecting an entity's objectives and goals. The selection of organizational goals precedes departmental objective design (i.e., stated policies and procedures; Davis, 2011). Subsequently, management connects or interrelates concepts, parts, activities, and personnel in a manner that allows unified operations to achieve established goals (Davis, 2011). Objectives and goals transformations into unified operations are commonly known as processes.

Entity objectives and goals should be ISG drivers. Therefore, an assigned IT auditor should obtain a detailed understanding of the:

- entity's and Information Security Office's mission,
- entity's and Information Security Office's vision,
- core entity and Information Security Office employee values,
- entity's and Information Security Office's strategy, and
- entity's and Information Security Office's objectives.

In preparing entity mission statements, manager-leaders should consider the environment, organizational capabilities, and the intended customer service (Davis, 2011). The

Information Security Office's mission statements should have congruence with the entity's mission statement. Understanding an entity's mission provides assigned IT auditors with the ability to assess organizational and control objectives' alignment.

Most information security processes have goals resonating with general entity-level objectives. Manager-leaders typically enable a management information system with objectives designed and implemented to comply with external and internal security requirements. Similarly, manager-leaders design and deploy processes to achieve specific objectives (Davis, 2011). An assigned IT audit team member should review long-range and strategic plans to determine the alignment of objectives and control consideration.

Deploying appropriate controls requires complete inscription. Control inscription supports managerial intentions concerning the entity's control system. Inscribed and communicated policies, directives, and procedures for ensuring controls, when carried out, represent control activities (Davis, 2011). Primary inscriptions for obtaining an ISG audit understanding of operational activities unification are system flowcharts, process maps, and data flow diagrams (Davis, 2011).

Assessing the entity's and the Information Security Office's mission, vision, values, strategies, and objectives' alignment is critical to determining information security management's ability to achieve the entity's objectives and goals. During the ISG study and evaluation of controls, the assigned IT audit team members should evaluate whether there is an entity strategic planning process by considering whether:

- There are clear mission and vision definitions;
- There is a utilized strategic planning methodology;
- The level of the individuals involved in the planning process is appropriate; and
- The planning is periodically updated (Davis, 2011).

Organizationally, a comprehensive and integrated strategic plan is typically crucial to defining information sharing, authorizing creation, and data use appropriate for the operating environment (Davis, 2011). In many cases, information security is critical to a for-profit's and not-for-profit's success in providing timely responses to adverse circumstances. Therefore, ensuring a strategic plan that encompasses IAP considerations and information security alignment with the entity's objectives enables effective and efficient administration.

Entity strategic plans derive from entity objectives (Davis, 2011). Consequently, as a foundational justification for ensuring ISG deployment, an indifferent attitude toward information security strategic alignment with the entity's strategic plans can have a detrimental impact on achieving the entity's objectives. A control environment factor that can contribute to information security strategic alignment apathy is lack of awareness. Specifically, when manager-leaders possess the full authority to acquire IAP systems for a unit, a myopia infection often emerges. In other words, whether the selected IAP will meet entity-wide needs is frequently overlooked since process owners commonly only consider their areas of responsibility when requesting resources. A myopic managerial focus regarding IAP often results in configurations that do not meet entity-wide objectives, disabling connectivity to external access points or restricting services sharing with other internal units.

The primary task of manager-leaders is to effectively and efficiently accomplish organizational goals linked to the entity's overall objectives (Davis, 2011). Effectiveness refers to the degree to which the goal or objective is achieved (Davis, 2011). Efficiency refers to maximizing output for a given input (Davis, 2011). In practice, effectiveness is of prime importance, and efficiency may be secondary since tradeoffs frequently occur (Davis, 2011). Nonetheless, entities usually have multiple objectives that are often contradictory. For example, the objectives for value realization and maximizing service delivery could be mutually exclusive within a given year because the expense might hamper or preclude service (Davis, 2011).

Lack of transparency in objectives will lead to uncertainty in planning, structuring, and staffing the entity. Moreover, the lack of transparency can lead to uncertainty in developing an information and communication control system to measure administrative decision effectiveness (Davis, 2011). Whether for-profit or not-for-profit, all entity missions and purposes should be clearly defined and strategically aligned with every organizational function supporting the entity (Davis, 2011). Contextually, all entities have a hierarchy of objectives that effectively determine priorities for investment decisions and management actions (Davis, 2011). For the policy level, objectives are usually broadly stated and embodied in the entity's strategic design (Davis, 2011). Primary entity objectives provide the initial guidelines and the unifying force that directs all activities and enables a baseline for control and accountability through policies (Davis, 2011).

At the operational level, examining audit area objectives to ensure correspondence to the type of operations and technology deployed for processing and the relationship to entity objectives are the IT audit team's focal points. When evaluating the information security strategic planning process, the assigned IT auditor needs to consider whether:

- There is a clear definition of the Information Security Office's mission and vision (Davis, 2011).
- There is a deployed strategic Information Security Office planning methodology (Davis, 2011).
- The planning methodology correlates operational objectives and goals to information security objectives and goals (Davis, 2011).
- The plan identifies major IAP initiatives and resources needed (Davis, 2011).
- The planning process is updated at least once a year (Davis, 2011).
- The level of the individuals involved in the planning process is appropriate (Davis, 2011).

The organizational structure needs evaluation for appropriate segregation-of-functions and segregation-of-duties. The organizational unit and employee job descriptions analysis are necessary for determining authority, responsibility, and accountability for assuring the individuals involved in the functional unit, and information security strategic planning processes are appropriate. Moreover, policies and procedures need evaluation for addressing a structured planning approach (Davis, 2011).

Assessment of management's effectiveness and efficiency is paramount during an IT auditor's information security and functional unit objectives' and goals' examination. When examining information security tactical planning, the assigned IT auditor should evaluate deployed project management practices by considering:

- the usage extent of project management methods,
- the project management controls applied,
- the project management tools used,
- the integration of entity functional unit employees along the various stages of projects, and
- change management methods used for large projects, involving significant organizational changes (Davis, 2011).

Project management controls govern planning, organizing, and directing IAP plans. Optimally, IAP controls address technological changes and the project environment. Technological change controls address modifications to information security resources, including change priority and content. Whereas the project environment controls pertain to assurance that no one person who has overwhelming project authority and controls receive proper emphasis within the project (Davis, 2011).

Information Security Value Delivery

After deploying safeguarding mechanisms, critical operational and ISG strategy alignments must occur for subsequently improved entity performance (Davis, 2017; Wu et al., 2015). To obtain an understanding of the processes and facilitate analysis to ensure ISG service delivery alignment with the entity's strategic drive, each operational phase needs a congruence appraisal to available resources (Davis, 2011, 2017). Through this assessment, ISG effectiveness can reflect the proper perspective for achieving defined entity objectives (Davis, 2011, 2017). With effective ISG deployment, once ethical manager-leaders adopt a strategic objective, subordinate courses of action should reflect attempts to achieve the desired end (Davis, 2011, 2017) through prevention and promotion mindsets (Neubert et al., 2013). Therefore, ISG effectiveness induces doing the right thing (Davis, 2017).

Operational plans can be formal or informal (Davis, 2011). Nevertheless, managerial accountability and responsibility can require information security delivery within a specified timeframe to help achieve entity objectives. Usually, the requirement for information security delivery timeliness corresponds to information value in the decision process. Consequently, when examining the information security delivery process, an assigned IT auditor must consider whether

- an analyst determines the financial and nonfinancial resource implications of institutionalizing a new or updated policy,
- the information security policies effectively address the risks identified in the IAP risk assessments,
- relevant information security policies are included in all third-party contracts,
- clear communication and enforcement of consequences for noncompliance with entity policies occur, and
- information security issues come under consideration in all material or significant entity decisions (Davis, 2017).

Assessing changes and maintaining existing systems are critical information security service elements contributing to value delivery (Davis, 2008). An assigned IT auditor must assess the entity's ISG efforts to meet the entity's needs and supporting operational goals to determine the control effectiveness of the security development methodology. Reviewing the security development methodology to ensure alignment with the entity's strategic objectives helps determine IAP planning and acquisition control appropriateness. Additionally, to determine project management control efficiency, the assigned IT auditor must assess whether a control achieves more than one objective and the estimated amount of time required to perform the control.

Information Security Risk Management

Information security manager-leaders plan, direct, and manage deployed IAP. Information security manager-leaders typically establish the Information Security Office's policies, procedures, and standards considering the organizational structure. Consequently, IAP deployment opportunities should reduce potential entity risks. Appropriate IAP risk management addresses the identification and treatment of potential unacceptable events. Whether the risk management process is formal or informal, minimally, the assigned IT auditor must evaluate:

- deployed risk management framework existence,
- entity-wide objective inclusion in the risk identification process,
- probability, frequency, and threat analysis technique inclusion in the risk identification process,
- IAP risk assessment updating frequency,
- implementation of appropriate countermeasures to mitigate information asset threat, vulnerability, and opportunity risks, and
- the level of the individuals involved in the risk assessment is appropriate.

Information Security Resource Management

Processes should be visible through the roles and responsibilities of Information Security Office personnel and need inscription at some level (Davis, 2011). Furthermore, each process should have an owner with clear responsibilities (Davis, 2011). Entity manager-leaders should install proper process models (Davis, 2011). An assigned IT auditor can refer to the available models to determine appropriateness in supporting the auditable processes and job descriptions (Davis, 2011). Alternatively, where acceptable process models and job descriptions are absent, ISG-related inscriptions might refer to some high-level criteria describing roles and responsibilities that in-turn require IT audit study and evaluation for appropriateness.

Personnel quality affects ISG. Therefore, an assigned IT audit team member must determine if existing personnel can complete assigned tasks, and long-term personnel plans are in place to effectively address future issues (Davis, 2011). Consequently, an assigned IT audit team member should evaluate whether information security personnel have the skills, experience, and resources to fulfill their roles. Specifically, the IT auditor evaluation must test whether specialist staff or functions are appropriate for enabling the best use of IAP tools and techniques in achieving information security objectives. Moreover, the IT auditor evaluation must consider whether the administration of IAP specialist and non-specialist with IAP responsibilities is adequate for addressing the risks to the entity of errors, mistakes, omissions, irregularities, and illegal acts.

Information Security Performance Management and Measurement

The entity's oversight committee and management should periodically evaluate the effectiveness of ISG by reviewing program survey responses, control activities, monitoring activities, and the ability to prevent, detect, and deter irregularities and illegal acts. Reviewing meeting minutes and executive memorandums usually indicate the commitment level for ensuring an appropriate ISG program deployment and sustainment.

For outsourced activities, management should have processes to govern the third-party provider relationship and performance (Davis, 2011). An entity's outsourced process monitoring can detect contractual risk (Davis, 2011). An assigned IT auditor should identify and review the outsourcing process components, including performance management and measurement (Davis, 2011). Consequently, to enhance an assigned IT auditor's understanding, a list of all active third-party contractors and associated documentation (including contracts) necessitate acquisition for study (Davis, 2011). Specifically, relationships and services need reviews to understand vendor-supplied information asset security requirements (Davis, 2011). If available, documentation particulars, minutes of meetings' recording outsourcing, confidential agreements, and security access listings (with profiles and resources available to vendors) need studying for determining control adequacy (Davis, 2011).

An IT auditor's ISG process examination must ascertain whether entity management reviews third-party providers against the performance standards or criteria outlined in the contract and any standards specified by regulatory bodies. The ISG process should include examining

- third-party provider financial performance,
- compliance with contract terms,
- changes in the control environment,
- results of control reviews performed by others, and
- maintaining appropriate insurance levels.

Service level agreements usually specify minimum acceptable internal and external performance criteria (Davis, 2011). Therefore, the inscribed service level agreements may permit performance management and measurement evaluation (Davis, 2011). Administratively, performance measurement for an activity requires a careful selection to prevent unintended employee behavior. However, complete performance measurement for information security activities is often impossible, undesirable, or inappropriate.

Other Auditable Information Security Units

ISG audit assessments should include (a) fiduciary requirements, (b) quality requirements, and (c) technology requirements. Entity management's monitoring of deployed controls helps ensure fulfillment of the established fiduciary relationship with stakeholders. IAP necessitates deployment as managerially required and with a sufficient level of formality, coverage, and control completeness. Occupational fiduciary requirements' measurement can include operational efficiency, operational effectiveness, information reliability, and compliance with laws and regulations.

- Operational efficiency receives evaluation in terms of optimum output for a given input and traceability (Davis, 2011). Typically, operational efficiency monitoring enables determining if IAP sustains a cost-benefit.

- Operational effectiveness receives evaluation in terms of how specific performance contributes to achieving entity objectives and goals in the desired manner (Davis, 2011). Typically, operational effectiveness monitoring enables determining if IAP sustains information security strategic alignment, value delivery, risk management, performance measurement, and resource management for meeting stakeholder expectations.
- Information reliability receives evaluation in representational faithfulness to ensure assertions and supporting purported events agree (Davis, 2008). Typically, information reliability monitoring enables determining if IAP sustains complete, accurate, and valid information for conducting entity affairs and reporting responsibilities.
- Compliance with laws and regulations receives evaluation in terms of adherence to statutory requirements when conducting organizational affairs. Typically, compliance monitoring of laws and regulations helps determine if IAP sustains mandated managerial, operational, and technical responsibilities.

Environmental and information quality requirements usually address IAP fitness for purpose. In other words, the right IAP solution deployment and maintenance should help meet the entity's objectives and goals. Quality requirements' measurement includes quality, delivery, and cost (Davis, 2011). Quality management services need deployment through inspections before, during, and after IAP installation to avoid information and environmental deterioration. Specifically, periodic external and internal review performance is necessary for sustaining IT availability while conjunctively ensuring effective and efficient service delivery (Davis, 2011). Internal reviews can transpire using quality control, self-assessment, and internal audit personnel. Minimally, an assigned IT auditor should assess an entity's internal audit function's involvement in ISG projects and ISG-related self-assessments.

An assigned IT auditor must evaluate policies, directives, standards, procedures, and rules for information and environmental quality. Information quality should be transparent. However, information quality is reliant on the deployed IAP. Information transparency relates to presentation form (Davis, 2011). In contrast, technological transparency represents delivery fashion. Environmental quality refers to hardware designed to counteract problems caused by dust, temperature, and humidity when defined narrowly (Davis, 2011). An entity should deploy temperature, humidity, and air quality climate controls to supplement IT hardware-designed environmental quality measures (Davis, 2011). Sustaining integrity is an essential IAP information and environmental form and fashion support criteria.

Cost as an efficiency issue exists when considering optimal productive and economical resource usage versus IAP valuation. A selected IAP investment financial projection, with associated potential returns, is a management responsibility. Commonly, IAP investments have an unknown result associated with a known probability of a projected outcome. Budgets help determine when the actual cost is inconsistent with the expected cost, thereby conveying IAP investment financial efficiency. Given that cost optimization is usually a critical driver for ISG, an assigned IT auditor should consider evaluating IAP costing methods and measurements to determine performance transparency.

IT requirements measurement include confidentiality, integrity, and availability. Given the cost of maintaining effective and efficient IT and the IT capability to create a strategic advantage when appropriately deployed, having a sound entity IAP architecture is vital to effective and efficient IT service delivery. Operational plans may vary from software test methodologies to approval processes. However, based on significance, inadequate or uninscribed policies, procedures, directives, standards, or rules are IT audit findings (Davis,

2011). When examining the information security delivery process, an assigned IT auditor must consider deployed application development operational controls, the development or modification process, and the deployed project management process. Regarding the IT application development methodology, practices, and the controls applied to the development process, an IT auditor's examination includes quality issues and infrastructure features, metrics utilized to estimate project size and progress, and techniques used to examine testing issues for project process improvements.

Technologically, during an ISG audit, an IT auditor should address standards associated with system tools and utilities. Tools and utilities are useable for system release management, configuration management, change control, database management, software development, software modeling, software monitoring, and other situations. If system tool or utility deployments are inconsistent, incompatibilities can potentially create inefficiencies. Complying with standards usually translates into operational procedures that improve the information security control environment and governance.

ISG Audit Testing and Evaluation of Controls

IT audit testing completes what is commonly called audit fieldwork (Davis, 2010). Logically, after completing the IT audit study and evaluation of control processes, auditors are prepared to perform selected statistical or nonstatistical testing of transactions, cycles, or events (Davis, 2010). Testing an ISG auditable unit, statistically or nonstatistically, is the culmination of the in-charge IT auditor's desired audit assurance concerning the direct subject matters, related subject matters, and management's assertions (Davis, 2010). Auditable unit test materiality rates should exceed the testing threshold before inscribing testing procedures (Davis, 2010). Consequently, test procedures should have a stated objective and reflect predetermined test timing, nature, and extent (Davis, 2010).

ISG audit materiality affects audit nature, timing, and extent (Davis, 2010). Consequently, ISG audit test materiality influences the audit testing nature, timing, and extent (Davis, 2010). Audit testing nature represents the type of performed testing (Davis, 2010). Testing performance is reflective of predetermined risk associated with the ISG auditable units (Davis, 2010), whereby ISG audit testing timing is when audit testing performance occurs (Davis, 2010). Furthermore, audit testing extent is the amount or range of testing (Davis, 2010). If the assigned in-charge IT auditor accurately forecasted auditable unit-required control effectiveness assurance, actual test results should approximate expected test results' assurance (Davis, 2010).

Ordinarily, audit test materiality aligns with audit design materiality (Davis, 2010, 2020). However, the substantive test materiality-levels can be below the design materiality to achieve ISG audit assurance objectives under certain circumstances. Conditionally, lower substantive test materiality can occur for:

- locating an expected significant misstatement;
- assertions, direct subject matter, or related subject matter when an audit includes a multiple organizational location sample;
- auditable unit tests classified as sensitive to financial statement users;
- auditable unit tests classified as sensitive to technology users; and
- specific line items when an audit includes a multiple organizational location sample.

ISG audits are general control examinations. Consequently, IT audit team testing of general controls skews toward performing manual procedures, statistically or nonstatistically

(Davis, 2011, 2020). Once a decision is made to use audit sampling, assigned IT auditors must choose between statistical and nonstatistical testing methodologies (Davis, 2010). The testing choice is primarily a cost–benefit consideration (Davis, 2010). Statistical audit testing methodologies aid the assigned IT auditors in designing efficient samples, measuring obtained evidential matter sufficiency, and evaluating sample results (Davis, 2010). With statistical audit testing methodologies, some sampling risk is always present (Davis, 2010). Statistical audit testing methodologies use mathematical probability to gauge sampling risk (Davis, 2010). Any audit testing methodology that does not benchmark sampling risk is a nonstatistical test application (Davis, 2010). If an auditor selects a sample yet does not make a statistical evaluation of sample results, the audit testing methodology is a nonstatistical audit test treatment (Davis, 2010).

Foremost in performing audit testing is defining the population under examination (Davis, 2010). An auditable unit test population is the group of data on which inferences are made based upon sample results (Davis, 2010, 2020). In other words, the auditable unit population represents the entire dataset from which the assigned IT auditor decides to sample to conclude on the target population (Davis, 2010, 2020).

Upon understanding and defining an auditable unit test population, the assigned IT auditor performs an appropriateness and completeness alignment assessment (Davis, 2010, 2020). The alignment assessment addresses IT audit test objectives and audit objectives to avoid completing the assurance task under a mistaken assumption (Davis, 2011; Soltani, 2007). Moreover, to exhibit professional due care for each IT audit test objective, detailed audit sampling plans require inscription. The detailed plans must reflect test goals supporting the audit test objectives (see Appendix D) and population composition and location driving the sample selection technique (see Appendix E; Davis, 2010).

Next, the assigned IT auditor defines sampling items (Davis, 2010, 2020). One individual item within the auditable unit test population represents a sampling unit. Audit sampling unit definitions are dependent on sample objectives (Davis, 2010). As a corollary note, population physical sample representation is a sample frame (Davis, 2010).

Statistical test sampling is an objective methodology attempting to represent the test population (Davis, 2010). Statistical test denotation forms the premise for classifying the result (Davis, 2010). Thus, a statistical parameter is a characteristic of a population that is a numeric value computed using every population element (Davis, 2010). A statistic is also a characteristic of a sample taken from the population that is a numerical value computed using only the sample population elements (Davis, 2010). Sampling is vital to ISG audits because a complete census is usually costly, time-consuming, and error-prone (Davis, 2010).

Statistical audit testing design can be fixed or sequential (Davis, 2010, 2020). Acceptance, Discovery, and Attribute are subclassifications available for Fixed Testing (Davis, 2010, 2020). Contrastingly, Stop-or-Go testing uses a Sequential Testing methodology and requires a lower confidence level than Fixed Testing methodologies (Davis, 2010, 2020). Nonetheless, Acceptance, Discovery, and Stop-or-Go Testing are unique attribute sampling applications (Davis, 2020). Systematic, random, stratified, and cell sampling methods are employable options for fixed and sequential testing methodologies (Davis, 2010, 2020).

Judgmental and Haphazard Sampling is available for nonstatistical testing (Davis, 2010). If nonstatistical testing is selected, an IT auditor cannot state the event occurrence probability in scientific terms (Davis, 2010). As a deterrent for nonstatistical testing usage, haphazard and judgmental methodologies do not quantify statistical precision and reliability, thus, preventing audit population conclusions based on the sample examined by the assigned IT auditor (Davis, 2010). Nevertheless, Haphazard and Judgmental Samplings are acceptable approaches for performing compliance and substantive testing under the same audit assurance provisioning considerations as statistical testing methods (Davis, 2010, 2020).

The Judgmental Sampling approach depends on decisions reflecting the individual's experience or conjecture for item selection (Davis, 2010, 2020). Thus, central to the validity of Judgmental Sampling is an IT auditor's organizational and personal experience (Davis, 2010, 2020) or deductive reasoning reliability. The Judgmental Sampling approach is a nonstatistical application that can have a high bias conclusion effect on an IT audit (Davis, 2010, 2020). In other words, Judgmental Sampling is a nonstatistical method that may rely on tainted subjectivity in reaching an opine (Davis, 2020; Hall et al., 2000).

Haphazard Sampling is a procedural attempt to remove subjectivity from population item selection (Davis, 2010, 2020; Glen, 2015). Nonetheless, like Judgmental Sampling, using the Haphazard Sampling approach does not quantify statistical reliability and precision (Davis, 2010, 2020). With the Haphazard Sampling approach, to actively eliminate conscious bias and choice predictability, demonstration of item selection true randomness is crucial (Bragg, 2019; Davis, 2005, 2011; Glen, 2015). However, unconscious biases and predictability can affect item selection decisions (Bragg, 2019; Davis, 2010, 2020; Glen, 2015). Therefore, Haphazard Sampling can generate a bias conclusion effect on an IT audit (Davis, 2010, 2020; Hall et al., 2000).

Information Security Compliance Testing

Unless otherwise dictated by the IT audit risk assessment or audit management, extensive compliance testing is the norm for ISG audits. The compliance testing high-level objective should support the preliminary control effectiveness assessment and address obtaining evidence supporting the auditor's report on controls (Davis, 2010). When obtaining audit evidence from a test of controls, the assigned IT auditor should consider the audit evidence completeness to support the assessed level of control risk (Davis, 2010). If financial statements are under examination, an additional high-level objective is obtaining support for the preliminary control risk assessment as moderate or low (Davis, 2010).

Attribute Testing is a fixed statistical attribute sampling method (Davis, 2020). A condition exists or does not exist for the sampling units with Attribute Testing (Davis, 2020). Attribute Testing requires the use of a probabilistic sample selection method. After drawing a sample, then using the sample for testing, if the maximum deviation rate is larger than the defined tolerable deviation rate, the sampling frame has an unacceptable control condition (Davis, 2020). Thus, the assigned IT auditor must conclude that the auditable unit control design and operation are insufficient.

A fixed attribute sampling statistical method is Discovery Testing (Davis, 2010, 2020). Foundationally, Discovery Testing is generally employed to infer an audit population's irregularities or illegal acts' probability (Davis, 2010, 2020). The purpose of Discovery Testing is the enablement of stating that the population error rate is below the predetermined error level with a stated degree of confidence (Davis, 2010, 2020). However, if detection of one error occurs during Discovery Testing, sampling stops, and the assigned IT auditor must initiate appropriate auditor actions (Davis, 2010, 2020). Stopping discovery testing due to error detection reflects a nonexistence hypothesis regarding auditable unit irregularities or illegal acts (Davis, 2010, 2020).

Acceptance Testing is a fixed statistical attribute sampling method (Davis, 2010, 2020). Consequently, the Acceptance Testing method only permits yes or no, and existence or nonexistence decisions regarding sampling units (Davis, 2010, 2020). Specifically, an IT auditor draws a sample for testing (Davis, 2010, 2020). If the defined sample does not exceed the exception rate limit, the sampling frame has an acceptable control condition (Davis, 2010, 2020). Given an acceptable control condition, the Acceptance Testing method allows the IT auditor to conclude that the population error rate is below the predetermined error level with a stated degree of confidence (Davis, 2010, 2020).

Stop-or-Go Testing is a sequential statistical attribute sampling method (Davis, 2010, 2020). Discovery and Acceptance Testing elements are present in Stop-or-Go Testing (Davis, 2010, 2020). As with all sequential sampling, Stop-or-Go Testing performance happens in multiple steps, with each step conditional on the preceding step results (Davis, 2010, 2020). The similarity to Discovery Testing is in only inspecting enough sample items for enabling the IT auditor to state the actual population error rate is below a predetermined error level, with a pre-specified confidence level (Davis, 2010, 2020). Testing using this method also allows stating the population error rate is below the predetermined error level with a stated degree of confidence, consistent with Acceptance and Discovery Testing (Davis, 2010, 2020). Furthermore, employing Stop-or-Go Testing enables concluding on the upper precision limit of the sampling frame.

Stop-or-Go Testing has premises and methodology departures from Discovery and Acceptance Testing (Davis, 2010, 2020). For instance, dissimilar to Discovery Testing, Stop-or-Go Testing is not usually employed for detecting irregularities or illegal acts (Davis, 2010, 2020). Furthermore, statistically, the Stop-or-Go Testing inference statement structure concerning a population differs from an Acceptance Testing projection (Davis, 2010, 2020). Nonetheless, Stop-or-Go Testing plans provide an opportunity to design a minimum sample size, anticipating a low population deviation rate (Davis, 2010, 2020). The expected low population deviation rate translates into a lower confidence level requirement (Davis, 2010, 2020). Therefore, dissimilar to Acceptance and Discovery Testing, Stop-or-Go relies on smaller sequential sample sizes and a lower confidence level (Davis, 2010, 2020).

Information Security Substantive Testing

Substantiation of the risk to control objective non-attainment is a primary substantive testing locus for an assigned IT auditor (Davis, 2010, 2020). Substantive testing subcategories are analytical procedures and tests of details (Davis, 2010, 2020). Analytical procedures and tests-of-details are options available for increasing audit assurance (Davis, 2010, 2020). Analytical procedure performance can occur to verify or determine IT auditable unit accomplishment of control objectives (Davis, 2010, 2020). Audit analytical methods can encompass ascertaining policy compliance, abnormalities, and inefficiencies (Davis, 2010, 2020). However, analytical procedures alone may not be sufficient when performing an IT audit (Davis, 2020).

Like analytical procedures, tests-of-details can verify or determine IT auditable unit control objective accomplishment (Davis, 2010, 2020). The objective of tests-of-details is to support relevant assertions or detect material misstatements at the relevant assertion level. However, tests of details are generally used in combination to enable sufficient substantive assurance regarding an assertion (Davis, 2010, 2020). Beneficially, a single detail test might provide substantive assurance concerning more than one assertion (Davis, 2010, 2020).

Information Security Evidence Assessment

Usually, inscribed ISG-related policies, procedures, and standards are available to assess operating effectiveness. Evidentially, IT audit team members should consider whether information obtained from the ISG audit planning, study and evaluation, and testing processes indicates appropriate coverage. Sufficient evidence determination should include evaluation of:

- ISG mission statement for IAP activities;
- agreed goals for IAP activities;
- objectives for IAP activities;
- risk assessments associated with IAP resource usage;
- the risk management approach for IAP resource usage;
- strategic plans for strategy implementation;
- monitoring strategic plans for strategy deployment progress;
- information security budgets;
- variance monitoring of information security budgets;
- high-level information asset use policies;
- high-level IAP policies;
- high-level compliance monitoring policies for information asset use and protection policies;
- relevant IAP performance indicator comparisons, including benchmarks from similar entities, functions, appropriate international standards, maturity models, or recognized best practices;
- regular performance monitoring against agreed performance indicators;
- evidence of periodic information security reviews by the ISG function, with action items identified, resolution assignment, and tracking; and
- evidence of efficacy and meaningful links between ISG auditable units.

ISG Audit Control Reporting

The performance of evidence identification usually occurs during the ISG audit planning, study, and testing processes (Davis, 2010, 2020). Collected evidence from the ISG audit planning, study, and testing processes usually satisfy sufficiency, reliability, relevancy, and usefulness expectations (Davis, 2020). Thus, additional audit evidence identification is rare during the reporting process (Davis, 2010, 2020). However, when additional audit evidence is necessary while performing the audit reporting process, an assigned IT auditor must update the audit evidence catalog and working papers to ensure accurate condition representation (Davis, 2010, 2020).

Preceding audit report preparation, audit area finding's condition, criteria, cause, possible effect(s), and recommendation(s) analysis ensures an appropriate risk scoring for the ISG audit (Davis, 2010). IT audit team members address ISG statutory compliance and control objective achievement. Whether corroboration is mandatory or discretionary, supporting evidence for an audit opine can take the form of physical existence, observed process, documentary, or representation (Davis, 2010, 2020). Nonetheless, corroborating evidence for oral representations may be remiss in some circumstances (Davis, 2010, 2020). Additionally, upon discovering inconsistencies and departures from applicable accounting principles during the ISG audit, the assigned IT auditor should request a qualified financial auditor review.

Reporting materiality represents a threshold for determining an opinion expression regarding the area under audit (Davis, 2010, 2020). The ISG audit report author inscribes an opinion regarding whether, in all material respects, the design and operation of control procedures concerning the audit area were effective (Davis, 2010, 2020; ISACA, 2014). When the IT audit team members undertake an engagement to enable inscribing an assurance statement, as shown in Table 7.2, an IT audit area opinion can be deemed unqualified, qualified, adverse, or disclaimer by considering specific audit events (Davis, 2020; ISACA, 2014). The expressed audit report opinion depends on whether the audit had an (a) Ambit Limitation, (b) Uncertainty, (c) Material Control Weakness, (d) Reportable Condition, or (e) Other Weakness.

- Ambit Limitation: represents a constraint to obtaining sufficient appropriate evidence concerning an engagement audit area component (Davis, 2020).
- Uncertainty: is insufficient audit evidence collection (Davis, 2020).
- Material Control Weakness: existence precludes the enterprise from providing reasonable assurance that errors, mistakes, omissions, irregularities, or illegal acts will be prevented or detected on a timely basis by employees in the ordinary course of performing their assigned responsibilities (Davis, 2020).
- Reportable condition: conveys a material or significant weakness in which the design and operation of one or more control components do not reduce to a relatively low level the risk that errors, mistakes, omissions, irregularities, or illegal acts potentially occurring and not detected timely by employees in the ordinary course of assigned duties (Davis, 2020). Moreover, for a reportable condition, causation by noncompliance or a performance measure or aggregation of related performance measures does not matter (Davis, 2020).
- Other weakness: indicates a material or significant non-control weakness that singularly or in combination with other non-control weaknesses will not prevent, or detect and correct, on a timely basis an error, mistake, omission, irregularity, or illegal act from potentially occurring.

Table 7.2 Audit Area Condition–Potential Control Report Opinion Matrix

Audit Area Condition	Potential Control Report Opinion			
	Unqualified	Qualified	Adverse	Disclaimer
Ambit Limitation		X		X
Uncertainty		X	X	X
Material Control Weakness		X	X	
Reportable Condition	X	X	X	
Other Weakness			X	X

Note: X, opinion consideration. Adapted from *IT Auditing: An Adaptive System* by R. E. Davis, 2011, Lulu. Copyright 2011 by Robert E. Davis. Adapted with permission.

Unqualified Opinion

An unqualified ISG audit opinion concerning control adequacy represents procedural design and operational deployments under appropriate control practices for meeting audit area control objectives (Davis, 2010, 2020). Moreover, an unqualified opinion concerning control adequacy avers the absence of material control weaknesses (Davis, 2010, 2020). In other words, an unqualified ISG audit report exists when the audit function concludes that, in all material respects, the design and operation of control procedures concerning the audit area were effective and congruent with actionable criteria (Davis, 2020; ISACA, 2014). However, an unqualified opinion may have nonmaterial reportable conditions (Davis, 2010, 2020).

Qualified Opinion

A qualified ISG audit opinion concerning control adequacy represents audit area control effectiveness except for weaknesses affecting the audit area control objectives (Davis, 2010, 2020). The ISG audit report author expresses a qualified opinion after reviewing sufficient and appropriate evidence that enable concluding that control weaknesses (individually, in combination, or the aggregate) are material, yet not pervasive to the IT audit objectives (Davis, 2020; ISACA, 2014). Moreover, a qualified opinion concerning control adequacy is issuable when IT audit team members cannot obtain sufficient and appropriate evidence as a decisional foundation (Davis, 2020). Even so, IT audit team members concluded that the possible effects on the IT audit objectives emanating from undetected weaknesses could be material but not pervasive (Davis, 2020; ISACA, 2014). A qualified ISG audit opinion inscription occurs through a separate report paragraph with reasons for the qualification (Davis, 2010, 2020; ISACA, 2014). If a separate ISG audit report is necessary, the author includes recommendations for corrective action (Davis, 2010, 2020).

Adverse Opinion

An adverse ISG audit opinion concerning control adequacy represents a material control weakness existing at the end of the audit period (Davis, 2005, 2010). The difference between a qualified and adverse ISG opinion directly corresponds to the degree audit subject matters or assertions reflect appropriate control deployments and control weakness pervasiveness (Davis, 2010, 2020). Consequently, the ISG audit report author expresses an adverse opinion when one or more significant deficiencies present a pervasive and material weakness (Davis, 2020; ISACA, 2014). When a material control weakness exists, the ISG audit report author can conclude that the controls are ineffective for achieving the information security control objectives (Davis, 2010, 2020). Summarily, an ISG adverse opinion is a message to information asset users that information security controls may be unreliable when making decisions.

Disclaimer Opinion

A disclaimer ISG audit opinion concerning control adequacy represents a limited degree of assurance concerning controls (Davis, 2010, 2020). The ISG audit report author expresses a disclaimer opinion when IT audit team members cannot obtain appropriate and sufficient evidence to base an opinion (Davis, 2020; ISACA, 2014). Moreover, The ISG audit report author expresses a disclaimer opinion when IT audit team members conclude that the possible effects on the IT audit objectives emanating from undetected weaknesses could be material and pervasive (Davis, 2020; ISACA, 2014). The ISG audit report author also considers a disclaimer opinion if information security controls are not the primary engagement objective (Davis, 2010, 2020). Nevertheless, the ISG report author inscribes a detailed explanation for the disclaimer opinion (Davis, 2010, 2020).

Degree of Correspondence

Ascertaining the degree of correspondence between assertions or direct subject matter and audit criteria is a professional mandate (Davis, 2010, 2020; Marius et al., 2009). Nonetheless, assurance methodologies have similarities and differences in practice (Davis, 2010, 2020). The similarity between IT audits and non-IT audit types exists because determining the degree of correspondence requires objective and subjective judgment concerning what constitutes a material deficiency in the control system under examination (Davis, 2010, 2020). The difference between IT audits and manual audit types exists because the control system is commonly more complex (Davis, 2010, 2020). Additionally, IT audits are more challenging because the assigned IT auditor must ascertain whether the computer programs and data files under examination have representational validity (Davis, 2010, 2020).

Control deficiency causation may be linkable to the entity's design or operating condition (Davis, 2010, 2020). On the one hand, a design deficiency exists when a necessary control is missing (Davis, 2010, 2020). A design deficiency also exists when the existing control has an improper design so that even when the control is operating, the control objective is not always met (Davis, 2010, 2020). On the other hand, an operating deficiency exists when a properly designed control is not operating as intended. An operating deficiency also exists when the individual performing a control does not possess the necessary authority or qualifications to effectively execute the control (Davis, 2010, 2020). A digitized data or related technology control deficiency could adversely affect the managerial ability to initiate, inscribe, process, and report information consistent with organizational management's assertions (Davis, 2010, 2020).

IT audit findings can be favorable or unfavorable (Davis, 2010, 2020). Favorable IT audit findings need to be brief and transparent inscriptions (Davis, 2010, 2020). Unfavorable IT audit findings necessitate relevant and explanatory inscriptions while sustaining simplicity and brevity (Davis, 2010, 2020). Moreover, unfavorable IT audit findings typically transfer to reportable conditions needing corrective actions (Davis, 2010, 2020). Regardless of the IT audit finding type, the in-charge IT auditor must consider the discovered, projected, and potential error materiality when assessing audit findings for report inclusion (Davis, 2010, 2020).

If an IT audit team member identifies a material error, control deficiency, or misstatement, an appraisal must occur regarding whether the discovery denotes irregularity or illegal act existence (Davis, 2010, 2020). If, after evaluation, audit evidence indicates irregular act occurrence, the in-charge IT auditor can recommend a thorough investigation or other appropriate action (Davis, 2013, 2020). With proper authorization, when the known facts warrant additional investigation, an assigned IT auditor determines irregularity nature, timing, and extent (Davis, 2013, 2020). When there is an indication that an irregularity or illegal act exists, the in-charge IT auditor must consider the effect on other audit aspects (Davis, 2013, 2020). Notably, the assigned IT auditor assesses the irregularity's effect on the audit objectives and evidence reliability (Davis, 2013, 2020). When the effect of an irregularity appears so significant that sufficient or reliable evidence is unobtainable, the in-charge IT auditor evaluates the need for engagement continuance (Davis, 2013, 2020). Furthermore, when audit evidence suggests managerial irregularity complicity, the in-charge IT auditor must consider engagement discontinuance (Davis, 2013, 2020).

Audit area directing and monitoring activities should reflect the managerial strategy for ensuring an appropriate control system (Davis, 2011, 2020). Audit evidence classification by governance level delineates managerial responsibility. Policies, directives, standards, procedures, and rules should have a one-to-one or one-to-many correspondence with entity management's risk appetite (Davis, 2011, 2020). Since entity manager-leaders plan, direct, and support technology deployments, audit area administrative duties should include establishing or enforcing policies, procedures, standards, and rules for ensuring the right-sizing of information asset controls.

Engagement Report Structuring

Direct reporting audit engagements exist when management does not inscribe an assertion concerning the effectiveness of control procedures, and the IT auditor provides an opinion (Davis, 2011, 2020). Conversely, attest reporting audit engagements happen when management inscribes an assertion regarding the effectiveness of control activities, and the IT auditor provides an opinion about the stated assertion (Davis, 2011, 2020). Whether the IT audit team members engage in direct or attest reporting, IT audit team members must complete assignments assuming IT auditing is a methodical examination of auditable units (Davis, 2020).

Regardless of the ISG examination type, the oversight committee and management need to be comfortable with the audit assurance level and determine whether to classify the ISG audit report as privileged information. Reporting on ISG involves auditing at the highest level in the entity. Generally, the assigned IT auditor should address ISG reports to the audit committee and executive manager-leaders. Where inadequacies occur in ISG design or deployment, the auditor should immediately report a significant deficiency to the appropriate individual or group defined in the audit charter or engagement letter.

Contextually, in addition to compliance with de facto and de jure reporting standards, the ISG audit report should include following the organizational terms-of-reference with:

- a statement that executive manager-leaders are responsible for the entity's control systems;
- a statement that a control system can only provide reasonable assurance against material misstatements or losses;
- a description of the primary procedures that executive manager-leaders established to provide an effective ISG system and the related supporting documentation;
- information on any noncompliance with the entity's policies or any relevant laws and regulations or industry codes of practice for entity governance;
- information on any material or significant uncontrolled risks;
- information on any ineffective or inefficient control structures, controls, or activities, together with the IT auditor's recommendations for improvement; and
- the IT auditor's overall conclusion on the deployed ISG, as defined in the terms-of-reference.

ISG Audit Follow-Up

IT auditors should comply with generally accepted follow-up procedures addressing the wide range and high risks associated with an ISG system. Naturally, the ISG follow-up procedures include carrying out sufficient, timely follow-up to verify that management actions address deficiencies and weaknesses. One commonly used dissemination technique is sending audit reports to the managers responsible for acting when engagement issues arise (Davis, 2020). Of the managerial responsibilities for acting on findings, specifying audit recommendation treatment through a written response within a reasonable time after receiving the audit report is crucial (Davis, 2010, 2020).

If appropriate, the IT audit unit can carry the recipient selection process a step further by assigning ISG audit recommendation responses to specific employees (by name or job title) after conferring with the designated information security manager (Davis, 2011). Regardless of the recipient selection approach, the information security manager enforces best practices by ensuring the inscription of the intended actions and specific time frames for finding resolutions so that the audit unit manager can direct follow-up activities accordingly (Davis, 2010, 2020).

While information security management is responsible for addressing ISG audit engagement findings and recommendations as well as tracking resolution status, audit management is responsible for establishing policies, procedures, standards, and rules for engagement follow-up activities (Davis, 2008, 2010, 2020). Audit management is also responsible for determining the adequacy of previous findings and recommendations resolution and consideration when planning future engagements (Davis, 2008, 2010, 2020).

ISG Audit Follow-Up Responsibilities

Procedurally, after distributing the final audit report, an assigned IT auditor must request and assess relevant information to conclude whether appropriate actions were taken by ISG management promptly for all audit report findings (Cascarino, 2012; Davis, 2010, 2020). Moreover, an assigned IT auditor can request and receive periodic updates from information security management to evaluate the progress made toward carrying out agreed-upon corrective actions (Davis, 2010, 2020). An IT audit periodic corrective action update request is most appropriate for ISG high-risk issues and remedial actions with long lead times (Davis, 2010, 2020).

IT audit follow-up activities include response evaluation and, if appropriate, response verification (Davis, 2010, 2020). Follow-up nature, timing, and extent are dependent on audit materiality and control criticality (Cascarino, 2012; Davis, 2010, 2020). An IT auditor assigned to tracking and assessing follow-up activities must understand the audit materiality of ISG findings and corrective actions (Davis, 2010, 2020). As for control criticality, an IT auditor assigned to tracking and assessing follow-up activities must also understand each ISG reportable condition effect magnitude relative to other audit area risks (Davis, 2010, 2020). By acquiring an ISG audit and control understanding, the assigned IT auditor has explicit knowledge of an acceptable response and the nature, timing, and extent of response verification (Davis, 2020; Thornton, 2013).

Influencing specific follow-up activities is materiality (Davis, 2020). IT audit follow-up materiality is corrective action strength in the context of entity entirety (Davis, 2020). The assessment of materiality for follow-up is a professional judgment matter (Davis, 2020). Nonetheless, the assigned IT auditor's assessment requires considering the effect or potential effect on meeting organizational objectives in the event of an error, mistake, omission, irregularity, or illegal act that may arise because of control weaknesses within the ISG program. ISG audit follow-up activities by an assigned IT auditor need to reflect the materiality of reportable conditions and the effect of inactions (Davis, 2010, 2020). Materiality influences the follow-up nature, timing, and extent of an IT audit (Davis, 2010, 2020). Using appropriate follow-up procedures allows the assigned IT auditor to determine what, when, and how of a corrective action deployment (Davis, 2010, 2020).

As part of the ISG management discussions concerning findings, the IT audit team members must attempt to obtain agreement on the audit results and an action plan to improve deficient systems, processes, activities, or tasks (Davis, 2010, 2020). The IT audit team members have no responsibility or authority to prescribe or direct ISG corrective actions for control defects (Davis, 2010, 2020). Ethically, once an individual is assigned an ISG IT auditor role, the prescribing or directing corrective actions impair engagement independence and objectivity (Davis, 2010, 2020). Prescribing or directing corrective actions also creates a practice conflict of interest if the assigned IT auditor previously held a position or currently holds a position directly or indirectly within the entity ISG function until reaching an appropriate redesignation time (Davis, 2010, 2020).

ISG corrective actions commonly mirror the findings' cost–benefit and risk analyses (Davis, 2010, 2020). When ISG administrative actions for deploying or otherwise addressing recommendations and comments are discussed with or provided to the assigned IT auditor, the proposed corrective actions should minimally receive inscription as a management response in the final audit report with a deployment commitment statement (Davis, 2010, 2020). Moreover, the ISG finding responses should provide an implementation date for each proposed corrective action (Davis, 2010, 2020). At the reporting process conclusion, the assigned IT auditor must update the audit function follow-up database with ISG manager responses to potential control improvements and an estimate for recommendation deployment dates (Davis, 2010, 2020).

An ISG audit finding may be reportable on an ongoing basis, often in the form of issue statements (Davis, 2010, 2020). Consequently, monitoring corrective actions to resolve ISG audit issues must occur continuously (Davis, 2010, 2020). When corrective action recommendations are operational or complete implementing an inscription against the ISG audit recommendation in the final audit report is acceptable (Davis, 2010, 2020). Nevertheless, completed or implemented ISG recommendations are reportable to the appropriate management level (Davis, 2010, 2020).

General ISG Audit Follow-Up Activities

One of the more pivotal aspects of an ISG audit engagement is IT audit follow-up (Davis, 2010, 2020). ISG audit follow-up are the activities pursued when a reportable condition exists that presents an audit area risk in achieving a control objective (Davis, 2020). IT auditor follow-up of ISG activities are process elements for determining the adequacy, efficacy, and timeliness of deployment actions by information security management concerning reportable engagement conditions (Davis, 2010, 2020). Upon the corrective action presentation, a procedural enactment of follow-up activities must occur (Davis, 2020). The follow-up activities include evaluating management responses and, if appropriate, response verification (Davis, 2010, 2020). As shown in Figure 7.3, an automated engagement tracking system with a findings database can help carry out IT audit follow-up activities (Davis, 2010, 2020; Gantz, 2013).

As a task within the follow-up activities, the IT auditor-assigned responsibility for tracking and assessing ISG audit responses evaluates whether unimplemented findings are still relevant (Davis, 2010, 2020; Gantz, 2013). Furthermore, the discovery of inconsistencies and departures from applicable accounting principles during the IT audit follow-up procedures can drive a corrective action review with a qualified financial auditor (Davis, 2010, 2020). When the Chief Audit Executive or Practice Partner concludes that a follow-up report response or action was unsatisfactory after professional consideration and necessary

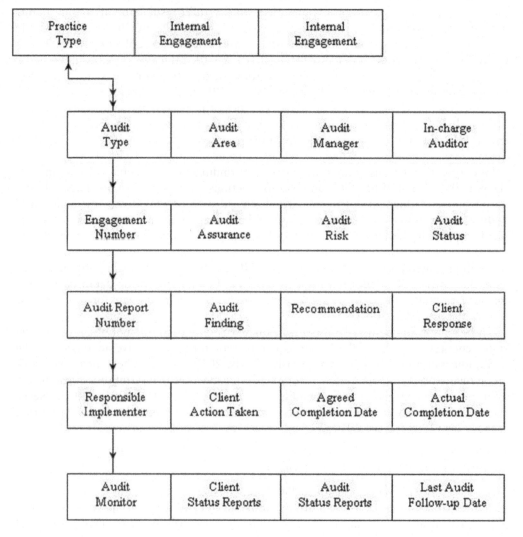

Practice Type	Internal Engagement	Internal Engagement	
Audit Type	Audit Area	Audit Manager	In-charge Auditor
Engagement Number	Audit Assurance	Audit Risk	Audit Status
Audit Report Number	Audit Finding	Recommendation	Client Response
Responsible Implementer	Client Action Taken	Agreed Completion Date	Actual Completion Date
Audit Monitor	Client Status Reports	Audit Status Reports	Last Audit Follow-up Date

Figure 7.3 Engagement Tracking System with Relational Database View.

Note: Adapted from *IT Auditing: An Adaptive System* by R. E. Davis, 2010, Amazon.com. Copyright 2010 by Robert E. Davis. Adapted with permission.

consultation, the appropriate entity management level needs to receive an inadequate outcome notification (Davis, 2010, 2020).

The IT auditor assigned responsibility for tracking and assessing ISG audit responses must give information security management a reasonable timeframe to provide details of actions undertaken to deploy recommendations (Davis, 2010, 2020). Moreover, the IT auditor assigned responsibility for tracking and assessing ISG audit responses needs to know in advance acceptable corrective actions (Davis, 2020). To assist in the follow-up activity determination, the IT auditor assigned responsibility for tracking and assessing ISG audit responses must request status information from the responsible implementer (Davis, 2010, 2020). The status request needs to happen soon after the expected deployment date passes for some, or all, of the agreed corrective actions (Davis, 2010, 2020).

Follow-up procedures necessitate aligning with the culture of the entity (Davis, 2010, 2020). In a formal entity culture, the assigned IT auditor might begin follow-up by sending a Request for Status of Corrective Actions letter to the responsible implementer (Davis, 2020). A Request for Status of Corrective Actions is a formal inscription asking appropriate audit area personnel about agreed-upon action plan progressions. Contrastingly, in the informal entity culture, ISG audit follow-up procedures might only entail asking appropriate information security personnel about the progress of agreed corrective actions (Davis, 2010, 2020). Whether a formal or informal entity culture exists, the assigned IT auditor's task pursuance necessitates responders to a corrective action status request to submit proof of recommendation deployment progression (Davis, 2010, 2020).

The most effective way to receive ISG audit follow-up responses from management is through inscription (Davis, 2010). Receiving an ISG audit follow-up response helps reinforce managerial responsibility and confirm progress achievement for corrective actions (Davis, 2010, 2020). Written responses are an evidential record of actions, responsibilities, and status of corrective actions (Davis, 2010, 2020). Nevertheless, depending on response delivery, follow-up activity may involve reformatting the final report to give information security management a section in the ISG audit communication to inscribe details of corrective actions undertaken to implement recommendations (Davis, 2010, 2020).

Alternatively, the assigned IT auditor can receive and record oral responses to status requests (Davis, 2010, 2020). When an assigned IT auditor investigates a reportable condition after ISG audit report issuance, using a follow-up form is the best means to inscribe oral responses for placement in working papers (Davis, 2020). As a minimum IT auditor practice, information on the ISG audit follow-up form needs to include:

- the point in time of exception discovery;
- the ISG corrective action under investigation;
- the auditable unit name;
- the name of the item needing corrective action;
- the finding and recommendation from the ISG audit report;
- the titles of the individual(s) contacted for determining the reportable condition disposition;
- the corrective action, if any, taken by information security management;
- the recommendation for additional activities, if any, when the responsible implementer has not taken appropriate action; and
- the agreed-on point in time for performing additional procedures when information security management has not taken corrective action as of the activity period (Davis, 2010, 2020).

Follow-up activity performance occurs to verify corrective action effectiveness in reducing ISG deficiencies after a reasonable time-lapse (Davis, 2008, 2020). Corrective actions commonly reflect audit recommendations that enable bringing reportable conditions to an alignment level with standards or best practices (Davis, 2010, 2020). If an information security manager conveys the actions taken for recommendations, and the assigned auditor is skeptical about the response or action efficacy, appropriate testing or other audit procedures should confirm the actual position or status before concluding ISG audit follow-up activities (Davis, 2010, 2020). To validate an acceptable corrective action, whenever possible, the assigned IT auditor obtains audit evidence of the design and operation actions in response to the ISG audit (Davis, 2020).

Audit management is responsible for establishing follow-up procedures to determine whether ISG management addressed reportable conditions and considerations in planning future audit engagements within the accountability ambit (Davis, 2010, 2020). Consequently, the in-charge IT auditor must ensure that follow-up activities exist for the ISG audit engagement (Davis, 2010, 2020). Factors for determining appropriate follow-up procedures are:

- the time involved,
- the complexity of the corrective action,
- the significance of the reported finding,
- the cost to correct the reportable condition,
- the significance of the finding recommendation,
- the degree of effort necessary to correct the reportable condition,
- the effect that can result from corrective action failure,
- any changes in the environment that may affect the significance or materiality of a reportable condition, and
- any changes in the environment that may affect the significance or the materiality of a recommendation (Davis, 2010, 2020).

The in-charge IT auditor is responsible for scheduling follow-up activities for an IT audit engagement (Davis, 2010, 2020). As part of the work scheduling responsibility, the in-charge IT auditor must design and deploy a corrective action notification procedure that reminds the assigned IT auditors to follow-up on pre-designated dates or fixed intervals (Davis, 2010, 2020). The ISG audit follow-up schedule needs to reflect the risk and exposure as well as the difficulty level and timing significance in deploying corrective action (Davis, 2010, 2020). Thus, the assessed materiality and criticality influence follow-up nature, timing, and extent (Cascarino, 2012; Davis, 2010, 2020).

IT audit follow-up nature addresses the type of procedural performance considering ISG auditable unit risk magnitude (Davis, 2010, 2020). IT audit follow-up timing confers when procedural performance will occur, considering the ISG audit report date. IT audit follow-up timing also is usually a matter of professional judgment dependent on such issues as nature and cost to the entity (Davis, 2010, 2020). IT audit follow-up extent conveys the amount or range of the assessment through weighing materiality, or significance, of the control weakness or deficiency (Davis, 2010, 2020). Concerning follow-up nature, timing, and extent, audit materiality typically reflects monetary magnitude relative to other assets (Davis, 2020). Simultaneously, control activity criticality infers the assessed item effect magnitude relative to other risks (Davis, 2010, 2020).

Assessing audit risk is a recurring IT auditor task (Davis, 2010, 2020). Audit risk inscription for ISG audit follow-up occurs during the IT audit planning process and represents the preliminary integration of tolerable risk rates for auditable units (Davis, 2010, 2020). If the follow-up actual rate exceeds the follow-up tolerable rate, the in-charge IT auditor must conclude that follow-up nature, timing, and extent require additional comparative analysis or follow-up audit assurance adjustment (Davis, 2010, 2020). When the in-charge IT auditor reexamines ISG, individual and overall corrective action assessments are necessary (Davis, 2020). The assessment outcomes permit inscribing follow-up audit assurance conveyance within the status report (Davis, 2020).

As a task within the audit follow-up activities, the assigned IT auditor evaluates whether undeployed corrective actions are still relevant or have a more considerable significance (Davis, 2010, 2020). Upon completing the follow-up activities, a reportable audit condition's status can change (Davis, 2020). Reportable condition significance or materiality can also change (Davis, 2020). Consequently, after a suitable analysis of ISG audit report responses, corrective actions, and current conditions, the assigned IT auditor can unilaterally decide that the deployment of an ISG recommendation is no longer appropriate (Davis, 2010, 2020). An effect on the assigned IT auditor recommendation decision could occur where information assets change, with a compensating or mitigating control deployment, or entity objectives morph in such a way as to significantly reduce the audit area risk (Davis, 2010, 2020). Inversely, a change in the entity environment may increase an IAP risk and the need for resolution. Thus, procedural communication escalation regarding remiss and unsatisfactory responses or corrective actions to appropriate management levels is fitting (Davis, 2010, 2020).

There may also be instances where an assigned IT auditor judges that oral or written responses to reportable conditions show corrective actions before audit report issuance was sufficient when weighed against deployment criticality (Davis, 2010, 2020). On such occasions, verification activity performance may become part of the next ISG audit engagement that addresses the relevant issue (Davis, 2010, 2020). Nevertheless, a status report on agreed corrective actions arising from the ISG audit report warrants presentation to the audit committee or those responsible for entity governance.

Follow-up activities can produce nonaddressable areas of concern (Davis, 2010, 2020). Nonaddressable areas of concern are situational IT auditor discoveries where the effect is not evident during current follow-up activities (Davis, 2010, 2020). Nonaddressable areas of concern may exist because the ISG issues exceed the audit ambit or are outside entity management's correction authority or control perimeter (Davis, 2010, 2020). Furthermore, due to circumstance uncertainty or limited audit work, the discovery of potentially unfavorable situations are not classifiable as acceptable ISG audit findings (Davis, 2010, 2020).

Items classified as nonaddressable areas of concern must have transparent inscription with adequate detail to prevent the misconstruing of audit information (Davis, 2010, 2020). The assigned IT auditor summarizes nonaddressable areas of concern and includes reasons for the conception (Davis, 2010, 2020). However, as nonaddressable areas of concern, recommendation inscription within the ISG audit follow-up status report usually does not occur (Davis, 2010, 2020).

When the deployment of all the agreed corrective actions occurs, an assigned IT auditor can forward the status report detailing all the deployment actions to the audit committee or those responsible for entity governance and information security management (Davis, 2010, 2020). Additionally, information security executive manager-leaders or senior manager-leaders may appreciate receiving a yearly recap report presenting significant recommendations and status along with recommendations from prior years that remain remiss of corrective actions (Davis, 2010, 2020).

References

Bragg, S. (2019, August 24). Haphazard Sampling. *Accounting Tools*. www.accountingtools.com/articles/2019/8/24/haphazard-sampling

Cascarino, R. E. (2012). *Auditor's guide to IT auditing* (2nd ed.). John Wiley & Sons.

Davis, R. E. (2005). *IT auditing: An adaptive process*. Pleier.

Davis, R. E. (2008). *IT auditing: Assuring information assets protection.* Pleier.

Davis, R. E. (2010). *IT auditing: An adaptive system.* www.amazon.com

Davis, R. E. (2011). *Assuring IT governance.* www.amazon.com

Davis, R. E. (2013). *Assuring IT legal compliance.* Lulu.

Davis, R. E. (2017). *Relationship between corporate governance and information security governance effectiveness in United States corporations* (Publication No. 10603383) [Doctoral Study, Walden University]. ProQuest Dissertations Publishing.

Davis, R. E. (2020). *IT auditing using a system perspective.* IGI Global.

Farahmand, F., Navathe, S. B., Sharp, G. P., & Enslow, P. H. (2005). A management perspective on risk of security threats to information systems. *Information Technology and Management, 6*(2–3), 203–225. https://doi.org/10.1007/s10799-005-5880-5

Flores, W. R., Antonsen, E., & Ekstedt, M. (2014). Information security knowledge sharing in organizations: Investigating the effect of behavioral information security governance and national culture. *Computers & Security, 43*, 90–110. https://doi.org/10.1016/j.cose.2014.03.004

Gantz, S. D. (2013). *The basics of IT audit: Purposes, processes, and practical information.* Elsevier.

Glen, S. (2015, June 25). What Is Haphazard Sampling? *Statistics How To.* www.statisticshowto.datasciencecentral.com/haphazard-sampling/

Guadalupe, M., Li, H., & Wulf, J. (2014). Who lives in the C-suite? Organizational structure and the division of labor in top management. *Management Science, 60*, 824–844. https://doi.org/10.1287/mnsc.2013.1795

Haislip, J. Z., Peters, G. F., & Richardson, V. J. (2016). The effect of auditor IT expertise on internal controls. *International Journal of Accounting Information Systems, 20*, 1–15. https://doi.org/10.1016/j.accinf.2016.01.001

Hall, T. W., Hunton, J. E., & Pierce, B. J. (2000). The use of and selection biases associated with non-statistical sampling in auditing. *Behavioral Research in Accounting, 12*, 231–255. https://aaajournals.org

Hitt, L. M., & Brynjolfsson, E. (1997). Information technology and internal firm organization: An exploratory analysis. *Journal of Management Information Systems, 14*(2), 81–101. https://doi.org/10.1080/07421222.1997.11518166

ISACA. (2013). IS audit and assurance standard 1202 risk assessment in planning. *ITAF: Information Technology Assurance Framework.* www.isaca.org/resources/frameworks-standards-and-models

ISACA. (2014). IS audit and assurance guideline 2202 risk assessment in planning. *ITAF: Information Technology Assurance Framework.* www.isaca.org/resources/frameworks-standards-and-models

Islam, M. A., Bagum, M. N., & Rashed, C. A. (2012). Operational disturbances and their impact on the manufacturing business-an empirical study in the RMG sector of Bangladesh. *International Journal of Research in Management & Technology, 2*(2), 184–191. www.iracst.org

Lucas, H. C., & Baroudi, J. (1994). The role of information technology in organization design. *Journal of Management Information Systems, 10*(4), 9–23. https://doi.org/10.1080/07421222.1994.11518018

Mahadeen, B., Al-Dmour, R. H., Obeidat, B. Y., & Tarhini, A. (2016). Examining the effect of the organization's internal control system on organizational effectiveness: A Jordanian empirical study. *International Journal of Business Administration, 7*(6), 22–41. https://doi.org/10.5430/ijba.v7n6p22

Marius, P., Cristian, T., & Amancei, C. (2009). Characteristics of the audit processes for distributed informatics systems. *Informatica Economica, 13*(3), 165–178. http://revistaie.ase.ro/

Meyer, J. W., & Rowan, B. (1977). Institutionalized organizations: Formal structure as myth and ceremony. *American Journal of Sociology, 83*(2), 340–363. https://doi.org/10.1086/226550

Neubert, M., Wu, C., & Roberts, J. (2013). The influence of ethical leadership and regulatory focus on employee outcomes. *Business Ethics Quarterly, 23*, 269–296. https://doi.org/10.5840/beq201323217

Quain, S. (2019, February 12). Basic types of organizational structure: Formal & informal. *Houston Chronicle.* http://smallbusiness.chron.com

Samson, D., Terziovski, M., & Lai, A. (2005). *Intellectual property strategy and business strategy: Connections through innovation strategy* (Working Paper 08/05). Intellectual Property Research Institute of Australia. www.researchgate.net/profile/Daniel_Samson2/publication/228740384_Intellectual_Property_Strategy_and_Business_Strategy_Connections_through_Innovation_Strategy/links/0046352c3c37f86e49000000.pdf

Schryen, G. (2013). Revisiting IS business value research: What we already know, what we still need to know, and how we can get there. *European Journal of Information Systems*, 22(2), 139–169. https://doi.org/10.1057/ejis.2012.45

Soava, G., & Raduteanu, M. (2014). Digital economy-economy of the new millennium. *Economics World*, 2(1), 45–57. www.davidpublisher.org

Soltani, B. (2007). *Auditing: An international approach*. Pearson Education.

Sor, R. (2004). Information technology and organisational structure: Vindicating theories from the past. *Management Decision*, 42(1/2), 316–329. https://doi.org/10.1108/00251740410513854

Thornton, T. (2013). Tacit knowledge and its antonyms. *Philosophia Scientiæ. Travaux d'histoire et de philosophie des sciences*, 17(3), 93–106. https://journals.openedition.org/philosophiascientiae/890

Wu, S. P. J., Straub, D. W., & Liang, T. P. (2015). How information technology governance mechanisms and strategic alignment influence organizational performance: Insights from a matched survey of business and IT managers. *MIS Quarterly*, 39, 497–518. www.misq.org

Yaokumah, W. (2015). Evaluating the effectiveness of information security governance practices in developing nations: A case of Ghana. In *Standards and standardization: Concepts, methodologies, tools, and applications* (pp. 1317–1333). IGI Global. https://doi.org/10.4018/978-1-4666-8111-8.ch062

Recommended Reading

Dzuranin, A. C., & Mălăescu, I. (2016). The current state and future direction of IT audit: Challenges and opportunities. *Journal of Information Systems*, 30(1), 7–20. https://doi.org/10.2308/isys-51315

Năstase, P., Năstase, F., & Ionescu, C. (2009). Challenges generated by the implementation of the IT standards CobiT 4.1, ITIL v3 and ISO/IEC 27002 in enterprises. *Economic Computation & Economic Cybernetics Studies & Research*, 3, 1–16. www.ecocyb.ase.ro/

Sheikhpour, R., & Modiri, N. (2012). A best practice approach for integration of ITIL and ISO/IEC 27001 services for information security management. *Indian Journal of Science and Technology*, 5(2), 2170–2176. https://doi.org/10.17485/ijst/2012/v5i3.1

Spremić, M. (2012). Governing information system security: Review of approaches to information system security assurance and auditing. In C.-G. Carstea (Ed.), *3rd international conference on applied informatics and computing theory (AICT '12): Latest trends in applied informatics and computing* (pp. 42–48). WSEAS.

Trites, G. (2013). Information integrity. *AICPA Assurance Services Executive Committee's Trust Information Integrity Task Force and the Canadian Institute of Chartered Accountants*. www.aicpa.org/InterestAreas/FRC/AssuranceAdvisoryServices/DownloadableDocuments/ASEC-Information-Integrity-White-paper.pdf

Control Environment Characteristics – Internal Policies Matrix

Audit Area Security Policy Template

Security Policy	Control Environment Attribute				
	Ethical Values	Operating Style	Competence	Commitment	Human Resources
Code of Conduct					
Security Awareness Program					
Security Operations Center					
Incident Response Program					
Security Training Program					
Oversight Committee					
Audit Committee					

Entity Culture – Audit Area Personnel Matrix

Audit Area Qualitative Rating Template

Awareness	Chief Operating Officer	Chief Security Officer	Chief Information Officer	Chief Financial Officer
Ethical Values	___High ___Moderate ___Low	___High ___Moderate ___Low	___High ___Moderate ___Low	___High ___Moderate ___Low
Operating Style	___High ___Moderate ___Low	___High ___Moderate ___Low	___High ___Moderate ___Low	___High ___Moderate ___Low
Competence Commitment	___High ___Moderate ___Low	___High ___Moderate ___Low	___High ___Moderate ___Low	___High ___Moderate ___Low
Human Resources Practices	___High ___Moderate ___Low	___High ___Moderate ___Low	___High ___Moderate ___Low	___High ___Moderate ___Low
Compliance	___High ___Moderate ___Low	___High ___Moderate ___Low	___High ___Moderate ___Low	___High ___Moderate ___Low
Total	___High ___Moderate ___Low	___High ___Moderate ___Low	___High ___Moderate ___Low	___High ___Moderate ___Low

ISG Audit Risk Assessment Template

Auditable Units	Audit Risk Categories			
	Inherent	Control	Detective	Total
Strategic Alignment				
• Entity Strategy				
• Application Architecture				
• Technical Infrastructure				
• Sourcing/Staffing				
• Funding				
Sub-Total				
Value Delivery				
• Timeliness				
• Usability				
• Financial Compliance				
• Non-Financial Compliance				
Sub-Total				
Risk Management				
• Strategic Objectives				
• Risk Assessments				
• Risk Reporting				
• Risk Appetite				
• Risk Treatment				
• Risk Monitoring				
Sub-Total				
Resource Management				
• People				
• Processes				
• Information				
• Infrastructure				
Sub-total				
Performance Management and Measurement				
• Customer Satisfaction				
• Competitive Advantage				
• Employee Productivity				
• Employee Profitability				
• Fiduciary Requirements				
• Technology Requirements				
• Quality Requirements				
Sub-Total				
Total				

Testing Methodology Options Table

Sample Goal	Testing Methodology
To estimate, with a specific degree of confidence, the characteristics of the population	Attribute/Dollar Unit
To determine, with a specific degree of confidence, the reasonableness of information	Variables
To estimate, with a specific degree of confidence, the value of the population	Variable/Dollar Unit
To estimate, with a specific degree of confidence, the value of a specific population characteristic	Variable/Dollar Unit
To understand the characteristics of the population	Judgmental
To determine whether a control activity is in operation	Judgmental/Haphazard
To obtain information regarding population characteristics through selecting a minimal sample size	Stop-or-Go
To distinguish, with a specific degree of confidence, good or bad item lots	Acceptance
To acquire evidence of at least one irregular transaction in the population	Discovery

Sampling Selection Options Table

Population	Selection Method
Numbering of items in a file	Random Number
Listing of items in a file	Random Number
Random number sampling presents an unacceptable burden	Fixed Interval/Cluster/Cell
Items have no pattern in the population that will bias the sample and missing items are identifiable	Fixed Interval/Cell
Items have considerable variation	Stratification
Increased confidence is achievable by grouping similar items	Stratification
Increased confidence is achievable by grouping comparable items	Stratification
Groups have physical dispersion, yet contiguous items exist	Cluster/Cell
Groups have logical dispersion, yet contiguous items exist	Cluster/Cell

Chapter 8

Cyber Security Governance Audit

Abstract

Evaluating IT solutions with an appropriate cybersecurity control over the information assets requires a detailed understanding of security principles and practices. Confidentiality, integrity, and availability are information security principles. Regarding practices, utilizable information should provide accurate and complete disclosure of available data while maintaining expected confidentiality. Information integrity and reliability are necessary for decisions that affect entity operational costs. Moreover, where there is an undue focus on compliance, an entity's IAP risk analysis can distort risk priorities and agendas, convey a false sense of security, and permit mistakes in resource allocations. Assessing Cyber Security Governance (CSG) is a critical audit service element contributing to an entity's access management, network infrastructure, risk analysis, technological environment controls, and protecting confidential information assets. Chapter 8 presents how to apply important IT audit methods from a system perspective when examining CSG operational processes.

Introduction

Failure of an entity to take proper safeguarding precautions can lead to significant operational problems and substantial asset losses (Davis, 2008). Recorded incidents throughout the world continuously reiterate that entities should not ignore cybersecurity risks and need processes to ensure appropriate redressing of IAP requirements. Cyber Security Governance (CSG) is a crucial element for providing an effective information security program. Due to CSG controls usually inscribed within ISG – including identity management, vulnerability management, threat management, and encryption management – a cybersecurity management system is not an inconsequential organizational structure.

Retrospectively, cybersecurity audits are a routine matter for internal auditors but sometimes a controversial issue among external auditors. External auditors typically do not consider cybersecurity auditable unit examinations beyond access controls necessary for formulating an opinion on financial statements (Davis, 2008). The controversy centers on cybersecurity controls as accounting controls rather than administrative controls (Davis, 2008). Though most external auditors accept access controls as accounting controls, there is a division of opinions when considering other cybersecurity controls (Davis, 2008).

Other cybersecurity controls that receive treatment as administrative controls by external auditors include off-premise file storage, environmental protection mechanisms, and data processing insurance (Davis, 2008). Usually, auditors with an administrative control abstraction level agree that such controls might receive an examination for managerial improvement recommendations (Davis, 2008). Contrary to the administrative control perspective, where a cybersecurity examination encompassing governance aspects is part of an entity financial statement audit, a cybersecurity assessment provides a comprehensive effort to evaluate the controls over the reliability and integrity of reported financial data (Davis, 2008) and constructed information.

Like ISG assurance services, CSG can be an individual audit area examination or an auditable unit examination for every cybersecurity function engagement. During the CSG audit planning process, all, or segments, of an entity's IAP-related frameworks are selectable as auditable units. Furthermore, CSG audits may cross geographical, divisional, functional, or departmental demarcations as with an ISG audit. This chapter presents IT audit planning, studying and evaluating controls, testing and evaluating controls, reporting, and follow-up processes that drive specific CSG assurance activities.

CSG Audit Planning Process

CSG audits usually have an operational focus addressing general controls. Operational-based CSG audits examine departmental personnel adherence to policies and procedures while simultaneously evaluating the economy, effectiveness, and efficiency of assigned tasks, relative to the fore stated control group (Davis, 2010). General technology control classification can include organizational structures, hardware configurations, operating systems, physical facilities, development methodologies, change management, and operational continuity (Davis, 2010). When during operational-based planning, the IT auditor discovers a CSG framework is remiss, the audit planner should consider using the ISO/IEC 27000 standards as a baseline for setting objectives.

Reflective of ensuring cybersecurity, as illustrated in Figure 8.1, IAP confidentiality and integrity are the primary information criteria. Simultaneously, availability, compliance, and reliability are secondary IAP information criteria, even when other audit measurement standards are within the audit ambit. For instance, information privacy may be within the CSG audit ambit and considered a material or significant auditable unit. However, privacy

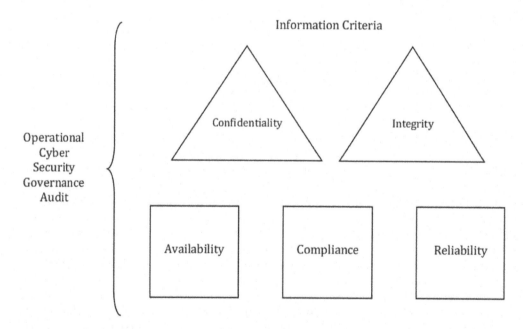

Figure 8.1 Operational Cyber Security Governance Audit.

Note: Adapted from *IT Auditing: Assuring Information Assets Protection* by R. E. Davis, 2008, Pleier. Copyright 2008 by Robert E. Davis. Adapted with permission.

compliance and effectiveness information criteria should remain secondary for the CSG audit, even when other distinct secondary auditable unit identification occurs.

Alternatively, CSG may be within the ambit of other audit areas. Under these circumstances, a functional-based, application-based, or compliance-based examination may be appropriate. Functional-based audits address identified processes as auditable units that can include objectives, goals, ownership, replication, roles, and responsibilities (Davis, 2008). Application-based audits address identified areas where IT is superposed to complete a task that can accommodate completeness, accuracy, validity, authorization, and segregation-of-duties (Davis, 2008). In the end, compliance-based audits redress adherence to externally and internally imposed entity requirements that can encompass national laws and regulations, as well as policies, directives, procedures, standards, and rules.

Primary drivers for CSG audit planning are verifying safeguarding existence, adequacy, and risk management. However, as with other IT audits, a general control environment, information systems, and an understanding of control procedures should be obtained during engagement planning to comply with assurance standards and guidelines as well as other applicable attestation, audit, accounting, and IT standards. Neglecting adherence to standardized professional practices can result in an unsupportable audit opinion.

Control Assessment

Typically, deploying a generally accepted framework that incorporates responsibility, accountability, and authority will ensure the CSG control environment, confidentiality, integrity, and availability adequacy. Therefore, audit risks may be reducible through understanding deployed IAP framework design elements (Davis, 2008). For example, where an entity has adopted the ISO/IEC 27000 security standards as a framework, IAP is probably well structured and has appropriate controls to significantly reduce risks associated with information assets (Davis, 2008).

When preparing and assessing CSG control environment risks, the focal points for consideration are management's attitude, awareness, and actions. Critical to an effective information security control environment is management's acknowledgment of IAP violation potential that can receive offsets with appropriate ethical values, operating style, competence commitment, human resource practices, and compliance commitment (Davis, 2008). An entity's oversight committee and subordinate management should also periodically assess the effectiveness of ISG program services, controls, and monitoring activities, as well as the ability to detect criminal and unethical conduct (Davis, 2008). Furthermore, the entity oversight committee should monitor control activities for ongoing relevance and effectiveness as well as responses to information security recommendations (Davis, 2008).

Assessing how much control environment risk is associated with a particular entity may be known using various techniques and tools, including Entity Policies – Control Environment Characteristics and Entity Culture – Audit Area Personnel matrices (Davis, 2008). Consequently, the in-charge IT auditor may ascertain a general profile of an entity's culture and personnel associated with a particular engagement; then subsequently place this information in an Entity Culture – Audit Area Personnel Matrix.

Essential to a CSG audit are managerial, operational, and technical procedures reflecting the assessed risk to information assets. When comparing an IT audit risk assessment with management's IAP risk assessment as well as processes for identification, monitoring, and response, the in-charge IT auditor should include examining:

- entity characteristics,
- entity history,

- recent changes in management,
- recent changes in operations,
- recent changes in IT,
- organizational asset risks,
- organizational service risks,
- strength of relevant controls,
- applicable regulatory requirements,
- applicable legal requirements,
- previous audit findings,
- findings rendered outside the audit ambit,
- findings detected during daily operations,
- IT technical sophistication, and
- IT technical complexity (Davis, 2008).

Control Environment

Control environment IAP means categories, once evaluated, determine expected depth and breadth of entity control norms (Davis, 2008). System reliability, information accuracy, and asset safety are dependent on adequate information protection controls (Davis, 2008). Weakness in financial information protection can result in unauthorized transaction processing, inaccurate data records, vital data loss, asset loss, and sensitive information disclosure (Davis, 2008). Information protection controls are crucial for financial information because IT assets are vulnerable to destruction, error, and abuse (Davis, 2008). Additionally, nonfinancial information has the same decision-making exposures as financial information (Davis, 2008). Therefore, non-financial information requires provisioning similar IAP.

Control environment scanning to produce a viable CSG audit plan is fundamental to planning an IT audit. The primary consideration regarding the control environment's operating style is IT auditability (Davis, 2008). As with most audit situations, verifiability is heavily dependent on auditability (Davis, 2008). IT auditability considerations should precede IT-integrated process deployment (Davis, 2008). In other words, the design of IT and the digitized information should include an auditability requirement for operational units before deployment. Consequentially, if not postponing a planned audit, auditability can help or hinder an IT assurance effort.

Information collection for a CSG audit should include obtaining relevant:

- incident reports;
- job descriptions;
- planning reports;
- organization charts;
- building floor plans;
- performance reports;
- key personnel listing;
- assets inventory listing;
- training documentation;
- awareness documentation;
- legislation and regulations;
- internal contractual agreements;
- external contractual agreements;
- physical access points' schematics;

- audit trail retention listings;
- audit trail archiving schedule listings;
- deployed control framework manuals;
- system data diagrams and flow charts;
- results of previous audits and reviews;
- process data diagrams and flow charts;
- high-level security and IAP risk assessments;
- recent management meeting reports or minutes;
- policies, directives, procedures, standards, and rules; and
- configuration management database documentation (Davis, 2008).

In addition to reviewing documentation and analyzing performance information, some standard techniques for gaining enhanced IAP understanding include visiting physical sites and observing operations (Davis, 2008, 2010, 2020). Moreover, interviewing personnel at various organizational levels and external subject matter experts may help understand the entity's IAP architecture.

Information Systems

Information system deployments contain the complete organization, infrastructure, people, and other elements that collect, process, disposition, store, transmit, display, and disseminate useful data (Davis, 2017, 2020; Schryen, 2013). Information systems are built on task configurations enabling data gathering, processing, and arranging for conveyance to accessing users or placement in a storage medium (Davis, 2017, 2020). A primary purpose for entity information systems is accurate, reliable, and timely data dissemination (Davis, 2010, 2020). Information systems and associated technology deployments can provide a competitive advantage and increase control requirements (Davis, 2010, 2020). On the one hand, if properly integrated, among other benefits, IT can provide a competitive advantage through an innovative application (Davis, 2017, 2020; Samson et al., 2005; Soava & Raduteanu, 2014). On the other hand, overly complex information systems using IT can reduce efficiency and effectiveness (Davis, 2020).

Technologies that link information systems can make intra- and inter-organizational communication almost seamless (Davis, 2017, 2020; Farahmand et al., 2005; Guadalupe et al., 2014). IT-based systems, processes, activities, and tasks are essential supporting elements for providing effective and efficient information and communications. Resultingly, the seamless IT network capability has influenced organizational structures (Davis, 2020). Interpretively, an entity's information systems represent the infrastructure to collect data, process transactions, and communicate operational results (Davis, 2010, 2020). In other words, an entity's management information systems represent the aggregation of resources with associated policies and procedures, allowing data processing to generate utilizable information for decision-making (Davis, 2011).

Whether inscribed or not, the in-charge IT auditor should acquire an understanding of the entity's information systems strategies, including:

- long-range plans to fulfill the entity's mission and goals,
- short-range plans to fulfill the entity's mission and goals,
- long-range strategies and plans for IT and systems to support entity plans,
- short-range strategies and plans for IT and systems to support entity plans,
- approach to setting the information security strategy,

- approach to developing plans,
- approach to monitoring progress against entity plans,
- approach to change control for information security strategies and plans,
- information security mission statement and agreed objectives and goals for activities, and
- assessments of existing information security activities and systems.

Control Procedures

Controls are procedural and classifiable as preventive, detective, corrective, directive, compensating (Cascarino, 2012), or mitigating measures (Davis, 2008, 2020). Procedures define tasks for accomplishing an activity (Davis, 2010, 2020). A control procedure conveys organizational personnel performance expectations during an undertaken activity or task (Davis, 2020). IAP controls comprise the procedures adopted or devised to furnish management with some degree of comfort regarding the achievement of information security objectives. Thus, IAP control procedures often provide for the safeguarding of organizational information assets. Regardless, a CSG audit planner centers on substantiating control existence in the engagement area that minimizes potential risks (Davis, 2020).

IAP control debacles can lead to financial loss, competitive position reduction, buyer trust elimination, image destruction, or reputation damage. Manager-leaders address the effectiveness of IAP controls for two main reasons. The main reasons are: (a) control weaknesses can lead to undetected material misstatements (Haislip et al., 2016) and (b) ensuring prevention, detection, or correction by organizational employees for perceived potential threats to information (Davis, 2020). Deploying effective IAP control procedures permits more efficient and effective information security management to emerge.

Control procedures should be considered performance processes for accomplishing control objectives and goals (Davis, 2011). Control procedures attempt to assure that management's operational intentions happen (Davis, 2011). Like policies, control procedures should provide organizational asset safeguarding expectations and promote effectiveness and efficiency (Davis, 2011).

Audit Risk Assessment

CSG audit risk assessments should take into consideration the life cycle phase under examination [e.g., pre-implementation (design), implementation, or post-implementation (operational) stage]. However, specific to a CSG audit, the planning risk assessment should include categories for addressing access controls, network infrastructure security, risk analysis, environmental controls, and confidential information assets (see Appendix A).

When performing a risk-based assurance engagement, the in-charge IT auditor should consider each auditable unit category's training and awareness at the detailed risk assessment level. Moreover, the in-charge IT auditor should simultaneously maintain a separate classification for sub-categorial items in the audit plan's auditable unit level for working papers if a risk assessment item is within the audit ambit. Furthermore, the in-charge IT auditor should understand the mechanisms used to obtain, monitor, and ensure compliance with pertinent laws and regulations. After that, the in-charge IT auditor should consider and apply the acquired understanding to the CSG audit risk assessment unless the CSG audit is part of a financial statement audit.

Laws and Regulations

Entity manager-leaders should ensure legal compliance with privacy, intellectual property, trans-border data flow, and cryptographic regulations applicable to entity-centric IT practices (Davis, 2008). Deploying a CSG framework may inhibit illegal acts by employees.

However, instituting a CSG framework is not an absolute deterrent for illegal employee actions. Although compliance is a secondary CSG audit information criterion, the in-charge IT auditor should inscribe a preliminary understanding of IAP-related laws and regulations affecting the entity, auditable units, and practices.

The identification of relevant laws and regulations demonstrates auditor due diligence consistent with practice requirements (Davis, 2008). Obtaining pertinent information concerning applicable laws and regulations may require the in-charge IT auditor to interview legal experts, accessing the Internet, and visiting libraries (Davis, 2008, 2010, 2020). Nonetheless, legal counsel should be the primary source of identification of applicable IAP laws and regulations (Davis, 2008). Possible IAP issues to explore during assurance planning include, but are not limited to:

- protection of employee legal rights when convicted of a crime;
- general awareness, appreciation, and understanding of the entity's ISG program;
- knowledge of entity personnel in the centralized compliance and ethics office;
- confidentiality of information handled by the central compliance and ethics office;
- IT auditor's access to information handled by the entity's compliance and ethics office;
- protection of employee legal rights when they are subject to investigational procedures;
- coordination between the central compliance and ethics office and organizational units;
- consistency and integration of IAP compliance requirements among different organizational units within the entity; and
- division of roles and responsibilities among the compliance and ethics office, human resources, legal, and IAP organizational units.

Analytical Procedures

Circumstantially, understanding IAP risks and associated control objectives can be a critical aspect of performing competent CSG audit planning. An entity may or may not have a deployed control framework to facilitate CSG audit planning. Therefore, to inscribe the CSG audit, the in-charge IT auditor may have to rely on knowledge obtained from other sources considered best practices. Additionally, a preliminary audit area analytical review may be necessary to assess risk correctly (Davis, 2008).

Information systems, from an IT audit perspective, are an inherent organizational risk. IT audit inherent risk may exist even if manager-leaders implement appropriate controls, such as firewalls and anti-virus software (Davis, 2008). Coincidently, deployed firewalls and anti-virus software routines reduce control risk when planning CSG audits. The Four Disciplines of Security Management: Information Security Reference Model (Lindstrom, 2004) can drive the cybersecurity mission and objectives for safeguarding an entity's information assets (Davis, 2008). Trust Management, Identity Management, Vulnerability Management, and Threat Management categorize the Four Disciplines of Security Management: Information Security Reference Model (Davis, 2008; Lindstrom, 2004; Omoyiola, 2020).

As shown in Table 8.1, through association with other IAP-related objectives (Davis, 2008), the in-charge IT auditor could use the Lindstrom (2004) reference model to determine appropriate CSG audit coverage. Vulnerability Management is a comprehensive approach to limiting weaknesses in resource-users, computing systems, and IT applications, as well as physical locations (Davis, 2008; Lindstrom, 2004; Omoyiola, 2020). Identity Management uses managerial techniques and tools for identifying objects (Davis, 2008; Lindstrom, 2004; Omoyiola, 2020). Trust Management is a comprehensive approach to ensuring the reliability of resources utilized for performing authorized functions (Davis, 2008; Lindstrom, 2004; Omoyiola, 2020). Threat Management is a comprehensive approach to identifying and responding to inappropriate or malicious activity within a computing environment (Davis, 2008; Lindstrom, 2004; Omoyiola, 2020).

Table 8.1 Control Objectives – Four Disciplines of Security Management Matrix

Control Objectives	Security Management Categories			
	Vulnerability	Trust	Identity	Threat
Management of Cybersecurity	S	P	S	S
Cybersecurity Plan	S	P		
Identity Management	S	S	P	
User Account Management		P	P	S
Security Testing, Surveillance, and Monitoring	P			P
Security Incident Definition				P
Protection of Security Technology	P	P	S	
Cryptographic Key Management		S	P	
Malicious Software Prevention, Detection, and Correction	P			S
Network Security	P	P	S	S
Exchange of Sensitive Data	S	P	S	

Note: P, Primary; S, Secondary. Adapted from *IT Auditing: Assuring Information Assets Protection* by R. E. Davis, 2008, Pleier. Copyright 2008 by Robert E. Davis. Adapted with permission.

Audit compliance gap analysis seeks to disclose any inherent impediments to the stated objectives and goals of entity-applicable legislation or regulation and conflicts between applicable legislation and regulations (Davis, 2008). Legal noncompliance could place an entity in violation of requirements for maintaining proper controls (Davis, 2008). Thus, an IAP-assurance risk assessment should consider management's control methods over compliance with laws and regulations as risk factors (Davis, 2008).

Gap analysis of laws and regulations should illuminate mandatory controls, potential sanctions, as well as deployment weaknesses (Davis, 2008). Specifically, the in-charge IT auditor should assess the CSG program's managerial, operational, and technical risks associated with legal requirements. To accomplish the legal risk assessment task, the in-charge IT auditor should consider analyzing audit risks by independently summarizing applicable IAP laws and regulations, then subsequently comparing the prepared information to management's applicable IAP laws and regulations assessment (Davis, 2008). If available, the in-charge IT auditor should obtain the entity laws and regulations Traceability Matrix to ascertain what legal compliance issues are under consideration (Davis, 2008). A Traceability Matrix provides baseline links that required a many-to-many relationship verification to ensure completeness (Gotel et al., 2012).

CSG Audit Study and Evaluation of Controls

Control objective deployment occurs through control practices (Davis, 2008). Practices are most useful when applied as a set of principles and a starting point for tailoring specific procedures (Davis, 2008). Similarly, risk management should be under consideration for the initial design of control procedures (Davis, 2008). Therefore, through logical association, using an effectual risk management framework allows an entity to determine which control practices are crucial and subsequently develop the most appropriate set of governance principles (Davis, 2008).

IAP should be an entity's uppermost concern because cybersecurity incidents may compromise financial and operational confidentiality, integrity, and availability (Davis, 2008). Employees with sanctioned authorizations may commit nefarious acts tarnishing an entity's reputation or image (Davis, 2008). IAP threats can be a person, thing, or event (Davis, 2008). Thus, potential threats that can convert to incidents include phishing, spyware, pharming, electronic piracy, and computer viruses.

- Phishing utilizes a deceptive technology-based medium to maneuver individuals into disclosing sensitive information (Davis, 2008). For instance, an individual might seek usernames, passwords, and account numbers for online banking websites through fraudulent emails (Davis, 2008).
- Spyware is software secretly or surreptitiously accessing IT to gather information on individuals or entities without the user's informed consent (Davis, 2008). Spyware can exploit technology for commercial gain (Davis, 2008). For instance, Van Eck Phreaking is a form of eavesdropping using special equipment to extract telecommunication signals or data within a computing device by monitoring and capturing electromagnetic fields produced by the signals or data movement (Davis, 2008).
- Pharming attacks occur through domain hijacking or by Domain Name Service poisoning (Davis, 2008). Domain hijacking is the practice of stealing an entity or individual website name (Davis, 2008). Alternatively, Domain Name Service poisoning involves corrupting or tainting a domain name system table by replacing a legitimate Internet address with a fraudulent website address (Davis, 2008).
- Electronic piracy involves the unauthorized copying or sharing of digitized files for which an appropriate licensing fee payment was not submitted and accepted by the licenser (Davis, 2008).
- Computer viruses can be malicious or non-malicious, depending on programmer intent (Davis, 2008). Computer viruses are typically considered unauthorized self-replicating computer programs that distribute reproductions to other files, programs, systems, and networks through insertion or attachment (Davis, 2008). For instance, malicious hackers create computer viruses to disrupt workflows and network access (Davis, 2008).

Generally, information criticality, sensitivity, and impact should receive identification and ranking by an entity's information owners (Davis, 2008). Junior manager-leaders should predict the adverse effects of lost information and interrupted operations as well as determine time limits regarding specific IT suspensions or postponements for situations such as irregularities, illegal acts, and exposure to the elements (Davis, 2008). However, obtaining executive and senior management's agreement with operational determinations and concurrence from affected groups is also necessary (Davis, 2008). The more manager-leaders understand and communicate potential threats, the better equipped the entity's personnel can be for providing precautionary measures to defend against likely security breaches (Davis, 2008).

Entity administrators need CSG risk management that enables Vulnerability Management, Trust Management, Opportunity Management, Access Management, and Threat Management to accomplish protection expectations (Davis, 2008). Moreover, the deployed risk management process should include a consideration for third-party providers, the service provided by third-party providers, and how management governs the relationship with other entities (Davis, 2008). Third-party assessments are critical because they contribute to ensuring all threats and vulnerabilities are identified and considered, the most significant risks identified, and appropriate decision-making accomplished regarding risk acceptance, reduction, transference, or avoidance treatment (Davis, 2008). A comprehensive high-level risk assessment should be the starting point for developing or modifying an entity's IAP policies and plan (Davis, 2008). Minimally, entities should perform an IAP risk assessment every 3 months (Davis, 2008). As a corollary activity, an inscription of quantitative or qualitative analysis should occur when performing risk assessments to gauge an information asset's value (Davis, 2008).

Management's pursuit of opportunities presents risks to the entity (Davis, 2008). Opportunity risks can be threats to the established system of safeguarding controls (Davis, 2008). Threats associated with an opportunity need evaluation to determine the viability of pursuit (Davis, 2008). Meticulous opportunity impact consideration relative to established or created threats should be a critical success factor (i.e., hurdle point) for justifying the pursuit of an opportunity (Davis, 2008). Diagnostically, unless the information asset's threat value exceeds the information asset's opportunity value, the item under assessment should remain classified as an information asset opportunity by the individual or individuals responsible for the risk analysis (Davis, 2008).

Good IAP risk management addresses potential unacceptable event identification and treatment while recognizing the strategic implications of multiple flashpoints such as increases in electronic crimes, infusions of new laws or regulations, and escalations in litigation activity (Davis, 2008). Consequently, independent risk assessments performance and inscription should occur regularly or whenever systems, facilities, or other conditions change (Davis, 2008). Therefore, whether the risk management process is formal or informal, minimally, the IT auditor should evaluate

- deployed IAP risk assessment framework existence;
- operational, IT, security, and IAP risk assessment updating frequency;
- risk assessment policies, directives, procedures, standards, and rules;
- the inclusion of entity-wide objectives in the IAP risk identification process;
- whether the level of the individuals involved in the IAP risk assessment is appropriate;
- the objectivity of personnel who performed and reviewed the IAP assessment;
- implementation of appropriate measures to mitigate IAP risks;
- inclusion of probability, frequency, and threat analysis techniques in the risk identification process;
- whether the IAP risk assessment considers information sensitivity, criticality, and impact;
- whether the IAP risk assessment considers the range of risks to the entity's information assets, and
- whether final IAP risk determinations and related management approvals are documented and maintained on file (Davis, 2008).

Responsibility designation enhances the ability to assure information assets are appropriately protected. An entity's executive manager-leaders should assign information assets to information owners and technology owners (Davis, 2008). After that, appointed information owners should have the responsibility for establishing rules concerning the appropriate use and protection of subject data. In contrast, designated technology owners should be responsible for coordinating development life cycle activities specific to subject technologies (Davis, 2008). Given the delineated assignment circumstances, the information owners for data stored within, processed by, or transmitted through technology may not be the same as the technology owners (Davis, 2008). Also, a single technology may use data obtained from multiple information owners (Davis, 2008). However, information owners should retain assigned responsibilities, even when data sharing with other entities (Davis, 2008).

Cybersecurity manager-leader duties normally include establishing unit policies, procedures, and standards for information assets, based on the organizational structure (Davis, 2008). To effectively fulfill the cybersecurity manager-leader's role and assumed responsibilities, IT threats and opportunities need evaluation, organization, and administration to reduce potential entity risks using available resources (Davis, 2008). Studying and evaluating CSG roles considering associated responsibilities are critical to determining whether adequate segregation-of-functions and segregation-of-duties exist to reduce the risk of security breaches (Davis, 2008). Employees, including direct superordinate management, should understand assigned occupational responsibilities and prohibited activities (Davis, 2008). Nonetheless, responsibility and accountability for ensuring employee occupational duties' comprehension ultimately reside with executive manager-leaders (Davis, 2008). Various control techniques can selectively or collectively enforce segregation-of-functions and segregation-of-duties, including:

- asset custody,
- role identification,
- information access,
- user authentication, and
- transaction authorization (Davis, 2008).

Safeguarding encompasses two primary categories: responsibilities separation and protection-of-information-assets (Davis, 2008). Regarding CSG audits, obtaining or creating an IAP Responsible, Accountable, Consulted and Informed or Responsible, Accountable, Supportive, Consulted, and Informed Chart can help an assigned IT auditor assess segregation-of-functions and segregation-of-duties implementations (see Appendix B). When an IT auditor inserts items for a Responsible, Accountable, Consulted and Informed or Responsible, Accountable, Supportive, Consulted, and Informed Chart, potential activities are policies and procedures established to ensure entity employees follow management's orders and instructions in an appropriate manner (Davis, 2008).

Segregation-of-functions ensures organizational responsibilities do not impinge upon independence or corrupt information asset integrity. However, segregation-of-duties is generally a key control measure for manual and automated systems and processes (Davis, 2008). The deployment of IAP segregation-of-duties controls reduces the opportunities for errors, mistakes, omissions, irregularities, and illegal acts' perpetration and concealment that can affect information integrity (Davis, 2008). Achieving appropriate segregation-of-duties may be a formidable administrative task in a centralized IT environment (Davis, 2008). Consequently, depending on the control environment, an autonomous function for data entry may exist within an entity to address responsibilities delineation (Davis, 2008). However, segregation-of-duties should exist, even if an entity distributes the data entry responsibility to employees within different organizational units (Davis, 2008). Furthermore, origination, processing, verification, signoff, and distribution responsibilities should receive monitoring and evaluation for violating segregation-of-duties control to ensure appropriate IAP (Davis, 2008).

An IT auditor should obtain the inscribed set of Rules-of-Behavior for each information system and specific elements within the CSG audit ambit. Furthermore, an assigned IT auditor should study and evaluate whether the Rules-of-Behavior delineates responsibilities and the expected behavior of individuals with access to information assets, states the consequences of inconsistent behavior or noncompliance, and sets appropriate limits on interconnections and information integrations (Davis, 2008). If segregation-of-functions and segregation-of-duties control technique expectations are remiss within a CSG audit area, an assigned IT auditor should investigate compensating and mitigating controls after completing the control study and evaluation process.

Cybersecurity Access Management

Information asset value is continuously increasing in the information age due to integration into decision-making processes (Davis, 2008). Decision-making process assistance is containable in an IT decision support system (Davis, 2008). Useable decision-support information should provide accurate and complete disclosure of available data while maintaining expected confidentiality and integrity (Davis, 2008). Therefore, an IT auditor should study and evaluate IAP procedural deployments to manage and maintain information confidentiality and integrity throughout the information life cycle (Davis, 2008).

IAP mechanisms are necessary to aid in ensuring information trust (Davis, 2008). When inadequate or inappropriate integrity management exists, incidents compromising data can generate unreliable information on which to base decisions, permit noncompliance with regulatory or third-party requirements, and allow misleading external report distributions (Davis, 2008). Primary information integrity attributes encompass authenticity, nonrepudiation, and accountability (Davis, 2008).

Technological implementations are diverse and complex (Davis, 2008). However, all IT deployments need protection from unauthorized usage by applying appropriate information asset access controls (Davis, 2008). Given IT interconnectivity, entities must protect information assets from unauthorized manipulation to safeguard investments and protect information assets from resource misuse risks (Davis, 2008). Consequently, information asset access control is typically viewable from two abstraction perspectives: physical and logical security (Davis, 2008).

Physical security provides tangible asset protection, whether an item is at rest or in transit (Davis, 2008). Physical information security is a critical aspect of appropriate perimeter and interior controls (Davis, 2008). Nevertheless, physical controls alone cannot ensure effectual IAP when remote data access points exist (Davis, 2008). Physical access controls should address the area containing hardware and wiring locations used to connect system elements, supporting services, backup media, and other items required for IT operational effectiveness (Davis, 2008). As a case in point, controls over access to IT devices may not be effective in online environments unless access to the data communication system is also restricted (Davis, 2008).

Considering that most entity IT configurations deploy online or real-time communication capabilities, establishing logical security controls that rebuff information confidentiality, integrity, and availability threats, such as wiretapping, is crucial (Davis, 2008). Distinctively, logical security focuses on safeguarding intangible assets, whether data is at rest or in transit (Davis, 2008). Information delivery channels usually define access levels to applications and systems, based upon the network medium used for data transfer (Davis, 2008). Essential elements for adequate logical access control are identification, authentication, authorization, and accountability (Davis, 2008).

Technology attacks and attendant security compromises are never easily managed (Davis, 2008). Parallel to the ingenuity of attackers and proportional to the value placed on entrusted information assets, effective and efficient access controls are imperative (Davis, 2008). Since physical and logical security techniques usually have primary objectives to provide appropriate asset protection, manager-leaders should consider deploying cost-effective processes for protecting data files, application programs, and hardware by combining the access security types (Davis, 2008). Due to technological and operational diversity, standard processes to control information asset access that permits economies of scale are critical. Potential candidates for access control convergence include:

- tokens,
- biometrics,
- passwords,
- smart cards,
- tracking systems,
- intrusion detection systems, and
- radio frequency identification cards (Davis, 2008).

Critical to maintaining information confidentiality and integrity are access controls (Davis, 2008). Logical and physical access control policy integration should occur at the managerial, operational, and technical levels to enable compliance with external and internal IAP requirements (Davis, 2008). Whether logical and physical access control policies are distinct or converged, minimally, during a CSG audit, the entity's designed and operating information asset access processes require an assessment. The IT auditor assessment needs to address identification, authenticity, authorization, accountability, and non-repudiation measurements at the summary and detail levels.

Integrated access control policies are necessary to sustain safeguarding capabilities. An entity's access control policy must clearly define responsibilities, roles, and procedures for employee status changes, such as changing positions and tasks (Davis, 2008). Specifically, establishing procedural requirements for managing user status changes and communicating changes to owners, supervisors, or any individual or group responsible for defining, granting, eliminating, or changing entitlements or privileges are crucial (Davis, 2008). Additionally, an entity's designated Chief Information Security Officer should have overall responsibility for IAP administration. Therefore, an assigned IT auditor should examine the system administration unit for assigned employee roles and responsibilities.

When physical and logical penetration protection mechanisms are converged under a unified access control policy, the resulting combination can operate as a customized baseline to redress entity-centric needs for effective threat countermeasures (Davis, 2008). To enable organizational coexistence with technological convergences, an entity's Chief Security Officer should assume responsibility for deploying and sustaining blended physical and logical access controls (Davis, 2008). Beneficially, regarding operational complexity, access control convergence can simplify entity security administration (Davis, 2008).

Appropriate access restrictions are prohibitive irregularities or illegal acts controls (Davis, 2008). Typically, discretionary access control policies align with identity-based access controls, while nondiscretionary access controls align with rule-based controls (Davis, 2008). When logical and physical access is under examination as one auditable unit, the primary information criteria most relevant to responsibility, authority, and accountability are effectiveness, efficiency, and confidentiality. Simultaneously, availability, integrity, and reliability are secondary considerations (Davis, 2008). Pervasively, employing a competent cybersecurity manager-leader can ensure continuous monitoring of local and remote access (Davis, 2008).

Depending on localized procedures, platforms, utilities, and the design of associated IAP technological resources, access administration can vary within entities (Davis, 2008). However, in all circumstances, entities should minimally include

- formally inscribed access requests for all actions with adequate rationales and appropriate approvals,
- requirements for user administrators receiving requests to verify proper approval recording on access requisitions,

- time frames for processing user administration operations from defined and accepted requestors,
- processes denoting passcodes remission to users for additions or resets, and
- controls to ensure passcode destruction after a specified time if the passcode does not reach the intended recipient (Davis, 2008).

Classification of protection mechanisms can help determine data sensitivity, information processed by an entity using IT, and an appropriate defense strategy deployment (Davis, 2008). An assigned IT auditor should consider control classification analysis to provide additional IAP control system insight and determine CSG audit testing nature, timing, and the extent to enable sufficient audit assurance. As constructed in Appendix E, IAP mechanisms are classifiable to ensure an appropriate defense against errors, mistakes, omissions, irregularities, and illegal acts for informational assets (Davis, 2008). Assessing physical and logical controls can involve highly technical issues, especially for large integrated systems and systems that involve telecommunications (Davis, 2008). Consequently, even an experienced IT auditor may need to seek technical advice from an expert on some issues (Davis, 2008). Nonetheless, an assigned IT auditor should study and evaluate whether the IT access process provides appropriate identification, authentication, and authorization (Davis, 2008).

Identification

Subject and object identification are essential for appropriate access control (Davis, 2008). Effective identity management establishes trust in an entity's technological environment (Davis, 2008). Moreover, proof-of-identity enables entity personnel to trust that the presented credentials are accurate representations of validated users (Davis, 2008). IAP identification policies should inscribe classifications and attributes of acceptable users, user groups, processes, and devices acting on behalf of individuals as well as accessible resources (Davis, 2008). In other words, designed entity identity policies should guide behaviors by defining the uniqueness of accessible objects and subjects requesting access (Davis, 2008). Therefore, as minimum procedures, an IT auditor should study and evaluate implemented IAP controls limiting the number of unknown users accessing information assets and controls enabling credentials' usage oversight and monitoring throughout the computing environment (Davis, 2008).

Authentication

Proper subject authentication is vital to safeguarding an entity's infrastructure (Davis, 2008). Controls for authenticating users based on entity-centric policies need deployment in ensuring appropriate access (Davis, 2008). Typically, no single authentication mechanism acts as a panacea for providing total protection from all potential threats. Thus, an assigned IT auditor should study and evaluate any inherent, control, and residual risks that are part of an entity's applied identification verification solution set (Davis, 2008).

Authorization

Entity authorization authority should reflect an assessment of managerial, operational, and technical control requirements (Davis, 2008). As a CSG activity, the audit of relevant Identity and Access Management controls should include authorization authority (Davis,

2008; McQuaide, 2003). Accordingly, authority re-authorization for an entity's information systems needs a review within 3 years (Davis, 2008). Coincidently, the 3-year authority re-authorization period coincides with most strategic audit planning cycles (Davis, 2008). An assigned IT auditor should note that the absence of standards for measurement is an indicator of an uncontrolled IAP processing environment (Davis, 2008). Consequently, an assigned IT auditor should study and evaluate whether the IT access process provides appropriate authentication and authorization (Davis, 2008).

Cybersecurity Network Infrastructure

Management's insufficient network infrastructure knowledge is partly attributable to custom-entity-developed-software and commercial-off-the-shelf-software user transparency spanning an entity's organizational structures (Davis, 2008). User transparency has released most managers from acquiring detailed familiarity with underlying entity systems and associated risks (Davis, 2008). Cybersecurity manager-leaders should ensure adequate expenditures directed toward acquiring, training, and retaining qualified IAP subject matter experts to close the potential network infrastructure knowledge gap (Davis, 2008).

Besides subject matter expert expenditures, cybersecurity manager-leaders should also deploy network security technologies minimally fulfilling identification, authentication, non-reputation, comprehension, and analysis requirements (Davis, 2008). Toward network security technologies achieving fulfillment, a unique tool available to manage and understand networks is the traceroute utility created at Lucent Technologies (Davis, 2008). The traceroute utility enables determining packet paths from a source computer to some destination (Davis, 2008). The traceroute utility is also employable for mapping the Internet or for tracing networking growth in regions of the world (Davis, 2008). Furthermore, cryptographic tools aid in access control by rendering data unintelligible to unauthorized users and protecting the confidentiality and integrity of transmitted or stored data (Davis, 2008). Characteristically, cryptographic tools are especially useful in network environments because potential usage includes providing decoded electronic signatures to assist in message authentication and ensuring file probity (Davis, 2008). Ensuring effectual technical IAP controls is a defendable cybersecurity program starting point that permits IT auditor recognition of supportive governance activities (Davis, 2008).

Universally, audit profession governing bodies accept network infrastructure controls as general controls that can significantly affect application controls (Davis, 2008). General control efficacy is dependent on the extent of inherent risks, control environmental factors, communication, and monitoring, which directly affect deployed IT (Davis, 2008). Serious IAP risks can exist because inadequate control installments or specific controls are remiss within an entity's network infrastructure (Davis, 2008). Even when sanctioned controls are available as software options, use may not occur because personnel responsible for control deployments are unaware of the risk or impact of allowing a control gap to exist (Davis, 2008).

Most IT software provides parameters enabling technical personnel to use privileges that can override controls (Davis, 2008). Audits of available cybersecurity parameters should include considering management's security policies, security responsibility allocations, risk assessment procedures, and monitoring compliance with security policies. Even where a privileged parameter does not comply with the IT auditor's view of best authorization practice, the parameter allocation may receive an endorsement for appropriateness considering the risk identified by entity management and the management policies directing how to address risk levels (Davis, 2008). Subsequently, any IT audit recommendations for improvement should address the risk management practices or policies and the parameter issue (Davis, 2008).

IT decentralization increased the need for effectual network security (Davis, 2008). In response, entities typically deploy several layers of information security technologies, including robust authentication and roving intrusion detection (Davis, 2008). Understanding network infrastructure concepts and linkages to other auditable units ensures an appropriate security evaluation when performing CSG audits (Davis, 2008). Pointedly, an assigned IT auditor must study and evaluate cybersecurity management software deployments that address the entity network configuration elements during CSG audits.

Typically, an entity's network infrastructure integrates diverse software and hardware solutions, each designed to achieve a specific function (Davis, 2008). As a critical ingredient to designing, implementing, and sustaining entity-wide efficacy, the network infrastructure requires in-depth IAP (Davis, 2008). Specifically, the network infrastructure should have appropriate IAP for IT hardware, operating systems, configuration systems, facilities, and support structures (Davis, 2008).

Hardware

Errors can occur due to IT hardware configuration item failure (Davis, 2008). An electronic element failure can affect the electrical values used in data processing, storage, and communication between different IT configuration components (Davis, 2008). If the failure leads to a change in the timing, strength, shape, or pulse frequency, the result could modify or destroy data used to construct information (Davis, 2008). Some IT hardware controls are typically built into equipment by the manufacturer, such as automatic error diagnosis and automatic retry routines to rebuff data manipulation and corruption (Davis, 2008).

Critical to appropriate information assets' protective posturing are control deployments addressing transmission confidentiality, integrity, and availability (Davis, 2008). If an assigned IT auditor plans to rely on deployed hardware controls as general technology controls (Davis, 2008), the following tasks should occur during the audit study and evaluation process.

- Document the make, model, size, and the number of IT hardware devices (Davis, 2008).
- Review vendor literature or other reliable information to determine what hardware controls are available (Davis, 2008).
- Inquire of management and IT personal regarding the available controls used by the entity.
- Review error logs to determine the frequency and types of hardware-induced errors (Davis, 2008).
- Evaluate the effectiveness of hardware controls (Davis, 2008).

Operating Systems

Usually, IT network environments orchestrate direction and control through an operating system installed to coordinate processes, including application software (Davis, 2008). In other words, an operating system performs most administrative functions for IT processes (Davis, 2008). Operating systems are the primary catalyst for computerization. Given the importance of computing, entity manager-leaders should ensure appropriate cybersecurity hardware and software control installations (internally and externally) for operating systems (Davis, 2008).

Regarding entity software controls, all the functions utilizing the Central Processing Unit and associated storage, as well as connected input and output devices, are potential candidates for operating system defense strategies (Davis, 2008). Tactically, five primary operating system protection mechanisms are deployable: memory, input, output, processor, and user program controls. In most instances, the purpose of operating system protection mechanisms is to prevent programs from interfering with each other during processing. Operating system protection mechanisms also ensure error-free referencing of subroutines in the program library and ensure no unauthorized changes occur to authorized instructions (Davis, 2008). Therefore, during the study and evaluation of operating system protection mechanisms, minimally, the IT auditor should determine if

- visual error messaging occurs, as opposed to other technological action taken when reference occurs to unauthorized subroutines, or when external references are unsolved;
- the operating system maintains a log of program usage; and
- the operating system's linkage editor maintains a processing history of each program, including control statements used (Davis, 2008).

Support Structures

For a network infrastructure, identification is typically an act or process that enables identifier presentation to an authentication system to recognize the access-requesting object and distinguish the requestor from other objects (Davis, 2008). Network infrastructure identification is a sequence of items (including a specific identifier) assigned to a subject or object for use when identifying a subject or object (Davis, 2008). At the network communications level, identification protocols are client-server rules for learning the identity of users of connections (Davis, 2008). Network infrastructure identification and authentication are technical controls ensuring user validation to enable access to information assets when combined (Davis, 2008).

Information systems typically use either shared known data or an organizational authentication solution to identify and authenticate devices on local and wide area networks (Davis, 2008). Architecturally, IT networks incorporate protocols and a general scheme driving IT networking rules (Davis, 2008). Single-function and multifunction protocols may apply to an Internet, Intranet, Extranet, or Peer-to-Peer architecture and enable IAP technical controls (Davis, 2008). Therefore, an IT auditor should study and evaluate the standardized rules set or protocols that, when followed, will allow orderly information exchange with adequate network infrastructure protection (Davis, 2008).

Configuration Management

Insecure configuration management presents network infrastructure vulnerabilities primarily through control weaknesses in IT managerial functions (Davis, 2008). In implementing an appropriate IAP level for the network infrastructure, identifying and controlling all IT access paths are vital to an entity (Davis, 2008). Simply sending any user who asks for an account a token or a certificate does not provide identification certainty (Davis, 2008; Wiesmann et al., 2005). Therefore, robust, trusted enrollment paths are necessary for ensuring that the authentication system is reliable for sustaining non-repudiation expectations (Davis, 2008; Wiesmann et al., 2005).

An assigned IT auditor should study and evaluate authentication processes to ensure appropriate network infrastructure security supplied through configuration management (Davis, 2008). Moreover, an assigned IT auditor should study and evaluate network infrastructure non-repudiation adequacy for ensuring eventual operational or legal use where information exchanges occur (Davis, 2008). Architectural security issues are classifiable according to action, perpetrator, and target to assist in assessing whether IT connectivity protection gaps exist (Davis, 2008; Gelbstein & Kurbalija, 2005). A classification based on action type can include data observation, data redirection, data interference, illegal access, and identity theft (Davis, 2008; Gelbstein & Kurbalija, 2005). Wherefore, possible perpetrators might encompass crackers, hackers, cyber-criminals, cyber-warriors, or cyber-terrorists (Davis, 2008, 2017; Gelbstein & Kurbalija, 2005). Potential ultimate targets are numerous; thus, categories can range from individuals, partnerships, and corporations to devices, buildings, and infrastructures (Davis, 2008; Gelbstein & Kurbalija, 2005).

Facilities

Network infrastructure facilities are the areas where IT hardware and software reside and require access controls (Davis, 2008). Consistent with logical access controls, users of the entity's information processing facilities should undergo authentication and authorization as per a formal policy and method (Davis, 2008). An entity's physical access methods' selection should align with the adopted information classification scheme and take the least privilege approach when granting rights and permissions (Davis, 2008). During a CSG audit, to adequately examine facility integrity risks, an assigned IT auditor should study and evaluate relevant controls concerning authentication, communication, processing, as well as ensuring non-repudiation for appropriate informational or transactional data (Davis, 2008).

Cybersecurity Risk Analysis

Resilient and repeatable risk management processes are critical success factors relative to fulfilling mandated security program responsibilities (Davis, 2008). Determining the IAP assessment ambit requires analysis of system boundaries and organizational responsibilities (Davis, 2008). However, the basis for system boundaries should not reflect physical configuration connectivity (Davis, 2008). To support IAP deployment decisions, safeguarding mechanisms for every technology or group of related technologies needs descriptions in the entity's information security plan (Davis, 2008). Potential premises for performing cybersecurity risk analysis can include operational or legal mandates (Davis, 2008).

Directly related to accomplishing information security strategic objectives is the inscription and assessment of the high-level cybersecurity objective providing control over the protective processes safeguarding information against unauthorized access, use, disruption, disclosure, modification, and damage (Davis, 2008). To achieve the cybersecurity safeguarding objective, some of the expected risk analysis process outcomes are:

- financial and nonfinancial values' assignment to information assets,
- comprehensive itemization of perceivable and significant threats,
- comprehensive itemization of perceivable and significant vulnerabilities,
- probabilities of the occurrence rate of each threat,

- probabilities of the occurrence rate of each vulnerability,
- loss potentials the entity can endure per threat in 12 months, and
- recommended countermeasures and action plan (Davis, 2008).

Where an IT risk management implementation project is underway, a participating cyber-security representative can:

- categorize information assets based on an inscribed impact analysis,
- select an initial set of IAP controls for information assets based on security categorization and apply tailoring guidance as appropriate,
- supplement the initial set of tailored IAP controls based on assessing risks that include entity-specific security requirements, specific threat information, cost–benefit analyses, and particular circumstances, and
- inscribe the agreed-upon IAP control set in the information security plan, including the justification for any refinements or adjustments to the initial control set (Davis, 2008).

Providing an appropriate cybersecurity mission and strategic objectives for delivery and support requires performing cybersecurity risk assessments that consider the entity's people, processes, infrastructure, and information (Davis, 2008). IAP policies should reflect an assessment of risks (Davis, 2008). However, the cybersecurity risk assessment personnel do not need to quantify risk precisely (Davis, 2008). Minimally, the cybersecurity risk assessment should include consideration of the entity's IAP processes for:

- access management,
- firewall deployments,
- user profiles,
- trusted paths,
- authorization,
- authentication,
- virus detection,
- virus prevention,
- incident handling,
- user identification,
- incident reporting,
- incident follow-up, and
- cryptographic key management (Davis, 2008).

IAP risk analysis should directly affect IT controls deployed (Davis, 2008). Consequently, a recent IAP risk analysis will commonly support entity management's assertion of a conscientious effort to provide the best protection for organizational information assets (Davis, 2008). However, compliance risks can be overestimated or underestimated by a lack of process standardization throughout the entity's control system. Thus, an assigned IT auditor should inscribe, study, and evaluate the IAP risk analysis process (Davis, 2008). Additionally, an assigned IT auditor should study and evaluate management's analysis and assessment of critical resources and the types of protection implemented (Davis, 2008). In the end, an assigned IT auditor should also evaluate if the IAP risk analysis is consistent with subject matter-related departmental, program, and entity-wide risk assessment frameworks (Davis, 2008).

Cybersecurity Environmental Controls

Technological environment controls refer to hardware designed to counteract problems caused by dust, temperature, and humidity that can be a conduit for electrostatic discharge (Davis, 2008). Electrostatic discharge is an electric shock generated through static electricity buildup (Davis, 2008). Conductive material contact releases the shock associated with an electrostatic buildup (Davis, 2008). Upon release, electrostatic discharge events can generate extreme heat through as much as 3000 Volts of electricity (Davis, 2008). The potential for electrostatic discharge warrants safety precautions, considering IT component damage can occur by a 20–30 Volt surge (Davis, 2008). There are also other hazards capable of corrupting or corroding information assets (Davis, 2008). An entity should install temperature, humidity, and air quality climate controls to supplement hardware-designed environmental controls (Davis, 2008). Deployed technological environment monitoring systems need capabilities for historical trend analysis (Davis, 2008). IT environmental form and fashion support the sustainment of information integrity criteria and address information asset availability requirements for an entity (Davis, 2008).

Entity manager-leaders should never mistake Plug-and-Play IT for Install-and-Forget hardware. Though technology operations personnel are traditionally responsible for IT hardware implementations, monitoring environmental appropriateness falls within the realm of cybersecurity due diligence (Davis, 2008). In particular, accurate and comprehensive monitoring of environmental support equipment and installation conditions is critical for reliable processing within complex and sensitive hardware configuration areas (Davis, 2008).

Climatically, strategizing optimum technological environment conditions for information assets is a managerial safeguarding responsibility (Davis, 2008). Environmental conditions such as heat production, airflow, and humidity are factors that should come under consideration during IT site preparation and operational sustainability (Davis, 2008). Concerning heat production, equipment using energy releases thermal units that can substantially increase ambient temperature (Davis, 2008). Air movement must occur, or otherwise the temperature and humidity will naturally escalate within an unregulated confined space (Davis, 2008). When the ambient temperature is at the manufacturer's recommended level, there is usually adequate cool airflow to minimize IT availability risks (Davis, 2008). Low humidity can generate static electricity, causing shocks, electrical malfunctions, paper jams, and recording media errors (Davis, 2008). Too dry a climate generates dust, which can accumulate on IT boards, where the first components typically affected are the Central Processing Unit modules, thus potentially causing system reliability problems that translate to availability issues (Davis, 2008).

When the relative humidity is high, water particulates form corresponding to the heat index (Davis, 2008). High humidity can warp hardware configuration cards (Davis, 2008). Additionally, any conditions that cause moisture deposits on equipment will eventually depreciate hardware functionality without adequate insulation (Davis, 2008). Maintaining the optimal temperature and humidity ensures that the mean time between failures is plannable with a minimum user impact (Davis, 2008).

IT can, and does, operate within a wide humidity range (Davis, 2008). Seasonal humidity changes are typically easier to control than hourly fluctuations (Davis, 2008). Under either humidity circumstance, typically, the primary environmental concern is preventing conditions that permit alterations where condensation results (Davis, 2008). Data culled from an analysis of historical psychrometer readings can help determine seasonal changes or outside influences (Davis, 2008). A psychrometer consists of two thermometers with bulbs, one wet and one dry (Davis, 2008). One bulb stays wet, so the cooling that results from evaporation permits a lower temperature registration than the dry bulb (Davis, 2008). The difference between the two readings constitutes a measure of atmospheric dryness (Davis, 2008).

Decreasing IT hardware replacement cost does not eliminate the need for adequate environmental protection (Davis, 2008). To avoid humidity corruption, cybersecurity managers should verify humidity and temperature level sustainment within the operating range specified in supplier documentation for deployed IT (Davis, 2008). Periodically, a cybersecurity professional should inspect the entity's IT sites for obvious external influences such as close placement to air conditioners, elevator shafts, industrial equipment, or other sources of potential atmospheric variations (Davis, 2008). If there is a high level of reliability requirement, then entity personnel should maintain optimal technological environment conditions (Davis, 2008). Maintaining equipment at the optimum climate range aids in protecting hardware from corrosion problems associated with high humidity levels and operational failures caused by static discharge when humidity is too low (Davis, 2008).

Technological environment controls are a subset of physical security controls that prevent or mitigate damage to the network infrastructure and service interruptions (Davis, 2008). Where necessary, footwear, floor-matting, and wrist-straps are controls for reducing the chance of an electrostatic discharge damaging IT (Davis, 2008). Smoke detectors, fire-resistant facilities, fire alarms, fire extinguishers, water sprinklers, waterproof covers, water drains, water pumps, maintaining appropriate temperatures for facilities, surge protectors, and deploying uninterruptible power supplies are some examples of other environmental controls (Davis, 2008).

Usually, equipment manufacturers specify noncondensing atmospheric conditions for purchased network configuration items (Davis, 2008). Information assets and the personnel who operate them need a reasonably well-controlled operating environment (Davis, 2008). Electric power, heating, cooling, water, sewage, and other utility system failures will usually cause a service interruption as well as damage hardware (Davis, 2008). Therefore, an assigned IT auditor should evaluate policies, directives, standards, procedures, and rules for IT environmental controls. Moreover, an assigned IT auditor should evaluate procedures to ensure that environmental utilities function properly (Davis, 2008).

Cybersecurity Confidential Information Assets

Information systems can include elements protected by data privacy, copyright, patent, and trademark laws (Davis, 2008). Entity property in information systems may cross borders virtually imperceptibly and can be vulnerable, without requiring original content extraction or leaving a trace of intrusion (Davis, 2008). Therefore, appropriate protective measures are necessary to maintain information assets in a properly controlled and secured environment (Davis, 2008, 2013). Specifically, a physically and logically secure environment should exist at the general technology controls level (Davis, 2008, 2013).

Cybersecurity manager-leaders should develop classification categories that meet legal and entity requirements for confidentiality in selecting the most appropriate IT controls (Davis, 2008). Consequently, when ensuring legislative or regulatory compliance, there may be an imperative to protect information confidentiality and subordinate other criteria for some storage media (Davis, 2008). Classifications can involve hierarchically delineating confidentiality levels, such as minimally sensitive, moderately sensitive, and highly sensitive (Davis, 2008). Critical success factors for suitable confidential information control deployments are careful classification formulation and operational implementation based on perceived risks (Davis, 2008).

Implementing a privacy classification system exemplifies an entity's commitment to protecting customer information (Davis, 2008). Nonetheless, not all data is equally sensitive due to differences in mission relevance, entity culture, competitive effect, financial worth, brand loyalty, and legal risks, among other factors (Davis, 2008). Moreover, certain data types are more sensitive in a particular industry (Davis, 2008). Through delegated information asset responsibilities, owners should determine which classifications are most appropriate for assigned resources (Davis, 2008). Information asset classification determination should flow directly from risk assessment results that identify threats, opportunities, vulnerabilities, and the potential adverse effects that could ensue from disclosing confidential information (Davis, 2008). Additionally, all confidential information classifications should receive a review and approval by an appropriate senior manager-leader, then maintained on file, and periodically assessed to ensure current environment correspondence (Davis, 2008).

Spyware can pose a severe threat to confidential digitized information storage and transmission (Davis, 2008). Typical spyware tactics include keylogger insertion, monitoring web browsing, and eavesdropping on voice communication (Davis, 2008). Entities should install anti-spyware programs designed to block, detect, and remove spyware to reduce unauthorized disclosure risks (Davis, 2008).

Telecommunication vehicles frequently transport confidential information (Davis, 2008). Technology allows encrypting or otherwise protecting data at different networking levels when transporting confidential information (Davis, 2008). Particularly pertinent to sustaining network infrastructure IAP is protocol and network architecture encryption (Davis, 2008). As an additional confidentiality protection, encryption can occur within entity software applications (Davis, 2008). Application encryption contributes to IAP at the network infrastructure interface level (Davis, 2008). Technologically, highly confidential applications need protection by a message authentication code or digital signature method, with requestor verification failure preventing software use (Davis, 2008). Selecting the appropriate level for invoking encryption and other protection mechanisms may involve considering currently deployed security as well as resource requirements (Davis, 2008). Regarding maintaining confidentiality, management should assess the level of trust in the transport medium (Davis, 2008).

Entity manager-leaders should ensure that sensitive transaction data are exchanged only over trusted paths or mediums with controls to provide authenticity of content, proof-of-submission, proof-of-receipt, and origin non-repudiation (Davis, 2008). When electronic telecommunication trustworthiness is an issue, entity cybersecurity manager-leaders should also ensure that data encryption occurs before network transmission (Davis, 2008). Specifically, entity cybersecurity manager-leaders should endeavor to encrypt data as close as possible to the source (Davis, 2008).

When disposing of or redeploying IT, entity manager-leaders should have procedures to eradicate confidential information (Davis, 2008). If complete sensitive information destruction does not transpire, confidential information recovery and inappropriate use or disclosure can be accomplished by individuals who have access to the discarded or transferred IT (Davis, 2008). The responsibility for removing confidential information needs exact assignment (Davis, 2008). After confidential data processing completion, the operating system should clear invoked memory usage (Davis, 2008). Applying a memory clearance procedure reduces the risk of sensitive information being available for subsequent access by other programs (Davis, 2008; Wiesmann et al., 2005). Furthermore, standard forms or logs are necessary for inscribing a discarded or transferred asset examination occurred for confidential information. Moreover, the standard forms or logs for discarded or transferred

IT assets should permit certifying that confidential information contained therein received a complete eradication treatment before asset release (Davis, 2008).

Compliance with laws, regulations, and internal policies is essential to ensuring adequate IAP (Davis, 2008). Therefore, an assigned IT auditor should consider individual-compliance, multiple-compliance, and cross-compliance during the study and evaluation process of a CSG audit addressing confidentiality. For applications processing transactions and payments as well as accepting and displaying any personal details confidential in nature, the assigned IT auditor should verify the application of appropriate encryption technologies or mechanisms in transmissions between users and applications (Davis, 2008).

CSG Audit Testing and Evaluation of Controls

IT audit testing completes what is commonly called audit fieldwork (Davis, 2010). Logically, after completing the IT audit study and evaluation of control processes, auditors are prepared to perform selected statistical or nonstatistical testing of transactions, cycles, or events (Davis, 2010). Testing a CSG auditable unit, statistically or nonstatistically, is the culmination of the in-charge IT auditor's desired audit assurance concerning the direct subject matters, related subject matters, and management's assertions (Davis, 2010). Auditable unit test materiality rates should exceed the testing threshold before inscribing testing procedures (Davis, 2010). Consequently, test procedures should have a stated objective and reflect predetermined test timing, nature, and extent (Davis, 2010).

CSG audit materiality affects audit nature, timing, and extent (Davis, 2010). Consequently, CSG audit test materiality influences the audit testing nature, timing, and extent (Davis, 2010). Audit testing nature represents the type of performed testing (Davis, 2010). Testing performance is reflective of predetermined risk associated with the CSG auditable units (Davis, 2010). Whereby CSG audit testing timing is when audit testing performance occurs (Davis, 2010). Furthermore, audit testing extent is the amount or range of testing (Davis, 2010). If the assigned in-charge IT auditor accurately forecasted auditable unit-required control effectiveness assurance, actual test results should approximate expected test results' assurance (Davis, 2010).

Ordinarily, audit test materiality aligns with audit design materiality (Davis, 2010, 2020). However, the substantive test materiality levels can be below the design materiality to achieve CSG audit assurance objectives under certain circumstances. Conditionally, lower substantive test materiality can occur for:

- locating an expected significant misstatement;
- assertions, direct subject matter, or related subject matter when an audit includes a multiple organizational location sample;
- auditable unit tests classified as sensitive to financial statement users;
- auditable unit tests classified as sensitive to technology users; and
- specific line items when an audit includes a multiple organizational location sample.

CSG audits are typically general control examinations. Consequently, IT audit team testing of general controls skews toward performing manual procedures, statistically or nonstatistically (Davis, 2011, 2020). Once a decision is made to use audit sampling, assigned IT auditors must choose between statistical and nonstatistical testing methodologies (Davis, 2010). The testing choice is primarily a cost–benefit consideration (Davis, 2010). Statistical audit testing methodologies aid the assigned IT auditors in designing efficient samples, measuring obtained evidential matter sufficiency, and evaluating sample results (Davis,

2010). With statistical audit testing methodologies, some sampling risk is always present (Davis, 2010). Statistical audit testing methodologies use mathematical probability to gauge sampling risk (Davis, 2010). Any audit testing methodology that does not benchmark sampling risk is a nonstatistical test application (Davis, 2010). If an auditor selects a sample yet does not make a statistical evaluation of sample results, the audit testing methodology is a nonstatistical audit test treatment (Davis, 2010).

Foremost in performing audit testing is defining the population under examination (Davis, 2010). An auditable unit test population is the group of data on which inferences are made based upon sample results (Davis, 2010, 2020). In other words, the auditable unit population represents the entire dataset from which the assigned IT auditor decides to sample to conclude on the target population (Davis, 2010, 2020).

Upon understanding and defining an auditable unit test population, the assigned IT auditor performs an appropriateness and completeness alignment assessment (Davis, 2010, 2020). The alignment assessment addresses IT audit test objectives and audit objectives to avoid completing the assurance task under a mistaken assumption (Davis, 2011; Soltani, 2007). Moreover, to exhibit professional due care for each IT audit test objective, detailed audit sampling plans require inscription. The detailed plans must reflect test goals supporting the audit test objectives and population composition and location, which drive the sample selection technique (Davis, 2010).

Next, the assigned IT auditor defines sampling items (Davis, 2010, 2020). One individual item within the auditable unit test population represents a sampling unit. Audit sampling unit definitions are dependent on sample objectives (Davis, 2010). As a corollary note, population physical sample representation is a sample frame (Davis, 2010).

Statistical test sampling is an objective methodology attempting to represent the test population (Davis, 2010). Statistical test denotation forms the premise for classifying the result (Davis, 2010). Thus, a statistical parameter is a characteristic of a population that is a numeric value computed using every population element (Davis, 2010). A statistic is also a characteristic of a sample taken from the population that is a numerical value computed using only the sample population elements (Davis, 2010). Sampling is vital to CSG audits because a complete census is usually costly, time-consuming, and error-prone (Davis, 2010).

Statistical audit testing design can be fixed or sequential (Davis, 2010, 2020). Acceptance, Discovery, and Attribute are subclassifications available for Fixed Testing (Davis, 2010, 2020). Contrastingly, Stop-or-Go testing uses a Sequential Testing methodology and requires a lower confidence level than Fixed Testing methodologies (Davis, 2010, 2020). Nonetheless, Acceptance, Discovery, and Stop-or-Go Testing are unique attribute sampling applications (Davis, 2020). Systematic, random, stratified, and cell sampling methods are employable options for fixed and sequential testing methodologies (Davis, 2010, 2020).

Judgmental and Haphazard Sampling is available for nonstatistical testing (Davis, 2010). If nonstatistical testing is selected, an IT auditor cannot state the event occurrence probability in scientific terms (Davis, 2010). As a deterrent for nonstatistical testing usage, haphazard and judgmental methodologies do not quantify statistical precision and reliability, thus, preventing audit population conclusions based on the sample examined by the assigned IT auditor (Davis, 2010). Nevertheless, Haphazard and Judgmental Sampling are acceptable approaches for performing compliance and substantive testing under the same audit assurance provisioning considerations as statistical testing methods (Davis, 2010, 2020).

The Judgmental Sampling approach depends on decisions reflecting the individual's experience or conjecture for item selection (Davis, 2010, 2020). Thus, central to the validity of Judgmental Sampling is an IT auditor's organizational and personal experience (Davis, 2010, 2020) or deductive reasoning reliability. The Judgmental Sampling approach is a nonstatistical application that can have a high bias conclusion effect on an IT audit (Davis, 2010, 2020). In other words, Judgmental Sampling is a nonstatistical method that may rely on tainted subjectivity in reaching an opine (Davis, 2020; Hall et al., 2000).

Haphazard Sampling is a procedural attempt to remove subjectivity from population item selection (Davis, 2010, 2020; Glen, 2015). Nonetheless, like Judgmental Sampling, using the Haphazard Sampling approach does not quantify statistical reliability and precision (Davis, 2010, 2020). With the Haphazard Sampling approach, to actively eliminate conscious bias and choice predictability, the demonstration of true randomness of item selection is crucial (Bragg, 2019; Davis, 2005, 2011; Glen, 2015). However, unconscious biases and predictability can affect item selection decisions (Bragg, 2019; Davis, 2010, 2020; Glen, 2015). Therefore, Haphazard Sampling can generate a bias conclusion effect on an IT audit (Davis, 2010, 2020; Hall et al., 2000).

Cybersecurity Compliance Testing

Unless otherwise dictated by the IT audit risk assessment or audit management, extensive compliance testing is the norm for CSG audits. The compliance testing high-level objective should support the preliminary control effectiveness assessment and address obtaining evidence supporting the auditor's report on controls (Davis, 2010). When obtaining audit evidence from a test of controls, the assigned IT auditor should consider the audit evidence completeness to support the assessed level of control risk (Davis, 2010). If financial statements are under examination, an additional high-level objective is obtaining support for the preliminary control risk assessment as moderate or low (Davis, 2010).

Attribute Testing is a fixed statistical attribute sampling method (Davis, 2020). A condition exists or does not exist for the sampling units with Attribute Testing (Davis, 2020). Attribute Testing requires the use of a probabilistic sample selection method. After drawing a sample, then using the sample for testing, if the maximum deviation rate is larger than the defined tolerable deviation rate, the sampling frame has an unacceptable control condition (Davis, 2020). Thus, the assigned IT auditor must conclude that the auditable unit control design and operation are insufficient.

A fixed attribute sampling statistical method is Discovery Testing (Davis, 2010, 2020). Foundationally, Discovery Testing is generally employed to infer an audit population's irregularities or the probability of illegal acts (Davis, 2010, 2020). The purpose of Discovery Testing is the enablement of stating that the population error rate is below the predetermined error level with a stated degree of confidence (Davis, 2010, 2020). However, if detection of one error occurs during Discovery Testing, sampling stops, and the assigned IT auditor must initiate appropriate auditor actions (Davis, 2010, 2020). Stopping discovery testing due to error detection reflects a nonexistence hypothesis regarding auditable unit irregularities or illegal acts (Davis, 2010, 2020).

Acceptance Testing is a fixed statistical attribute sampling method (Davis, 2010, 2020). Consequently, the Acceptance Testing method only permits yes or no and existence or nonexistence decisions regarding sampling units (Davis, 2010, 2020). Specifically, an IT auditor draws a sample for testing (Davis, 2010, 2020). If the defined sample does not exceed the exception rate limit, the sampling frame has an acceptable control condition (Davis, 2010, 2020). Given an acceptable control condition, the Acceptance Testing method allows the IT auditor to conclude that the population error rate is below the predetermined error level with a stated degree of confidence (Davis, 2010, 2020).

Stop-or-Go Testing is a sequential statistical attribute sampling method (Davis, 2010, 2020). Discovery and Acceptance Testing elements are present in Stop-or-Go Testing (Davis, 2010, 2020). As with all sequential sampling, Stop-or-Go Testing performance happens in multiple steps, with each step conditional on the preceding step results (Davis, 2010, 2020). The similarity with Discovery Testing is in only inspecting enough sample items for enabling the IT auditor to state that the actual population error rate is below a predetermined error level, with a pre-specified confidence level (Davis, 2010, 2020). Testing using this method also allows stating that the population error rate is below the predetermined error level with a stated degree of confidence, consistent with Acceptance and Discovery Testing (Davis, 2010, 2020). Furthermore, employing Stop-or-Go Testing enables concluding on the upper precision limit of the sampling frame.

Stop-or-Go Testing has premises and methodology departures from Discovery and Acceptance Testing (Davis, 2010, 2020). For instance, dissimilar to Discovery Testing, Stop-or-Go Testing is not usually employed for detecting irregularities or illegal acts (Davis, 2010, 2020). Furthermore, statistically, the Stop-or-Go Testing inference statement structure concerning a population differs from an Acceptance Testing projection (Davis, 2010, 2020). Nonetheless, Stop-or-Go Testing plans provide an opportunity to design a minimum sample size, anticipating a low population deviation rate (Davis, 2010, 2020). The expected low population deviation rate translates into a lower confidence level requirement (Davis, 2010, 2020). Therefore, dissimilar to Acceptance and Discovery Testing, Stop-or-Go relies on smaller sequential sample size and a lower confidence level (Davis, 2010, 2020).

Rules-of-Behavior

Most CSG audit compliance testing lists include procedures for confirming if rules-of-behavior are made available to information asset users before receiving access, and the rules contain a signature page to acknowledge receipt (Davis, 2008). Additionally, where a set of behavior rules exists, an assigned IT auditor should consider verifying use during security training sessions (Davis, 2008).

Authorization

Authorization structures enable the tracing of permissions to process information, accuracy assurance, and procedure compliance when implementing modifications (Davis, 2008). Inscribed permission requests to process data and information permits source validity assurance for authorizations. However, IT audit personnel should not assume that the information submitted for IT authorization processing is accurate. Therefore, compliance testing is ordinarily necessary for information asset authorizations (Davis, 2008). Additionally, if warranted, an assigned IT auditor should test physical access control effectiveness for information assets during regular operating hours and other times (Davis, 2008).

Risk Analysis

Commonly, the CSG audit risk results suggest that the CSG risk analysis reports of assessed threats, potential vulnerabilities, impacts, and countermeasures for identified risks need testing to opine on accuracy and completeness (Davis, 2008). Regarding manual CSG risks, an assigned IT auditor needs to examine garbage disposal areas and bins for sensitive security and general organizational information that may be useful in compromising confidentiality (Davis, 2008). Furthermore, an assigned IT auditor needs to test accessible recycling paper bins for sustaining confidentiality requirements (Davis, 2008).

Cybersecurity Substantive Testing

Substantiation of the risk to control objective non-attainment is a primary substantive testing locus for an assigned IT auditor (Davis, 2010, 2020). Substantive testing subcategories are analytical procedures and tests of details (Davis, 2010, 2020). Analytical procedures and tests-of-details are options available for increasing audit assurance (Davis, 2010, 2020). Analytical procedure performance can happen to verify or determine IT auditable unit accomplishment of control objectives (Davis, 2010, 2020). Audit analytical methods can encompass ascertaining policy compliance, abnormalities, and inefficiencies (Davis, 2010, 2020). However, analytical procedures alone may not be sufficient when performing an IT audit (Davis, 2020).

Like analytical procedures, tests-of-details can verify or determine IT auditable unit control objective accomplishment (Davis, 2010, 2020). The objective of tests-of-details is to support relevant assertions or detect material misstatements at the relevant assertion level. However, tests of details are generally used in combination to enable sufficient substantive assurance regarding an assertion (Davis, 2010, 2020). Beneficially, a single detail test might provide substantive assurance concerning more than one assertion (Davis, 2010, 2020).

Audit Trails

An assigned IT auditor should normally verify that adequate audit trails exist (Davis, 2008). Typically, audit trails are legally protected evidence that require logging to high-integrity destinations for preventing intentional or unintentional tampering and destruction (Davis, 2008). Therefore, an assigned IT auditor should consider performing substantive tests to determine if audit trails are adequate (Davis, 2008). The CSG audit substantive tests can include addressing whether:

- logs in transit maintain probity between the logging host and the destination,
- logs have a tamper-proof mechanism to prevent changes from the time of the logging activity until a review, and
- relevant logs are easily extracted in a legally sound fashion to assist with prosecuted cases (Davis, 2008).

Mitigating and Compensating Controls

Cross-sectional audit area testing may be within the CSG audit ambit. Therefore, an assigned IT auditor may need to perform sufficient testing to confirm a data quality program addresses data integrity, standardization, consistency, one-time data entry, and storage (Davis, 2008). For financial and record count analysis addressing information integrity, an assigned IT auditor should calculate totals for comparison with independent and application-maintained control totals (Davis, 2008). Where direct controls are absent, detailed CSG compensating controls can include

- passwords,
- inquiry only access,

- logs,
- dual authorization requirements, and
- inscribed reviews of input and output (Davis, 2008).

Cybersecurity Evidence Assessment

Usually, inscribed CSG-related policies, procedures, and standards are available to assess operating effectiveness. Evidentially, IT audit team members should consider whether information obtained from the CSG audit planning, study and evaluation, and testing processes indicate appropriate coverage. Sufficient evidence determination should include evaluation of:

- CSG mission statement for IAP activities;
- agreed goals for IAP activities;
- objectives for IAP activities;
- risk assessments associated with IAP resource usage;
- the risk management approach for IAP resource usage;
- strategic plans for strategy implementation;
- monitoring strategic plans for strategy deployment progress;
- information security budgets;
- variance monitoring of information security budgets;
- high-level information asset use policies;
- high-level IAP policies;
- high-level compliance monitoring policies for information asset use and protection policies;
- relevant IAP performance indicator comparisons, including benchmarks from similar entities, functions, appropriate international standards, maturity models, or recognized best practices;
- regular performance monitoring against agreed performance indicators;
- evidence of periodic information security reviews by the CSG function, with action items identified, resolution assignment, and tracking; and
- evidence of efficacy and meaningful links between CSG auditable units.

CSG Audit Control Reporting

The performance of evidence identification usually occurs during the CSG audit planning, study, and testing processes (Davis, 2010, 2020). Collected evidence from the CSG audit planning, study, and testing processes usually satisfy sufficiency, reliability, relevancy, and usefulness expectations (Davis, 2020). Thus, additional audit evidence identification is rare during the reporting process (Davis, 2010, 2020). However, when additional audit evidence is necessary while performing the audit reporting process, an assigned IT auditor must update the audit evidence catalog and working papers to ensure accurate condition representation (Davis, 2010, 2020).

Preceding audit report preparation, the condition, criteria, cause, possible effect(s), and recommendation(s) analysis of the audit area finding ensure an appropriate risk scoring for the CSG audit (Davis, 2010). IT audit team members address CSG statutory compliance and control objectives' achievement. Whether corroboration is mandatory or discretionary, supporting evidence for an audit opine can take the form of physical existence, observed process, documentary, or representation (Davis, 2010, 2020). However, corroborating evidence for oral representations may be remiss in some circumstances (Davis, 2010, 2020). Additionally, upon discovering inconsistencies and departures from applicable accounting principles during the CSG audit, the assigned IT auditor should request a qualified financial auditor review. Reporting materiality represents a threshold for determining an opinion expression regarding the area under audit (Davis, 2010, 2020). The CSG audit report author inscribes an opinion regarding whether, in all material respects, the design and operation of control procedures concerning the audit area were effective (Davis, 2010, 2020; ISACA, 2014). When the IT audit team members undertake an engagement to enable inscribing an assurance statement, as shown in Table 8.2, an IT audit area opinion can be deemed unqualified, qualified, adverse, or disclaimer by considering specific audit events (Davis, 2020; ISACA, 2014). The expressed audit report opinion depends on whether the audit had an (a) Ambit Limitation, (b) Uncertainty, (c) Material Control Weakness, (d) Reportable Condition, or (e) Other Weakness.

- Ambit Limitation: represents a constraint to obtaining sufficient appropriate evidence concerning an engagement audit area component (Davis, 2020).
- Uncertainty: is insufficient audit evidence collection (Davis, 2020).
- Material Control Weakness: existence precludes the enterprise from providing reasonable assurance that errors, mistakes, omissions, irregularities, or illegal acts will be prevented or detected on a timely basis by employees in the ordinary course of performing their assigned responsibilities (Davis, 2020).
- Reportable Condition: conveys a material or significant weakness in which the design and operation of one or more control components do not reduce to a relatively low level the risk that errors, mistakes, omissions, irregularities, or illegal acts potentially occurring and not detected timely by employees in the ordinary course of assigned duties (Davis, 2020). Moreover, for a reportable condition, causation by noncompliance or a performance measure or aggregation of related performance measures does not matter (Davis, 2020).
- Other Weakness: indicates a material or significant non-control weakness that singularly or in combination with other non-control weaknesses will not prevent, or detect and correct, on a timely basis an error, mistake, omission, irregularity, or illegal act from potentially occurring.

Table 8.2 Audit Area Condition-Potential Control Report Opinion Matrix

Audit Area Condition	Potential Control Report Opinion			
	Unqualified	Qualified	Adverse	Disclaimer
Ambit Limitation		X		X
Uncertainty		X	X	X
Material Control Weakness		X	X	
Reportable Condition	X	X	X	
Other Weakness			X	X

Note: X, opinion consideration. Adapted from *IT Auditing: An Adaptive System* by R. E. Davis, 2011, Lulu. Copyright 2011 by Robert E. Davis. Adapted with permission.

Unqualified Opinion

An unqualified CSG audit opinion concerning control adequacy represents procedural design and operational deployments under appropriate control practices for meeting audit area control objectives (Davis, 2010, 2020). Moreover, an unqualified opinion concerning control adequacy avers the absence of material control weaknesses (Davis, 2010, 2020). In other words, an unqualified CSG audit report exists when the audit function concludes that, in all material respects, the design and operation of control procedures concerning the audit area were effective and congruent with actionable criteria (Davis, 2020; ISACA, 2014). However, an unqualified opinion may have nonmaterial reportable conditions (Davis, 2010, 2020).

Qualified Opinion

A qualified CSG audit opinion concerning control adequacy represents audit area control effectiveness except for weaknesses affecting the audit area control objectives (Davis, 2010, 2020). The CSG audit report author expresses a qualified opinion after reviewing sufficient and appropriate evidence that enable concluding control weaknesses (individually, in combination, or the aggregate) are material, yet not pervasive to the IT audit objectives (Davis, 2020; ISACA, 2014). Moreover, a qualified opinion concerning control adequacy is issuable when IT audit team members cannot obtain sufficient and appropriate evidence as a decisional foundation (Davis, 2020). Even so, IT audit team members concluded that the possible effects on the IT audit objectives emanating from undetected weaknesses could be material but not pervasive (Davis, 2020; ISACA, 2014). A qualified CSG audit opinion inscription occurs through a separate report paragraph with reasons for the qualification (Davis, 2010, 2020; ISACA, 2014). If a separate CSG audit report is necessary, the author includes recommendations for corrective action (Davis, 2010, 2020).

Adverse Opinion

An adverse CSG audit opinion concerning control adequacy represents a material control weakness existing at the end of the audit period (Davis, 2005, 2011). The difference between a qualified and adverse ISG opinion directly corresponds to the degree audit subject matters or assertions reflect appropriate control deployments and control weakness pervasiveness (Davis, 2010, 2020). Consequently, the CSG audit report author expresses an adverse opinion when one or more significant deficiencies present a pervasive and material weakness (Davis, 2020; ISACA, 2014). When a material control weakness exists, the CSG audit report author can conclude that the controls are ineffective for achieving the information security control objectives (Davis, 2010, 2020). An adverse opinion is appropriate even if the entity's management asserts that controls are adequate except for the material weakness or weaknesses (Davis, 2010, 2020). Notably, an adverse opinion is appropriate when the audit report author determines that the material weakness or weaknesses represent ineffective control procedures (Davis, 2010, 2020).

Disclaimer Opinion

A disclaimer CSG audit opinion concerning control adequacy represents a limited degree of assurance concerning controls (Davis, 2010, 2020). The CSG audit report author expresses a disclaimer opinion when IT audit team members cannot obtain appropriate and sufficient evidence to base an opinion (Davis, 2020; ISACA, 2014). Moreover, The CSG audit report author expresses a disclaimer opinion when IT audit team members conclude that the possible effects on the IT audit objectives emanating from undetected weaknesses could be material and pervasive (Davis, 2020; ISACA, 2014). The CSG audit report author also considers a disclaimer opinion if information security controls are not the primary engagement objective (Davis, 2010, 2020). Nevertheless, the CSG report author inscribes a detailed explanation for the disclaimer opinion (Davis, 2010, 2020).

Degree of Correspondence

Ascertaining the degree of correspondence between assertions or direct subject matter and audit criteria is a professional mandate (Davis, 2010, 2020; Marius et al., 2009). Nonetheless, assurance methodologies have similarities and differences in practice (Davis, 2010, 2020). The similarity between IT audits and non-IT audit types exists because determining the degree of correspondence requires objective and subjective judgment concerning what constitutes a material deficiency in the control system under examination (Davis, 2010, 2020). The difference between IT audits and manual audit types exists because the control system is commonly more complex (Davis, 2010, 2020). Additionally, IT audits are more challenging because the assigned IT auditor must ascertain whether the computer programs and data files under examination have representational validity (Davis, 2010, 2020).

Control deficiency causation may be linkable to the entity's design or operating condition (Davis, 2010, 2020). On the one hand, a design deficiency exists when a necessary control is missing (Davis, 2010, 2020). A design deficiency also exists when the existing control has an improper design so that even when the control is operating, the control objective is not always met (Davis, 2010, 2020). On the other hand, an operating deficiency exists when a properly designed control is not operating as intended. An operating deficiency also exists when the individual performing a control does not possess the necessary authority or qualifications to effectively execute the control (Davis, 2010, 2020). A digitized data or related technology control deficiency could adversely affect the managerial ability to initiate, inscribe, process, and report information consistent with organizational management's assertions (Davis, 2010, 2020).

IT audit findings can be favorable or unfavorable (Davis, 2010, 2020). Favorable IT audit findings need to be brief and transparent inscriptions (Davis, 2010, 2020). Unfavorable IT audit findings necessitate relevant and explanatory inscriptions while sustaining simplicity and brevity (Davis, 2010, 2020). Moreover, unfavorable IT audit findings typically transfer to reportable conditions needing corrective actions (Davis, 2010, 2020). Regardless of the IT audit finding type, the in-charge IT auditor must consider the discovered, projected, and potential error materiality when assessing audit findings for report inclusion (Davis, 2010, 2020).

If an IT audit team member identifies a material error, control deficiency, or misstatement, an appraisal must occur regarding whether the discovery denotes irregularity or illegal act existence (Davis, 2010, 2020). If, after evaluation, audit evidence indicates irregular act occurrence, the in-charge IT auditor can recommend a thorough investigation or other appropriate action (Davis, 2013, 2020). With proper authorization, when the known facts warrant additional investigation, an assigned IT auditor determines irregularity nature, timing, and extent (Davis, 2013, 2020). When there is an indication that an irregularity or illegal act exists, the in-charge IT auditor must consider the effect on other audit aspects (Davis, 2013, 2020). Notably, the assigned IT auditor assesses the irregularity's effect on the audit objectives and evidence reliability (Davis, 2013, 2020). When the effect of an irregularity appears so significant that sufficient or reliable evidence is unobtainable, the in-charge IT auditor evaluates the need for engagement continuance (Davis, 2013, 2020). Furthermore, when audit evidence suggests managerial irregularity complicity, the in-charge IT auditor must consider engagement discontinuance (Davis, 2013, 2020).

Audit area directing and monitoring activities should reflect the managerial strategy for ensuring an appropriate control system (Davis, 2011, 2020). Audit evidence classification by governance level delineates managerial responsibility. Policies, directives, standards, procedures, and rules should have a one-to-one or one-to-many correspondence with entity management's risk appetite (Davis, 2011, 2020). Since entity manager-leaders plan, direct, and support technology deployments, audit area administrative duties should include establishing or enforcing policies, procedures, standards, and rules for ensuring the right-sizing of information asset controls.

Engagement Report Structuring

Direct reporting audit engagements exist when management does not inscribe an assertion concerning the effectiveness of control procedures, and the IT auditor provides an opinion (Davis, 2011, 2020). Conversely, attest reporting audit engagements happen when management inscribes an assertion regarding the effectiveness of control activities, and the IT auditor provides an opinion about the stated assertion (Davis, 2011, 2020). Whether the IT audit team members engage in direct or attest reporting, IT audit team members must complete assignments assuming IT auditing is a methodical examination of auditable units (Davis, 2020).

Regardless of the CSG examination type, the oversight committee and management need to be comfortable with the audit assurance level and determine whether to classify the CSG audit report as privileged information. Reporting on CSG involves auditing at the highest level in the entity. Generally, the assigned IT auditor should address CSG reports to the audit committee and executive manager-leaders. Where inadequacies occur in CSG design or deployment, the auditor should immediately report a significant deficiency to the appropriate individual or group defined in the audit charter or engagement letter.

Contextually, in addition to compliance with de facto and de jure reporting standards, the CSG audit report should include following the organizational terms-of-reference with:

- a statement that executive manager-leaders are responsible for the entity's control systems;
- a statement that a control system can only provide reasonable assurance against material misstatements or losses;
- a description of the primary procedures that executive manager-leaders established to provide an effective CSG system and the related supporting documentation;
- information on any noncompliance with the entity's policies or any relevant laws and regulations or industry codes of practice for entity governance;
- information on any material or significant uncontrolled risks;
- information on any ineffective or inefficient control structures, controls, or activities, together with the IT auditor's recommendations for improvement; and
- the IT auditor's overall conclusion on the deployed CSG, as defined in the terms-of-reference.

CSG Audit Follow-Up

As with an ISG audit, IT auditors should comply with generally accepted follow-up procedures addressing the wide range and high risks associated with a CSG system. Naturally, the CSG follow-up procedures include carrying out sufficient, timely follow-up to verify that management actions address weaknesses. One commonly used dissemination technique addresses the audit report to the managers responsible for acting when engagement issues arise (Davis, 2020). Of the managers responsible for acting, a determining factor for selection is the responsibility of specifying audit recommendation treatment through a written response within a reasonable time after receiving the audit report (Davis, 2010, 2020). If appropriate, the IT audit unit can carry the recipient selection process a step further by assigning CSG audit recommendation responses to specific employees (by name or job title) after conferring with the designated information security manager (Davis, 2011). Regardless of the recipient selection approach, the information security manager enforces best practices by ensuring the inscription of the intended actions and specific time frames for finding resolutions so that the audit unit manager can direct follow-up activities accordingly (Davis, 2010, 2020).

While information security management is responsible for addressing CSG audit engagement findings and recommendations as well as tracking resolution status, audit management is responsible for establishing policies, procedures, standards, and rules for engagement follow-up activities (Davis, 2008, 2010, 2020). Audit management is also responsible for determining the adequacy of previous findings and recommendations' resolution and consideration when planning future engagements (Davis, 2008, 2010, 2020).

CSG Audit Follow-Up Responsibilities

Procedurally, after distributing the final audit report, an assigned IT auditor must request and assess relevant information to conclude whether appropriate actions were taken by CSG management promptly for all audit report findings (Cascarino, 2012; Davis, 2010, 2020). Moreover, an assigned IT auditor can request and receive periodic updates from information security management to evaluate the progress made toward carrying out agreed-upon corrective actions (Davis, 2010, 2020). An IT audit periodic corrective action update request is most appropriate for CSG high-risk issues and remedial actions with long lead times (Davis, 2010, 2020).

IT audit follow-up activities include response evaluation and, if appropriate, response verification (Davis, 2010, 2020). Follow-up nature, timing, and extent are dependent on audit materiality and control criticality (Cascarino, 2012; Davis, 2010, 2020). An IT auditor assigned to tracking and assessing follow-up activities must understand the audit materiality of CSG findings and corrective actions (Davis, 2010, 2020). As for control criticality, an IT auditor assigned to tracking and assessing follow-up activities must also understand each CSG reportable condition effect magnitude relative to other audit area risks (Davis, 2005, 2011). By acquiring a CSG audit and control understanding, the assigned IT auditor has explicit knowledge of an acceptable response and the nature, timing, and extent of response verification (Davis, 2020; Thornton, 2013).

Influencing specific follow-up activities is materiality (Davis, 2020). IT audit follow-up materiality is corrective action strength in an entire entity context (Davis, 2020). The assessment of a material or an immaterial item for follow-up is a professional judgment matter (Davis, 2020). Nonetheless, the assigned IT auditor's assessment requires considering the effect or potential effect on meeting organizational objectives in the event of an error, mistake, omission, irregularity, or illegal act that may arise because of control weaknesses within the CSG program. IT audit area follow-up activities need to reflect the materiality of reportable conditions and the effect of inactions on the entity (Davis, 2010, 2020). Materiality influences the follow-up nature, timing, and extent of an IT audit (Davis, 2010, 2020). The assigned IT auditor can determine what, when, and how of a corrective action deployment using appropriate follow-up procedures (Davis, 2010, 2020).

As part of the CSG management discussions concerning findings, the IT audit team members must agree on the audit results and an action plan to improve deficient systems, processes, activities, or tasks (Davis, 2010, 2020). The IT audit team members have no responsibility or authority to prescribe or direct CSG corrective actions for control defects (Davis, 2010, 2020). Ethically, once an individual is assigned a CSG IT auditor role, prescribing or directing corrective actions impairs engagement independence and objectivity (Davis, 2010, 2020). Prescribing or directing corrective actions also creates a practice conflict of interest if the assigned IT auditor previously held a position or currently holds a position directly or indirectly within the entity CSG function until reaching an appropriate redesignation time (Davis, 2010, 2020).

CSG corrective actions commonly mirror cost–benefit and risk analyses of the findings (Davis, 2010, 2020). When CSG administrative actions for deploying or otherwise addressing recommendations and comments are discussed with or provided to the assigned IT auditor, the proposed corrective actions should minimally receive inscription as a management response in the final audit report with a deployment commitment statement (Davis, 2010, 2020). Moreover, the CSG finding responses should provide an implementation date for each proposed corrective action (Davis, 2010, 2020). At the reporting process conclusion, the assigned IT auditor must update the audit function follow-up database with CSG manager's responses to potential control improvements and an estimate for recommendation deployment dates (Davis, 2010, 2020).

CSG audit findings may be reportable on an ongoing basis, often in the form of issue statements (Davis, 2010, 2020). Consequently, monitoring corrective actions to resolve CSG audit issues must occur regularly (Davis, 2010, 2020). When corrective action recommendations are operational, completed or implemented inscription against the CSG audit recommendation in the final audit report is acceptable (Davis, 2011). Nevertheless, completed or implemented CSG recommendations are reportable to the appropriate management level (Davis, 2010, 2020).

General CSG Audit Follow-Up Activities

One of the more pivotal aspects of a CSG audit engagement is IT audit follow-up (Davis, 2010, 2020). CSG audit follow-up pursuit occurs when a reportable condition exists that presents an audit area risk in achieving a control objective (Davis, 2020). IT auditor follow-up of CSG activities comprises process elements for determining the adequacy, efficacy, and timeliness of deployment actions by information security management concerning reportable engagement conditions (Davis, 2010, 2020). Upon the corrective action presentation, a procedural enactment of follow-up activities must transpire (Davis, 2020). The follow-up activities include evaluating management responses and, if appropriate, response verification (Davis, 2010, 2020). An automated engagement tracking system with a finding database can help carry out IT audit follow-up activities (Davis, 2010, 2020; Gantz, 2013).

As a task within the follow-up activities, the IT auditor-assigned responsibility for tracking and assessing CSG audit responses evaluates whether unimplemented findings are still relevant (Davis, 2010, 2020; Gantz, 2013). Furthermore, the discovery of inconsistencies and departures from applicable accounting principles during the IT audit follow-up procedures can drive a corrective action review with a qualified financial auditor (Davis, 2010, 2020). When the Chief Audit Executive or Practice Partner concludes that a follow-up report response or action was unsatisfactory after professional consideration and necessary consultation, the appropriate management level needs to receive an inadequate outcome notification (Davis, 2010, 2020).

The IT auditor-assigned responsibility for tracking and assessing CSG audit responses must give information security management a reasonable timeframe to provide details of actions undertaken to deploy recommendations (Davis, 2010, 2020). Moreover, the IT auditor-assigned responsibility for tracking and assessing CSG audit responses should know in advance acceptable corrective actions (Davis, 2020). To assist in the follow-up activity determination, the IT auditor-assigned responsibility for tracking and assessing CSG audit responses must request status information from the responsible implementer (Davis, 2010, 2020). The status request needs to happen soon after the expected deployment date passes for some, or all, of the agreed corrective actions (Davis, 2010, 2020).

Follow-up procedures necessitate aligning with the culture of the entity (Davis, 2010, 2020). In a formal entity culture, the assigned IT auditor might begin to follow up by sending a Request for Status of Corrective Actions letter to the responsible implementer (Davis, 2020). A Request for Status of Corrective Actions is a formal inscription asking appropriate audit area personnel about agreed-upon action plan progress. Contrastingly, in the informal entity culture, CSG audit follow-up procedures might only entail asking appropriate information security personnel about the progress of agreed corrective actions (Davis, 2010, 2020). Whether a formal or informal culture, the assigned IT auditor's task pursuance necessitates responders to a corrective action status request submitting proof of recommendation deployment progression (Davis, 2010, 2020).

The most effective way to receive CSG audit follow-up responses from management is by an inscription (Davis, 2011). Receiving a CSG audit follow-up response helps reinforce managerial responsibility and confirm progress achievement for corrective actions (Davis, 2010, 2020). Written responses are an evidential record of actions, responsibilities, and status of corrective actions (Davis, 2010, 2020). Nevertheless, depending on response delivery, follow-up activity may involve reformatting the final report to give information security management a section in the CSG audit communication to inscribe details of corrective actions undertaken to implement recommendations (Davis, 2010, 2020).

Alternatively, the assigned IT auditor can receive and record oral responses to status requests (Davis, 2010, 2020). When an assigned IT auditor investigates a reportable condition after CSG audit report issuance, using a follow-up form is the best means to inscribe oral responses for placement in working papers (Davis, 2020). As a minimum IT auditor practice, information on the CSG audit follow-up form needs to include:

- the point in time of exception discovery;
- the CSG corrective action under investigation;
- the auditable unit name;
- the name of the item needing corrective action;
- the finding and recommendation from the CSG audit report;
- the titles of the individual(s) contacted for determining the reportable condition disposition;
- the corrective action, if any, taken by information security management;
- the recommendation for additional activities, if any, when the responsible implementer has not taken appropriate action; and

- the agreed-on point in time for performing additional procedures when information security management has not taken corrective action as of the activity period (Davis, 2010, 2020).

Corrective actions commonly reflect audit recommendations that enable bringing reportable conditions to an alignment level with standards or best practices (Davis, 2010, 2020). To validate an acceptable corrective action, whenever possible, the assigned IT auditor obtains audit evidence of the design and operation actions in response to the CSG audit (Davis, 2020). After a reasonable time-lapse, follow-up activities performance can occur to verify corrective action effectiveness in reducing CSG deficiencies of the entity (Davis, 2008, 2020). Specifically, information security management can submit information on actions taken to deploy recommendations (Davis, 2008, 2020). However, the assigned IT auditor can be skeptical about the response or action efficacy (Davis, 2008, 2020). Consequently, the assigned IT auditor should perform appropriate testing or other audit procedures to confirm the recommendation's actual position or status before concluding CSG audit follow-up activities (Davis, 2010, 2020).

Audit management is responsible for establishing follow-up procedures to determine whether CSG management addressed reportable conditions, giving response consideration in planning future audit engagements within the accountability ambit (Davis, 2010, 2020). Consequently, the in-charge IT auditor must ensure follow-up activities exist for the CSG audit engagement (Davis, 2010, 2020). Factors for determining appropriate follow-up procedures are:

- the time involved,
- the complexity of the corrective action,
- significance of the reported finding,
- cost to correct the reportable condition,
- the significance of the finding recommendation,
- degree of effort necessary to correct the reportable condition,
- the effect that can result from corrective action failure,
- any changes in the environment that may affect the significance or materiality of a reportable condition, and
- any changes in the environment that may affect the significance or the materiality of a recommendation (Davis, 2010, 2020).

The in-charge IT auditor is responsible for scheduling follow-up activities for an IT audit engagement (Davis, 2011). As part of the work scheduling responsibility, the in-charge IT auditor must design and deploy a corrective action notification procedure that reminds the assigned IT auditors to follow-up on pre-designated dates or fixed intervals (Davis, 2010, 2020). The CSG audit follow-up schedule needs to reflect the risk and exposure, as well as the difficulty level and timing significance in deploying corrective action (Davis, 2010, 2020). Thus, the assessed materiality and criticality influence follow-up nature, timing, and extent (Cascarino, 2012; Davis, 2010, 2020).

IT audit follow-up nature addresses the type of procedural performance considering CSG-auditable unit risk magnitude (Davis, 2010, 2020). IT audit follow-up timing confers when procedural performance will occur considering the CSG audit report date and is usually a matter of professional judgment dependent on such issues as nature and cost to the entity (Davis, 2010, 2020). IT audit follow-up extent conveys the amount or range of the assessment through weighing materiality or significance of the control weakness or deficiency (Davis, 2010, 2020). Concerning follow-up nature, timing, and extent, audit materiality typically reflects monetary magnitude relative to other assets (Davis, 2020). Simultaneously, control activity criticality infers the assessed item effect magnitude relative to other risks (Davis, 2010, 2020).

Assessing audit risk is a recurring IT auditor task (Davis, 2010, 2020). Audit risk inscription for CSG audit follow-up occurs during the IT audit planning process and represents the preliminary integration of tolerable risk rates for auditable units (Davis, 2010, 2020). If the follow-up actual rate exceeds the follow-up tolerable rate, the in-charge IT auditor must conclude that follow-up nature, timing, and extent require additional comparative analysis or follow-up audit assurance adjustment (Davis, 2010, 2020). When the in-charge IT auditor reexamines CSG, individual and overall corrective action assessments are necessary (Davis, 2020). The assessment outcomes permit inscribing follow-up audit assurance conveyance within the status report (Davis, 2020).

As a task within the audit follow-up activities, the assigned IT auditor evaluates whether undeployed corrective actions are still relevant or have a more considerable significance (Davis, 2010, 2020). Upon completing the follow-up activities, a reportable audit condition's status can change (Davis, 2020). Reportable condition significance or materiality can also change (Davis, 2020). Consequently, after a suitable analysis of CSG audit report responses, corrective actions, and current conditions, the assigned IT auditor can unilaterally decide that the deployment of a CSG recommendation is no longer appropriate (Davis, 2010, 2020). An effect on the assigned IT auditor recommendation decision could occur where information assets change, with a compensating or mitigating control deployment, or entity objectives morph in such a way as to significantly reduce the audit area risk (Davis, 2010, 2020). Inversely, a change in the entity environment may increase the significance of an IAP risk and the need for resolution. Thus, procedural communication escalation regarding remiss and unsatisfactory responses or corrective actions to appropriate management levels is fitting (Davis, 2010, 2020).

There may also be instances where an assigned IT auditor judges that oral or written responses to reportable conditions show corrective actions before audit report issuance was sufficient when weighed against deployment criticality (Davis, 2010, 2020). On such occasions, verification activity performance may become part of the next CSG audit engagement that addresses the relevant issue (Davis, 2010, 2020). Nevertheless, a status report on agreed corrective actions arising from the CSG audit report warrants presentation to the audit committee or those responsible for entity governance.

Follow-up activities can produce nonaddressable areas of concern (Davis, 2010, 2020). Nonaddressable areas of concern are situational IT auditor discoveries where the effect is not evident during current follow-up activities (Davis, 2010, 2020). Nonaddressable areas of concern may exist because the CSG issues exceed the audit ambit or extend beyond entity management's correctional authority or control perimeter (Davis, 2010, 2020). Furthermore, due to circumstantial uncertainty or limited audit work, the discovery of potentially unfavorable situations is not classifiable as acceptable CSG audit findings (Davis, 2010, 2020).

Items classified as nonaddressable areas of concern must have transparent inscription with adequate detail to prevent the misconstruing of audit information (Davis, 2010, 2020). The assigned IT auditor summarizes nonaddressable areas of concern and includes reasons for the conception (Davis, 2010, 2020). However, as nonaddressable areas of concern, recommendation inscription within the CSG audit follow-up status report usually does not occur (Davis, 2010, 2020).

When the deployment of all the agreed corrective actions occurs, an assigned IT auditor can forward the status report detailing all the deployment actions to the audit committee or those responsible for entity governance and information security management (Davis, 2010, 2020). Additionally, information security executive (or senior) manager-leaders may appreciate receiving a yearly recap report presenting significant recommendations and status along with recommendations from prior years that remain remiss of corrective actions (Davis, 2010, 2020).

References

Bragg, S. (2019, August 24). Haphazard sampling. *Accounting Tools*. www.accountingtools.com/articles/2019/8/24/haphazard-sampling

Cascarino, R. E. (2012). *Auditor's guide to IT auditing* (2nd ed.). John Wiley & Sons.

Davis, R. E. (2005). *IT auditing: An adaptive process*. Pleier.

Davis, R. E. (2008). *IT auditing: Assuring information assets protection*. Pleier.

Davis, R. E. (2010). *IT auditing: An adaptive system*. www.amazon.com

Davis, R. E. (2011). *Assuring IT governance*. www.amazon.com

Davis, R. E. (2013). *Assuring IT legal compliance*. Lulu.

Davis, R. E. (2017). *Relationship between corporate governance and information security governance effectiveness in United States corporations* (Publication No. 10603383) [Doctoral Study, Walden University]. ProQuest Dissertations Publishing.

Davis, R. E. (2020). *IT auditing using a system perspective*. IGI Global.

Farahmand, F., Navathe, S. B., Sharp, G. P., & Enslow, P. H. (2005). A management perspective on risk of security threats to information systems. *Information Technology and Management, 6*(2–3), 203–225. https://doi.org/10.1007/s10799-005-5880-5

Gantz, S. D. (2013). *The basics of IT audit: Purposes, processes, and practical information*. Elsevier.

Gelbstein, E., & Kurbalija, J. (2005). *Internet governance: Issues, actors and divides*. Diplo Foundation.

Glen, S. (2015, June 25). What Is Haphazard Sampling? *Statistics How To*. www.statisticshowto.datasciencecentral.com/haphazard-sampling/

Gotel, O., Cleland-Huang, J., Hayes, J. H., Zisman, A., Egyed, A., Grünbacher, P., Dekhtyar, A., Antoniol, G., Maletic, J., & Mäder, P. (2012). In *Software and systems traceability* (pp. 3–22). https://doi.org/10.1007/978-1-4471-2239-5_1

Guadalupe, M., Li, H., & Wulf, J. (2014). Who lives in the C-suite? Organizational structure and the division of labor in top management. *Management Science, 60*, 824–844. https://doi.org/10.1287/mnsc.2013.1795

Haislip, J. Z., Peters, G. F., & Richardson, V. J. (2016). The effect of auditor IT expertise on internal controls. *International Journal of Accounting Information Systems, 20*, 1–15. https://doi.org/10.1016/j.accinf.2016.01.001

Hall, T. W., Hunton, J. E., & Pierce, B. J. (2000). The use of and selection biases associated with non-statistical sampling in auditing. *Behavioral Research in Accounting, 12*, 231–255. https://aaajournals.org

ISACA. (2014). IS audit and assurance guideline 2202 risk assessment in planning. *ITAF: Information Technology Assurance Framework*. www.isaca.org/resources/frameworks-standards-and-models

Lindstrom, P. (2004, May). The four disciplines of security management: Information security reference model. *Information Security Magazine*. http://spiresecurity.com/poster/Spire%20Poster%20-%20Four%20Disciplines.pdf

Marius, P., Cristian, T., & Amancei, C. (2009). Characteristics of the audit processes for distributed informatics systems. *Informatica Economica, 13*(3), 165–178. http://revistaie.ase.ro/

McQuaide, B. (2003). Identity and access management, transforming E-security into a catalyst for competitive advantage. *Information Systems Control Journal, 4*. www.isaca.org/

Omoyiola, B. O. (2020). The evolution of information security measurement and testing. *IOSR Journal of Computer Engineering, 22*(3, Series II), 50–54. www.iosrjournals.org

Samson, D., Terziovski, M., & Lai, A. (2005). *Intellectual property strategy and business strategy: Connections through innovation strategy* (Working Paper 08/05). Intellectual Property Research Institute of Australia. www.researchgate.net/profile/Daniel_Samson2/publication/228740384_ Intellectual_Property_Strategy_and_Business_Strategy_Connections_through_Innovation_ Strategy/links/0046352c3c37f86e49000000.pdf

Schryen, G. (2013). Revisiting IS business value research: What we already know, what we still need to know, and how we can get there. *European Journal of Information Systems, 22*(2), 139–169. https://doi.org/10.1057/ejis.2012.45

Soava, G., & Raduteanu, M. (2014). Digital economy-economy of the new millennium. *Economics World, 2*(1), 45–57. www.davidpublisher.org

Soltani, B. (2007). *Auditing: An international approach.* Pearson Education.

Thornton, T. (2013). Tacit knowledge and its antonyms. *Philosophia Scientiæ. Travaux d'histoire et de philosophie des sciences, 17*(3), 93–106. https://journals.openedition.org/philosophiascientiae/890

Wiesmann, A., Curphey, M., van der Stock, A., & Stirbei, R. (Eds.). (2005). *A guide to building secure web applications and web services* (2.0 Black Hat ed.). The Open Web Application Security Project. www.owasp.org

Recommended Reading

Al-Matari, O. M., Helal, I. M., Mazen, S. A., & Elhennawy, S. (2020). Integrated framework for cybersecurity auditing. *Information Security Journal: A Global Perspective*, 1–16. https://doi.org/ 10.1080/19393555.2020.1834649

Burgemeestre, B., Hulstijn, J., & Tan, Y. H. (2013). Value-based argumentation for designing and auditing security measures. *Ethics and Information Technology, 15*(3), 153–171. https://doi. org/10.1007/s10676-013-9325-2

Gupta, P. P. (2011). *Auditing the control environment.* The Institute of Internal Auditors.

Li, H., No, W. G., & Boritz, J. E. (2020). Are external auditors concerned about cyber incidents? Evidence from audit fees. *Auditing: A Journal of Practice & Theory, 39*(1), 151–171. https://doi. org/10.2308/ajpt-52593

Maleh, Y., Sahid, A., Ezzati, A., & Belaissaoui, M. (2017). A capability maturity framework for IT security governance in organizations. In A. Abraham, A. Haqiq, A. Muda, & N. Gandhi (Eds.), *International conference on innovations in bio-inspired computing and applications: Vol. 735. Advances in intelligent systems and computing* (pp. 221–233). https://doi.org/10.1007/978-3- 319-76354-5_20

Von Solms, S. H. (2010). The 5 waves of information security: From Kristian Beckman to the present. In K. Rannenberg, V. Varadharajan, & C. Weber (Eds.), *Security and privacy: Silver linings in the cloud: IFIP advances in information and communication technology* (pp. 1–8). https://doi. org/10.1007/978-3-642-15257-3_1

CSG Audit Risk Assessment Template

Auditable Units	Audit Risk Categories			
	Inherent	Control	Detective	Total

Access Management

Logical Access
• Identification
• Authentication
• Restriction
• Provisioning

Physical Access
• Identification
• Authentication
• Restriction
• Provisioning
Sub-Total

Network Infrastructure Security
• Security Devices
• Security Protocols
• Security Techniques
• Incidence Monitoring
• Incidence Response
• Encryption Management
Sub-Total

Risk Analysis
• Design
• Implementation
• Monitoring
Sub-Total

Environmental
• Human Occurrences
• Non-Human Occurrences
Sub-Total

Confidential Information Assets
• Storage
• Retrieval
• Transport
• Disposal
Sub-Total

Total

IAP Functions or Duties Templates

Segregation-of-Functions

Activities	IAP Functions						
	[Dept. 1]	[Dept. 2]	[Dept. 3]	[Dept. 4]	[Dept. 5]	[Dept. 6]	[Dept. 7]
Identification							
Classification							
Valuation							
Recording							
Safeguarding							
Disposal							
Reconcilement							

Legend: R, Responsible; A, Accountable; C, Consulted; and I, Informed

or

Legend: R, Responsible; A, Accountable; S, Supportive; C, Consulted; and I, Informed

Segregation-of-Duties

Activities	IAP Duties						
	[Job Title 1]	[Job Title 2]	[Job Title 3]	[Job Title 4]	[Job Title 5]	[Job Title 6]	[Job Title 7]
Identification							
Classification							
Valuation							
Recording							
Safeguarding							
Disposal							
Reconcilement							

Legend: R, Responsible; A, Accountable; C, Consulted; and I, Informed

or

Legend: R, Responsible; A, Accountable; S, Supportive; C, Consulted; and I, Informed

IAP Control Classification Template

Deployed Controls	Control Types		
	[Type 1]	*[Type 2]*	*[Type 3]*
[Deployment Type 1]			
[Deployment Type 2]			
[Deployment Type 3]			
[Deployment Type 4]			
[Deployment Type 5]			
[Deployment Type 6]			
[Deployment Type 7]			
[Deployment Type 8]			
[Deployment Type 9]			

Potential Deployed Controls:

- Firewalls,
- Intrusion Detection Systems,
- Intrusion Prevention Systems,
- Provisioning Procedures,
- Content Scanners,
- Security Incident Policy,
- IAP Training Program,
- Cryptographic Key Management, and
- Virus Protection.

Potential Control Types:

- Preventive, Detective, or Corrective
- Management, Operational, or Technical
- Governance, Management, or Operational
- Strategic, Tactical, or Operational
- Confidentiality, Integrity, or Availability

Index